"This is the stuff memories can be duplicated from."
— Karen Krebsbach, *Foreign Service Journal*

"Like gourmet chefs sampling the produce in an overstocked French market, the editors of *Traveler's Tales* pick, sift, and prod their way through the weighty shelves of contemporary travel writing, rejecting the second rate and creaming off the very best. They have impeccable taste—a very welcome addition to the genre."
— William Dalrymple, author of *City of Djinns* and *In Xanadu*

"I can't think of a better way to get comfortable with a destination than by delving into *Travelers' Tales*...before reading a guidebook, before seeing a travel agent. The series helps visitors refine their interests and readies them to communicate with the peoples they come in contact with...."
— Paul Glassman, Society of American Travel Writers

"The *Travelers' Tales* series should become required reading for anyone visiting a foreign country who wants to truly step off the tourist track and experience another culture, another place, first-hand."
— Nancy Paradis, *St. Petersburg Times*

"Like having been there, done it, seen it. If there's one thing traditional guidebooks lack, it's the really juicy travel information, the personal stories about back alleys and brief encounters. The *Travelers' Tales* series fills this gap with an approach that's all anecdotes, no directions."
— Jim Gullo, *Diversion*

"...The essays are lyrical, magical and evocative: some of the images make you want to rinse your mouth out to clear the dust."
— Karen Troianello, *Yakima Herald-Republic*

"*Travelers' Tales* delivers something most guidebooks only promise: a real sense of what a country is all about..."
— Steve Silk, *Hartford Courant*

TRAVELERS' TALES BOOKS

Country and Regional Guides
America, Australia, Brazil, Central America, Cuba, France, Greece,
India, Ireland, Italy, Japan, Mexico, Nepal, Spain, Thailand;
American Southwest, Grand Canyon, Hawai'i,
Hong Kong, Paris, San Francisco, Tuscany

Women's Travel
Her Fork in the Road, A Woman's Path, A Woman's
Passion for Travel, A Woman's World, Women in the Wild,
A Mother's World, Safety and Security for Women
Who Travel, Gutsy Women, Gutsy Mamas

Body & Soul
The Spiritual Gifts of Travel, The Road Within,
Love & Romance, Food, The Fearless Diner, The Adventure
of Food, The Ultimate Journey, Pilgrimage

Special Interest
Not So Funny When It Happened,
The Gift of Rivers, Shitting Pretty, Testosterone Planet,
Danger!, The Fearless Shopper, The Penny Pincher's
Passport to Luxury Travel, The Gift of Birds, Family Travel,
A Dog's World, There's No Toilet Paper on the Road
Less Traveled, The Gift of Travel, 365 Travel

Footsteps
Kite Strings of the Southern Cross, The Sword of Heaven,
Storm, Take Me With You, Last Trout in Venice, The Way of
the Wanderer, One Year Off, The Fire Never Dies

Classics
The Royal Road to Romance,
Unbeaten Tracks in Japan, The Rivers Ran East

TRAVELERS' TALES

FRANCE

TRUE STORIES

TRAVELERS' TALES

FRANCE

TRUE STORIES

Edited by

JAMES O'REILLY   LARRY HABEGGER

SEAN O'REILLY

Series Editors
JAMES O'REILLY AND LARRY HABEGGER

TRAVELERS' TALES
SAN FRANCISCO

Cover design: Michele Wetherbee
Interior design: Kathryn Heflin and Susan Bailey
Cover photograph: © Joe Cornish / Stone. Vineyards at Pernand-Vergelesses,
    Burgundy, France
Illustrations: Nina Stewart and David White
Map: Keith Granger
Page layout: Cynthia Lamb, using the fonts Bembo and Boulevard

Distributed by: Publishers Group West, 1700 Fourth Street, Berkeley, California
94710

Library of Congress Cataloging-in-Publication Data
    Available upon request

First Edition
Printed in the United States of America
10 9 8 7 6 5 4

La parole humaine est comme un chaudron fêlé où nous battons des mèlodies à faire danser les ours, quand on voudrait attendrir les étoiles.

Human speech is like a cracked kettle on which we tap crude rhythms for bears to dance to, while we long to make music that will melt the stars.

—GUSTAVE FLAUBERT, *Madame Bovary*

Table of Contents

Part Two
SOME THINGS TO DO

Part Three
GOING YOUR OWN WAY

Part Four
IN THE SHADOWS

Part Five
THE LAST WORD

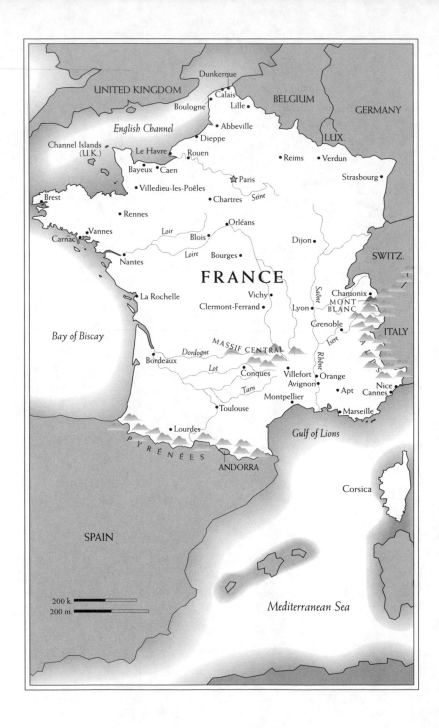

France: An Introduction

France is, of course, the heart of Western civilization. And much as the heart gives life and meaning to the rest of the body, so France gives life and meaning to what we call culture, history, and worthwhile experience; France is the loyal guardian of civilization with a capital C, despite constant assault by the spreading global monoculture and its twin engines, television and advertising.

Much in France and French culture is immediately familiar to the first-time visitor: we have all been exposed one way or another to its exquisite art and architecture, to images and stories of Paris or the south of France, to memories of the invasion of Normandy and the battle of Verdun, to French cuisine and wine, and to manifold stereotypes of the French people. Many of us also have a romantic fantasy of France that is hard to shake, even after repeated visits, simply because we want to believe that a place such as France exists, that a people such as the French exist, that a language such as French is still spoken and written, that a way of life one can still experience all over France is still possible.

Travelers' Tales France opens a series of anecdotal windows to life in France—the life of centuries but more important for the traveler, the life of the day. For while you can indeed go to France for museums, châteaus, and cathedrals until the sight of one induces coma, while you can indeed stuff yourself with *foie gras,* cheese, wine, and the world's best bread, while you can cycle and barge and balloon and hike till you're blue in the face, these aren't the real reasons for going to France. The real reason is to experience Life As It Should Be. And then in your own way, you can return home and set about making your life The Way It Ought To Be. And if you must return over and over again for further inspiration, the French will forgive you, and you will be infinitely rewarded each time.

But countries, like individuals, don't stand still. They change, they endure crises and bad leaders, they grow old and die, perhaps to be reborn, or to evolve and accept new missions in the world and the life of the mind and spirit. France, much like its ally and nemesis, England, has gone from being one of the world's largest empires to being (almost) just another country in Europe after being shredded by two World Wars in the same century. It is a great power no more in the old sense, but as the rest of the world devolves into a new century of barbarism, stupidity, and historical amnesia, France still has the power to influence, to civilize, to teach, and to inspire.

Yet as more and more people visit the shrine of culture and good living, the French face monumental challenges. It is no easy thing to host 60 million guests each year, nor is it an easy thing to absorb a multitude of immigrants from recent history—the Algerians, the West Africans, the Vietnamese, to name a few. It is no easy thing for a country which has been and still is so Catholic, to absorb and integrate Islam without being changed, nor to digest the post-socialist neo-pagan who worships only financial success. It is no easy thing for a people so in love with their language to see it threatened and usurped by the rampant weed of worldwide English. It is no easy thing for the French to master tourism on a massive scale, which is both an economic blessing and a modern disease. It is no easy thing to see the standards and traditions of French farming change, perhaps irrevocably, in the face of the needs of the European Union.

We can only hope, for the sake of the rest of us, that the spirit of France prevails, and that the French continue to live with undying *savoir-faire*.

PART ONE

ESSENCE OF FRANCE

JOHN FRASER

✦ ✦ ✦

There Is this Street

An ordinary byway may lead to all
things French, if you let it.

SHORTLY AFTER SEVEN A.M., THE METAL SHUTTERS ON THE
ground floor of an unsurprising apartment building on rue St-
Jacques creak open. Very slowly. Pushed out from the interior, they
screech like chalk run backwards on the blackboard. Not the nicest
of waking sounds in Paris, or anywhere. Not even an improvement
on the wailing ambulances that nightly whip down this old and
very long street to the nearby hospitals in the heart of the Fifth
Arrondissement. The fighting Fifth. The anarchic Fifth. The
glorious Fifth.

"It's raining, my little darlings. I won't put you on the ledge
yet."

The voice, normally sharp and rasping, sounds gluey with trea-
cle and floats heavily up the two floors to my bedroom window.
More horrible screeches from the shutters confirm that the morning has indeed arrived and Madame C., the concierge, is preparing
to give her three feathery, closely caged friends their first airing of
the day.

Like a liturgical response, opening shutters from across the narrowness of rue St-Jacques answer back. This time though they are
smart, wooden shutters, well-oiled on their hinges. Like the build-

3

ing whose windows they service, these superior shutters bespeak
something finer than mere utility.

"It's raining again," shouts Madame C. to Madame R. across the
street.

"The garbage is still uncollected," says Madame R., in an irri-
tated voice. "A little rain and the whole system collapses."

Two concierges of rue St-Jacques are in window-to-window
communication. The day has officially begun. God is in his
heaven.

I know this street well, but as an outsider, so unlike many
Parisians I have never taken it for granted. For three years, off and
on, I lived in the apartment building atop Madame C.'s empire of
the threshold. The memory of the smells and noises of St-Jacques
always bring back waves of nostalgia. How I loved it! It is a lost
street, lost in normality and therefore buzzing with life, from the
local office of the Socialist Party to the fruit stalls, cafés, and hard-
ware and book stores that punctuate the sidewalks with outdoor
stalls or other extensions of premises, bringing the life of the city
outdoors. It is a street that has seen nearly everything in Paris's
long history, but it divulges little to those who need instant grati-
fication and much to those who linger.

Its ordinariness is not comprehensive, for St-Jacques does have
occasional, almost hidden epiphanies, like the revelation of Val-de-
Grâce, where the street abruptly opens up into a little square and
you are transfixed before the forecourt of one of the great classical
ecclesiastical structures of Paris—the 17th-century chapel of Val-
de-Grâce military hospital, with its imposing dome and noble
flanks. Facing the chapel are the only truly elegant apartment
buildings along the whole length of the street, the ground floors of
which are all smart little shops that airily ignore down-market
neighbours like the Vietnamese restaurant just to the north or the
run-down laundry just to the south.

Yet the glories of Val-de-Grâce are the exception on St-Jacques
and its essential appeal contradicts grandiloquent statements.
Instead, it is a street caught up with the stuff of everyday Paris,
wearing its long history with no affectation and getting on with

the business of survival. For an outsider, it takes a special state of mind to walk its length and resist all the wonderful tourist traps hovering just beyond. Yet the re-wards for perseverance are com-pletely satisfying, for St-Jacques is nothing less than an invitation to partake in the real city.

Noisy, often dusty and chaotic, the street cuts through the Fifth Arrondissement like a shaky surgeon's scalpel. In theory it runs due south from Ile de la Cité and the Seine, the northern boundary of the Fifth, all the way to boulevard de Port Royal, the southern end. It has run the same course since its earliest days in medieval Paris and was once the longest continuous street in the city. It is also one of the very few streets to have survived intact after the massive renovation of Paris's street grid carried out by Baron Georges Haussmann in the 1850s.

> *he heart of Paris is like nothing so much as the vast interior of a house. Buildings become furniture, courtyards become carpets and arrases, the streets are like galleries, the boulevards greenhouses.*
>
> *It is a house, one or two centuries old, rich, bourgeois, distinguished. The only way of going out, of shutting the door behind you, is to leave the city's center.*
>
> —John Berger, "Imagine Paris," *Harper's Magazine*

Its "straight line" therefore ambles off indirectly every now and then. Also, the prevailing narrowness gets even narrower at certain key points, especially just south of rue Gay-Lussac, and the thought occurs that a very modern traffic engineer has cleverly concocted an effective speed barrier. The people who rent apartments right here do not have to pay much for their premises. Late at night, when the ambulances tear down St-Jacques heading for the hospital district, they have to slow down to five or ten kilometers at this particular pinched spot, and the sirens' wails are good for at least 400 francs' rental rebate a month.

The bizarre thing about walking along rue St-Jacques is that you are constantly being beckoned off it. At its southern end, for example, many of the intersecting streets from the west lead directly to boulevard St-Michel and the Luxembourg Gardens and palace. There is a particularly grotty collection of commercial enterprises at the corner of St-Jacques and rue Royer-Collard—a games arcade, an unappealing café, a never-open second-hand bookstore—but off in the clear distance the dreamlike, leafy haze of the Luxembourg makes the park seem like a mysterious island. Or farther north, at rue Soufflot, when St-Jacques is trying desperately to put on some bourgeois airs in preparation for its apotheosis—the Sorbonne and some of the faculties of the old University of Paris—you are abruptly confronted by the nearby Panthéon, which is a very heavy scene indeed, one demanding an immediate response and luring you away from St-Jacques's humble charms. I mean, there you are taking a modest look at a few antique stores and soaking in the calm atmosphere when suddenly the whole dead weight of the *gloire* of France and its pantheon of heroes falls on your shoulders. It's like bumping unexpectedly into General de Gaulle and a mounted division of the *Garde républicaine* after you've had a wee gossip with a news vendor.

Yet, whenever you make the mistake of veering off, whether it is to the Panthéon, or a little farther north to the wonderful Cluny Museum, you are usually—and quite abruptly—reminded that you have entered tourist Paris. St-Jacques is a street tourists cross to get somewhere else but where Parisians linger to get something. This is the difference between going and being.

As rue St-Jacques sheds its domestic guise and enters the world of academia, its character changes—and not subtly. Don't let people tell you this part of the Fifth is not like it used to be. This is still Left Bank student territory. There may not be a hint now of riots on the street or self-righteous attacks on the apostasy of ruling cliques, but the territory still belongs to scholars and books and irreverent chat. Your average Paris university student is no longer institutionally enraged, and this quarter reflects an undeniable drift into Gallic yuppiedom.

For example: at the juncture of St-Jacques and rue des Ecoles, there is a cluster of twelve boutiques calling themselves Au Vieux Campeur, each specializing in some aspect of the up-market sporting life. The best is the boot shop, where you can get ski boots, climbing boots, walking boots, jogging shoes, running shoes, tennis shoes, and even newly designed *boule* shoes (remembering that one's oldest battered footwear was once thought adequate for the world's most delightful stand-up sedentary sport).

As for the spirit of revolt, its emblem can still be found—albeit mutely—on rue St-Jacques when you reach the Faculty of Law building, where bills and posters of all descriptions are pasted on a side wall, directly above an official notice that reads:

DEFENSE D'AFFICHER
Loi du 29 juillet 1881
Article 15

If you are fortunate enough to live some small or large part of your life in Paris, two of the useful secret experiences for the outsider are learning to deal with Parisian rudeness and savouring French hypocrisy.

Hypocrisy is the easier to handle because, generally speaking, it is something to observe quietly and usually requires no action. For example, I cherish the little charity coin box on the counter of the butcher's store six premises down from the apartment building I once lived in. With blood coursing down the butcher's chopping boards; with pigs' heads surmounting stainless steel platters; with sides of newborn calves hung from large hooks; with livers, intestines, and hearts neatly arranged on glass trays; with all these gory reminders that we humans remain red in tooth and claw, where on earth do the coins go that are placed in the box whose only written appeal is "*Pour nos amis, les bêtes*"?

Along rue St-Jacques there is also ample opportunity to experience numerous little acts of rudeness, from outdoor food vendors who purposely spit on the sidewalk just before you cross their shadow to a vitriolic concierge who will scream at you for merely whistling a happy tune (upsetting her birds, no doubt). The street's narrowness and the convivial, if miserly sized, sidewalks force you into much greater proximity with the local world than is usual on an important street in Paris. As a result, you quickly learn the Parisian remedy for rudeness, which is simply to give back as good as you got—as quickly as possible. I have not yet spat upon a concierge's pet canaries, but the threat of doing so once proved to be cathartic and immediately salutary.

The only mistake you can make on St-Jacques is to take the rudeness and hypocrisy seriously. To do so is to allow the worm of doubt to creep into your consciousness, doubt that Paris is the only place in the world to be (if you actually happen to be there), and doubt that St-Jacques is at the heart of Paris. The rudeness and hypocrisy are necessary warts, transmuting an infatuated outsider's cultural awe into the matrix of complicated reality.

After all, it is Paris and it is the Fifth. Why linger on the negative? The morning has returned. Again. The shutters are opening. Madame C. is trilling and Madame R. is grousing. Again. Bread and croissants are waiting at the nearby *boulangerie*. *Le Figaro, Libération,* and the *International Herald-Tribune* are waiting to be purchased at the news kiosk. Large pots of rich, dark coffee are being prepared at the corner café to assuage the assault of sirens and the screeches. And rue St-Jacques? It is happily getting on with the business of being the most consistently underappreciated thoroughfare in the entire city.

John Fraser is a Canadian journalist, author, and teacher who in his varied career has been a music and dance critic, a foreign correspondent in Europe and China, editor of Saturday Night, *Canada's oldest and most distinguished magazine, and author of five books, including* Private View: Inside Baryshnikov's American Ballet *and* Saturday Night Lives. *Currently he is Master of Massey College, Toronto, where he lives with his wife and three daughters.*

★

They've all come to Paris. The Gauls, the Romans, Chou En-lai and Ernest Hemingway, Pol Pot and F. Scott Fitzgerald, Pablo Picasso and Dwight Eisenhower, the Czar of Russia and Lenin, the Queen of England and Benjamin Franklin, Buffalo Bill and George Gershwin. Some have even tried to capture the city. Attila the Hun wanted to take Paris but failed. Charlemagne tried to move the capital of France, and for a short period of time the city was abandoned. Hitler wanted the city he considered the jewel of the world—and he grabbed it. But when the Americans were approaching to liberate Paris, he wanted to destroy it. His general refused to carry out the order. For the general, Paris had to live. Nobody, even the most powerful, was going to stop the city from existing. And now everyone wants to come to Paris, millions of tourists each year, motivated by the desire to see the most beautiful city in the world.

—Pierre Salinger, "Paris," *Travel & Leisure*

RICHARD GOODMAN

✦ ✦ ✦

A Question of Water

In France, matters of the garden
border on the numinous.

YOU MIGHT NOT EXPECT SOMETHING AS ORDINARY AS WATERING would be controversial, but it was. In the south of France, it was. And especially in St-Sébastien de Caisson. The controversy revolved around what time of day to water, morning or evening. This was no very small matter, as it turned out. Actually, I didn't fully understand how important it was until later, when it grew hotter. The villagers were roughly divided in half on this question, and the passion with which each expressed his or her point of view served to bewilder me. Villagers without gardens also felt free—obliged, I would say—to express themselves openly on the subject.

You won't find the name St-Sébastien de Caisson on a map—the author made it up to protect the privacy of its inhabitants—but the town is real.

—JO'R, LH, and SO'R

This was an issue for one simple reason: *le Lion,* the Sun. As the days grew hotter, and even hotter, and the sun turned into a dangerous fire to be respected and feared, it became essential not to water in its presence. How can I convey the sun's relentless brutality now, its "blank and piti-less stare," so many months and so many miles away? The sun,

10

whose lovely light had often caressed us in the winter months, became, during the long summer days, a tireless killer. If, for example, you made the stupid mistake of watering the garden *anytime* after seven a.m., random droplets that splashed onto the leaves would be converted into tiny magnifying glasses, and the sun would sizzle the leaves into a wilted mess.

So from the beginning it had been made clear to me by numerous St-Sébastieners that the question of *when* to water was a profound one. What should I do? Naturally, I first asked Monsieur Noyer. This short, broad-headed man with massive hands, skeptical eyebrows and gray hair was the former president of the *cave coopérative* and St-Sébastien's most celebrated gardener. When I asked him what time to water, he spoke without hesitating.

"You must water at dawn, Richard. Before the sun rises. Then the earth is cool. The roots can better accept the water." He looked at me sharply. This was more than advice. This was a pronouncement.

We were, in fact, in his garden. It was strictly kept, well watered, and produced plants of such health you might see them displayed at the Iowa State Fair.

"*Exactly* what time should I water, Monsieur Noyer?" I asked.

"Before six-thirty. No later. Even at that hour, you are taking a chance. The sun is already past the horizon." He glanced over to the low hills in the east where the sun came up.

"Wouldn't it be better to water in the evening? After it's cooled down a bit?"

"No! Never!" The words shot out of his mouth like bullets. Since his garden adjoined the town square, they resounded off the town hall, furthering their effect. "Even after the sun has set, the land is still warm." He moved his fingers together cautiously, as if he were feeling the baked earth. "When you water then, it's bad for the roots. It shocks them."

He stepped closer to me and put aside his hoe. "Who told you to water your garden in the evening, Richard?"

"Oh, well…" I had to think quickly. "Somebody…from another village," I blurted. People from other villages always knew nothing.

He snorted and looked at me carefully. Then he pointed an instructing finger. "Never water in the evening, Richard. Never!"

Of course, it wasn't somebody from another village who had told me to water in the evening. It was Marcel Lécot, St-Sébastien's second-best gardener. As I said, Monsieur Noyer was acknowledged to be St-Sébastien's best gardener, and so his advice had a weighty authority. But Marcel had his champions, too; I had seen his garden, and it was impressive. Marcel was a retired plumber who had worked ten years in Lyon. He disliked Lyon: "It's too big, Richard! St-Sébastien, it's much better." Marcel was a balding, robust man, animated and kind, with burly forearms and a wide, generous smile that confounded his 73 years. I liked him very much. He was always friendly to me, and to Iggy [the author's girlfriend]. When we talked, he looked at me intently, his head tilted slightly to one side, and he had the habit of mouthing my words with me as I spoke them. It was as if he wanted to help me somehow in my feeble efforts at speaking French with some of his boundless energy, and this always endeared him to me, though unfortunately it never seemed to help my French.

Marcel felt very strongly that a garden should be watered in the evening.

"*Exactly,* what time in the evening should I water, Marcel?" We were having our conversation in the square, next to his house. It was a warm spring day, and the sun bathed us luxuriously. A car sped down the road in the distance, its tires spitting out bits of gravel. We glanced at it. I had already begun to acquire the village habit of noting carefully the most ordinary occurrences.

"Eight o'clock in the evening, Richard," Marcel said. "No earlier. Even later, perhaps."

"That's pretty late."

"The later the better, Richard. The land will guard the water then. Even through the night."

"Why can't I water in the morning, before the sun gets too hot?"

"Never!" He made a step backwards in alarm.

"Why not?" I was startled by his passion.

"At six-thirty the sun rises and—poof!—the heat sucks up all the water." Here he made a pulling-up motion with both hands. "There's nothing left. And if any water gets on the plants' leaves, it can be very bad for them. Very bad." He shook his head seriously. "No, never. Never water in the morning." He peered at me closely to see if I comprehended.

"I see, Marcel," I said. He mouthed those few words with me. Then he nodded. But he was still not convinced.

"Who told you to water in the morning, Richard?"

"Uh...nobody, Marcel. Really. I just...heard it." It was the truth. I hadn't yet had my audience with Monsieur Noyer. I did, however, already know through my general investigations that some people watered their gardens in the early morning.

Marcel looked at me. It was a dubious look. Then he slapped me on the shoulder. "Take care, Richard." He grinned and pointed upward. "The sun!"

What was I going to do? What a dilemma! After much seeking of advice and much anxiety over the question—even the man who sold me my newspaper in a nearby town had an opinion; everyone did!—I decided to water in the evening, when the power of the scorching sun had abated. It suited my temperament better, for one thing. And I found the land did guard the water—even though it was still warm when I arrived—all through the night and far into the next morning. And I could splash the leaves inadvertently, without fear. Thus began my ritual. At eight o'clock every evening, when the sun was just beginning to set, I went and watered my garden.

Monsieur Noyer didn't let this most crucial decision pass unnoticed, however. Whenever he saw me loading my car in the evening, obviously on my way to the garden, he would look at me for a few devastating seconds, snort, and glance away. He always made me feel as if I had disobeyed the Master. And I always wondered if I made the wrong decision about watering, especially when my plants began to suffer from the violent heat.

Watering my garden was not easy. It was a complicated, laborious job and a frustrating one. Since my land was away from the

town, I had no *robinet,* no faucet that provided ready water. I did
have a stream that flowed near my land, but it ran in a ravine about
ten feet below the plot, off to one side. So there was only one way
to get the water: by hand. The main device in this process was a
thick, fifteen-liter green rubber bucket Jules had loaned me. I simply attached a rope to its handle, tossed it the ten feet or so below
into the stream and then pulled it back up, full. This required a certain technique. If the bucket was tossed out just any way, the bottom would probably strike the water first and the bucket would remain floating—i.e., remain empty. I had to learn to toss the bucket
outward in such a way that, falling downward, its rim would strike
the water first and cut into the stream, allowing water to enter and
sink the bucket. After hauling it back up, I carried the full
bucket—or nearly full, since some water always sloshed out on the
way up—to the garden and watered my plants.

Now the obvious question is: why didn't I rig up some sort of
pulley system? Or go and buy a pump, even a primitive one? I had
no money for a pump. And even if I had, spending so much money
for a pump to grow my own vegetables *just one time* seemed a bit
indulgent. Especially when you could buy beautiful things in the
market so cheaply. The central idea here wasn't to save money, I
agree; but it wasn't to waste it, either. As for pulleys, well, even if I
could have *found* a hook and tackle, it wouldn't have worked. As I
said, no bucket simply lowered would have picked up water. The
stream was not moving fast enough to tilt the bucket by itself.

Generally, the entire process, including the hauling and the actual watering, took about an hour. By the end of that hour, the
bank was slippery from spilt water, and I was exhausted. My back
and arms were aching, not only from hauling dead weight, but
from the forced angles I had to place my body in to keep the
bucket from banging against the side and spilling as it was pulled
up. The process then became very tricky. I nearly slid off the
muddy bank and into the stream several times. Once I actually did
slide off, rescuing myself like Harold Lloyd grabbing the arm of
that huge clock. I grasped an exposed tree root that grew nearby.
I wish I had a photograph of that moment.

Even though it was difficult and time-consuming, I loved to water my plants. There was something eminently satisfying about giving *water* to them. I hesitate to use the word spiritual, but...I loved the pure, colorless liquid, spraying out from my vessel and splashing to the ground, this strange substance that made things grow. It was mysterious to me. And still is.

There were times when, for whatever reason—a dinner at someone's house or a visit to another village—that I couldn't water my garden until very late. Sometimes I arrived at my garden as late as midnight—once, even at two-thirty a.m. If there

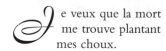

e veux que la mort me trouve plantant mes choux.

I want death to find me planting my cabbages.

—Michel de Montaigne, *Essays*

was no moon, then I turned my car toward the garden and left my headlights on. The two Peugeot beams more or less provided enough illumination to work by, though one was astigmatic, and so it sprayed its light a bit wildly into the tops of bushes.

If there was a full moon, though, I didn't need to use my car lights. Watering my garden late on a soft summer night in the empty French countryside was a rapturous experience. As the moon led me, I walked back and forth to the bank near the stream, threw my bucket in, and hauled up bucket after bucket of cool water from the stream. I couldn't see the stream, or the bucket when it landed, but I could hear the splash. Once they got used to me, the frogs continued their mad barking and gave me my metronome. The air was remarkably soft.

The light from the moon was just strong enough so most of the time I didn't trip over a root or a bulging stone. But the glow was also just weak enough to blur outlines of trees and bushes and make it difficult to judge distances properly. Was that plant ten feet away from me, or two? Was that a basil plant or an eggplant? Moonlight is a light that's not quite there, like a red light in the darkroom of a photographer. It was all like a dream. I often felt my life in St-Sébastien was like a dream, and this moonlight ritual only made it seem more so. But there was something wonderfully subterranean about it all. Being at my garden so late, guided only by the light of the moon, was like working in a pale, white sea, and my motions, somewhat tentative and groping, made me feel as if I were swimming in the night.

Richard Goodman is a writer who lives in New York. He has apprenticed as a French chef and has worked on film projects, but he's more interested in writing books. He is the author of French Dirt: The Story of a Garden in the South of France, _from which this piece was excerpted._

★

Thoughts of a summer garden are never far from fears of a summer drought—and the water problems. Water, in the Midi, is the currency of friendship. Without it, you need friends. With it, you make friends. Our own well dried up one August. Guests from the north arrived to stay. "Not _any_ water?" they exclaimed, extra white. "Only from the village fountain," we said. Luckily they were old friends, and the twice daily jerrycan run added a chin-up-and-carry-on zest to their holiday, like the Desert Rats with their half-glass of water a day.

Eventually a proper water supply had to be piped from 150 metres below ground; there was no guarantee of striking it either, no diviner, just blind faith and a geologist's survey to encourage painless payment as we drilled deeper and deeper.

It paid off, in more ways than water. In exchange for letting our drainage disappear beneath his vines, our neighbour Pierre gets a supplementary water supply from us; the pipeline is like a blood-link between us, an artery of friendship.

—Julian More, _Views From a French Farmhouse_

MORT ROSENBLUM

River of Light

If Paris is the heart of France,
the Seine is the aorta.

A GLANCE AT THE RIVER IN PARIS TELLS YOU WHAT IS GOING ON in France. If it is not slopping over its stone quais at the new year, farmers had a bad time with drought. When it runs fast, high, and cocoa brown in April, the skiing was terrific; keepers had to drop the sluice gates on the Marne to drain off melting snow. When France is happiest, for a bicentennial celebration of the revolution or on Bastille Day, barges and barks jam the Seine on their way to the fireworks.

You can gauge the crop of tourists by counting heads hanging over the rails of *bateaux-mouches.* When barges are so heavy with gravel that water splashes over their gunwales, construction is booming. Seine watchers knew France was hooked on American television when the police began blasting past in hot little patrol boats, driver erect at the wheel, bound for lunch à la *Miami Vice.*

And downstream past Rouen, that glance at the Seine can tell you the state of the world. Long before most people got their lips around a new household word, *perestroika,* Jacques Mevel knew the curtain was coming down. A river pilot, he travels the world each day without leaving the Seine. He noticed that Soviet sea captains suddenly started smiling and talking to strangers.

17

From the beginning, the French soul has bobbed in the waters of the Seine. On its bridges, love blooms; beneath them, lives end. Hardly anyone can tell you exactly where the river starts, or much else about it, but it flows through every romantic's spirit. It nourished Maupassant's pen and watered Monet's lily pond.

Paris was the City of Light long before there were switches to flip. The *rayonnement,* that radiance which the French have always beamed to the less enlightened, emanates from the pinks and oranges and sparkling flashes of the sun sinking into the Seine. When Baudelaire wrote that all around was nothing but *"ordre et beauté; luxe, calme et volupté,"* he was looking at the river off the Ile Saint-Louis.

A few generations ago, Guillaume Apollinaire mused:

Beneath the Pont Mirabeau flows the Seine
And our love...
While passes beneath the bridge of our arms
The eternal gaze of the sultry waves.

But the river is not always as the poets would have it, voluptuous and unchanging. In late winter, its mood shifts. When only slightly aroused, it floods the fast lanes along the Left Bank, gridlocking traffic from Saint-Michel to the Eiffel Tower. In 1910, hell-bent on mayhem, it went knee-deep into the fancy shops off the Champs-Elysées. A century ago, by the placid banks of a Normandy village, the current swallowed Victor Hugo's daughter Léopoldine, who toppled from a boat and sank in her Sunday best.

For 2,000 years, the Seine was alimentary canal to a nation that took its nourishment seriously. Grain moved upriver, passing cargoes of wine headed downstream. Most food travels by road and rail these days, but a look at the Seine suggests that it is still at least France's digestive tract. By the time it reaches Paris, the river carries enough detritus of civilization to sicken your average sewer rat. This, of course, does not deter the swimmers who race periodically from Notre-Dame toward Neuilly, emerging undissolved. The Seine will confound you every time.

Visitors have never gotten enough of the river. Gertrude Stein ran her dogs by the Seine. Henry Miller walked off his excesses along it; in a houseboat, Anaïs Nin took hers to new levels. Fish was the first course of Hemingway's moveable feast; he loved to watch the anglers along the Pont des Arts footbridge: "It was easier to think...seeing people doing something they understood." The idea of Seine sushi is pretty revolting, but the old guys are still there in late spring when fishing is best.

Today's generation, if less lost than Hemingway's, still comes to the Seine in summer to shed inhibitions. Parisians strip down to nothing and sunbathe on its warm stone banks. They hide their wine in brown bags only when embarrassed by the label. On certain stretches of the quaiside, Paris is gay. On others, kids and dogs frolic. Aging pigeon feeders occupy the benches by day, but lovers claim them at night.

Even its small mysteries intrigue. One evening a black wingtip shoe floated past my boat, dry inside, sole flat on the surface. Enough Parisians insist they can walk on water; would one of them shortly stride past?

*Y*ou have to be a little odd to remember rats fondly, but there they were. One night, my travel companion and I ended up down by the water level on the bank of the Seine. We were drinking cheap wine and waxing philosophical about the future when the rats showed up. We shouted and waved our arms, but the rats refused to scamper away. Several of them hunkered down at a medium distance to keep an eye on us.

My boyfriend rose to his feet and ran toward the waiting rats, hoping to chase them away. I was impressed. The rats were not. Lacking anything larger, we began heaving our pistachio shells at them. Singularly ineffective, but entertaining.

Perhaps it was the wine, perhaps it was the company, perhaps it was France, but we were not as afraid as we probably should have been. I rather thought rats lent a distinctive air to the scene. Such is the alchemy of travel. What would be horrifying in an alley in New York City becomes part of the ambiance in Paris.

—Katherine Walcott,
"A Moment in Paris"

My upstream neighbor, Pierre Richard, did well as the lead in a film called *The Tall Blond Man with One Black Shoe*. Who knows?

People mark their history with memories of the Seine. One night in 1958, my friend Jo Menell stood on the Pont-Neuf and watched mysterious loglike shapes bobbing by the dozen in the swift current. France was at war to keep Algeria under her wing, and the shapes were Algerians murdered by French zealots who countered terror in Algiers with terror in Paris. Bodies, as tradition demanded, were dumped in the river.

Politics changed, but the eternal waves flowed on. A few years after Jo stood on the Pont-Neuf, Algeria and most other French colonies went free, and people of two dozen cultures crowded into the *métropole*. By 1993, France decided it was no longer a land of asylum. On that same bridge, police stopped an African and demanded his papers for a routine identity check. He flung himself over the stone parapet and drowned in the Seine.

"The Seine is the great receptacle which first receives the victims of assassination or despair," wrote Fanny Trollope in 1836. "But they are not long permitted to elude the vigilance of the Parisian police; a huge net, stretched across the river at Saint-Cloud, receives and retains whatever the stream brings down; and anything that retains a trace of human form which is found amidst the product of the fearful drought is daily conveyed to La Morgue;—DAILY; for rarely does it chance that for four-and-twenty hours its melancholy biers remain unoccupied; often do eight, ten, a dozen corpses at a time arrive by the frightful caravan from '*les filets de Saint-Cloud*.'"

These days, the number is down. During 1992, Paris police recovered thirteen bodies from the Seine. They rescued another twenty-three people who had fallen in, accidentally or on purpose. And they extracted nine cars. It was an average year.

The net at Saint-Cloud is also down. Today, God knows what would shred it, or fill it, in minutes. When the current is fast, huge trees are hurled downstream, like battering rams. Other items, smaller than trees and sometimes unspeakable, also float down the Seine. Here, for example, is a brief sampling from the log of a young visitor to *La Vieille* [the author's boat and home] who watched for half an hour: one mattress, countless Styrofoam containers, a bloated pig, several condoms, dead fish, live ducks, a television set, someone's jacket, someone else's trousers, many people's lunch—at one stage or another....

When I moved to the river, I found a cast of the old characters right off the end of my gangplank. Jean Privat looked after the quai at the Touring Club de France, where 50 converted barges and boats are settled in a floating community between the Pont de l'Alma and the footbridge just above the Pont de la Concorde. His job was to make sure nothing sank.

Winter and summer, he wore an increasingly off-white yachting cap and an American bomber jacket he picked up while working with U.S. forces in the war. A dashing figure, even when a liquid breakfast slurred his sentences, he always managed to have the last word. He spoke river, and urban mariners depended upon him for translation. When Jean died in 1990, he left in character. It was a busy day at the crematorium, and his family, having paid extra, refused to be shunted off to a chapel annex. The mortician was firm and so was the family, but Jean, of course, had the last word. The heavy caisson bearing his coffin suddenly rolled on its track—across the undertaker's toes.

It troubles me to leave Paris, for I am separated from my friends: to leave the country, for then I am separated from myself.

—Joubert, *Pensees*

After Jean's ashes were scattered on the water, his boat hook went to Jacques Donnez, who spells his name Jack (no one else does). Jacques looks like a cross between Jean-Paul Sartre and Popeye, with a raspy voice and a craggy squint behind opaque glasses. At first, for me, he was mainly prime character material. Then I asked him to teach me to navigate. By the third time he spared me from making chopsticks of a fine old boat, he was Captain, sir, and a friend.

Jacques was born afloat in 1939, an eighth-generation Seine

boatman. He and his wife, Lisette, married on a floating church barge, made a decent income ferrying coal, sand, grain, and wine while their laundry flapped in the wind on the aft deck. But trucks and trains cut deeply into the market. In 1976, they sold the barge for scrap and came ashore. He took a job on the quai, where he can fix anything made by man and wait out anything delivered by nature. He starts early, works hard, and does his level best to help Burgundy vineyards prosper.

"*Ouuaais, je l'aime,*" says Jacques, a man of few words, when asked to rhapsodize on the Seine. The trick is to watch him look at the river; his eyes are as expressive as temperature gauges. When he furrows his brow at the rising current, it is time to get your car off the quai. He is like most hearty old marine equipment, utterly dependable as long as you check the meters. When his nose flashes red, for example, it is not the time to have him change your bilge pump.

In no time at all, the river bewitched me. Most likely, it happened that July morning when I was wakened by a mother duck giving hell to eight fuzzy ducklings. With a fresh cup of coffee, I sat on deck to survey my new neighborhood. The Seine was calm but by eight a.m. *La Vieille* was rocking gently, like a cradle. The air bore a pleasant nip and fresh river scent. The bridge statues gleamed gold. Suddenly, sweet notes of music wafted down to the deck. Up in the trees, masked by leaves, I saw a bandsman in blue and red with shiny brass buttons tuning a French horn.

On balmy summer nights, we sat on deck until the Eiffel Tower blinked off at one a.m. Then we drank wine and giggled, forgetting to go to bed, until it was time for sunrise and the duck serenade.

Soon, I started talking funny. When I remarked to a normal person, "I've got dry rot in my head," he nodded in agreement, not aware that I was referring to the bathroom ceiling. At the time, the world was in turmoil, and my job as a reporter kept me nearer the Volga, the Vltava, and Victoria Falls. But every time I came home, the Seine had a new surprise. I decided I had to learn more about this magical river and the people who live on it.

The books lined up in *La Vieille*'s saloon were of some help. Mostly, they confirmed a single bit of nautical knowledge: deck leaks make pages stick together. Within a year I had hired storage space for a library that would have capsized the boat: old musings in heavy leather, mildewed maps and slim volumes of verse. I spent afternoons gazing at paintings to see what had captivated the impressionists. I studied the river's moods, attuned to rising currents and falling barometers. With the help of Captain Jacques, I got *La Vieille* ready to roll, and we snooped into the river's innermost secrets. The more I realized that the depths were unfathomable, the more I loved the mission.

Looking around, I found the river's rich history bubbled regularly to the surface, refusing to lie dead in books. One morning I returned to Paris to find a Viking longboat—gargoyles, oars and all—docked at the visitors' quai. This being the Seine, it would not have surprised me to find it full of hairy Norwegians in animal skins and pointy helmets looking for loot after a thousand-year time warp. It was a replica, part of an exhibition at the Grand Palais.

> *When I think of Paris now it is with affection. I lived there longer than in any city except the one in which I was born, and when I come into its streets it is like renewing an old love affair. I know where everything is. I feel alert and alive. I don't regret not having lived in Paris as a young man, because I did.*
>
> *But this was not my mood at the time. Once back in America I wrote an article for the old* Saturday Evening Post *called "I Hate Paris in the Springtime." I got $1,500 for it, and I have never been able to remember it without shame. It mentioned the bad weather, the roaring inflation, the constant one-day strikes, and of course the balloting for or against heat. It mentioned a good deal else too, but not what was most important: that Paris—the French—had taught me everything I know about how to live.*
>
> *"Every man has two countries,"* Benjamin Franklin said, *"his own and France." Not every man, certainly. Some. One, anyway.*
>
> —Robert Daley, *Portraits of France*

Since Roman times, the Seine was an Old World thoroughfare. Norsemen routinely plundered riverside abbeys and towns until

Charles the Simple bought off King Rollo in 911 with a spare daughter and Normandy. The Vikings turned their energies into taming the river; their channels and dikes lasted ten centuries. On the Seine, William the Conqueror put together the flotilla that invaded England. He chased his cousins back to Scandinavia, and they have yet to return, except for Wimbledon.

Among the old stones of Paris are traces of walls built to repel the Vikings and remnants of later medieval forts that Napoléon III blasted away last century to let the river run free. By Notre-Dame, for instance, the Petit Pont has been around in one form or another since the birth of Christ. It was once flanked by wooden buildings, but they went in 1718, in a Parisian precursor to the Mrs. O'Leary cow incident. When things got lost in the Seine, back then, people went to a local convent for a hunk of bread blessed with a prayer to St. Nicolas. This, balanced on a plank along with a lighted candle, was placed in the river. Wherever the candle went out was the spot to look. A widow who lost her only son in the current launched a plank to find his body. The candle did not go out. It ignited a hay barge which struck the bridge, setting a three-day fire. Twenty-two houses burned to the pilings.

As the French went from monarchy to republic to empire to monarchy to empire to republic, the Seine remained their centerpiece. I had not only a river to explore but also a few thousand years of the soul of France.

The Seine that is synonymous with Paris is actually 482 miles long. In a straight line, it travels only 250 miles, but the Seine is in no hurry. It wells up from three cracks at the foot of a limestone hill in a forest glade in the Côte d'Or province of Burgundy, 30 miles northwest of Dijon. The Gauls, knowing magic when they saw it, built a temple at the source to the river goddess, Sequana, whose name was later smoothed out into Seine. Until the 4th century A.D., when German invaders destroyed the temple, pagan Perrier cured ancient ailments. A few believers remain convinced.

For the first mile or so, you can pop a cork across the Seine while *déjeunering sur l'herbe*. By the time it reaches Le Havre, after

25 locks in all, the river has broadened to an estuary hardly distinguishable from the English Channel beyond. From source to mouth, the Seine drops only 1,600 feet. At its widest, it can be dead calm, translucent in deep green hues. Or it can look like café au lait on the boil.

"La Seine" is sanctified by signboard on an old stone bridge in the village of Billy-les-Chanceaux, eight miles from the source. The water beneath is crystal clear and hardly deep enough to drown a dwarf. It twists and turns, picking up the odd stream, until it reaches the bottom of Champagne country. By then, its banks are dotted with the remains of wooden wheels that once ground flour or cranked up a few watts of electricity.

Châtillon-sur-Seine is a miniature Paris, Seine-wise; its oldest part nestles between two branches of the river. But neither branch is wider than ten yards or more than a yard deep. Navigation starts at Marcilly, 120 miles from the source. River traffic once reached the medieval port at Troyes via canal, but the grand waterway ordered by Napoléon was closed less than a century after it opened, one more casualty of a vanishing way of life.

At Montereau, the Seine gets significant. The Yonne joins in, doubling the flow and adding traffic from canals and rivers that reach the Mediterranean. Farther on, at the impressionists' paradise of Moret, there is the Loing. Soon after, the Essonne. Then the Marne empties in, bringing water from the mountains of the Vosges and barges from beyond the Rhine, as far away as the Black Sea. The Seine is swift and murky and ready for Paris.

From the City of Light, the Seine winds into the heart of darkness. Past the abandoned hulk of a Renault factory on the Ile Séguin outside Paris, the riverside homes peter out. Suddenly, it is as if you are on Conrad's steamer among mangrove swamps on the Congo. And then, just as abruptly, the river turns and you sense the luminosity that inspired so many painters.

The Oise comes in below Paris, and the Eure and others. Long past the wrought-iron terrace of La Fournaise, where Renoir painted the luncheon clientele and Maupassant scribbled on the walls, it passes near the village near Rouen where Flaubert's Emma

Bovary learned home economics the hard way. Plaques along the way mark where battered Englishmen went home after their Hundred Years' War and where, a long time later, the English helped run off Germans. A little tower marks the spot where Napoléon's ashes came ashore, for a carriage ride to Paris, after sailing up the Seine in a frigate painted black.

On a map of Normandy, Sequana looks like an earthworm with stomach cramps. The river snakes among spectacular castles and abbeys, set against a backdrop of plunging white escarpments and thick woods. In spring, its lazy loops are flanked in the shocking pink of cherry orchards. It changes again and again, meandering through history and humdrum, on toward open waters.

No statesman has missed the significance of this varied thoroughfare. "Le Havre, Rouen, and Paris are a single town," Napoléon said, "and the Seine is Main Street." He planned to build canals so that boats from lesser states to the east could visit the capital of Europe by inland waterway.

The Rhône, wild and wide, was once a Roman freeway. The Loire, lovely and long, winds among sumptuous châteaux. Next to either, the Seine is a stream. Its normal flow, 400 cubic meters a second, is a fifth of the Rhône's and a sixth of the Danube's. But the Seine and its tributaries water an area totaling 78,878 square kilometers, 15 percent of France. Seventeen million inhabitants, almost a third of the French population, live within its reach. More than half of France's heavy industry, 60 percent of the phosphoric acid plants, 37 percent of the petroleum works, and a pair of nuclear reactors flank the greater Seine. The port of Paris handles 26 million tons of freight a year, equal to a million truckloads.

With all that, the people who live and work on the Seine reject the geographers' term *fleuve,* the French word for a river that feeds into the sea. Instead, the Seine is *la rivière,* which is supposed to apply only to gentle inland waterways. Sequana was a lady, Seine people insist, and so is their river.

If you live on the Seine, you are constantly asked two questions: Isn't it damp? (The answer is yes) and Where do you get your croissants in the morning? (The answer is: At the bakery). Occasionally, some kindred spirit has a third: When are you going to die and leave this to me?

It is agreeable, as the French say, to take a candlelight cruise without leaving home. You can go away for a weekend and not pack. Your morning alarm is those ducks quacking. Friends visit without coaxing. My pal Barbara Gerber fled a Stockholm winter and dropped into the nearest deck chair. When a *bateau-mouche* passed, she flung out her arms and yelled, "Envy me...."

But then there is the secret life of the Seine, a separate *arrondissement* of the spirit. For years, when I watched the Seine from above, I treasured the river as a lovely but inanimate path through the center of the most thrilling settlement I knew. It took moving onto it, having it seep into my bilges and turn my underwear green, for me to realize that it was alive, a settlement in its own right, peopled by an elaborate class system of citizens who pledged allegiance to it.

Where else in Paris can you love thy neighbor? Late one night, I was washing dishes in the galley and heard someone bellowing my name. It was Olivier, who lives just aft, setting off in his little red boat with a load of nubile friends and his habitual shit-eating grin. They were off to the mysterious Ile d'Amour upriver and around the bend, accessible only by water. He just wanted to wave good-bye. John D. MacDonald's character Travis McGee insists that the *Alabama Tiger* hosts the world's longest permanent floating party. He obviously does not know Olivier.

Close to the madding crowd, Paris wakes to fumes, snarls, bent fenders and coffee splashing on silk ties. Olivier de Cornois, however, grins so wide you'd think he was crazed except for that glimmer which suggests he knows why he is smiling. "Ahhhh," he says each morning to anyone close enough to hear, breathing deeply and showing an extra molar on either side of his grin, "the river."

Scion to a sugar-aristocracy family from Picardy, Olivier fell for the river in 1970. "*J'ai flashé*," he puts it. He'd been living in an apartment on the rue Vavin in Montparnasse, studying drama, and fighting with his neighbors over loud parties; it is not clear whether the parties were theirs or his. But one night he went to a small orgy on a large boat and never looked back.

"My life has been paradise ever since," he told me one morning, grinning that grin which suggests Captain Blood on the way to bury doubloons. He lives on a red runabout that bobs like a cork in a dishwasher anytime something serious churns past. He paints for the few odd francs, but lives, essentially, on nothing. The Seine is his only love, except perhaps for women of tender age, and for riding his motorbike while standing up on the seat.

Olivier is tall and spare, with a rugged, handsome face and a shag of curls. He yells endearments at passing women, the kind that get your arm broken in California, and a lot of the women seem to like it. One of them married him.

For a brief time, Olivier and his much-younger wife were a model of bourgeois bliss. They had a daughter and moved ashore. "You know, the bouncing, the tight space, it's not so good for an infant," he said at the time, as if trying to convince himself more than me. When I next saw him, his crazed grin had matured to a beatific beam. He explained to me how it felt to nurture a tiny girl, and his eyes watered.

A little later, a touch of rue flavored his smile. In his 40s, he was finding it hard to boogy all night and change diapers in the morning. But he was trying. Then I went away for a long time and came back to find him living alone on the boat. He was almost the old Olivier again, up with a grin, a few turns around the quai standing up on the motorbike, and a sacred thoughtful hour on the park bench under the trees in the late afternoon. But not quite.

I asked no questions, but soon enough the news came. Olivier's baby had died. His wife was with her family. He was back to his first love, the Seine.

At the time, Olivier was tied up behind me, next to a steel-hulled *péniche.* This is a 126-foot barge, the standard French work-horse. Its master is Philippe, a perfect neighbor who was not wild about my writing this book. When I told him the title, he recoiled:

"But if you write about it, it's not secret. Be sure to tell them about floods and leaks." I resolved to spare his privacy, just as anyone aboard *La Vieille* is schooled not to see into his uncurtained windows. In France you can do it.

"Please understand if I do not seem to see you when we look at each other," Philippe said when we first met. I loved him instantly. Two boats tied alongside are like Siamese twins, and I am no Rotarian. Imagine the perils of proximity. You cannot get to my boat without walking across the bow of Philippe's. He can't leave the quai unless I go first.

Carefully, like a couple of porcupines sharing a den, we found a happy symbiosis. I don't sand my rails when he is sleeping in. He shrugs when I park my car on his hose during his shower. Every so often he comes aboard to dislodge debris about to tear off my port-side prop, a hazard I tend not to notice, and he mutters in English: "Unaware. Completely unaware."

You never know. The other Sunday, he emerged blearily at five p.m., unwound six feet of hung-over party victim, wandered below to get my guitar, and announced, in G, "I'm a little red rooster."

My neighbors began to settle along the quai in the 1960s when few people lived on the Seine. By now, the old-timers know the river's every mood and who sells the best rope and the cleanest fuel. One barge has a rose garden worthy of Versailles.

Depending on the season, early morning on the quai produces a trickle of joggers—once Madonna and goons trotted by—or a few diehard lovers or a Dutch camper that sneaked through the gate. But you will always see Bernard, Captain Jacques's sidekick, and his burly German shepherd. Bernard will be in a greasy black seaman's cap and blue coveralls. The dog will be drooling.

Bernard was one of those *clochards* who live under the bridges, friendly trolls of a time-honored class of Parisian bums. In *Boudou Saved from Drowning,* a classic film about the river, Michel Simon plays a *clochard* who is saved from the Seine. Bernard, however, was saved by the Seine. One morning, Philippe gave him a few francs to clean up in front of his boat. Then another neighbor hired him, and so did someone else. Soon, Bernard had a steady job working for the port, and his bum days were behind him.

One of life's pleasures is a chat with Bernard as he leans on his broom or scratches his dog's ears. It's too bad I can understand only one in every ten words of his Gabby Hayes delivery.

A lot of characters along the river have only walk-on parts. Someone is always making a movie, or modeling underwear or uncorking a primal scream. It seems that a section of the Seine is reserved for every proclivity, and our quai is for lovers. Mostly, old-fashioned pairs stroll past. But one particular bench in the trees is noted for world-championship brazen coupling.

As the lyricists have it, Paris makes love to the Seine. At least, the city embraces its waterways like nowhere else on earth. New York ignores two rivers. London turns its back on the Thames. Comparisons with Venice are more than hyperbole. The Canal Saint-Martin loops deep into the Right Bank, carrying barges past chestnut trees and dramatic old landmarks to the Ourcq and Saint-Denis canals. From these, you see a Paris that most Parisians would swear vanished decades ago. There is the hulking Grands Moulins de Paris, which made the flour for bread no one could match. And the Hôtel du Nord, which gave its name to another film classic. When Arletty leaned from a bridge and rasped to Louis Jouvet, "*Atmosphère, atmosphère…,*" Parisians cried a river. The city's Grand Canal, the Seine itself, winds among parks and fancy mansions you reach by crossing water.

Venetian waterways are public thoroughfares, but their edges are jealously guarded. Vaporettos carry gawkers past private landings and closed wooden doors. But you can get off a Parisian Bat-O-Bus at any stop and walk along like you own the quai. On the upper level, *les bouquinistes* offer best-sellers from the 1930s and travelogues of Timbuktu from open-air stalls. Down below, you can converse amiably with corn-fed tourists off the bus or play AIDS roulette with the rough trade. You'll hear French and English and Japanese, but also Catalan and Lapp and Dari.

On the Ile St-Louis or the Ile de la Cité, you can walk by the river and peer into mysterious worlds when someone swings open any of those massive double doors. At 17 Quai d'Anjou, for instance, Baudelaire and the *club des hashishins*—a play on *assassins*—met to smoke dope and plot the discomfiture of stuffy citizens. Rilke and Wagner and Delacroix were regulars; Hugo took a few hits and dropped off to sleep. Balzac didn't inhale.

Today's bohemians still gravitate to the river. So do most other Parisians. If most moored boats are people's homes or cargo haulers, and you approach uninvited on pain of death, others are there to be visited. Floating restaurants offer everything from tempura to tacos. By Notre-Dame, the *Metamorphosis* has been transformed from a sand barge to an Italian-style magic theater.

Every night, until the early hours, dozens of men can be seen hanging around along the avenue Foch, within a stone's throw of the Arc de Triomphe. They are, or so I have been told, waiting for invitations to orgies, where they serve as paid participants. I once asked a savvy Frenchwoman exactly what so many people were doing in all those parked cars that I had noted late at night in the Bois de Boulogne. Of course, I suspected what was going on in them. And yet, I appreciated the matter-of-fact precision of her answer. "They are fucking," she said.

—Richard Bernstein, *Fragile Glory: A Portrait of France and the French*

Down any quai, you can let your imagination run wild. Ask a few questions, and people are likely to misinform you about neighbors they hardly know. They guess by default; etiquette frowns on their prying in any obvious manner. Also, affairs are seldom as they seem. The Doges' Venice was straightforward as a Boy Scout troop next to a Seine-side boat community. People on the river by and large treasure their status as characters.

Among the Seine's colorful cast is *La Vieille*, that cranky but lovable aging matron with whom I spent a rough first night when I moved onto the river in July 1987.

La Vieille was built from Burmese hardwood and English hard-

ware at the turn of the century as an admiral's gig for the Royal
Navy. Driven by a steam engine, she plowed her deep V-shaped
hull into heavy seas as flag officers pottered about their fleets.
Doubtless she had a rich, noble history: seamen rolling depth
charges overboard at lurking U-boats, daring rescues in the North
Sea, the Dunkirk evacuation—that sort of thing. Doubtless.

All I know is that after World War II, someone turned her into
a motor yacht. She had a lot of new names. The first was *Namouna*.
Another evoked a port in Andalusia, an arid stretch of Spain not
unlike my home country in Arizona. One of her names, I was told,
meant "freedom" in Arabic. This appealed to me. When you can
unplug a few lines and head toward anywhere in the world you
have the fuel to reach, *Freedom* is a pretty good name to have
painted across your fantail. But I prefer the nickname. *La Vieille*,
like a lot of French terms, means whatever you want it to mean:
the old bitch; your mother; or the woman you love.

The boat is 54 feet long and 13 feet wide. Her hull of double
teak planking over closely spaced ribs is solid as a mountainside.
Deep below the wheelhouse lurk two BMC Commodore diesel
engines, slightly modified versions of what powered London taxi-
cabs in the 1950s. What used to be the engine room is a saloon,
fitted out in mahogany cabinets and built-in benches. There is an
aft cabin, a decent-sized galley and a head with a tiny tub, another
cabin, and a fo'c'sle ("foxhole," as one friend kept calling it).

My friends, Paul and Jill, found the old girl moldering in a boat
yard on the River Dart in the mid-1960s. Their knowledge of
water was limited to baths and whisky mix. Nonetheless, they
pointed her toward France and steamed up the Seine. When Paul
and Jill signed over the boat, I went on a trip to give them time to
wrap up the eighteen years they had spent on board. They left
quickly, and the boat remained empty for weeks while the sun
blazed down, preparing my welcome.

At some point, *La Vielle's* deck had been laid in soft-wood
planking, which was later covered with fiberglass sheets. This, I
learned, is not such a great combination. If the air is humid, the
decking swells and seals itself. When the sun bakes down, it dries

out. Planks contract and fiberglass cracks, unless someone regularly waters down the deck. That July, no one did.

I went aboard in a raging downpour and found it raining nearly as hard belowdecks as it was up top. Deep cracks had opened everywhere. Fat drops splashed off the mahogany cabinets and the fancy folding table. The foam mattress was soaked in the aft cabin. All hatches leak a little; mine were streaming water.

Suddenly, I had a terrible thought: the deck would be leaking the length of the boat, pouring water into the bilge. I lifted the sodden carpet and pulled up a floorboard. The Seine was two inches below my feet. Like a maniac, I started to bail with a pot. Calming down, I pondered a call to the *pompiers,* a noble crew with sturdy pumps. Instead, I switched on both bilge pumps and waited. The level slowly dropped. I found a small dry patch, curled into a ball and slept until the rain stopped.

In the morning, I found the gift that Paul and Jill had left playfully behind. It was a huge wooden carving of the up-yours finger, yet one more treasure they had plucked from the Seine.

Mort Rosenblum is the former editor-in-chief of the International Herald Tribune *and the author of* Mission to Civilize, A Goose in Toulouse and Other Culinary Adventures in France, *and* Olives: The Life and Love of a Noble Fruit. *This story was taken from his book* The Secret Life of the Seine.

✳

Bypassing rue Descartes
I descended toward the Seine, shy, a traveler,
A young barbarian just come to the capital of the world.
                    —Czeslaw Milosz, "Bypassing Rue Descartes,"
                    The Collected Poems, 1931-1987

NICHOLAS DELBANCO

April Fool

*In which the tables are turned
in the south of France.*

WE GAVE A TEA PARTY ON APRIL 1. WE INVITED FOUR COUPLES—
all elderly, all Europeans—to the little house. They had entertained
us often, turn by turn; it was our chance to reciprocate. We bought
pâtisserie by the box-full, tarts and fruit and cake. They were engineers, and brokers and retired chemists, grave and kindly citizens,
courtly men with stiff-brimmed hats, the women wearing gloves.

What imp of the perverse possessed me I can no longer tell. But
it came to me, preparing, that this was April Fool's Day and we
should observe it; we could introduce them to the time-honored
custom of practical jokes. "A custom better honored in the
breach," Elena said, and I said, no, we ought to do it, it would be
terrific fun. We would start the meal with joke food and then re-
pair to the real treats that waited covered on the sideboard or in
the chill *cave.*

So we did the whole thing wrong—preparing coffee and tea,
then spicing it, pouring vinegar in wine and pepper in the chocolate sauce, adding mustard to the jam. All the uproarious tricks of
a ten-year-old returned to me—the whoopee cushion, the
preshredded napkin, salt in the sugar bowl, dirt on the fork. I could

scarcely contain my excitement; it seemed like the most fun in years.

When they arrived, we were waiting. We were mannerly, polite. We showed them the house, the flowers, the grounds; we discussed the weather and politics and how innocent the American people were as to corruption, how we failed to take it for granted, making molehill-mountains out of fraud and greed. They said that we were lucky, marvelously fortunate, and that youth—ourselves excepted, *naturellement*—is wasted on the young.

We sat. We offered wine, cake, and tea. Tittering, I poured while Elena cut and served. They tasted the first mouthful, expressionless, then ate. I had been waiting for the burst of laughter, the telltale recognition, dawning joke, the way we'd grin and explain it away, the proper feast to come.

Instead, and to my horror, they proceeded with the meal. They said how skilled we were, how domestically practiced; they even asked Elena for the recipe. "Where did you learn to cook?" one woman inquired—at whose house we had consumed a splendid six-course supper just the week before. Her question did not sound sarcastic. She drank the undrinkable brew. When her husband asked for seconds, I had had enough. I said the joke was over now, my little game was stupid, they did not need to continue. The cake was inedible, clearly; my own piece lay untouched.

"*Mais non,*" they said. "Don't be unkind. It's an excellent *gâteau.*"

"*Gâté,*" I said. "It's spoiled. We made it this way on purpose. It's April Fool's, you see."

"April Fool's?"

"The first of April. *Un gâteau gâté*—a spoiled cake. On this day we play practical jokes."

"How sweet of you," they said, "to make excuses for your wife. But she doesn't require them, truly. She will learn to bake."

"She knows it already," I said.

"How very sweet."

"How gallant. *Les jeunes mariés.*"

"I'll have some more," said the excellent cook, "of your excellent coffee. *Merci.*"

I have not played an April Fool's joke since.

Nicholas Delbanco is a novelist and essayist, the author of several books including Fathering, In the Middle Distance, *and* Running in Place: Scenes from the South of France *from which this story was excerpted.*

★

The French in general are elaborately, almost ritualistically polite, an attribute that accompanies their attachment to elegance, with which *politesse* is linked. They are among the rare people who use the slightly formal but nonetheless entirely courteous sir, miss, and madame as they address people with whom they are not familiar.

—Richard Bernstein, *Fragile Glory: A Portrait of France and the French*

* * *

Covert Operations

Dust off the windows of your soul: flirting
abounds in the City of Light.

MY BEST PARISIAN ROMANCE TO DATE ENDURED THE LENGTH OF a traffic light, but the memory will bring a smile to my lips when I'm a grandmother in a rocking chair.

It began and ended on a hot August afternoon in the shadow of St. Augustin Church in what could be described as the august 8th Arrondissement of the fashionable French capital. I had driven to Charles de Gaulle airport to pick up a friend arriving from overseas, and, when we stopped at the fated *feu rouge,* I was in fact quite preoccupied with his horror stories of connections missed. Yet, feeling the magnetic pull that often accompanies the sudden awareness of being watched, I swung my head to the left toward the car abreast of me—and to its owner.

In retrospect, I am reminded that it was the French who gave us the phrase *coup de foudre* (love at first sight). The man at the wheel was staring at me with such intensity that, handsome as he was, I had to look away. I'm talking about a sexual energy that could be measured in megawatts. Of course, I couldn't resist stealing another glance in a few seconds, and yes, indeed, those mesmerizing eyes locked again with mine. I nearly swooned. I can't even tell you what kind of car he was driving.

I tried to maintain my cool—after all, my friend in the car with me had still been talking all the while—but the next time I looked back, I could not look away. Then, when the ensuing thrill was getting to be almost too exquisite, I slowly smiled at him. The man smiled back with a warmth that surprised me, since I'd taken him for a mere predator. I was intrigued.

*D*oes your lovelife need to spice up its nightlife? *Make a journey to the temple of close dancing, Le Balajo. The blinking red neon lights and scarlet swinging doors on rue de Lappe have welcomed Hemingway, Zelda and Scott Fitzgerald, Mistinguette, Edith Piaf, and streams of other characters who have craved the bawdiness of this low-down Paris dance hall.*

In the 1930s this shadowy bal musette was the hangout of macho toughs who liked to throw their girls around the dance floor and steal kisses in the dark corners. Many jealous battles, knifings and shootings have taken place on the premises. One can easily visualize a "Frankie and Johnny" episode occurring here. Violence seldom flares among the clientele nowadays, although the seedy interior with its wooden booths, slick dance floor, mirrorball and hefty bouncers has changed very little.

—Edith Kunz, Paris Passion Places: A Guide to Romantic Paris

The light changed, however, jolting me back to reality, and it was with no small regret that I watched the man of my dreams disappear in the traffic on Boulevard Malescherbes.

Later on, when my pulse had slowed to a manageable rate, I reflected that I had experienced what a friend of mine in New York and I used to refer to as Grand Eye Contact. When you're lucky enough to have it, Grand Eye Contact at the very least can change your whole day, put a spring in your step, make you feel the blood in your veins. The really good cases, such as that of my traffic light Lothario, become fodder for fantasies and can be replayed in memory for years afterward.

I had not lived in Paris for long when that particular Grand Eye Contact occurred. Yet I since came to realize that this harmless but potent pastime, so rare in New York that it really did warrant an upper-case epithet, was the biggest game in town in Paris.

Men and women *flirt* in Paris! This is one of the things I love most about my new home, right up there with open-air markets and the view from Pont de l'Alma. I'm not talking about blatant come-ons but about the fleeting yet electric encounters that can recharge one's batteries as nothing else can. Once a woman who's coming from a more rigid society realizes that, in Paris, an intimate glance from a man is not necessarily an invitation to the boudoir, the potential for fun is endless, not to mention the accompanying affirmation of femininity and the ego boost.

In Paris, it can happen anywhere, out of nowhere. It can be nothing more than a meeting of the eyes when two people are crossing the street. Once, at the local swimming pool, I shared Grand Eye Contact with a robust man who was tending to his two children but looked over just long enough to let me know without words that he thought we could have had a pretty good time together, had life turned out differently. Another day, I was jogging toward three men who appeared to be in deep discussion, except that the one facing in my direction waited until I was nearly past, then dropped a discreet wink without skipping a beat of the conversation, as if we shared a private joke.

"Private" is a key word here. Absent in Paris are the kinds of catcalls American women dread at construction sites; this game between the sexes seems more of an undercurrent in Paris street life. Or, if words are forthcoming, they are designed to make a woman feel appreciated, not demeaned. One magazine editor I know, for example, recounts an outing during which she became acutely aware of an attractive man watching her as he walked down the street in the opposite direction. As they drew parallel, the man said to her in French, "What lovely legs you have, madame! Congratulations!" And he disappeared, never to be seen again, but more important, never to be forgotten.

The anecdotes from my American friends alone are enough to convince me that we've found a great thing going here in Paris. And, really, how dismal can one's love life seem when one has access to this particular variety of street entertainment?

Recently a handsome businessman in a long, elegant coat saw

me looking at *him* from my car when I was stuck in heavy traffic on Avenue de la Grande-Armée near L'Etoile. He not only switched into Grand Eye Contact mode, but then leaned down and rapped on the car window on the passenger side, gave me a devastating smile, and departed. At the risk of being dubbed a dizzy dame, I confess that I became so unhinged that, less than a minute later, I bumped into the car in front of me and busted a headlight on my car.

It is hard to say where the word "flirt" comes from, but my bet, especially after what I've seen in Paris, is on the French. Consider the verb *fleureter;* it means "to say sweet nothings" or "to flirt" (*fleurette* means floweret), and *un fleuret* can mean "foil" in fencing terms. Isn't flirting, after all, a sort of innocent, sexual swordplay?

The French form of flirtation seems to be a Latin phenomenon, as it is something I have not noticed as much in London or more northern European cities. One thing is certain, however: it is something I find sadly absent in the United States, at least among adults adequately above the age of consent. Just to make sure, I've tried to play this game when I returned to New York and failed miserably. OK, granted, one has to be careful in the Big Apple about to whom one grants access to one's windows of the soul, but after Paris, New York seemed sexless and drab. So did other, safer American cities, in fact.

Feeling subdued and anxious to get back to Paris, I have wondered what happened to American men and women. A phrase such as "Say, baby, you look swell," which I recall from movies from my parents' era, no longer seems quaint, but instead rather appealing, making me believe that relations between the sexes were not always so strained in America. Without trying to place the blame on either sex, I simply wish that American men and women could play the way they do in Paris; that Americans were more fluent in the unspoken romantic languages; that an American man could feel more at ease letting women know he found them attractive without feeling he had to make some sort of *commitment*.

I recently sought the opinion of my friend David Leddick, an American and a longtime resident of Paris. A respected international advertising creative director who is now an advertising consultant to Revlon, he has long kept a watchful eye on both fashion and sociological trends.

Leddick agrees with me about Parisians versus Americans. "America is much more of a matriarchy than we realize, and American men feel that, if they flirt, there is a fundamental commitment at the end of the line," he says. "Europeans are much more subtle—they can handle degrees of interaction. I think Americans are very black-and-white, all-or-nothing. Either you're not interested, or you're completely interested.

"I think American men are far more concerned about other men's opinion of them than women's opinion of them," Leddick continues. "Power is the big drive in America, not sex. Men are very intimidated by women, and I think they prefer withdrawing into a buddy relationship. A 'power trip' is something they can get their mitts on. Women? They don't seem to know how to deal with them."

Leddick, warming to the topic, offers many theories about why there is more flirtation in Paris, from the fact that the French have café life, whereas Americans don't, to his view that the primary self-image a French adult maintains is male/female rather than parental, and that he or she is always testing to see how viable an image that is. Or, suggests Leddick, perhaps the French flirt more simply because they don't watch television as much as Americans do. "The long history of flirting in Europe has continued because it's never been interrupted by passive entertainment," he declares.

Yet Leddick has one observation about flirtation that seems especially apt in Paris: "It's art appreciation," he asserts. "It's the Louvre for the man in the streets. It's the way they acknowledge beauty, and they're not afraid to express it. In New York, a woman can't really go out on the street put together at her best because, in America, it means wolf whistles from construction crews and rude remarks from taxi drivers. In Paris, a woman can put herself together and go out on the street, and men really will appreciate her beauty."

I couldn't disagree, especially because this called to mind a story told to me by my friend Wendy, a pretty blond American who works in Paris. One night on the way home on the bus, she relates, she was talking with a friend when she spied a man staring at her. Fond of flirting herself, she smiled but later regretted this when her admirer got off at the same stop. In fact, as he approached her, she was ready with sharp words to keep him at bay, until the man smiled shyly and handed her a page torn out of a magazine he had been holding.

There, sketched in the corner of the page, was Wendy's profile. "*Excusez-moi, mademoiselle, je ne peux pas résister,*" the man apologized before, thanking her, he disappeared into the night.

Debbie Seaman is a freelance writer who found the man of her dreams while flirting in Paris. Now she lives in Sydney, Australia with her husband and twin boys, where she is a frequent contributor to WHO Weekly.

★

A Frenchman who had been married to an American for several years said, "I love my wife...but she will always be an intimate stranger to me." An American woman who had lived with a Frenchman summarized her experience in these terms: "If I had wanted to have a child, I would have liked to have it with him, but never in a million years would I have wanted him to be the father of my child." Thus in a single sentence, she had managed to separate the genetic being from the cultural being.

—Raymonde Carroll, *Cultural Misunderstandings:*
The French-American Experience

War and Remembrance

The horrors of the D-Day invasion
are still vivid in Normandy.

MOISSY IS NO MORE THAN A HAMLET ON A ROAD TO NOWHERE IN Normandy. It lies in a shallow valley, rich with three of the region's crops: wheat, sunflowers, and grazing grass. Cows with creamy café au lait coats and brown patches around their eyes get fat on saturated pastures. It seems that nothing much has disturbed this scene in a thousand years, except, perhaps, a greater sophistication in the farming.

A dairy tanker pulls out from a farmyard, its silver gut bulging wide in a narrow lane. The lane was never intended for two-way traffic. It was part of an intensively woven pattern of field and lanes called *bocage*. Even today, most of this lane is fringed by the deep-rooted and embanked hedgerows and shade trees arching into a canopy of foliage that characterizes *bocage*.

Bocage is a Norman delineation of turf, describing the earliest pattern of European feudalism. It set boundaries as permanently as stone walls, and it provided windbreaks and contained herds. *Bocage* has also left a military reputation: it entangled one of the most formidable armies on earth, and severely hindered that army's pursuers.

Where Moissy begins, as an easily overlooked turnoff on the D13 road between two modest agricultural towns, Trun and Chambois, there is a small hand-painted sign, dark blue lettering on a ground the color of dried blood. It reads: AOUT, 1944 LE COULOIR DE LA MORT.

Corridor of death?

Everything around speaks of abundant life. Pumpkins swollen by too many summer rains border a chicken wire fence at the foot of the sign, and behind it, a vegetable patch is knee-deep in zucchini plants. Tomatoes are set out on the sills of cottage windows, seeking the fleeting sun to ripen. It has been a poor year for ripening on the vine, but a good one for the chemistry of meadow and udder that gives such weight to Norman creams and cheeses.

All this is too much for the imagination. I cannot easily make the link between what I see and what I know. I know that down this very lane on August 21, 1944, remnants of a once-invincible German Army (lethal Panther tanks of the 21st Panzers, half-tracks, trucks, horse-drawn wagons, motorcycles, and a curious vehicle that the French called a Chenillette, combining a motorcycle with Caterpillar tracks—all these and foot soldiers) attempted a headlong retreat from the encircling Allied armies who had, two and a half months earlier, landed on the Normandy beaches.

There is a terrible molecular focus to this army in flight, locked in one lane, one path, one track that would turn out to be, with literal truth, a dead end. The Third Reich met its nemesis as much here as it did—albeit in far greater numbers—at Stalingrad. Bottled in the *bocage*, the Wehrmacht was strafed without mercy from the sky, raked by artillery, and pursued by tanks. Normandy closed in on its occupier and exacted a withering revenge. German corpses were still being found in the fields fifteen years later; the carnage at Moissy and in the meadows around it effectively ended the Battle of Normandy, begun on June 6, D-Day, on the beaches named Utah, Omaha, Gold, Juno, and Sword.

In its darker moods, when rolling barriers of cloud seem to issue from the tree lines of its forests like smoke from peat fires,

Normandy can appear unrelentingly medieval, a place of Gothic temper. The Normans were great castle builders. Grim probity ruled the land, enforced by knightly sword. Steel, mud, and blood come to mind as you look at battlements built up from rock so that commanding heights were a meaningful statement of power.

From what remains of the castle at Domfront, above the Varenne River in Normandy's deep and somewhat Transylvanian interior, it's easy to imagine Arthurian squadrons clanking across the drawbridge with pennants flying. In fact, it was at Domfront, during the Christmas of 1166, that Archbishop Becket met Henry II as those lions of church and state sought truce; here also that Eleanor of Aquitaine's troubadours caroused.

This land fed armies well. Never was a feudal system better provisioned than from these heavy pasturelands, source of the richest creams and most pungent cheeses in the world. It has been Normandy's destiny and fate to feed great war machines—some of its own making, then that of an invader—and finally to suffer bombardment from the most vast armada ever assembled, to be the doormat of the liberators of Europe who came ashore on the D–Day beaches.

Beaches. How discordant the word is when matched with what befell the first men ashore that morning. Above the cliffs of Omaha, the Normandy American Cemetery has 9,286 white crosses aligned so that from any viewpoint they fall into perfect formation, armies of the dead on permanent parade. It was at Omaha that the invasion very nearly foundered. The overall plan having unraveled, a bridgehead was secured only by acts of heroic improvisation.

Europe has cause to remember. It was reclaimed from Nazi occupation by the men who fought their way from the Norman beaches to Berlin. The American commitment to the salvation of Europe was absolute; there was a messianic drive behind these battles (Eisenhower's memoir was called *Crusade in Europe*). Now, as always, Europeans are held accountable to that vision: Are they worthy of the sacrifices that were made for their liberation?

Of all the landscapes of war, Normandy appears at first sight to have healed as completely as say, the killing fields of the Civil War,

places like Antietam Creek or the slopes and meadows of
Gettysburg. From its harbors to the deep *bocage*, the restaurateurs
of northern France take their pick of catches and crops. The
Range Rover crowd from Paris and London buy barns and farms
for their weekends. But take a second look. In almost every village and in many
towns, few buildings more than 50 years old survive. For a place
with a past stretching into dim mists, this is the architectural equivalent of a historical death. In Caen, an ancient regional center
caught in the direct path of the Allied armies, 80 percent of the
city was destroyed by bombing and bombardment.

It is only when you go beyond the area of the major battles—
extending from the Cotentin peninsula eastward for 50 miles to
the estuary of the river Orne, and 60 or so miles southward from
the beaches—that the missing past begins to reappear.

But even beyond, you can find the remnants of precisely selected targets of violence. Soon after the landings, the distant
château at Thury-Harcourt, a 17th-century ducal seat sheltered in
a gorge and rich in treasures, was detected by the Allies as the op-
erational headquarters of Panzer Group West. On the evening of
June 10, it was subjected to surgical bombing. More than 150
paintings in the château burned, along with the furnishings. The
German survivors fled to Paris. Today, the shell of the château is
crudely bricked up. Two forlorn little mansarded gatehouses lead
to the gardens, carefully restored, which convey a sense of a place
having once been gloriously able to host all the games of *les liaisons
dangereuses.*

Bayeux was luckier. Perilously close to the first landings and
battles, it was an ancient, compact city clustered around the small
but exquisite cathedral of Notre-Dame, on which work began in
the 11th century and ended in the 13th. The cathedral has three
towers, two spired and one with a domed campanile. In June 1944,
these towers were a dominant landmark for the Americans pushing in from Omaha beach and the British from Gold. As any army
would, the Germans were prone to use church and cathedral spires
as observation posts and sniping positions.

A Scene from the Bayeaux Tapestry

Fearsome naval barrages had been directed against German strongholds even far inland from the beaches, and might well have been directed at Bayeux; fortunately, the Allies found that there were virtually no Germans in the city, and it was taken on June 7, with minimal damage, by the British 50th Division. The core remains a vignette of Norman history, but Bayeux's place in the heraldic progress of France was secured not by stonemasons but by the weavers of a 224-foot-long strip of linen, technically known as Queen Mathilda's Tapestry but more universally as, simply, the Bayeux Tapestry.

In a series of vividly detailed *tableaux,* the tapestry legitimizes the conquest of England by Guillaume of Normandy, William the Conqueror. It is an engrossing document and breathes the martial confidence of this race of administrator-warlords who governed anarchic Britain into coherence. There was, therefore, a poignant symmetry in the fact that Bayeux

I t is possible to imagine that the most enduring record of D-Day is very low-tech indeed. It is 272 feet long, 3 feet high and made of bits of cloth. It was put together by 25 women of Britain's Royal School of Needlework, working for four years, and was dreamed up and paid for by a pioneer conservationist, a generous, irascible, dog-loving, stag-stalking, fox-hunting English lord. His aim was to commemorate Operation Overlord, D-Day and the Battle of Normandy. His explicit inspiration was another illustrated piece of cloth, 224 feet long, which tells the story of the Norman Conquest of England and has preserved it for nearly a thousand years. What Lord Dulverton wanted, he said, was "a Bayeux Tapestry in reverse."

—Timothy Foote, "Tapestried Tales of Two Channel Crossings," *Smithsonian* should be liberated by a British Army in 1944, reversing the mission of 1066, when William took 12,000 knights and foot soldiers across the English Channel in an armada of as many as 3,000 boats and routed King Harold at Hastings. (Harold's demise, with an arrow through an eye, is the *coup de grâce* of the tapestry).

The tapestry does not shrink from savage cameos of war: dismemberment, rape, pillage. Military historians study it for details of armor and weapons. Nine centuries grant a certain clinical detachment, until these one-dimensional Norman knights and decapitated Saxons begin to dance in the head along with scenes from monochrome documentaries of the Battle of Normandy in 1944, flickering in war museums. Then bodies merge, attitudes of combat and death look eerily similar, and humankind's learning curve seems pitiably shallow.

A few miles south of Bayeux, in a hollow of the rolling farmland and alongside a farm selling its own Calvados [apple brandy], is one of the smallest war cemeteries. Forty-six British and one Czech soldier lie here, in an immaculately tended plot given the name of a small hamlet nearby, Jerusalem. There was an intense firefight around the hamlet, repelling a German armored column trying to retake Bayeux. In its economy and concentration, Jerusalem is as poignant as the vista of massed crosses above Omaha. Cemeteries of every nationality involved in the Battle of Normandy crop up like this—men left near where they fell in clusters. The French honor and respect these places, and the flowers are always fresh. *N'oubliez pas.*

Do not forget.

In fact, Normandy is engaged in a perpetual struggle to preserve memory. By honoring the relics of an eviscerating battle, the Normans are also obliged to confront France with an ignominious chapter of its history. A superbly conceived museum in Caen meets this duty unflinchingly with a section, suitably subterranean and darkly lit, called the Dark Years. Here, you walk through the tunnel of France's deepest shame, the capitulation of its armies in 1940 and the craven Vichy regime that acted as Hitler's surrogates in France.

The moral rot of this collapse is caught in one shameful telephone conversation played on tape along with newsreel footage.

Hitler had summoned the French generals to the same *wagon-lit* in the forest at Compiègne, 50 miles from Paris, where France had accepted the German surrender in World War I, and here, contemptuously, he dictated the terms for the armistice with France in 1940. The French general Huntziger was sent back to Paris to call his chief, General Weygand, in Bordeaux. The Germans recorded the call, which you can hear today in the museum, scratchy with the static of Europe in collapse.

At first, Weygand is more concerned that he not take any further battering from the German army, and Huntziger assures him: "...the German command is going to give the order...to save Bordeaux in every way...."

And then to the emasculating terms agreed upon at Compiègne:

Huntziger: "I am sending the text by car to Bordeaux...the original German text...."

Weygand: "Yes."

Huntziger: "The text which has been signed. I will attach a copy in French...just so you can understand it. But it is the German text which is legitimate."

Weygand: "Yes."

I don't think the hideous intimacy of war ever quite came home to me until I visited the Peace Museum in Caen. It wasn't a picture of bodies blasted to bits, or gaunt prisoners, or tanks in flames, but of a 17-year-old girl about to be hanged in Warsaw. She was smiling, forgiving the whole thing with the beauty of her soul and her short life. But the most awful thing about the picture was the face of the German soldier with the noose. He looked so terribly unhappy. Poor bastard, I thought (standing there with my own daughters), he didn't want to do it. Perhaps he was even a father himself, and if he refused his orders, no doubt he would be shot. What awful set of events brought him to this moment? What daisy chains of evil and banality and failures of free will? What would I do in such a situation? What would you do? And then, a bit further down the hall, a photograph of Hitler in Paris, smiling.

—James O'Reilly, "On and Off the *Autoroute*"

In a few sentences, as though discussing the closing of a mortgage, they have given away France. And yet Weygand was able to tell 84-year-old Marshal Pétain, about to become the Nazi satrap in France, that the terms were "harsh but not dishonoring."

The Caen Memorial Museum frames this disaster as being "within six weeks the unprecedented collapse of a great power." But, of course, no truly great power collapses like that. In May 1940, shortly before the panzers rolled over northern France, *France Magazine* reviewed the French Army's state of parade and reported: "One look at the comfort and elegance of these new uniforms is enough to convince us that we shall soon have the best dressed army in the world."

Like the great milk cow she was, France was sucked dry by her Nazi occupiers. Then came the fires of liberation. Images of French landscape in the First World War are apocalyptic: the battles of the Second World War were twice as devastating, leveling or gutting not far short of two million buildings and, in Normandy, killing and maiming hundreds of thousands.

Those who walk through the dungeon of The Dark Years come out into the daylight and a minimalist public space called the Esplanade Dwight Eisenhower. All around are suburbs indistinguishable from those built in the America of the '80s. A few miles to the south, the fragments of old Caen are a museum of a different kind, with a memory of centuries, and where the clocks stopped on the night of July 7, 1944, when 450 British heavy bombers made it ground zero. Afterward, "a great silence fell over the town, broken only by the cries of the wounded and the sound of falling masonry from burning buildings," said a witness. Two thousand civilians died in Caen.

From these four years of dishonor and suffering, one figure emerges walking upright out of the smoke, possessed of an ego the size of his country and with no place for shame.

On June 13, 1944, two policemen riding bicycles on the outskirts of Bayeux were stopped by a military staff car. A French general asked them if they would mind riding into the center of the city ahead of him, announcing his arrival. They had not recognized him, since he was known to them only as a voice carried across the Channel in clandestine broadcasts to France from the BBC in London. Now, stunned to be told that they had met General Charles de Gaulle, they sped into Bayeux as his tribunes.

Forty-five minutes later, in a square now named for him, De Gaulle made his first speech on liberated soil: "We shall fight beside the Allies, with the Allies, and as an ally, and the victory we shall win will be the victory of liberty and the victory of France." In a notoriously untuneful voice, he then led the weeping citizens in singing the "Marseillaise."

The speech had been delicately constructed. De Gaulle was no favorite of the Allied leaders, nor of the generals leading the invasion of Normandy. Units of the Free French Forces were held back from the first landings and were used judiciously in other engagements until, taking the initiative, they were instrumental in the liberation of Paris, late in August. This had nothing to do with any deficiency of fighting spirit. It had a lot more to do with De Gaulle's conviction that he, and only he, could resurrect France. In the middle of a battle whose outcome was by no means certain, De Gaulle was a symbolic asset rather

As D-Day crowds remember fallen soldiers, bitter survivors gather at the 14,000 scattered and forgotten graves of civilians sacrificed in the name of the Liberation.

Most of them were victims of the "Transportation Plan," an essentially fruitless Allied effort to slow German reinforcements by bombing Norman cities and crossroads into heaps of rubble. People expecting deliverance watched in shock as explosives leveled urban centers that Resistance agents had reported were free of enemy concentrations.

"They aimed not to kill Germans but to cut the roads, which the French knew was impossible," said Jean Quellien, a historian who studied civilian casualties. "Everyone wondered: 'Why?'"

Because inaccurate bombing was worsened by bad weather and anti-aircraft fire, many more people died from the air raids than from the crossfire of battle, he added.

—Mort Rosenblum, "D-Day Survivors Decry Failed Attempt to Cut Roads," *Associated Press* than an emperor back from Elba, but of course—in the long run—his own estimate of himself was accurate.

Coming ashore in one of the amphibious vehicles called DUKWs, De Gaulle would have been mindful of what, by then, was an incredible feat of reinforcement and supply. Eisenhower's staff had effectively bridged the Channel. But the waters were not docile. The seas for De Gaulle's crossing were rough, and a three-day storm that broke on June 19 seriously damaged the stupendous fabricated harbors that had been shipped in pieces and dropped into place on the American and British beaches.

The dawn assaults on June 6 had shown one face of the Norman littoral: its diverse entrapments, from sheer cliffs and rock promontories to the tank-snarling *bocage* immediately beyond. But the English Channel—or, if you are French, *La Manche*—is another thing. Stand at its edge and it seems dense and sluggish with atomized gravel, as though the stone that gives Norman towns their graven composure has also, over millions of years, become a slurry that leadens the waves. But get out from the lee of cliffs and beyond harbor walls. Then this sea, squeezed by northern blasts through the narrows between Dover and Calais or driven from the west by Atlantic gales, becomes a churning, dark green broth that takes a sea dog's stomach to survive.

In the autumn of 1066, William's armada had set out once and then put back into harbor to await better seas; he could basically go only where the winds took him. In June 1944, Eisenhower also agonized through a Channel storm, keeping a fleet of 6,483 vessels in port a day and reluctantly committing the force to the landings during a predicted lull. In fact, come the dawn of June 6, the seas were rough. At the British Gold Beach, near Bayeux, a Force 5 wind whipped up waves of more than four feet.

All along the beaches, from the northeast-facing Utah, where the Cotentin peninsula gave some protection, to Sword at the Orne estuary, the seas had become a second enemy, often as lethal as the first. At Omaha, landing craft were swamped and sank. A force of Sherman tanks, called DDs, had been fitted with canvas collars and propeller drives, designed to be launched into the water and to sail onto the beaches, so that they could give much-needed covering fire to the exposed infantry. Twenty-nine were launched at Omaha: only two made it to the beach; many others sank like stones, taking their crews with them. At Gold, the British, who had conceived the DDs, didn't take the risk and landed the tanks directly on the beach.

Today, DD tanks are part of the archaeology of the battle. Two of those that sank at Omaha have been salvaged from the long ribbon of wrecks that lies under the coastal water. They sit, encrusted with barnacles and scabs of orange rust, a coating resembling peanut brittle, on plinths outside the spookiest of all the museums, the Musée des Epaves Sous-Marines du Débarquement, near the little fishing harbor of Port-en-Bessin.

Inside, displayed in the kind of glass case that in the British Museum holds Etruscan amulets or Parthian coins, are the prosaic artifacts of unlucky Allied invaders: a Gem razor made in Brooklyn; a pair of binoculars made in Rochester; a pair of wire-rim spectacles; a ship's canteen tray, billed as a *plat à ration,* with traces of noodles calcified on the dull metal. Remains of all kinds are a troubling kind of sediment. These, disinterred from the ocean's floor, are disturbingly personal.

Down the road, in Port-en-Bessin, a large billboard promotes the 27-hole Omaha Beach Golf Course, strung out along the dunes. The port is a natural cleft between high cliffs. It seemed to me strikingly Cornish, having the same economy of color that comes, I think, from enduring the same Atlantic gales, the habit of turning inward for comfort. There are Celtic links between the two places. However, it is not the Celts whom the Normans see as seeding the iron in their blood, but the Vikings.

In Bayeux, in the 17th-century seminary where the Bayeux Tapestry is handsomely mounted, a preamble to the saga of William makes much of the Viking colonization of northern France. An ethnic toughening is implied. And if you want to speculate where the fearsome marriage first occurred between armored knights and evangelism—the forging of barbarity, chivalry, and strutting Christendom—this could be it.

What is less conjectural is that once William, pumping his iron sword with Viking-like pectorals, conquered the Saxons, the courts of England and France were joined, and bred all those psychotic medieval intrigues that mark every castle and cathedral of the Anglo-Frankish world, not least in Normandy.

The Bayeux Tapestry is blatantly a Norman document. For hundreds of years it was thought to be the admiring work of Matilda, William the Conqueror's queen, who supposedly had it run up by the ladies of her court to honor her husband's crowning as king of subjugated England in December 1066. Only recently have experts decided (on the basis of the stitching work and the spelling of place-names in the Latin captions laced into its surface) that the Bayeux Tapestry was made in England by English hands. Because he appears prominently, the best guess is that Bishop Odo of Bayeux, the Conqueror's clerical half-brother, had it done to curry favor with William when he felt he was falling out of favor. William was a ruthless man as well as (literally and figuratively) a bastard, the son of Robert, Duke of Normandy, by a beautiful tanner's daughter. Falling from favor with him was not a good thing.

—Timothy Foote, "Tapestried Tales of Two Channel Crossings," *Smithsonian*

The country that has grown back over the moonscape has many textures. On the high plateau behind Omaha, golden grain crops mix with meadows, and the grid of *bocage* still imposes a tightness to the patchwork. The lanes dive and twist; no sweeps of one color are possible. Farther south, between Caen and Falaise, the sky opens up. There is a swath of broad and flat cereal fields and no *bocage*. The N158 is a prairie road, straight and true.

But south of Falaise, Normandy begins a geological upheaval. A line of increasingly steep ridges runs west to east, divided into two formations, the Collines de Normandie in the west and the Collines du Perche in the east. On the peaks of these ridges where vestiges of great medieval forests remain, are the old fortress towns, like Domfront. And within these heights, the terrain becomes more contorted. In several places the lateral ridges are ruptured by river gorges working north out of the hills to the sea.

Where the Orne pushes toward Caen, the gorge forms the axis of a peculiar pocket called La Suisse Normande. It isn't very Swiss—more like the foothills of Savoy. One small town, Clécy, breasting an escarpment over the river, is spectacularly sited, and another along the river, Pont-d'Ouilly, is as awash with flowers as the Hanging Gardens of Babylon, from its weir to every available surface in the town.

No matter what the seductions, however, a pattern of war is embedded in this topography. Every battle is a map. The major obstacles to armies are obvious. The prairie between Caen and Falaise was perfect tank country, open and clear—deep gorges are the enemy of mobility. But beyond these broad strokes, I began to see a wholly different scale of warscape: a church here, a copse there, any number of localized advantages and disadvantages according to whether you were the hunter or the hunted. At first, of all the Norman obstacles, *bocage* was the worst. The military historian John Keegan wrote: "*Bocage* came to mean the sudden, unheralded burst of machine-pistol fire at close quarters, the crash and flame of a *Panzerfaust* strike on the hull of a blind and pinioned tank."

But then came Sergeant Curtis G. Culin of the American 2nd Armored Division. Listening to the frustration of Sherman crews trapped in the *bocage*, Culin took up an idea that others ridiculed: to put large saw teeth on the front of the tanks. Using scrap from German beach obstacles, Culin improvised the teeth and found a way of mounting them on the Sherman's carapace. These Rhinos ate *bocage* in seconds, and Culin was hailed as the first technohero of the Battle of Normandy.

As the balance of the battle shifted, from securing the beachheads to stopping panzer counterattacks and smashing Hitler's Panzer Group West, the Norman topography was evenhanded in its punishments. Both sides suffered and learned, with grievous losses. In the Collines de Normandie, at Mortain, a natural fortress first exploited by the Romans defending northwest Gaul, the Germans staged their last serious counterattack. As the Blue Guide to Normandy puts it, the battle of 1944 "took a serious toll on the town."

From then on, at the height of summer, the Wehrmacht was pursued eastward into a trap whose terrain and nature seemed innocent enough.

Many great rivers have brought generals to their knees, forcing a battle where it was unwise, blocking retreat. It is hard to see the river Dives in that light. As it meanders, virtually out of sight, between Trun and Chambois, southeast of Falaise, it seems no more formidable than a ditch. It is bridged twice in a stretch of a few miles—each time in a utilitarian way, since the heaviest traffic likely to cross it is a tractor.

In late August 1944, the remnants of a German army that had once been half a million strong came to the banks of the Dives. The bridges were the only way over for the armor and the ragbag of vehicles still functioning. They had been forced into a pocket the shape of a deflating balloon. The neck of the balloon, barely six miles wide, lay across the Dives bridges.

The village of St-Lambert, at the southernmost of the two river crossings, has been rebuilt and is very much as it was, an agricultural backwater. In 1944 it found itself the focus of the German retreat. On August 20, bad weather had given the Wehrmacht some cover. From the belfry of the church at St-Lambert, General Von Luttwitz, commanding the 2nd Panzer Division, and General Straube, commanding the 47th Armored Corps, directed the traffic. It was a hellish spectacle. The roads were choked with wrecked vehicles and corpses. A charnel stench overlay everything. Those who made it through St-Lambert turned south toward Chambois, but that road was blocked by similarly grisly fusions of metal and flesh. Trying to break out across country, they wheeled, unsuspecting, northeast at Moissy and into the gates of Le Couloir de la Mort.

As the weather lifted, the columns in the lane at Moissy were fatally exposed. Rocket-firing Allied aircraft would hit the lead vehicle of a column, jamming the rest in the *bocage*, and then strafe them systematically. Men who broke into the surrounding fields came under fire from Canadian gunners. "We would see a group trying to run across a field from one wood to another, and watch some fall, some run on, some lie moaning in front us. It was more of an execution than a battle," recalled one of the gunners. "What a massacre," said another. "Terrified horses trying to break out of their harness, men trying to flee.... It was useless."

The lucky ones hid and emerged when it was safe to surrender. One group of more than a thousand Germans found the parish priest of the small village of Tournai and asked him to lead them to the Allied lines. Groping through the rolling smoke of the inferno, the priest came upon a lone Canadian. Against his own instincts for survival, this soldier was persuaded to take the Germans' white flags on faith and lead them to safety.

The design of the culminating battle was becoming starkly clear from the crest of a hill a few miles northeast of the Dives. On the Allied maps, the hill had a number, 262. Atop it sat 80 tanks and 1,500 infantry of the 2nd Polish Armored Regiment. The Poles were avengers; they fought the Germans with the specific fury of men whose country was the first to be blitzkrieged into submission in 1939. After an earlier error of map-reading, they had—they thought luckily—come up to this salient from which they could see the Germans caught in the narrowing gap below.

I saw my first German dead. He must have been killed while running. Even in death his body seemed to be trying to surge forward. His helmet and uniform were all in place. He had been dead for several hours. I could tell by the color of his skin. He was wearing glasses, still not broken.

I remember self-consciously saying to someone, "Well, he won't bother anyone again." Now I wonder whether he ever wanted to bother anyone.

—John Ausland,
Letters Home: A War Memoir

Canadian artillery was shelling the Germans from the north. The Polish tanks joined in from hill 262, but the Poles belatedly realized that they were in danger themselves: powerful German units, seeking to keep the escape route open, were coming up behind them. The Panzer divisions that had made it out of St-Lambert fought with suicidal ferocity, storming the Polish hill until it was rimmed with a bulwark of bodies.

There is a simple and powerful Polish memorial on hill 262 today. Etched into metal on a stone plinth is the disposition of the forces during the battle of August 20 and 21, 1944. Standing at the plinth, you can survey the landscape as the Polish commander must have done, except that it is still and verdant, not shrieking with shells and covered in the oiled smoke of burning tanks.

Four flags fly over the memorial: French, American, Polish, and Canadian. Early on the afternoon of August 21, the Poles, besieged for 24 hours, were relieved by a column of Shermans from the Canadian Grenadier Guards. The Poles had lost 325 men in the few days of the battle. More than a thousand were wounded, and 114 were missing—in total, twenty percent of the Polish combat strength. When the Canadians arrived, the Poles had no food left and very little ammunition. But the Battle of Normandy was over.

In four days, 10,000 Germans were put out of action and 40,000 captured. Bayerlein's elite Panzer Lehr had virtually ceased to exist. Nonetheless, as many as 50,000 men made it through the corridor, either during darkness, with the help of bad weather, or simply by fighting their way out. But they took with them nightmare memories, never lost.

On August 23, Eisenhower himself arrived at the killing fields. He said it was a scene that only Dante could have described. A French historian did his best: "For hundreds of metres one could walk only on decaying human remains, in ominous silence, in luxuriant countryside which life had suddenly deserted.... The trees had lost their leaves and branches and no bird sang."

The Normandy beaches saw the most perilous phase of the battle, the great Allied army barely getting its grip on land in time, before the Germans realized what was happening. But it is a mistake to think only of the beachheads. Two million Allied soldiers poured into Normandy, well over half of them American. As the battle tore its way through the hinterland and then into the ancient domains of medieval France, it became a vicious but finally decisive clash of titans. And it was a crusade. The Allies lost 206,703 men, but from Omaha to hill 262, one vision of Europe had purged another.

N'oubliez pas.

Clive Irving is a journalist and author who was born in England in 1933. He has been managing editor of The Sunday Times *of London, editor of numerous magazines, and he has worked in television. Since 1972 he has been a freelance writer and novelist, and his most recent book is* Wide-Body: The Triumph of the 747.

✳

One recalls that several weeks before the Allied invasion, a pair of German officers climbed to the belfry of the square stone steeple of the Catholic church to look over the countryside and check placement of coastal defenses.

They lay their map on a ledge outside the belfry and, absorbed in conversation for a moment, looked up just in time to see the wind catch it and lift it away from the balcony. Obviously aware of the importance of the document and the necessity of keeping its notations secret, they scurried down the steps from the belfry to find it.

But find it they could not. It had floated down from the sky and into the three-sided, unroofed public urinal near the town square where a local house painter was answering nature's summons.

The map fell right into his unoccupied hand, and he stashed it immediately in his pants.

Accosted by the frantic German officers, the painter denied having seen it. But it was one of the first French gifts bestowed upon arriving American soldiers as they pushed up from Utah Beach and into Sainte Marie-du-Mont.

—Mike Harden, "French Town Doesn't Miss Humor, Irony,
Tales Galore," *The Columbus Dispatch*

JUDY WADE

* * *

Love Among the Apples

On the back roads of Brittany,
an old man remembers.

I BICYCLED ALONG, HAPPILY, PAST ROWS OF SPROUTING CAULI-
flower and artichoke, along well-tended fields. I slowed at one particular pasture where a huge black and white Holstein tenderly
nuzzled her wobbly calf. The spring afternoon sun lay warm on
my back. I thought about the similarities between the farms here,
along France's Brittany coast, and the farm where I'd grown up in
central Minnesota.

At the top of a hill I paused to check my map for the village of
Lanloup where I'd meet the rest of my cycling group. It seemed to
be just ahead.

Within half an hour of pedaling I realized that either the map
was wrong or I'd miscalculated. Or, I could have missed Lanloup.
More than once I'd embarrassed myself by asking directions to a
village, only to be told I was standing in it.

Ahead I could see a stocky fellow in overalls checking his apple
orchard, his grey hair sprouting from beneath a navy beret.

In my best high school French I called, *"Où est Lanloup?"* He
turned slowly, regarded me for a moment, then broke into a glad-
dened grin and a torrent of incomprehensible French.

"*Américaine? Canadienne?*" he bellowed enthusiastically as he strode in my direction.

"*Américaine,*" I verified, clutching my handlebars.

Without warning he crushed me in a great bear hug as I struggled to keep myself and my bike erect. Garlic-scented French swirled around me as he released me, regarding me at arm's length with a delighted smile.

Gently, with great ceremony, he took my bike and propped it against a fence post. He led me to where his worn knapsack hung on a branch just beginning to bud with the new-season's apples. From the sack he extracted a heavy chipped tumbler and a casually corked bottle of unlabeled red wine.

With the care of a sommelier he filled the glass and offered it to me. "*Merci, merci,*" he repeated as he pantomimed a toast.

Thanks? For what? I shrugged back.

Slowly, carefully, he pronounced every syllable. "*Pour la guerre de votre père.*"

For the war of my father?

Suddenly it dawned. I remembered where I was. This delightful old gentleman was thanking me for the part my father may have played in liberating France during World War II. With tears slipping into the corners of my smile, I raised my glass in a second salute...to the circumstances that had made such a meeting possible, to my father who had indeed been a part of World War II, and to my new friend for remembering.

I hope he understood.

Judy Wade is the author of Arizona Guide, Seasonal Guide to the Natural Year, *and* Disneyland and Beyond, *among others. She is also a freelance travel writer who prefers to write about outdoor activities, including "mellow strolls through interesting countryside." She is a contributing editor of* Travel 50 & Beyond *and contributing writer for* Physicians Travel & Meeting Guide *and* Where to Retire. *She lives with her husband in Phoenix.*

"All my life I have been grateful for the contribution France has made to the glory and culture of Europe—above all for the sense of personal liberty and the rights of man that has radiated from the soul of France."

—Sir Winston Churchill, in a speech in the
House of Commons, August 2, 1944

REX GRIZELL

✦ ✦ ✦

In the Land of the Musketeers

An Englishman muses on life and change in Gascony.

THERE ARE TWO WAYS TO LIVE IN A COUNTRY THAT IS NOT YOUR own. You can take an interest in what goes on around you, the people, their customs, even their history, or you can ignore all that and create your own private "island." In France the *"liberté"* in the French national motto still means something and, once you have conformed to the regulations, no one will bother you. Personally, I have always been interested in other people's business, so Marie-Anne and I chose the first course, trying to understand the different ways of life, the different behaviour and customs, of our new neighbours. But even as we learned things changed around us.

This was farming country—fruit, vegetables, cereals, wine, and livestock. It has been so from time immemorial, and so it still is, but not in the same way. The rhythm and permanence, and the security, have gone from farming. In the past the farmers always had enough. They gave their labour, their expenses were limited, and as a rule they made a profit; some good farmers died rich. But in recent years the consumer society, inflation, increased mechanisation, and the establishment of EU quotas for various products have changed all that.

In this area the shock has been brutal. Only five or six years ago the farmers here had a good investment—the price of agricultural land had been rising every year. There was a shortage of farms to rent, and would-be tenants had to pay a heavy premium similar to "key money" to get one. Anyone from abroad seeking to buy a landed property risked seeing most of the land taken from them on compulsory purchase by the Sogaf, an official body which would then install young farmers on it. This organization no longer has money to spare. The value of the land is in steady decline and the farmers have additional problems.

In some other agricultural parts of France there has been a steady decline for years. In departments like the Hautes-Alpes of Provence, where life has always been hard, it is now almost impossible. Dozens of villages have died. Where there were hundreds of people there are now a few dozen ancients with nothing but bent backs and wrinkled and toothless faces to show for a life of incessant toil. Even in the fertile heart of France, in departments like the Cher, it's the same story: deserted villages, no shops, boarded-up houses, closed schools. Where there were 70 farmers, there are a dozen left, scraping a living.

There are as yet no dead villages in Gascony, but many are struggling, and the farmers are afraid. Much of the land in the river valleys is very fertile, but it is heavy. Traditionally it was ploughed with the aid of horses, sometimes oxen. As long as they worked, the beasts manured the ground, and when they were too old for work, the farmers sold them to the butcher for almost as much as they had paid for them in the first place. Now the farmer must have all the latest agricultural machinery. New tractors cost thousands, old tractors fetch almost nothing. But farming is said to be more efficient, more productive.

M. Caumont questions it all. "What I know is that I grew up in a happy family. True, we had fewer possessions. We knew less about farming than we know now. I am, perhaps, a better farmer than my father, advances have been made. But my father never owed money, while I float on a sea of debt, like every other farmer I know. Young people, sensibly, don't want to work on the land. Clever men invent machines to do their work, and the farmers must buy them, because they cannot get labour. Where do they get the money? They are obliged to borrow, and in a few years the machines must be replaced, and they borrow again. There is no way out."

Despite their initial scorn tourism has become an alternative source of income for many farmers, who offer bed and breakfast, or convert old farm buildings to holiday cottages. Down here they don't make the transition from turnips to tourism easily. In Normandy I once stayed with a successful farmer who had turned part of his land into a well-equipped camp site and was proud of it. He looked indulgently at his campers and said to me, "Far and away the best crop I ever had." In contrast a local farmer here asked me if I could help him get holiday visitors for a cottage on his land. I went to look at it. The walls were patterned with damp stains, there was no bathroom, the sideboard had lost part of a leg and was propped up with ancient books a lot more valuable than the furniture, and, if it had been London, I would have said the mattresses came from a skip. When I told him he would have to redecorate and refurnish throughout and put in a bathroom, his face fell.

ays begin and end in the dead of night.
They are not shaped long, in the manner
of things which lead to
ends—narrow road, man's life on earth.
They are shaped
round, in the manner of things eternal and stable—sun, world, God.
Civilization tries to persuade us we are going towards
something, a distant goal. We have forgotten that our only goal is to
live, to live each and every day, and that if we live each and every day, our true goal is achieved. All civilized people see the day
beginning at dawn or a little after or a long time after or
whatever time their work begins; this they lengthen according to their work, during what they call "all day long;" and end it when they close their eyes. It is they who say the days are long. On the contrary, the days are round.

—Jean Giono, *"Rondeur des Jours"* as quoted by Julian More in *Views from a French Farmhouse*

"But that would cost money," he said. He was typical of many peasant farmers. They have learned that if they want a good crop, they must invest in fertilizer, but they want a return from tourism without any investment.

One of the lovely sights of spring when we first came here was the great drifts of rose and pink blossom as the many peach orchards came into flower. But the farmers decided that they could no longer compete with Spanish growers who could get their peaches to market about two weeks before the first local peaches were ready. So many of the peach orchards have gone.

There is change everywhere. Even our peaceful river now boasts a beautifully converted barge on which holiday visitors, old people's clubs, and others enjoy a daily cruise in summer. In a comfortable dining saloon meals are supplied by one of the best local restaurants, and the strains of music float across the water, where before there was only the plop of a fish or the harsh squawk of the buzzard.

All these are physical changes and have altered the nature and the look of the countryside around us to some extent. But the difference is minor. Those visitors who have not seen it before find a lovely landscape of gently rolling hills, broad valleys with great rivers, smaller valleys with streams and lakes, and wooded slopes, as well as farm fields and orchards.

Yes, the land is beautiful and benevolent and spacious. But there is more to living in a foreign country than scenery and sunshine, and more than can be learned even in many holidays and business visits. There is another climate, that created by the people and their attitudes of mind. It would be a rash man who said he understands the French. Even after years of living among them they remain enigmatic, difficult to know in depth.

In general, certain characteristics are strongly marked. "The Gallic temperament is impetuous, unreliable, ingenious, inconsistent...brave but utterly devoid of the stern temper that survives defeat.... They are politically instable, and their plans follow an ever-varying pattern of emotionalism.... They stop every traveler, willing or not, and ask him what he knows on any topic that in-

terests them…. They are credulous, and slaves of superstition."
These comments and many others were made by Julius Caesar, one
of the shrewdest and most capable men in history, more than 2,000
years ago, and recorded in his own account of the conquest of
Gaul, *De Bello Gallico.*

Nothing much has changed through the centuries. Their politics are still chaotic; in sport they do well when winning but lose
heart as soon as they sense defeat. They still repeatedly question
everybody on everything—the public opinion poll is an obsession
in France, and no politician is interviewed without being faced
with the week's result on this or that. Judging by the large number of advertisements for fortune tellers, clairvoyants, and faith
healers, they are still credulous. In money matters they are avari-
cious, but their insistence on value for money has a good side. The
general high standard of workmanship throughout France is a direct result. In business they seek an advantage relentlessly and are
dissatisfied when their terms are met, thinking they might have
done better.

They live in this beautiful land, but they are not happy. Their
lives are clouded by mistrust. They have little confidence in each
other. Unlike Britain, where—another generalization—people
tend to be trusted until they show a good reason why they
should not be, in France all relationships begin in mistrust and
suspicion. Even marriage includes a written contract relating to
the material possessions of the couple. The French countryman
cannot take things at face value, he always suspects an underlying
motive.

When you live among them, you cannot help feeling that deep
down the French are a sad race. "Gay Paree" is a misnomer with a
touch of desperation about it. It was no accident that Françoise
Sagan's *Bonjour Tristesse* was a bestseller. Its title, a "*cri de coeur*" they
all recognized, would have sold it to the French, whoever had
written it. In *Madame Bovary,* Gustave Flaubert dispassionately describes another aspect of this same sickness. The French soul is
often like a caged animal, hopelessly moving around in search of a
way out. All their best songs, and there are many lovely ones, are

full of nostalgia, of *"tristesse,"* the sense of something lost from life. One of France's finest and most popular singers, Francis Cabrel, is a Gascon whose songs are poetic in their sadness.

Although we had found that people in the French countryside were unfailingly kind and generous once the ice was broken, we had also noticed that they seemed much more reserved than their counterparts in England, or indeed elsewhere in Europe, where it is quite normal to call out a greeting to a friend or stranger met on the road. Not only did the French tend not to do this, or only to return our greetings after a fractional hesitation, but those who did not know they had been observed would often step out of sight. Time and again we glimpsed a figure as we passed a village house or country farm furtively moving back behind a curtain or open doorway. We speculated as to whether this was the innate shyness of a peasant population or whether it might have something to do with their land having been occupied by foreign invaders twice within living memory. Most tourists to France have noticed how the initial reaction to strangers there is more reserved than elsewhere. We had found that off the beaten track the contrast was even more striking.

—Robin Hanbury-Tenison,
*White Horses Over France:
From the Camargue to Cornwall*

But there are many contradictions in the Gascon character. For me there is a touch of the Irish about them, always ready to be dramatic and voluble, and sometimes rash. I once worked for a time in a small town in the far west of Ireland, in county Mayo. The local hero was a young man who had inherited a country house and a fortune in his twenties. He was not envied or respected for that, but because in less than ten years he had gone through the lot, spent it all, in the correct Irish order, on horses, drink, and women. No true Gascon could bring himself to do that, they have too much respect for money, but like the men of Mayo, they would all like to and would have admired him for it. Even sober M. Caumont saw the point, when I told him this story before he made a trip to Ireland. "Ten years of good living is more than most of us ever get," he said.

The Gascons are fiercely independent, fiery and impetuous, and brave, and if these qualities sometimes degenerate into touchiness and a swaggering boastfulness with a somewhat cavalier regard for truth, it is never long before their joviality and natural courtesy return.

They do appreciate a good lie, and every year in the village of Moncrabeau a Liars' Festival is held and whoever, in the opinion of the judges, tells the most entertaining lie is crowned King (or on one occasion Queen) of the Liars for a year. It has become a popular event which now attracts competitors from all over France, but the point is that it was originally a local, purely Gascon festival.

The exaggeration, the boastfulness, the conscious geniality so often found in the Gascons is, perhaps, just the other side of the coin, a kind of defiance of underlying unhappiness. Perhaps their inability to keep a promise, proverbial in France, is another aspect of the same feeling, as if they ask themselves, What does it matter in the end? Yet they are not men of straw. They are traditionally great fighters. The Three Musketeers were Gascons. The famous d'Artagnan was from a poor farm—it still exists—in the heart of Gascony, though in real life he was a career soldier with no more flair or imagination than the average sergeant-major. He was one of the many younger sons of poor landowners whose only choice in the 17th and 18th centuries was between poverty on the land and a career with the sword, and who, as the *"cadets de Gascogne,"* won a reputation for bravery in the king's army. The courage of the Gascons was again evident in World War II when the region was a stronghold of the Resistance.

Another contradiction is that, though tight with money, like all the French, they can be hospitable to strangers. An aged relative of mine went for a walk on a summer's day, forgot where he was, and found himself adrift in a local farmyard. The farmer welcomed him, offered him a draught of some home-made nectar, and after an amiable but incoherent conversation—neither spoke the other's language—steered him in the right direction. He returned to the house even unsteadier on his feet than usual, and saying what re-markably good stuff it was they drink in these parts.

Although the Gascon is often intense and serious, and seldom light-hearted, he can show a spontaneous warmth. The local people, whatever their problems and however cautious they may be in friendship, are also unfailing in their courtesy in day to day matters. They would not dream of passing you or anyone they know without a friendly "*Bonjour*" and the inevitable handshake.

So life goes on, for the most part pleasantly and efficiently enough, though there is a continual round of strikes and demonstrations by the unhappy farmers. They pelt the Town Hall and the mayor, who has a food canning factory, with the tomatoes he hasn't bought from them, or tip tons of apples into the streets, or block the bridges across the Garonne with their tractors, as they have done once or twice. As the bridges are as much as twenty miles apart, this is a serious inconvenience to those who want to cross and go about their business, but down here the sympathy is with the farmers, and after a short grumble, the motorists wait patiently. They know quite well that no farmer is going to miss his lunch for a demonstration and that shortly before twelve the tractors will start to move.

These are the people we deal with every day, a mercurial race, full of awareness, who feel that life could and should offer a lot more than it does, and in consequence they feel cheated and often tend to react bitterly. Discontent is a very strong flavour in the French brew, and the Gascons are no exception.

Yet, and it is part of the enigma, as we have discovered, when they let go, they really know how to enjoy themselves. One occasion we shall always remember was the *méchoui* arranged by my friend, the lady of the bath, at the local auberge. *Méchoui* is a term originally used throughout the Maghreb—Arab North Africa— for barbecuing a whole sheep. What Madame was offering was an alfresco dinner based on such a barbecue. For 80 francs we would have aperitifs, soup, barbecued lamb, pudding, and free wine, followed by music and dancing. And that's what we had, plus some unexpected extras.

We had an English family on holiday in the *pigeonnier*. Dad was a highly placed aviation executive, Mum taught handicapped children and there were two small boys, six and nine years old, John and Peter. Marie-Anne and I thought they might find the *méchoui* interesting. An old friend of ours, a writer and artist, was actually staying in the inn, with his wife and son, so we bought our tickets and formed a small British delegation to this essentially French affair.

Having had a drink at the house, we arrived a few minutes later than the seven thirty advertised. The inn has a spacious courtyard, shaded by large chestnut trees. Long trestle tables had been set out in rows beneath the trees with places for about seventy people. In the courtyard between the parking area and the tables there was a pit with a whole sheep stretched on a spit above a miserable fire. Edward, the artist, and family, being resident, were already there, installed at a table facing the abandoned sheep, drinks at hand. Apart from a French family of five at the far end of a table, the place appeared deserted.

"Bit of a rave up," said our aviation friend laconically.

"Madame says not to worry," said Edward, "Plenty of people coming. Full house. Just southern time-keeping."

Madame of the bath spotted us and brought us a kir all round, and Coke for the boys. We chatted. Nothing happened for a while, then other guests began to arrive. On her way back from serving them we stopped Madame and asked her when things would get going.

"We can't start yet," she said. "The cooks are not here." Then she added, by way of explanation, "They are the local dustmen and they haven't finished their round yet."

"Did she say the cooks are the dustmen?" asked Edward's wife, tentatively.

"That's right."

"Just as well we are not having stew," said the aviation man.

Madame, who speaks no English, saw us smile and smiled herself. "Don't worry. They will soon be here. Have another kir."

Five minutes later the three Moroccan cooks, still in their boots and jerkins, appeared, and were greeted with a ragged cheer. One of them began kicking up the fire, and added more logs. A second produced a galvanized bucket full of oil.

"I saw him fetch that oil from the garage next door," said

Edward, improvising, as the third man produced a floor mop, dipped it in the bucket and began to slosh oil all over the sheep.

"I bet his wife's looking for that mop," said the aviation man, not to be outdone.

By now the tables were practically full, and a cloud of pungent blue smoke was drifting under the trees. Conversation all round was becoming animated, but there was no sign of the meal starting. Madame appeared again, as if in answer to a telepathic command.

"Won't be long now," she said. "Have another kir."

"I think I'd prefer a gin and tonic," said Edward. "All right, all round?" No one protested. "Okay. Six gin and tonics, madame, if you please."

They had barely arrived when the meal began. Madame's son went round putting open bottles of red wine on the table, one for every four guests. He was followed by his blonde wife, ladling out soup from a huge tureen. After the soup, there was what the French call a "*petite pause,*" which can last anywhere up to half an hour. The pause was naturally filled with glasses of red wine, conversation, and repetitions of the bucket of oil and mop routine. As we talked, we discovered that the lively lady opposite me and most of our immediate neighbours were from Calais.

"You are Eengleesh," said the man sitting next to her. "When ze Eengleesh arrive in Calais, we lock up our women," he added, glancing at his companion. From her subsequent behavior, it might have been an idea to lock her up whoever arrived in Calais.

Time went by, and we were beginning to lose interest in whether we had anything more to eat or not, but spirits were raised when the sheep was removed from the spit and placed on a butcher's table, where one of the cooks attacked it ferociously with a scimitar, or something very like it. While this was going on, to shouts of encouragement from the diners, and stares of incredulity from the two small boys, huge dishes of rice appeared and were placed at intervals along the tables. Gradually plates bearing roast lamb were passed down the table. Edward and the aviation man received beautifully cooked slices of leg, while Marie-Anne and I each had an interesting collection of bones with a few tatters of meat adhering. They came round again with more bottles of wine. And again. It was quite good, if you drank enough of it.

Some time after the main course, the moment for which the small boys had been patiently waiting all evening arrived—ice-cream was passed round, with double portions for them as the only small children present. While this was going on Madame's son and daughter went round the tables with a seemingly endless piece of string, linking all the diners together. The women were apparently told to loop it around a bra strap or through their blouse, and the men to attach it to their trousers. I had no idea what was going on but it was obvious that most of the diners had played this game before and knew what to expect. Marie-Anne had quickly appreciated how things were going to turn out and only pretended to attach it, and advised Edward's wife and Mrs. Aviation to do the same.

Eventually amid a good deal of hilarity the string was pulled, and when the confusion which followed had subsided, a number of the women, who had not been wearing much anyway on the hot summer evening, were in advanced stages of undress, and several of the men had lost their shorts or trousers. The lively lady across the table was topless and stood up waving her shirt.

It cannot be insignificant that the French not only have a female figure as the symbol of the Republic, Marianne, whose facial features adorn coins and city halls all over the country, but officially select an actual French-woman, usually a movie star, to be the model for the symbol. It used to be Brigitte Bardot; then it was Catherine Deneuve; in 1989, it became a model, Inès de la Fressange. I always felt that the attitude of the French toward the female breast was a sign of their skill in incorporating, without fanfare or triumphalism, a certain eroticism into everyday life. The French love breasts, which are photographically and artistically reproduced everywhere…but with none of the snickering and gloating that surrounds that part of the anatomy in the puritan countries, where the prurience of the interest is more blatant.

—Richard Bernstein, *Fragile Glory: A Portrait of France and the French*

"Oh, not again, Mum," said a pretty teenage girl a couple of places away to my left. Whether she meant that Mum did this every year, or every week, or wherever she could find a *méchoui,* we never knew. But Mum, who was directly opposite me, was bouncing around unrestrained, and for a woman with a teenage daughter she was remarkably well built and had nothing to be ashamed of. To keep up the liveliness, the man next to her, reduced to his colourful underpants, stood on the bench and sang, quite well, what Marie-Anne said was a distinctly lewd song. Nevertheless, almost everybody present, men and women, knew the chorus and joined in heartily.

Satisfied with his triumph, he sat down and said, "Now you give us Eengleesh song."

I demurred, thinking that we would make a very poor choral group, but Marie-Anne, among whose many qualities is the ability to smooth over awkward moments, broke into "Happy birthday to you," and in no time everybody joined in, and honour was saved. After this, there was a pause for breath and drinks, and a what now? feeling. Away to our left an oldish man, grey-haired, ordinary look-ing, stood up. There was a drop in conversation as people looked in his direction, and I heard a small voice say, "*Mais non, Pappy.*" But Grandpa took no notice. He remained standing and began to sing.

Whatever we expected, it was not what we got. The songs he sang were well-known, sentimental, musical comedy hits of the re-cent past, and he sang them in full tenor voice without the slight-est false note or hesitation. Each was greeted enthusiastically with a round of energetic applause. The word was passed around the ta-bles, "He's retired now, but for twenty years he was a soloist with the Opéra Comique in Paris." During the third song he encour-aged the diners to join in, and not for the first time I was surprised at the musicality and choral ability of the French. The old man bowed slightly and sat down, happy, like all performers with an ap-preciative audience. He had added a touch of champagne to an al-ready warm-hearted evening.

Madame came round to announce that the occasion would continue with music and dancing. People began to leave the tables and move to the bar. Mum was persuaded to put her shirt on to go indoors. "Good night, *les Anglais*," called her retrousered friend, entering the bar.

We took the small boys home, tired out, mystified by the unfamiliar goings-on, but well content with their ice-cream. Edward and family stayed behind, and reported later that the revelry continued until well after midnight.

Next time I saw Madame, I complimented her on the evening and said how much everyone had enjoyed themselves.

"It's the same every year," she said. "It's the sunshine and the air of Gascony. It goes to their heads."

Gascony is one of the last unspoiled regions of France. One of the things we like most of all is the feeling of space, that towns and villages are miles apart and not linked by ribbon development, the sense that there is room to live, and for people and places to evolve in their own way. I don't think the French could live happily in a small country, crowded together. The Dutch would manage very well in France, but the French in a space like Holland would be a total disaster. As it is the open spaces, the distances, are their consolation, their margin of liberty. They walk, they climb, they sail, and in the space and the open air something of that "*tristesse*" disperses.

We share this sense of liberty, and we like, too, a lifestyle where a village may have three bakers each baking their own "real" bread, and where farmers still have their own vineyard and make their own wine, and where there are markets in every town which have been taking place on the same days every week for a thousand years, and are still crammed with the produce of the local fields and woods and orchards.

And their land, their beloved Gascony, with its rolling hills, its forests and woods, its fertile fields, its countless streams and lakes, and its great rivers, all sheltered by the majestic barrier of the snow-capped Pyrénées, is itself a daily benediction.

Recently we were away for six weeks in London, the longest period we have ever been absent. It seemed to us that life was becoming increasingly stressful in London, and we were pleased to return to Gascony.

The baker calls three times a week. He is the epitome of peasant reserve and caution, always a formal *"bonjour,"* but rarely volunteering a comment of any kind, and in the years I have known him, I don't think he has ever handed me a loaf without first having the money for it in his hand. Then he gives me the change, if any is due, and then he gives me the loaf. When I returned, he started deliveries again. On the first day he said, *"Bonjour, monsieur,"* and held his hand out of the window of his van for me to shake, something he had never done before. "Did you have a good trip?"

"Very good," I said. "We have a grandson, our first. Everything's fine. My wife is staying on another week to help my daughter-in-law."

"That's good. All that's very good. I'll come by on Saturday as usual. It's nice to see you back."

Well, I thought, as I walked back into the house with the country loaf in my hand, perhaps I do belong here at last. On the other hand it might be just that I represent three loaves a week all year round, with extras for family and friends in the summer.

You never know with the Gascons. We don't mind. We took a leap in the dark, but looking back on our years here, it seems to us that, on the whole, like the man who fell off the precipice, we've been lucky.

Rex Grizell spent 30 years as a feature writer and executive on London's Fleet Street. He is the author of Auvergne and the Massif Central *and* A White House in Gascony: Escape to the Old French South *from which this story was excerpted. He lives with his French wife on a farm in Gascony.*

★

Hence the French peasant who has not money enough to buy even a horse, who has barely enough food to eat, can willfully assert his sense of personal being and worth: "Since I am too poor to buy any other horse, at least the Horse of Pride will always have a stall in my stable." This kind of defiance of circumstance and all others is common in Europe. Sometimes it verges on hauteur.

—Stuart Miller, *Understanding Europeans*

JENNY WOOLF

Cinéma en Plein Air

*Idealism found a home in a farmhouse-cum-hostel
in the south of France.*

IT WAS THE STRANGEST THING TO FIND IN AN ISOLATED COUNTRY field. It looked like a medium sized cow-shed, except that a black and white poster for *Lost Horizons* was propped up outside the door, and inside you could just glimpse row upon row of red plush-and-chrome, tip-up seats. It was completely empty, but neat and expectant: film stills decorated its walls, the floor was swept, the chrome gleamed.

We'd cycled for hours, an endless drone of bees sounding above the hissing of the wheels through the scent of lavender, pine, and cedar. A clear and sunny light grew more golden as evening drew on and we had at last found the bumpy track leading off the road. Through woodlands, past the little cinema alone in the field, and right to the edge of the cliff, there, a path led downwards and a rickety sign pointed over the edge: REGAIN.

As we wheeled our bikes to the edge, we saw a great handmade house built directly out of the cliff, connected together by steps and paths and staircases. It rambled and spread down the rockface, and, below, glimpsed through trees, a straw-roofed terrace reached out to a waterfall trickling down the rock. More steps wound down from that into the grass and trees of a shadowed evening valley.

It was the home of François Morenas and his painter wife, Claude. Neither spoke English—or wanted to speak it, perhaps—but with my mediocre French I learned that François had approved of communal living since the 1930s, and chose to open his home as a low-priced hostel to anyone who wanted to come, to enjoy the pleasures—preferably outdoors—of art, nature, and film.

He'd been young in the 1930s, gripped, like so many Europeans, by idealistic notions that had flourished before the War swept most of them away. Hiking, community, open air, internationalism: here they were, blended with that particularly Gallic love of culture that supports the structure of civilized French life.

He was old, now; frail, courteous, and modest. He asked about our trip, and allocated us a little room with vines growing over the windows and shading the sun: very simple, with Claude's paintings hung upon the walls.

The farmhouse had been a peasant's home when François found it, and he'd purchased the valley below for a few francs in the 1930s, long before Peter Mayle and hordes of foreign real-estate buyers had moved into the Luberon. He added rooms and his perfect miniature cinema as he went along. Inside, it was cool and dark, with big oil paintings, rough rock walls, and fine old furniture: a dark sideboard with flowers, gleaming brass bowls, a big desk, and one of those odd French bread-safes that looked as if it should house a couple of parrots.

L' amour est en ces lieux
enfant de la nature:
Partout ailleurs il est enfant
de l'art.

*Love in these places is a child
of nature:
Elsewhere it is a child of art.*

—Voltaire

The company was pleasant; conversation in many languages revolved around traveling, art, and films, but I had come for the countryside. The valley was wooded and grassy, dotted with scented stocks and wild sweet-peas, with walls of great lime-stone slabs, and caves big enough to live in. The insects were gorgeous: migraine-striped butterflies with zigzags and turquoise patches, metallic beetles, giant dragonflies, strange hopping things with bright blue wings, and monstrous brown armored creatures lumbering through the baking air, droning like small Lancaster bombers.

The nearest place of any size was Apt, ten kilometers down a precipitous road. François's principles didn't include edible food so I'd stocked up with chocolate and cheese before toiling up the hill.

Because it was July, François was planning to show a film that evening about the French Revolution. "To commemorate, but not celebrate it," he said carefully. He was taking his projector and screen out into the forest, so that people could watch the film in the open air. He seemed sad when I said I didn't want to attend but did not try to change my mind.

He was so shaky now that he made me nervous, but when he was younger and stronger he had marked hiking trails through his land and was glad we were using them. We explored the valley, detouring to the village of Sivergne. It was restored, with dark blue pitchers on many of the windowsills, each pitcher containing a bunch of spiky leaves. I thought it was too artful, but the valley itself shimmered untouched beneath clouds of butterflies. The farmhouse, when we returned seemed to be full of new kittens and wasps.

Most people wandered into the forest as night fell to see the film about the French revolution. I wasn't interested in revolutions, so sat on the terrace munching the chocolate. White light from the projector flickered through distant trees, and faint, canned, revolutionary sounds came on the breeze. I wished I wasn't going the next day.

Next morning, François sat drinking his coffee on the terrace and watching me load the bike. "Once," he said, "people came for several weeks, but now so many come just for a day or two.

"They are," he said slowly, "in such a hurry! They're on long distance walks, great adventures. They're too tired to socialize in the evening, and next day they leave at 6 a.m., in order to keep to their schedule. To the group, they contribute only the strange idea that walking in the countryside should be competitive." He shrugged. "It's not the way I ever wanted to live, of course."

As I packed, I wished again that I could stay. I suspected François might be dead by the time I could return another year. I had touched his strangely pre-war existence by a mere filament. He came from an era when people thought there was space and time to spare. But I had limited time, and tickets booked for home, and many kilometres to go before I got there.

Jenny Woolf is a freelance travel writer and contributing editor to Islands *magazine. She lives in London and travels to France often. She loves to cycle, which is good because she also loves to eat French food.*

★

"It's not that French people or Europeans generally don't know how to talk about things that are usually hidden—sex, shit, and what not. We did that before Americans, though you now do it more easily. But the deep tenderness, the *tendresse, that* we do not talk about. It would be a violation. We express it more subtly and, perhaps when we feel it, we feel it more profoundly....

"Let me give you an image. You put little bits of silver paper in a ball of water and shake it up. Everything glitters. Americans would be inclined to exclaim: 'Wow!' or 'Wonderful!' They don't wait until the glitter drops into a sediment. They see the pretty movement but not the deeper thing which doesn't glitter anymore. It's not something I say or do, you see, but something I am. If I get excited by it before I *am* it, it goes away."

—Hugo Potter, a French psychologist, quoted by Stuart Miller in
Understanding Europeans

LAWRENCE OSBORNE

Métro Metaphysics

A ride on the Paris Métro is a trip
through the city's subconscious.

IN PARIS THE PUBLIC TRANSPORTATION SYSTEM DOES NOT BEAR A
vernacular name. It is not the "Underground," or the "Subway," or
the "Unterbahn": it is the Métro, the *Métropolitain*. A word as
Greek as the word cosmopolitan. In fact, the system could easily
have been called the Cosmos, since the names of its stations pretend to encompass the entirety of human history, defining as they
do a mental geography that contains battlefields, poets, entire nations, capital cities, revolutionaries, animals, and scientists. A lithe
and elastic cosmopolitanism shines through the city in the names
of its Métro stations, all of which share in the dream of the
Universal City.

The Métro is above all a system of names, names which are a
thousand times more secretive than the places they supposedly de-
note. Filles du Calvaire, Bel-Air, Crimée, Danube, Pyramides,
Campo-Formio, Botzaris, Croix-de-Chavaux, Jasmin, Ourcq…the
mercurial names of the Métro, with the exoticism of the names of
extinct birds and buried cities. The three most mysterious to the
foreign ear are Exelmans, Télégraphe, and St-Ambroise, which are
ascetic and distant, like the white hills upon which monasteries are
built. Extravagantly politicized and willing to whisper propaganda,

catholic and Catholic, ready to act as stele to Great Men, palimpsestic and hermetic, the Métro names will be remembered in the future as a schoolchild's mnemonic for the ancient history of Europe or as a crazy hieroglyphic inscription over which scholars will shake their heads as dubiously as they once did confronted with the walls of Luxor. Why, they will ask, was Stalingrad included in the same city as Austerlitz; why was Bolivar thrown in with Charles de Gaulle, St-Sébastian with Marx—and where is Napoléon? A station for George V and Garibaldi but not Napoléon! Incredible self-effacement in the name of the spirit of the Métro! It will be concluded, of course, that the Métro was an idea, a religious idea, perhaps, or a pan-humanitarian one, but never a public transport system. That would be like saying the pyramid of Djerber was an ancient shopping mall. The Métro was an idea in the mind of 20th-century man and the astrological map around which his archaic spirituality revolved. In it, he tried to express his yearnings for unity and harmony in the face of the chaos of his history, and if people wished to drive around in trains along the configurations appointed by this divine map of reality that only showed how deeply the people of this age felt their pan-humanistic rituals. This undoubtedly explains why the system did not run in straight lines. What do straight lines have to do with enlightenment?

And the passengers on the Métro are themselves subject to various forms of wild daydreaming as they pass along the intertwining lines like Aborigines feeling their way along songlines. En route from Tolbiac to Brochant, from Corentin-Coriou to St-Mandé-Tourelle, from Marcel Sembat to Garibaldi, they gradually lose their sense of reality, bombarded as they are by hailstorms of associations evoked by the Métro's melodic names. The voyager travelling to Argentine or to Danube thinks, if only for seconds, of phantasmagoric pampas, tangos, strange-looking cowboy hats and snobs dancing waltzes in the warm evenings of the 19th century…barbaric images of history telescoped into millions of heads every day, countless times every minute of every day, and all because of these names dreamed up in the spirit of agnosia and urban philanthropy. Nowhere on earth is so much expendable dreaming occasioned by so much inadvertent linguistic exoticism. The Métro is a masterpiece of literature.

The Métro is best at night. After dark it loses its inhibitions and complexes and becomes as whorish as it is meant to be. The brilliant combustion of electricity in the air, the proliferation of gleaming surfaces and the artificial brightness of everything underground reminds you of the makeup of a successful tart while giving to the skins of clients the pale hue of troglodytes. It is now that the prudent user of the world's finest underground transportation system can best exploit its innate tendency towards dream. The multifarious races of the City's patchwork of peoples merge and blend against their will, and it has been known for some passengers at night to enter one station white and exit by another black, and vice versa.

he Paris Métro (RATP) has been in existence since the turn of the century and gained its name from its first line, the Métropolitain. It truly plays an essential role in the life of the city and is filled with its own character, energy and mythology. Some 5.5 million commuters use the system each day. You can get nearly everywhere in a relatively short period of time for a reasonable price in relative safety and security on the Paris Métro. Don't be afraid of it. At times it gets a bit overcrowded, odoriferous, noisy, and confused, but on the whole the Paris underground subway system is among the best in the world.

—David Applefield,
Paris Inside Out: The Insider's Guide for Visitors, Residents, Professionals & Students on Living in Paris

Not without a smile you remember the strange deaths that people meet underground—the general, for example, in the Métro's first years who died when his beard was caught in the new-fangled automatic doors, or the tramp stabbed in a frenzy by a well-heeled commuter who leaped across the tracks knife in hand in order to punish some drunken foul language. You remember the aboriginal crowds of frustrated rush-hour passengers who during the strike marched *en masse* from station to station along the live rails lynching RATP staff *en route*, behaving in ways that would have been impossible in the other Paris, the city up in the air. Apprehensively, you remember the Morlocks [from H. G. Wells's *The Time Machine*] who lived underground and fed on the reservoirs of white flesh from the upper world. You look more closely at the faces around, brutalized by the mere fact of being underground.

However, like our peasant, you are resolved to indulge in Métro dreams, and so you direct yourself to a station suitably conducive to the necessary initial suspension of disbelief. An admirable station for this purpose is Vaneau on the rue de Sèvres because outside, despite the overall smallness and shabbiness of this quiet stop on the Boulogne-Austerlitz line, it has the virtue of being equipped with a life-sized Egyptian water-carrier set into the wall by the entrance, the same wall that encircles the Hôpital Laennec. The blank gaze of this haunting statue gives rise in your mind, as you go down the steps, to the conjecture that Paris was once an Egyptian city, as can otherwise be confirmed by visiting the Place du Caire, with its crazy pharaonic heads set into the walls. This might at least be true of the Métro which is, despite what historians will tell you, by far the most ancient part of the city. Under the influence of this presentiment you look for and indeed find the hieroglyphs you have been expecting etched along the tunnels with spray cans and seeming to spell the English word "shark" *ad infinitum*. The décor of the Vaneau station does not bring you down to earth either, although admittedly it is less Egyptian than you had hoped. There is, for example, the tramp who is always asleep at night in the Austerlitz platform within a circle of orange peel, beer-bottle tops, arcs of frozen saliva, and fragmented teeth...he may be imitating the recumbent posture of a mummy, but you can tell he is alive by the curling of his naked toes. And then

Métro stop

there are the advertisements pasted the length of the curved walls within ochre-yellow scrolled frames.

We are aware of the temptation toward cheap and anti-capitalistic moralisms against the publicity in the Métro—where its presence is, it seems, most lamented. But let us say straight away that we are not indignant about it, nor are we moved to noble fury at the thought of the slow but irresistible degradation of our finer instincts by these profit-oriented buffooneries. Quite the contrary: we are in favor of these giant posters being made compulsory by law in all public places, and above all in all Métro stations. They are the outposts of the unconscious in the domain of public transport and as such should be rigorously imposed upon all urban travelers and visitors, whatever their supposed political preferences. For example, let us take the coffee ads. True, they are a little spoiled by their pseudo-sexual logos:

One afternoon on the Métro I saw an old madwoman sitting on the platform directing the trains at the top of her voice. When the doors opened, half of the people in my car stood up to get a better look; they pointed at the woman and broke into loud laughter. She had a better audience than mimes do in New York. It was a moment straight out of Norbert Elias: an underground lesson in the internationalization of restraint. In New York we would pretend not to notice; or if things got out of hand we would call the cops. We want that external authority still, whether it's television, transit police, or social programs. In Paris a chorus of laughter brought order to the scene. The madwoman might have joined in herself had she not been too busy keeping the trains running on time.

—Herbert Muschamp, "Paris and the Middle," *Artforum*

every one of them seems prepared to copulate with the consumer. Douceur Noire, the language of desire. Café Grand-Mère, the Arabica that strokes the drinker's scrotum while raping his epiglottis. Copacabana, the taste of creole thighs and aroused armpits. The texts are designed to elicit loathsome and reactionary responses in the regions of the lower bowels. And not one of them compares say the taste of Lavazza with the pleasures of a fishing trip, a to-

boggan ride, a Beethoven concerto, or a spring day in the
Appalachians. No, it is all orgasm, licking, sighs, and satin slips.
While this might offend the odd revolutionary, it has to be admitted that the images that go with these banal texts are viciously seductive: the pair of dark hands filled with coffee beans surging out
of a tropical blue sky with a globose orange moon and the shadowed tips of palm trees; a white hand loitering with intent against
the black rump of an evening dress suggesting a drop of cream in
an espresso; a pair of cochineal lips working their way around a
teaspoon while a vaguely female rose of the same colour sulks on
a saucer and a limp male mouth implants itself on the left cheek of
the owner of the lips. Who can deny that these compositions,
which suggest in no uncertain terms what will happen to you if
you happen to drink coffee in conjunction with your favourite
contraceptive on an evening when the moon is full, are infinitely
preferable to the bloated faces of tabby cats gorging themselves on
piles of excretal high-fibre tunny-flavoured nuggets, or those of
enamelled cocottes gulping down whole bottles of drinkable ac-
tive-ingredient yogurt? The founder of the Métro, Fulgence
Bienvenüe, made the following remark: "In another age the appearance of the Métro would have given rise to a special and particular mythology"; but isn't it truer to say that that mythology has
already come to pass and that its heroes, impossible animals,
demons, and beauties are already elevated to the status of Elgin
Marbles in the form of the station ads? The Métro is already a
giant brain sleeping through decades of history and filled with
endless unrepeatable nightmares.

   The neurons and nodes of this catastrophic dreaming organ are
the 429 stations, 80 kilometers of corridor and 295 kilometers of
track. And like any brain it is filled with heroes and villains. From
the beginning of its active life at the turn of the century it has been
capable of inflicting both terror and romance upon its users.
Despite the hysteria of the contemporary moralist, who sees in the
everyday manners and rising crime of the Métro the beginnings of
the disintegration of an entire civilization, it has always harboured
peripatetic sadists, Dalinian exhibitionists, lone avengers like the

Woman in Black with her sinister sharpened needle who terrorized the network more than half a century ago, the apaches of the Belle Epoque and its armies of homeless tramps. Its crimes are peculiar to it, whether they be the hold up of a train at Anvers station by Fantômas and the drugging of its passengers, who are later found wandering dazed and aimless around the City, or those prosaic but unsolved murders that rise to the surface of the Métro's dreaming mind like nefarious and misformed flowers.

From Vaneau, however, forgetting these alarming associations, you pass to Sèvres-Babylone, a station which holds no interest for you except in so far as the word Babylon encapsulates the ancient anima of the Métro, and here you encounter the chief pleasure of these ingenious systems of subterranean transport: the freedom of individual choice. At Babylon, as in the real city, roads cross and the traveller is free to indulge himself as far as his destination (which is the same as his destiny) is concerned. North to adventures in the exotic and treacherous regions of the Carrefour Pleyel or St-Lazare or east to the playgrounds of Cardinal Lemoine or St-Michel. Of course, the traveller in search of some decent oneiric activity can only choose the Porte de Clignancourt line, which he can join at Odéon and which takes him through landscapes of convulsive disobedience. The trip may begin anodynely enough, but soon an equinoctial disequilibrium enters the carriages with the influx of barbarism associated with Les Halles and reaches a climax of disorder between Etienne Marcel and Barbès. It is best to take this line during a strike, when the other lines are unexpectedly closed and when the carriages are so full of lemming-like night creatures that you feel you are on a freight train of human cattle bound for Auschwitz—with all the possibilities for witnessing spontaneous explosions of violence and social tension that a train without brakes imagined by Céline crashing through a landscape of marshes and pill-boxes could offer. You will not, however, always be so lucky. When the doors open at Les Halles a fresh intoxicating aroma of menace enters the carriages nevertheless, and always a small gnome with scrofula, who begins expounding to the crowd the evils of unemployment, social-security administration procedures, the problems of feeding seventeen children, or recovering from acute pyaemia and the necessity of transferring cash to his palm in exchange for haunting views of amazing scars traced over a belly distended by the ravages of lumbago. For it is in the Métro that the diseased of the City, having crawled heroically from their workhouse beds, reveal to a shocked and sympathetic public the evils of the supposedly superior metropolis above. It is only in the Métro that sociologists can observe the nation's silent lepers. It is only underground that the tentacular technological organ passing for the City's unconscious excretes its desperate and tragic human stools....

You could swear, as a matter of fact, that you see the same faces day after day. The Nefertiti, for example, always getting off at Madeleine and always winking at you as she sweeps down the platform; the snoring head of the banjo player on his way to Strasbourg-St-Denis who always magically wakes up when his station has arrived, his little gipsy nose partially eaten away by some epithelial cancer; the various physiognomies of Rama-pithecus Man flashing across screens of empty air lit by the ubiquitous and sickening electricity—a light as virile as an endless photographic flash and which burns them into memory with an insolent and persuasive violence; and most of all the old man who plays Italian songs on a mandolin in the long corridor at Sèvres-Babylone and whose begging cap never contains any coins except what our peasant, who enjoys his bad but heart-breaking playing, gives him.

You conclude that the Métro is a machine for processing faces, crossing and combining them, spewing them out senselessly in all directions and that it might have been more effective if the advice of the Ligue Parisienne du Métro Aérienne, which campaigned in the 1890s for an overhead instead of an underground system, had been heeded after all. For the only time when this monstrous discharge of disoriented faces becomes human once more, alert to its surroundings and suffused with some vaguely biological colour, is when the train shoots up from underground into the open air, borne up by the elegant and gay iron-vaulted overpasses whose supporting pillars are embellished with all kinds of anachronistic cartouches, scrolls, fluting and sculpted garlands. It can only be regretted that this Jules Vernian conception of the Métro, with its joy in technically advanced acts of levitation and naïve show-off bravura, was buried by the earnest Vulcian school of engineers content to work sombre and forbidding miracles underground. It is possible, of course, that in the future the system will be filled up with sand and the overhead bridges extended to cover the entire City, while the style of the confident and tasteful *avant-garde* of 1895 is retained so that, by a conscious act of municipal remembrance, a vast megalopolis of gravity-induced vehicles will circulate around, beneath, and next to a network of neo-Grecian pillars and romantic shadows. But, let us admit immediately, the chances of this happening in the vertigo of Futuropolis are as likely as the invention and mass-marketing of immortality. The travelling human unit will become more subterraneanly oriented, the human complexion will pale even further in re-

One night in the Paris Métro, I wait with my Belgian friend, Roland Dupont, for the train to come. He is a Belgian theoretical physicist with a strong humanistic education—a lover of history, literature, and wit. He is a good example of that small group of Europeans who have traveled the world and put together the two cultures of America and Europe and the other two cultures of science and humanities—not in a theoretical but in a personal way.

Across the tracks, a drunken bum, what the French call a clochard, *sits on a bench. We watch, and listen, for the drunk speaks to the gathering number of people waiting for the late-night trains on both platforms.*

The clochard *grumbles insults at the crowds. Then he looks into his little box and draws out things to eat. He holds them up to exhibit and grandly proclaims:* "C'est le pâté de chevreuil!" *And then,* "C'est du Boursin!" *He says, "It is the* pâté *of venison!" And then, "It is Boursin cheese," soft with garlic flavoring. "Like a duke," observes my friend Roland. "He is there like a duke. A disappointed duke, perhaps, but a duke just the same."*

—Stuart Miller,
Understanding Europeans

sponse to a necessary deprivation of ultra-violet rays and the physiognomy of the human face will grow more vegetal, chilling, and blank. We can only cross our fingers and hope that pornographic advertising will come to the rescue....

The other hope—one which frankly gives us the greatest sense of expectation and proleptic titillation—is the possibility that Fantômas will resurrect himself and commit an act of terrorism so great, so scandalous, so inadmissible and so useless that the days of mass hysteria will be brought back and the adventure of underground restored to its former virility. Nor should you smile at this childish and quaint idea. For if the Métro is the city's unconscious, its slumbering, nightmare-filled brain, its perpetual darkened bedroom where dreams go unhindered for decades and eventually centuries, then like any oversized head it can create any incubus it likes, nothing can stop it piling up lunacies...accidents and crimes, riots and epic arsons...even, if you like, a call-girl at the end of the line at midnight, although in this case you will never know for as you approach your destination, drooling with lust, you are suddenly overwhelmed by another desire altogether, one that has been conferred upon you by the closeness and sweatiness of the Métro itself, which always seems to be overheated, a desire which brusquely makes you forget all about your precious rendezvous and all it might have promised: namely to visit a Turkish bath. You needn't feel ashamed to want to plunge yourself into a hammam—on the contrary, our peasant feels exactly the same thing every time he takes a trip on the Métro. After all, the two experiences are not dissimilar, with the difference that the latter is infinitely more narcotic.

Lawrence Osborne is the author of The Angelic Game, Ania Malina, *and* Paris Dreambook: An Unconventional Guide to the Splendor and Squalor of the City *from which this story was excerpted. He lives in Paris.*

*

When I was in Paris, I fell in love with the Métro. Each morning, I waited eagerly for us to decide where we were going so that I could begin to plan the route. I was indifferent to the sights we were going to see; I merely wanted to get out the map and begin digging in.

The Paris Métro is complicated but simple. One ticket gets you anywhere. Trains are frequent and transfer points numerous. There are alternate routes from almost anywhere to almost anywhere else.

One day I was riding on the Métro with my younger daughter, Shana, an actual resident of Paris, taking the train back from La Défense. No one says much about La Défense; no one says (although this is true) that a trip there will plunge you into the breathless, weird grandiosity of the French commercial heart.

La Défense is a kind of overheated industrial park featuring a gigantic office building in the shape of an arch. It is littered with terrifying crystalline high-rises and plazas built for giants. It is somewhere between Louis Quatorze and Louis Ka-BOOM.

Shana and I were seated side by side on the hurtling Métro. A man came up to us and spoke in a thick Middle European accent. "Speakink English?" he asked hopefully.

"Absolutely," I said. "Where are you from?"

"Australia," he said. It seemed improbable.

Actually, he was born in what was at the time Czechoslovakia. It was his first time in Paris. He had been given written instructions about how to reach a specific Métro stop, but he had gone past the station where he needed to change and had wound up at La Défense.

Could I give him directions? Could I write them down?

Could I! I whipped out my little blue book and turned to the greasy page. He wanted Lamarck, so he could change at Charles de Gaulle and again at Pigalle, or, if that seemed too complicated, he could—"Change at Concorde and take direction Porte de La Chapelle," said Shana. She had her greasy Métro map out too; she too was tracing routes with her fingers and muttering under her breath. "Want me to write it down for you?"

"I was thinking," I said, "that he could change at Charles de Gaulle and…"

"This is just as fast and easier," she said. "Trust me."

She wrote the information down for the bouncing Australian Czech. He thanked her and moved off.

I realized that my daughter had fallen in love in just the same way I had. She too had become fascinated with the maps, had inspected the stations and the decorations, investigated the various entrances and exits.

It was in her blood, the pathfinding chromosome, the map gene. We shared a passion so obvious it was a secret. We didn't say a word to each other; it seemed like a good time to study our maps some more.

—Jon Carroll, "Notes From the Underground," *San Francisco Chronicle*

Three Women of Nice

A simple museum visit provides an opportunity
for hanging out with the natives.

I WAS SITTING IN A SECOND-FLOOR SALON AT THE MUSÉE MATISSE in Nice, scribbling in my notebook, when an attractive, middle-aged woman in an impeccably tailored peach-colored suit approached me and said in flawless French, "Excuse me, but do you speak French?"

I said I did, and she continued, "Well, forgive me for bothering you, but I'm wondering just what a foreign visitor thinks about this museum. You see, I'm from Nice, and I can't find anything worthwhile here, and I'm afraid that visitors who come all the way to Nice from far away to see this museum will be terribly disappointed."

"Whatever have you found to write about?" she said, gesturing at my notebook.

"Well," I began, hoping my trusty, rusty French was up to this adventure in art criticism, "there are certain valuable illuminations to be found—"

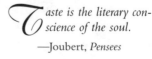

Taste is the literary conscience of the soul.

—Joubert, *Pensees*

"Illuminations!" she exploded, her pearl necklace trembling. "Have you been to the Matisse show in Paris?"

"Well, no," I said, "but I did see the Matisse exhibition in New York."

"New York!" she pouted, as if she had been one-upped by a neighbor. "And how does this compare to that?"

"Well, you really can't compare," I began, but then another well-dressed woman who had been hovering near us burst into speech.

"But you can't compare the two!" she exclaimed, fire in her voice and eyes. "I too am a native of Nice, and I think this is a very interesting museum, an extraordinary achievement given all the obstacles that had to be overcome, all the planning and work that went into it.

"You know," she continued, turning to me, "this museum was six years in the making. As you can see"—and her fiery gaze directed my eyes to the museum's grounds—"this villa is set on an area of Roman ruins. There were all manner of political problems and personality problems, permissions to be obtained, regulations to be followed—the plan had to be meticulous, absolutely perfect! It is a miracle this museum was ever finished!"

I almost expected the room to burst into applause.

"Well, yes," my original questioner countered, "but now that it is finished, I ask you, what is there to see? Some half-finished drawings, studies, a scattering of canvases. Where are the masterpieces? Where is the genius of Matisse?" and she thrust one diamond-bedecked hand toward the sky.

"Well," I said, "that canvas over there—'Fenêtre à Tahiti'—is a powerful composition, with those great blocks of color one associates with Matisse's masterpieces."

"Bravo!" said the second woman.

"Oh, that," said the first woman, flinging a finger at the painting as if it were the bones of yesterday's fish dinner, "yes, there are a few canvases of note here—but so few! Why cannot Nice, Matisse's home, produce a more distinguished tribute to an artist of such distinction?"

"But don't you know"—the second woman's friend now entered the fray—"how expensive it is to mount exhibitions these days? All the permissions that have to be obtained, and the shipping fees—and the insurance!" she exclaimed, her eyes rolling heavenward in horror.

"The insurance," muttered woman number one. "We are talking about art and genius and a suitable tribute—and you are talking about insurance!"

"Yes, I am. You have to be practical, realistic. I think this is a very charming tribute. It has a hometown feeling—"

"An intimacy," I said.

"Bravo for the American! Yes, an intimacy, that I think distinguishes it from larger, more impersonal exhibits."

"I agree," I said. "You feel closer to the soul of Matisse here."

"*Voilà!*" exclaimed woman number two.

"The soul of Matisse?" the first woman said, eyeing me suspiciously. "Are all Americans so kind?" She paused and smiled slightly.

"I think I would be—how shall I say?—deceived, disappointed, if I flew all the way across the ocean to see this."

"Well," I began expansively, "no one will fly all the way across the ocean just to see this. They will fly all the way across the ocean to see this!"—and I pointed

he French in general like to talk, and the language in all its richness gains much of its melodic quality from the long and circular phrases needed to express what could be said in a word or two in English or German. This love of words and dialogue, though, is reserved for specific places and contexts...the café, the dinner table, the table ronde, the conference. You might notice that people don't talk very loudly in subways, buses, streets, or public places. This comes from the French distinction between public and private life. Personal life is private and is handled discreetly. The French will not openly talk about or be overheard discussing family matters, emotions, or money. With this silent backdrop it's not surprising that tourists seem remarkably loud and obnoxious.

On the other hand, the French can be highly vocal and overt when in the public mode—partaking in a débat (debate), manifestation (demonstration), or grève (strike), for example.

—David Applefield,
Paris Inside Out: The Insider's Guide for Visitors, Residents, Professionals & Students on Living in Paris

grandly to the sunny seaside city outside the museum's walls.

"Ah," all three women said.

"So you like Nice?" asked woman number one.

"Oh, I love Nice," I said. "I love the winding alleyways in Old Nice, and the old shuttered buildings. I love the sidewalk cafés and the restaurants that have room for only four tables. I love the grand Promenade des Anglais and the fantastic hotels that look onto it."

"And the people of Nice?"

"Oh, yes," I began—"well, actually, you are the first Niçoises I've had the opportunity to talk at length with, but all the people I've encountered have been very friendly and courteous. One thing that amazes me is that people are so willing to speak English here. In Paris, even if they know some English, shopkeepers or waiters will often refuse to speak with foreign customers."

"We are not Parisians here, my dear," said woman number two.

"Gracious no!" added woman number one. "We have a temperament of the south, wouldn't you say?"

"Exactly," said woman number three. "We are more relaxed, more passionate,"—did she smile discreetly at me?—"more... In Paris, they work now to enjoy life later. In Nice, we enjoy life now!"

"Yes!" I said. "I'm sure that is exactly what Matisse felt!"

I suddenly realized that the visitors in the salon were paying more attention to our little group than they were to the paintings and drawings on the walls.

"So you like art?" woman number one asked.

"Yes," I said, "especially modern French art."

"Then you must go to Antibes to see the Picasso museum, and Cagnes-sur-Mer to see Renoir's former residence."

"And of course you must go to the Fondation Maeght in St-Paul," said woman number two.

"And the Chagall museum down the street," said woman number three, "and the Cocteau museum in Menton."

"Oh, and have you seen the Rosary Chapel in Vence?" asked woman number one. "It is Matisse's triumph!"

"And you must see the Cocteau chapel in Villefranche!" said woman number three.

"Yes," I lamented, "there is so much to see, and I have so little time."

I was waiting for the women to offer to take me in their Mercedes from museum to museum over the next few days. Barring that, I was waiting for them at least to invite me back to their homes for dinner or a drink.

But life never follows a set script.

"Oh!" said woman number two, looking at her watch. "I have to pick up the children!"

And the other two women, as if on cue, looked at their watches and exclaimed, "The time!"

"How quickly time passes with pleasant company," said woman number one, and winked at me. "Well, our new American friend," she continued with a broad smile, glancing at my still open notebook, "have you found something to write about now?"

As they made for the exit, she turned one last time and said, "*Au revoir!* Enjoy your stay in our lovely Nice!"

Then they were gone.

I walked once more around the suddenly intimate and enchanting museum, looked again at the artist's luminous, passion-filled pieces and thought: ah, Matisse—now I understand even better what you loved about Nice.

Don George was travel editor at the San Francisco Examiner *for nine years and founder and editor of "Wanderlust," Salon.com's award-winning travel site, from 1997 to 2000. He is currently the travel editor at Lonely Planet. In addition, he co-edited* Travelers' Tales Japan *and edited* Salon.com's Wanderlust: Real-Life Tales of Adventure and Romance. *His career as a peripatetic scribbler started in Paris, where he lived and worked and fell in love (several times) the summer between his junior and senior years at Princeton.*

✱

The Riviera was invented in 1925, so the legend has it, by a very rich, erudite, glamorous, and civilized young American couple named Sara and Gerald Murphy. They arrived one day from Paris and fell in love with the little walled town of Antibes, which then sat in a quilt of rose and carnation farms, jasmine fields, and canebrakes, its ramparts caressed by an as yet unpolluted sea.

Enraptured, they rented a small house in a pinewood just above the empty beach known as La Garoupe. Patriotically, they renamed the house Villa America and invited their host of American friends from Paris, who would arrive on the night train in the golden dawn, fall under the spell, and linger on and on. In time they all became a little too much. People had to be fed and wined. The picnics on La Garoupe had to be devised and catered. Sara's cast list was mostly very distinguished and demanding, as holiday guests so often are.

The Fitzgeralds, Picasso and his monumental Mamma dressed, as always, in deepest black plus high hat, Hemingway and whoever he brought with him, and a list of others all equally brilliant, glowing, and glamorous: writers, painters, musicians, and players. The Murphys asked the owners of the local hotel along the beach to stay open one summer to accommodate their guests. Normally the winter season finished at about the end of April, for no one wanted the heat and the blazing summer sunlight. The hotels would close until the cooler weather returned in September or October. The owners were somewhat astonished by the Murphys' suggestion, not believing that they would be filled, but they agreed to remain open for "just one summer." The trains brought, and continued to bring, the glittering crowds from Paris, the Hôtel du Cap remained open ever afterward, and thus was "the Riviera" born.

—Dirk Bogarde, "Beauty and the Beach," *European Travel & Life*

✦ ✦ ✦

The Arch of Orange

A monument commissioned by conquering Romans
reveals more about Roman barbarity than the
glory it was meant to celebrate.

I TURNED TO MY GUIDEBOOK TO SEE IF THERE WAS ANYTHING worth seeing in Orange. The only local offerings mentioned were some "vestiges of ancient Rome": a Roman triumphal arch "built to commemorate Julius Caesar's conquest of Gaul" and later rededicated to Tiberius, as well as a Roman theater "built during the reign of Augustus." Even though the guidebook stated that the arch was the best preserved of its kind and one of the first triple arches to be built, and that the theater was not only the best preserved but the most beautiful in existence, Henry James had not waxed ecstatic about these vestiges, so I was not particularly eager to see them. There were, however, three hours before lunch, and it was either the triple arch and the theater or three hours of pinball. I opted for the "vestiges of ancient Rome."

I decided to try the arch

Arch of Orange

first. On the map of Orange it appeared in a circle at the end of a long promenade. I decided to walk, presuming I would have an increasingly dramatic view of the arch as I approached it. However, as I walked down what I thought was going to be the "promenade," I wished I had taken the car. Unlike the rest of Orange, which is a bustling provincial town filled with delightful cafés and restaurants, the area leading to the arch was unpleasant: noisy with traffic, hot, smelly with fumes from cars and buses, a route crowded with gas stations and nondescript structures that made it impossible to get a good view of the arch from a distance. The arch was located in the middle of a traffic circle at the end of a broad street, and as I approached it, I could see big tour buses circling the traffic island on which it stood. I also noticed that although the buses were circling the arch, they were not bothering to stop. The fact that they were circling but not stopping led me to believe that I should have spent the morning drinking coffee and perfecting my pinball technique. However, having invested nearly an hour walking to the arch, I decided I might as well take a good look at it. Besides, it was a very hot morning, already in the high 80s, and the only shade—and I was in need of shade by this time—was under one of the three arches.

So, dodging buses and trucks, I ran across the road to the grassy island on which the arch was standing and found myself face-to-face with a sculptured relief that in all honesty is the cause of this book [*The Road from the Past: Traveling Through History in France*]. Since I had come on a sunny morning, the entire arch had a golden glow, and the sculpture on the eastern wall was brilliantly illuminated. I think the morning sun must have been important, because without it these reliefs on the eastern face would have been in shadow and hard to see, but with the sun spotlighting and illuminating them, they were so powerful that I was completely overwhelmed. In fact, I don't think any American, with his feelings about individual freedom—feelings that come close to religious passion—could help but be overwhelmed by the carving on the eastern wall.

What I saw was two captured Gauls chained to a tree: a man

and a beautiful woman. The woman is still beautiful after two thousand years. Her head bent slightly forward in despair, she is obviously yearning to be free. She is the most poignant captive I have ever seen. Above the two captives is a Roman legionnaire, his arms stretched wide above his head in victory like a tennis star who has just won the U.S. Open, holding not a tennis racket but two captured Gallic shields, one in each hand: arrogant and cruel in his victory. While the original intent of the arch was obvious— to impress the barbarian with Roman superiority—what I felt upon seeing this frieze was something more, transcending its original intent. What I felt must have been the emotions experienced by the artist who carved this work into stone two thousand years ago: compassion for the captives suffering the humiliation of subjugation; hatred for the Roman legionnaire so obviously elated by victory and domination. I had always thought of the advance of the Roman Empire as the advance of civilization. Not once before seeing these carvings had I thought of what it must have been like to lose one's freedom to a people as arrogant as this triumphant Roman soldier. I actually found it rather peculiar that a Roman Arch of Triumph commemorating and celebrating a Roman victory over the Gauls should arouse such strong feelings of compassion for the Gauls and corresponding feelings of hatred—rather than admiration or awe—for the Romans. I later learned a very poignant fact that explained my odd reaction: although the arch was designed by the Roman conquerors, it was executed and paid for by the defeated Gauls. The fact that the friezes were carved by native Gallic, rather than Roman, artisans explains why I felt such compassion for the Gauls' loss of freedom. And in this carving the artist had expressed his suffering so well that it was still vivid to me looking at it two thousand years later.

Gallic artisans were able to execute the Roman designs with such fine craftsmanship because they had been trained by Greek masters. As early as 600 B.C., Greek merchants began establishing peaceful trading posts, first in Marseille and then farther inland along the banks of the Rhône, intermarrying with the barbarians who were the forebears of today's Frenchmen. By the time the

Romans came to the area now known as Provence and forcibly made it a province of Rome, it had already been Hellenized and part of the Greco-Roman world for centuries. Its citizens dressed in Greco-Roman togas, attended schools established by the Greeks, and studied under Greek masters who taught, among other things, the art of sculpture.

The arch is a monument both to the melding of three cultures and to Roman political sophistication. In addition to commemorating the victory of the legions that had conquered Gaul, it was built to both impress and overawe the citizens held in subjugation. And not only did the Roman conquerors force Gallic artisans to carve the friezes on the arch; more subtly still, they forced the citizens of Orange to pay for the arch by having them hold a referendum authorizing funds for its construction. By holding this "election," the conquered people of Orange showed their "willing" submission to Rome.

If the Arch of Triumph at Orange was built to impress, it certainly must have done so. I was impressed, not only by its carvings but, when I started to think about it, by the fact that the Romans built so grand and majestic a structure in what was a very remote part of their empire. I was impressed—and I had just left a modern hotel. How must a Gallic barbarian have felt when he first saw the gleaming white marble triple arches of this Imperial structure, so Roman in nature. A barbarian arriving from the north would have just left his mud-and-wattle hut in the forest. That was what his civilization knew how to build. He must have been awed. Was he also grateful, as I had read in history books for years, for the generosity of the far-off and mysterious emperor in having bestowed on his city this monument with its graceful Corinthian columns and tablature and magnificent coffered vaulting? The barbarian would not have needed a guidebook to tell him that this was a triumphal arch, that this was a monument to victory, the victory of Roman legions over his fellow tribesmen. The Romans designed the arch to tell the illiterate barbarian of his defeat and to impress him with the civilization of his conqueror. The message was as clear today as it was when the arch was built two thousand years ago.

As I walked around the arch, I realized that the entire structure was covered with friezes: friezes of naval trophies symbolizing Roman supremacy at sea; friezes depicting Roman legionnaires defeating naked, hairy Gauls; and a collage of trophies from these battles hanging from trees to symbolize Roman supremacy on land. All the friezes celebrated Roman victory, and each would have evoked meaningful stories to the citizens living at the time during which the Republic of Rome was becoming the Empire, stories that began with Caesar's war in Gaul and ended with Actium, the great naval battle at which the forces of Augustus defeated those of Antony and Cleopatra.

oltaire observed that every city in France "competes with its neighbor for the honor of having been the first to which Caesar gave a flogging. We quarrel over what route he used to come and slit our throats, make love to our wives and daughters, and steal our tiny savings."

—Henry S. Reuss and Margaret M. Reuss, *The Unknown South of France: A History Buff's Guide*

I stopped and looked at the long bas-relief collage of captured trophies: torques (the bands of precious metal that Gallic warriors wore around their necks), shields, swords, and Gallic trousers. The Romans hung everything they captured from trees, including the pants worn by the Gauls. These trousers were actually quite a novelty to the toga-and-tunic-wearing Romans. Only the Gauls living in the north of France wore trousers. At the time that Caesar came, saw, and conquered Gaul, France was divided into two parts—the north and the south. The south, or Provence, had long been a fashionable and favorite resort for political exiles of the Greco-Roman world, Hellenized by the intellectual Greeks who had first settled there. It was prized for its climate, its wines, its fish soup, and its olives and spices. In the rest of France the Gauls still dressed unstylishly in trousers instead of the more chic white toga, didn't shave their faces, and wore their hair much too long and shaggy to be socially acceptable. Some of the ancients derisively referred to the northern half of France as "the trouser-clad place." It was Julius Caesar who arbitrarily labeled the area, which now contains northern France, Britain, and Belgium, "Gaul," which he divided into three parts and where he won the victory this arch commemorates. (This is a fact I wish I had known during my first year of Latin, when as a ninth-grader I parsed my way through Julius Caesar's *Commentaries on the Gallic War.* I was unable to find Gaul in my atlas and, considering the barbaric nature of the places Caesar described, could not figure out why he came, saw, and conquered it.)

In 36 B.C. Augustus gave Orange to the veterans of Caesar's Second Legion as a reward for their service in the Gallic Wars.

These wars, which lasted eight years, had begun in 58 B.C. Gallic chieftains asked Rome for help in driving off a tribe of 368,000 Helvetii who had migrated into France from Switzerland. For two years Republican Rome had ignored the request: in Republican Rome only defensive wars could be fought—wars of expansion were illegal, and the Helvetii posed no threat to Rome. But when Caesar became proconsul of Provence in 58 B.C., he realized he could use the two-year-old request to enrich and advance himself by conquering Gaul. He led 10,000 of his fierce, disciplined veterans against a huge horde of the Helvetii, killing 238,000 of them before he drove the rest back to Switzerland.

Vercingetorix, chief of the Averni, one of the many tribes of Gaul, watched Caesar's slaughter of the Helvetii and realized that although the Helvetii were gone, Caesar's legions were not. Vercingetorix realized that Caesar's "aid" meant the end of Gallic freedom. Traveling from tribe to tribe, appealing to his fellow Gauls' love of freedom, telling them "it was better to die fighting than to forfeit their ancient military glory and the liberty their ancestors had bequeathed them" (and cutting off ears and gouging out eyes when that appeal failed), he was able to unite the independent tribes of Gaul to fight Caesar and the Roman legions. His father, previously chief of the Averni, had been condemned to death for attempting to unite and make himself the king of these tribes, who shared a common culture and language. But Vercingetorix succeeded where his father had failed.

The Celts had defeated the Romans once, but that had been in

390 B.C., almost four hundred years before Caesar renamed them Gauls. At that time they had burst out of Central Europe, vanquishing and intermarrying with each of the tribes they encountered as they conquered western Europe and Britain. They were able to vanquish everyone because they had invented the double-edged sword, the atomic bomb of the Iron Age. Putting the second edge on a sword doesn't seem like much of an invention today, but twenty-four hundred years ago it gave the Gauls a definite edge over their enemies. (The double-edged sword symbolizes the Gallic double-edged temperament: warlike on the one hand and poetic on the other. War-like, they learned to extract iron ore from stone and turn it into this new kind of sword; poetic, they saw the taking of iron from stone and transforming it into a sword as a magical act—one that, as the centuries passed, was transformed into marvelous tales of chivalry in which God gives the hero a great sword—always embedded in a rock—with which to defeat his enemies. As time passed, pagan legends became Christian miracles: Roland, the personification of the perfect Christian knight, is able to hold off a hundred thousand Saracens because of the divine properties of his sword, Durendal, which—to prevent its capture by the infidels—he flings into the air before dying; it magically lands embedded in a rock at the pilgrimage site of Rocamadour. Across the English Channel, King Arthur proves his right to the throne by removing Excalibur, the magic sword, from a stone.)

But in 58 B.C., when the tribes of Gaul, united under Vercingetorix, faced Caesar's legions, the Romans were the superior military force. Vercingetorix realized he couldn't defeat them in open battle—he had witnessed Caesar's cunning and siegecraft when the Romans slaughtered the Helvetii and knew that unexpected tactics had to be devised. Vercingetorix's strategy was brilliant: a combination of modern guerrilla warfare and scorched-earth policy, in which he convinced his fellow Gauls to burn over twenty of their cities to deny the Romans shelter and food, and then to attack the Romans as they searched for food. He must have been a very charismatic leader to have convinced the peasants to

burn the homes, crops, and villages that lay in the path of the
Roman advance. According to Caesar, Vercingetorix told his people that "these measures might be
thought to be unfair and even
terribly cruel; but...the alternative was infinitely worse: slavery
for their wives and children,
death for themselves—the universal fate of conquered peoples."

*he Romans' Provincia
gave Provence its name,
super-imposed imperial pomposity
and lumpen bourgeois civilization
on a land in search of identity,
and did very little to help her find
it. The monuments perpetuate
the Roman presence as a far
vaster legacy than that of
any other stranger.*

—Julian More,
Views From A French Farmhouse

He almost succeeded in defeating Caesar and his invincible
legions. However, when fellow
Gauls begged him not to burn
Bourges, their most beautiful
city, he gave in. Since
Vercingetorix did not burn
Bourges, he had to defend it. He couldn't. Vercingetorix's defeat is
brilliantly described by Caesar. Before the battle of Bourges, the
Romans had been close to starvation and defeat, but Bourges's
capture gave the Romans its stores of food and gold. Accused of
cowardice in refusing to meet the enemy in open battle—
Vercingetorix had argued that "the Romans had not won by
courage in the open field, but by cunning and expert knowledge
of siegecraft, with which the Gauls had not much acquaintance"—
Vercingetorix finally was forced to fight a pitched battle against
Caesar on the field of Alesia, outside Beaune. Vercingetorix
watched the Roman legions slaughter his one hope for victory, the
Gallic calvary, as well as thousands of his fellow tribesmen, and realized that the eight-year struggle for freedom was lost.

On the following day Vercingetorix addressed a meeting of
Gallic chiefs and explained that "he had embarked upon this war
not for private ends but in his country's cause. 'Now,' he said, 'I
must bow to the decrees of Fate.'"

To prevent more of his men from dying, he bravely dressed
himself in his best armor, rode into Caesar's camp, and gave himself up in exchange for an end to hostilities. When Vercingetorix

offered himself to Caesar, he had expected—and wanted—instant death. But Caesar was the brilliant politician. Not only had he seen in the conquest of Gaul the source of the fame and wealth that would gain him control of Rome, but he also knew that the Gauls believed in instant reincarnation—they believed, he wrote, that "souls do not die but after death pass from one another"—and that the death of Vercingetorix would have to be delayed until he was forgotten. So Caesar kept him in a cage in Rome for six long years before having him strangled.

The bravery and love of freedom of this first great leader in the land that became France were not forgotten. Two thousand years later, during the Second World War, Vercingetorix would become a symbol of French resistance to the Nazi invaders.

Ina Caro is a writer and historian who has traveled throughout France since 1978 studying its history. She was the sole researcher on award-winning biographies of Robert Moses and Lyndon Johnson written by her husband, Robert A. Caro, and she is the author of The Road from the Past: Traveling Through History in France, *from which this story was excerpted.*

✳

Imagine yourself standing, as Petrarch once stood, on the top of Mont Ventoux to the east of the Rhône Valley, and look around you. To the west lies Roman Orange, to the south-west Nîmes, Avignon, city of the Popes, and Arles, perhaps the most typical of all Provençal towns. Turn now to the south, towards Aix-en-Provence and on further to Marseille and the Mediterranean. On a clear night it is possible to pick out the lighthouses that dot the coast stretching on and out of sight to the Riviera. From Ventoux's high peak one can see, as Petrarch saw, the wide and varied spread of Provence, with its special combination of hills and marshes, mountains and plains; the area most commonly known to travellers as the South of France. It is to this region that, as early as 600 B.C., colonists and settlers came, first by boat and later by horse and carriage (now car, train or aeroplane) crossing that invisible boundary where the olive trees begin and Northern Europe becomes the South.

—Laura Raison, *The South of France: An Anthology*

* * *

I Was Really Very Hungry

In a place where food is worshipped,
it's not easy to get a simple lunch.

ONCE I MET A YOUNG SERVANT IN NORTHERN BURGUNDY WHO was almost frighteningly fanatical about food, like a medieval woman possessed by a devil. Her obsession engulfed even my appreciation of the dishes she served, until I grew uncomfortable.

It was the off season at the old mill which a Parisian chef had bought and turned into one of France's most famous restaurants, and my mad waitress was the only servant. In spite of that she was neatly uniformed, and showed no surprise at my unannounced arrival and my hot dusty walking clothes.

Mary Frances Kennedy Fisher passed away in 1992, leaving behind many bereaved readers. This piece, written many years ago, is as true today as it was then.

—JO'R, LH, and SO'R

She smiled discreetly at me, said, "Oh, but certainly!" when I asked if I could lunch there, and led me without more words to a dark bedroom bulging with First Empire furniture and a new white bathroom.

When I went into the dining room it was empty of humans— a cheerful ugly room still showing traces of the petit bourgeois parlor it had been. There were aspidistras on the mantel; several small white tables were laid with those imitation "peasant-ware" plates that one sees in Paris china stores, and very good crystal glasses; a cat folded under some ferns by the window ledge hardly looked at me; and the air was softly hurried with the sound of high waters from the stream outside.

I waited for the maid to come back. I knew I should eat well and slowly, and suddenly the idea of dry sherry, unknown in all the village bistros of the last few days, stung my throat smoothly. I tried not to think about it; it would be impossible to realize. Dubonnet would do. But not as well. I longed for sherry.

The little maid came into the silent room. I looked at her stocky young body, and her butter-colored hair, and noticed her odd pale voluptuous mouth before I said, "Mademoiselle, I shall drink an apéritif. Have you by any chance—"

"Let me suggest," she interrupted firmly, "our special dry sherry. It is chosen in Spain for Monsieur Paul."

And before I could agree she was gone, discreet and smooth.

She's a funny one, I thought, and waited in a pleasant warm tiredness for the wine.

It was good. I smiled approval at her, and she lowered her eyes, and then looked searchingly at me again. I realized suddenly that in this land of trained nonchalant waiters I was to be served by a small waitress who took her duties seriously. I felt much amused, and matched her solemn searching gaze.

"Today, Madame, you may eat shoulder of lamb in the English style, with baked potatoes, green beans, and a sweet."

My heart sank. I felt dismal, and hot and weary, and still grateful for the sherry.

But she was almost grinning at me, her lips curved triumphantly, and her eyes less palely blue.

"Oh, in *that* case," she remarked as if I had spoken, "in that case a trout, of course—a *truite au bleu* as only Monsieur Paul can prepare it!"

She glanced hurriedly at my face, and hastened on. "With the trout, one or two young potatoes—oh, very delicately boiled," she added before I could protest, "very light."

I felt better. I agreed. "Perhaps a leaf or two of salad after the fish," I suggested. She almost snapped at me. "Of course, of course! And naturally our hors d'oeuvres to commence." She started away. "No!" I called, feeling that I must assert myself now or be forever lost. "No!"

She turned back, and spoke to me very gently. "But Madame has never tasted our hors d'oeuvres. I am sure that Madame will be pleased. They are our specialty, made by Monsieur Paul himself. I am sure," and she looked reproachfully at me, her mouth tender and sad, "I am sure that Madame would be very much pleased."

I smiled weakly at her, and she left. A little cloud of hurt gentleness seemed to hang in the air where she had last stood.

I comforted myself with the sherry, feeling increasing irritation with my own feeble self. Hell! I loathed hors d'oeuvres! I conjured disgusting visions of square glass plates of oily fish, of soggy vegetables glued together with cheap mayonnaise, of rank radishes and tasteless butter. No, Monsieur Paul or not, sad young pale-faced waitress or not, I hated hors d'oeuvres.

I glanced victoriously across the room at the cat, whose eyes seemed closed.

Several minutes passed. I was really very hungry.

The door banged open, and my girl came in again, less discreet this time. She hurried toward me.

"Madame, the wine! Before Monsieur Paul can go on—" Her eyes watched my face, which I perversely kept rather glum.

"I think," I said ponderously, daring her to interrupt me, "I think that today, since I am in Burgundy and about to eat a trout," and here I hoped she noticed that I did not mention hors d'oeuvres, "I think I shall drink a bottle of Chablis 1929."

For a second her whole face blazed with joy, and then subsided into a trained mask. I knew that I had chosen well, and somehow satisfied her in a secret and incomprehensible way. She nodded politely and scuttled off, only for another second glancing impatiently at me as I called after her, "Well cooled, please, but not iced."

I'm a fool, I thought, to order a whole bottle, I'm a fool, here all alone and with more miles to walk before I reach Avallon and my fresh clothes and a bed. Then I smiled at myself and leaned back in my solid wide-seated chair, looking obliquely at the prints of Gibson girls, English tavern scenes, and hideous countrysides that hung on the papered walls. The room was warm; I could hear my companion cat purring under the ferns.

The girl rushed in, with flat baking dishes piled up her arms like the plates of a Japanese juggler. She slid them off neatly in two rows onto the table, where they lay steaming up at me, darkly and infinitely appetizing. *"Mon Dieu!* All for me?" I peered at her. She nodded, her discretion quite gone now and a look of ecstatic worry on her pale face and eyes and lips.

There were at least eight dishes. I felt almost embarrassed and sat for a minute looking weakly at the fork and spoon in my hand.

"Perhaps Madame would care to start with the pickled herring? It is not like any other. Monsieur Paul prepares it himself, in his own vinegar and wines. It is very good."

I dug out two or three brown filets from the dish, and tasted.

One August, years ago, I was wandering around the spacious property of a château in Normandy, trying to work up a proper appetite for lunch. The land doubled as a horse farm, and a vicious brood mare had tried to bite me, an act I rewarded with a stone sharply thrown against her ass.

Two old men I hadn't seen laughed beneath a tree. I walked over and sat with them around a small fire. They were gardeners and it was their lunch hour, and on a flat stone they had made a small circle of hot coals. They had cored a half-dozen big red tomatoes, stuffed them with softened cloves of garlic, and added a sprig of thyme, a basil leaf, and a couple of tablespoons of soft cheese. They roasted the tomatoes until they softened and the cheese melted. I ate one with a chunk of bread and healthy-sized swigs from a jug of red wine. When we finished eating, and since this was Normandy, we had a sip or two of calvados from a flask. A simple snack but indescribably delicious.

—Jim Harrison,
Just Before Dark: Collected Nonfiction

They were truly unlike any others, truly the best I had ever eaten, mild, pungent, meaty as fresh nuts.

I realized the maid had stopped breathing, and looked up at her. She was watching me, or rather a gastronomic X-ray of the herring inside me, with a hypnotized glaze in her eyes.

"Madame is pleased?" she whispered softly.

I said I was. She sighed, and pushed a sizzling plate of boiled endive toward me, and disappeared.

I had put a few dull green lentils on my plate, lentils scattered with minced fresh herbs and probably marinated in tarragon vinegar and walnut oil, when she came into the dining room again with the bottle of Chablis in a wine basket.

"Madame should be eating the little baked onions while they are hot," she remarked over her shoulder as she held the bottle in a napkin and uncorked it. I obeyed meekly, and while I watched her I ate several more than I had meant to. They were delicious, simmered first in strong meat broth, I think, and then drained and broiled with olive oil and new-ground pepper.

I was fascinated by her method of uncorking a vintage wine. Instead of the Burgundian procedure of infinite and often exaggerated precautions against touching or tipping or jarring the bottle, she handled it quite nonchalantly, and seemed to be careful only to keep her hands from the cool bottle itself, holding it sometimes by the basket and sometimes in a napkin. The cork was very tight, and I thought for a minute she would break it. So did she: her face grew tight, and did not loosen until she had slowly worked out the cork and wiped the lip. Then she poured an inch of wine in a glass, turned her back to me like a priest taking Communion, and drank it down. Finally some was poured for me, and she stood with the bottle in her hand and her full lips drooping until I nodded a satisfied yes. Then she pushed another of the plates toward me, and almost rushed from the room.

I ate slowly, knowing that I should not be as hungry as I ought to be for the trout, but knowing too that I had never tasted such delicate savory morsels. Some were hot, some cold. The wine was light and cool. The room, warm and agreeably empty under the rushing sound of the stream, became smaller as I grew used to it.

My girl hurried in again, with another row of plates up one arm, and a large bucket dragging at the other. She slid the plates deftly onto the table, and drew a deep breath as she let the bucket down against the table leg.

"Your trout, Madame," she said excitedly. I looked down at the gleam of the fish curving through its limited water. "But first a good slice of Monsieur Paul's *pâté*. Oh yes, oh yes, you will be very sorry if you miss this. It is rich, but appetizing, and not at all too heavy. Just this one morsel!"

And willy-nilly I accepted the large gouge she dug from a terrine. I prayed for ten normal appetites and thought with amused nostalgia of my usual lunch of cold milk and fruit as I broke off a crust of bread and patted it smooth with the paste. Then I forgot everything but the exciting faint decadent flavor in my mouth.

I beamed up at the girl. She nodded, but from habit asked if I was satisfied. I beamed again, and asked, simply to please her, "Is there not a faint hint of *marc,* or perhaps cognac?"

"*Marc,* Madame!" And she awarded me the proud look of a teacher whose pupil has showed unexpected intelligence. "Monsieur Paul, after he has taken equal parts of goose breast and the finest pork, and broken a certain number of egg yolks into them,

or a thing about the French that fewer travellers notice is that they are born teachers. The result is a very high level of accomplishment. The tourist is likely to meet it in the motor-mechanic, the cobbler, the hairdresser. Handling machines appeals to most men, and a repair-shop where he can take an antique car to pieces, put it together lovingly nut by nut, and make it go, is the joy of the workman. The cordonnier *will look reproachfully at your shoes, tell you that you have worn them too long and crushed them too little, and explain at length what can be done for them, as though he were a doctor prescribing for an illness due to neglect. He will then mend them well and cheaply.*

—Freda White, *Three Rivers of France: Dordogne, Lot, Tarn*

and ground them very, *very* fine, cooks all with seasoning for some
three hours. But," she pushed her face nearer, and looked with fe-
rocious gloating at the *pâté* inside me, her eyes like X-rays, "he
never stops stirring it! Figure to yourself the work of it—stir, stir,
never stopping!

"Then he grinds in a suspicion of nutmeg, and then adds, very
thoroughly, a glass of *marc* for each hundred grams of *pâté*. And is
Madame not pleased?"

Again I agreed, rather timidly, that Madame was much pleased,
that Madame had never, indeed, tasted such an unctuous and exciting *pâté*. The girl wet her lips delicately, and then started as if she
had been pin-stuck.

"But the trout! My God, the trout!" She grabbed the bucket,
and her voice grew higher and more rushed.

"Here is the trout, Madame. You are to eat it *au bleu,* and you
should never do so if you had not seen it alive. For if the trout were
dead when it was plunged into the *court bouillon* it would not turn
blue. So, naturally, it must be living."

I knew all this, more or less, but I was fascinated by her absorp-
tion in the momentary problem. I felt quite ignorant, and asked
her with sincerity, "What about the trout? Do you take out its guts
before or after?"

"Oh, the trout!" She sounded scornful. "Any trout is glad, truly
glad, to be prepared by Monsieur Paul. His little gills are pinched,
with one flash of the knife he is empty, and then he curls in agony
in the *bouillon* and all is over. And it is the curl you must judge,
Madame. A false *truite au bleu* cannot curl."

She panted triumph at me, and hurried out with the bucket.

She is a funny one, I thought, and for not more than two or
three minutes I drank wine and mused over her. Then she darted
in, with the trout correctly blue and agonizingly curled on the
platter, and on her crooked arm a plate of tiny boiled potatoes and
a bowl.

When I had been served and had cut off the anxious breathings
with an assurance that the fish was the best I had ever tasted, she
peered again at me and at the sauce in the bowl. I obediently put

some of it on the potatoes: no fool I, to ruin *truite au bleu* with a hot concoction! There was more silence.

"Ah!" she sighed at last. "I knew Madame would feel thus! Is it not the most beautiful sauce in the world with the flesh of a trout?"

I nodded incredulous agreement.

"Would you like to know how it is done?"

I remembered all the legends of chefs who guarded favorite recipes with their lives, and murmured yes.

She wore the exalted look of a believer describing a miracle at Lourdes as she told me, in a rush, how Monsieur Paul threw chopped chives into hot sweet butter and then poured the butter off, how he added another nut of butter and a tablespoon of thick cream for each person, stirred the mixture for a few minutes over a slow fire, and then rushed it to the table.

"So simple?" I asked softly, watching her lighted eyes and the tender lustful lines of her strange mouth.

"So simple, Madame! But," she shrugged, "you know, with a master—"

I was relieved to see her go: such avid interest in my eating wore on me. I felt released when the door closed behind her, free for a minute or so from her victimization. What would she have done, I wondered, if I had been ignorant or unconscious of any fine flavors?

She was right, though, about Monsieur Paul. Only a master could live in this isolated mill and preserve his gastronomic dignity through loneliness and the sure financial loss of unused butter and addled eggs. Of course there was the stream for his fish, and I knew his *pâté* would grow even more edible with age; but how could he manage to have a thing like roasted lamb ready for any chance patron? Was the consuming interest of his one maid enough fuel for his flame?

I tasted the last sweet nugget of trout, the one nearest the blued tail, and poked somnolently at the minute white billiard balls that had been eyes. Fate could not harm me, I remembered winily, for I had indeed dined today, and dined well. Now for a leaf of crisp salad, and I'd be on my way.

The girl slid into the room. She asked me again, in a respectful but gossipy manner, how I had liked this and that and the other things, and then talked on as she mixed dressing for the endive.

"And now," she announced, after I had eaten one green sprig and dutifully pronounced it excellent, "now Madame is going to taste Monsieur Paul's special terrine, one that is not even on the summer menu, when a hundred covers are laid here daily and we have a headwaiter and a wine waiter, and cabinet ministers telegraph for tables! Madame will be pleased."

And heedless of my low moans of the walk still before me, of my appreciation and my unhappily human and limited capacity, she cut a thick heady slice from the terrine of meat and stood over me while I ate it, telling me with almost hysterical pleasure of the wild ducks, the spices, the wines that went into it. Even surfeit could not make me deny that it was a rare dish. I ate it all, knowing my luck, and wishing only that I had red wine to drink with it.

I was beginning, though, to feel almost frightened, realizing myself an accidental victim of these stranded gourmets, Monsieur Paul and his handmaiden. I began to feel that they were using me for a safety valve, much as a thwarted woman relieves herself with tantrums or a fit of weeping. I was serving a purpose, and perhaps a noble one, but I resented it in a way approaching panic.

I protested only to myself when one of Monsieur Paul's special cheeses was cut for me, and ate it doggedly, like a slave. When the girl said that Monsieur Paul himself was preparing a special filter of coffee for me, I smiled servile acceptance: wine and the weight of food and my own character could not force me to argue with maniacs. When, before the coffee came, Monsieur Paul presented me, through his idolater, with the most beautiful apple tart I had ever seen, I allowed it to be cut and served to me. Not a wince or a murmur showed the waitress my distressed fearfulness. With a stuffed careful smile on my face, and a clear nightmare in my head of trussed wanderers prepared for his altar by this hermit-priest of gastronomy, I listened to the girl's passionate plea for fresh pastry dough.

"You cannot, you *can*not, Madame, serve old pastry!" She seemed ready to beat her breast as she leaned across the table. "Look at the delicate crust! You may feel that you have eaten too much." (I nodded idiotic agreement.) "But this pastry is like feathers—it is like snow. It is in fact good for you, a digestive! And why?" She glared sternly at me. "Because Monsieur Paul did not even open the flour bin until he saw you coming! He could not, he *could* not have baked you one of his special apple tarts with old dough!"

She laughed, tossing back her head and curling her mouth voluptuously.

Somehow I managed to refuse a second slice, but I trembled under her surmise that I was ready for my special filter.

The wine and its fortitude had fled me, and I drank the hot coffee as a suffering man gulps ether, deeply and gratefully.

I remember, then, chatting with surprising glibness, and sending Monsieur Paul flowery compliments, all of them sincere and well won, and I remember feeling only amusement when a vast glass of *marc* appeared before me and then gradually disappeared, like the light in the warm room full of water-sounds. I felt surprise to be alive still, and suddenly very grateful to the wild-lipped waitress, as if her presence had sustained me through duress. We discussed food and wine. I wondered bemusedly why I had been frightened.

The *marc* was gone. I went into the crowded bedroom for my jacket. She met me in the darkening hall when I came out, and I paid my bill, a large one. I started to thank her, but she took my hand, drew me into the dining room, and without words poured more spirits into my glass. I drank to Monsieur Paul while she

*G*iven France's reputation as the land of good cooking, *every young Français believes he is a born chef, just as every young Englishman thinks, quite erroneously, that he is a born sailor in the mould of Drake and Nelson. Ce n'est pas vrai. Pas du tout. The French are quite as capable of cooking badly as the English are of being seasick. But neither will believe it.*

—Bill and Laurel Cooper,
A Spell in Wild France

watched me intently, her pale eyes bulging in the dimness and her lips pressed inward as if she too tasted the hot, aged *marc*.

The cat rose from his ferny bed, and walked contemptuously out of the room.

Suddenly the girl began to laugh, in a soft shy breathless way, and came close to me.

"Permit me!" she said, and I thought she was going to kiss me. But instead she pinned a tiny bunch of snowdrops and dark bruised cyclamens against my stiff jacket, very quickly and deftly, and then ran from the room with her head down.

I waited for a minute. No sounds came from anywhere in the old mill, but the endless rushing of the full stream seemed to strengthen, like the timed blare of an orchestra under a falling curtain.

She's a *funny* one, I thought. I touched the cool blossoms on my coat and went out, like a ghost from ruins, across the courtyard toward the dim road to Avallon.

In her long career, M. F. K. Fisher was a prolific writer of novels, poetry, and reflections on food and life. This story was excerpted from her book, As They Were.

★

Believe us, fellow peasants, food is not an innocent and sweet trifle to be played with, even though it appears to waltz so benignly upon our plates and tables. It is nature herself, stupid, cruel, and ruthless. Everything is food, including yourselves, even if it is only bacteria which eat you now. Nature, over which you naturally and melodiously coo and rub your hands, that plump and fertile part-time goddess who manures your unconscious and whose backside you would so dearly like to kiss, that fat cow of a deity whom you vaguely imagine as some tinkling ethnic icon or as a smiling dairymaid covered in gossamer and tentacles of ivy, is no other than the mindless sadist who has commanded all living things to eat all other living things with a perpetual and inane violence, that lobotomized designer who casually exterminates dinosaurs and dodos, sabretoothed tigers and hairy mammoths, and whose supposed capacity to maintain harmonious order is merely the effect of the relentless whip that ensures continual discontinuity, the stick which flagellates every beast on its path to consumption. Nature, as all true peasants are fully aware, is the greatest advocate of vulgar consumerism the universe has so far produced.

—Lawrence Osborne, *Paris Dreambook: An Unconventional Guide to the Splendor and Squalor of the City*

* * *

Les Invalides

*A sick visitor provides the occasion
for much mirth.*

I HAD BEEN TO A PHARMACY IN APT FOR TOOTHPASTE AND SUN-
tan oil, two innocent and perfectly healthy purchases. When I arrived home and took them out of the bag, I found that the girl
who served me had included an instructive but puzzling gift. It was
an expensively printed leaflet in full color. On the front was a picture of a snail sitting on the toilet. He looked doleful, as if he'd
been there for some time without achieving anything worthwhile.
His horns drooped. His eye was lackluster. Above this sad picture
was printed *La Constipation*.

What had I done to deserve this? Did I look constipated? Or
was the fact that I bought toothpaste and suntan oil somehow significant to the expert pharmacist's eye—a hint that all was not well
in my digestive system? Maybe the girl knew something I didn't. I
started to read the leaflet.

"Nothing," it said, "is more banal and more frequent than constipation." About twenty percent of the French population, so the
writer claimed, suffered from the horrors of *ballonnement* and *gêne
abdominale*. And yet, to a casual observer like myself, there were no
obvious signs of discomfort among the people on the streets, in the
bars and cafés, or even in the restaurants—where presumably

twenty percent of the clientele tucking into two substantial meals a day were doing so in spite of their *ballonnements*. What fortitude in the face of adversity! I had always thought of Provence as one of the healthier places in the world. The air is clean, the climate is dry, fresh fruit and vegetables are abundantly available, cooking is done with olive oil, stress doesn't seem to exist—there could hardly be a more wholesome set of circumstances. And everybody looks very well. But if twenty percent of those ruddy faces and hearty appetites were concealing the suffering caused by a traffic jam in the *transit intestinal,* what else might they be concealing? I decided to pay closer attention to Provençal complaints and remedies, and gradually became aware that there is indeed a local affliction, which I think extends to the entire country. It is hypochondria.

A Frenchman never feels out of sorts; he has a *crise.* The most popular of these is a *crise de foie,* when the liver finally rebels against the punishment inflicted by *pastis,* five-course meals, and the tots of *marc* and the *vin d'honneur* served at everything from the opening of a car showroom to the annual meeting of the village Communist Party. The simple cure is no alcohol and plenty of mineral water, but a much more satisfactory solution—because it supports the idea of illness rather than admitting self-indulgence—is a trip to the pharmacy and a consultation with the sympathetic white-coated lady behind the counter.

I used to wonder why most pharmacies have chairs arranged between the surgical trusses and the *cellulite* treatment kits, and now I know. It is so that one can wait more comfortably while Monsieur Machin explains, in great whispered detail and with considerable massaging of the engorged throat, the tender kidney, the reluctant intestine, or whatever else ails him, how he came to this painful state. The pharmacist, who is trained in patience and diagnosis, listens carefully, asks a few questions, and then

French pharmacies are easy to spot on the street of any town because of their bright green and white signs in the shape of crosses.

—JO'R, LH, and SO'R

proposes a number of solutions. Packets and jars and ampoules are produced. More discussion. A choice is finally made, and Monsieur Machin carefully folds up the vital pieces of paper that will enable him to claim back most of the cost of his medication from Social Security. Fifteen or twenty minutes have passed, and everyone moves up a chair.

These trips to the pharmacy are only for the more robust invalids. For serious illness, or imaginary serious illness, there is, even in relatively remote country areas like ours, a network of first aid specialists that amazes visitors from cities, where you need to be a millionaire before you can be sick in comfort. All the towns, and many villages, have their own ambulance services, on call 24 hours a day. Registered nurses will come to the house. Doctors will come to the house, a practice I'm told is almost extinct in London.

We had a brief but intense experience with the French medical system early last summer. The guinea pig was Benson, a young American visitor on his first trip to Europe. When I picked him up at the Avignon railroad station, he croaked hello, coughed, and clapped a handkerchief to his mouth. I asked him what was the matter.

He pointed to his throat and made wheezing noises.

"Mono," he said.

Mono? I had no idea what that was, but I did know that Americans have much more sophisticated ailments than we do—hematomas instead of bruises, migraine instead of a headache, postnasal drip—and so I muttered something about fresh air soon clearing it up and helped him into the car. On the way home, I learned that mono was the intimate form of address for mononucleosis, a viral infection causing considerable soreness of the throat. "Like broken glass," said Benson, huddled behind his sunglasses and his handkerchief. "We have to call my brother in Brooklyn. He's a doctor."

We got back to the house to find the phone out of order. It was the beginning of a long holiday weekend, and so we would be without it for three days, normally a blessing. But Brooklyn had to be called. There was one particular antibiotic, a *state of the art* antibiotic, that Benson said would overcome all known forms of mono. I went down to the phone booth at Les Baumettes and fed it with five-franc pieces while Brooklyn Hospital searched for Benson's brother. He gave me the name of the wonder drug. I called a doctor and asked him if he could come to the house.

He arrived within an hour and inspected the invalid, who was resting behind his sunglasses in a darkened room.

"*Alors, monsieur...*" the doctor began, but Benson cut him short.

"Mono," he said, pointing at his throat.

"*Comment?*"

"Mono, man. Mononucleosis."

"*Ah, mononucléose. Peut-être, peut-être.*"

The doctor looked into Benson's angry throat and took a swab. He wanted to run a laboratory test on the virus. And now, would Monsieur lower his trousers? He took out a syringe, which Benson peered at suspiciously over his shoulder as he slowly dropped his Calvin Klein jeans to half-mast.

"Tell him I'm allergic to most antibiotics. He should call my brother in Brooklyn."

"*Comment?*"

I explained the problem. Did the doctor by any chance have the wonder drug in his bag? *Non.* We looked at each other around Benson's bare buttocks. They jerked as Benson coughed painfully. The doctor said he must be given something to reduce the inflammation, and that side effects from this particular shot were extremely rare. I passed the news on to Benson.

"Well...OK." He bent over, and the doctor injected with a flourish, like a matador going in over the horns.

"*Voilà!*"

While Benson waited for allergic reactions to send him reeling, the doctor told me that he would arrange for a nurse to come twice a day to give further injections, and that the test results would be in on Saturday. As soon as he had them, he would make out the necessary prescriptions. He wished us a *bonne soirée.* Benson communed noisily with his handkerchief. I thought a *bonne soirée* was unlikely.

The nurse came and went, the test results came through, and the doctor reappeared on Saturday evening as promised. The young Monsieur had been correct. It was *mononucléose,* but we would conquer it with the resources of French medicine. The doctor began to scribble like a poet in heat. As prescription after prescription flowed from his pen, it seemed as though every single resource was going to be called into action. He passed over a wad of hieroglyphics, and wished us a *bon weekend.* That too was unlikely.

The Sunday of a holiday weekend in rural France is not the easiest time to find a pharmacy open for business, and the only one for miles around was the *pharmacie de garde* on the outskirts of Cavaillon. I was there at 8:30, and joined a man clutching a wad of prescriptions almost as thick as mine. Together we read the notice taped to the glass door: opening time was not until 10:00.

The man sighed, and looked me up and down.

"Are you an emergency?"

No. It was for a friend.

He nodded. He himself had an important *arthrose* in his shoulder, and also some malign fungus of the feet. He was not going to stand for an hour and a half in the sun to wait for the pharmacy to open. He sat down on the pavement next to the door and started to read chapter one of his prescriptions. I decided to go and have breakfast.

"Come back well before ten," he said. "There will be many people today."

How did he know? Was a Sunday morning visit to the pharmacy a regular prelunch treat? I thanked him and ignored his advice, killing time with an old copy of *Le Provençal* in a café.

When I returned to the pharmacy just before ten, it looked as though *le tout Cavaillon* had gathered outside. There were dozens of them standing with their voluminous prescriptions, swapping symptoms in the manner of an angler describing a prize fish. Monsieur Angine boasted about his sore throat. Madame Varices countered with the history of her varicose veins. The halt and the maimed chattered away cheerfully, consulting their watches and pressing ever closer to the still-locked door. At last, to a murmured accompaniment of *enfin* and *elle arrive,* a girl appeared from the back of the pharmacy, opened up, and stepped smartly aside as the stampede jostled through. Not for the first time, I realized that the Anglo-Saxon custom of the orderly queue has no place in French life.

I must have been there for half an hour before I was able to take advantage of a gap in the mêlée and give my documents to the pharmacist. She produced a plastic shopping bag and started to fill it with boxes and bottles, rubber-stamping each prescription as she worked her way through the pile, a copy for her, a copy for me. With the bag at bursting point, one prescription remained. After disappearing for five minutes, the pharmacists admitted defeat; she was out of stock of whatever it was, and I would have to get it from another pharmacy. However, it was not grave, because the important medication was all there in the bag. Enough, it seemed to me, to bring a regiment back from the dead.

Benson sucked and gargled and inhaled his way through the menu. By the next morning he had emerged from the shadow of the grave and was feeling sufficiently recovered to join us on a trip to the Ménerbes pharmacy in search of the last prescription.

One of the village elders was there when we arrived, perched on a stool while his shopping bag was being stuffed full of nostrums. Curious about what exotic disease the foreigners might have, he remained seated while our prescription was being filled, leaning forward to see what was in the packet as it was put on the counter.

The pharmacist opened the packet and took out a foil-wrapped object the size of a fat Alka-Seltzer tablet. She held it up to Benson.

"*Deux fois par jour,*" she said.

Benson shook his head and put his hand to his throat.

"Too big," he said. "I couldn't swallow anything that size."

We translated for the pharmacist, but before she could reply the old man collapsed with laughter, rocking perilously on his stool wiping his eyes with the back of a knobby hand. The pharmacist smiled, and made delicate upward motions with the foil-wrapped lump. "*C'est un suppositoire.*"

Benson looked bewildered. The old man, still laughing, hopped down from his stool and took the suppository from the pharmacist.

"Regardez," he said to Benson. *"On fait comme ça."*

He moved away from the counter to give himself space, bent forward, holding the suppository above his head, and then, with a flowing backwards swoop of his arm, applied the suppository firmly to the seat of his trousers. *"Toc!"* said the old man. He looked up at Benson. *"Vous voyez?"*

"Up the *ass?*" Benson shook his head again. "Hey, that's weird. Jesus." He put on his sunglasses and moved a couple of paces backwards. "We don't do that where I come from."

We tried to explain that it was a very efficient method of getting medication into the bloodstream, but he wasn't convinced. And when we said that it wouldn't give him a sore throat either, he wasn't amused. I often wonder what he told his brother the doctor back in Brooklyn.

Shortly afterward, I met my neighbor Massot in the forest and told him about the suppository lesson. It was droll, he thought, but for a truly *dramatique* episode there was nothing to touch the story of the man who had gone into the hospital to have his appendix out and had woken up with his left leg amputated. *Beh oui.*

I said it couldn't be true, but Massot insisted that it was.

"If I am ever ill," he said, "I go to the vet. You know where you are with vets. I don't trust doctors."

Fortunately, Massot's view of the French medical profession is as unlikely to reflect reality as most of his views. There may be doctors with a taste for amputation in Provence, but we have never met them. In fact, apart from our brush with mononucleosis, we've only seen the doctor once, and that was to combat an attack of bureaucracy.

It was the climax of months of paper shuffling that we had gone through in order to get our *cartes de séjour*—the identity cards that are issued to foreign residents of France. We had been to the *Mairie,* to the *Préfecture,* to the *Bureau des Impôts,* and back again to the *Mairie.* Everywhere we went, we were told that another form was required which, *naturellement,* could only be obtained somewhere else. In the end, when we were convinced that we had a full set of certificates, attestations, declarations, photographs, and vital statistics, we made what we thought would be our last triumphal visit to the *Mairie.*

Our dossiers were examined carefully. Everything seemed to be in order. We were not going to be a drain on the state. We had no criminal record. We were not seeking to steal employment from French workers. *Bon.* The dossiers were closed. At last we were going to be official.

The secretary of the *Mairie* smiled nicely and passed over two more forms. It was necessary, she said, to have a medical examination to prove that we were of sound mind and body. Doctor Fenelon in Bonnieux would be pleased to examine us. Off to Bonnieux we went.

Doctor Fenelon was charming and brisk as he X-rayed us and took us through the fine print of a short questionnaire. Were we mad? No. Epileptic? No. Addicted to drugs? Alcoholic? Prone to fainting? I was half-expecting to be interrogated about bowel movements in case we might be adding to the constipated sector of the French population, but that didn't seem to be a concern of the immigration authorities. We signed the forms. Doctor Fenelon signed the forms. Then he opened a drawer and produced two more forms.

He was apologetic. "*Bien sûr, vous n'avez pas de problème, mais...*" he shrugged, and explained that we must take the forms into Cavaillon and have a blood test before he could give us our *certificats sanitaires.*

Was there anything special that we were being tested for?
"*Ah, oui.*" He looked even more apologetic. "*La syphilis.*"

Peter Mayle spent fifteen years in advertising before turning to writing books. His work has been translated into seventeen languages, and he is best known for his books French Lessons, Encore Provence, A Year in Provence, *and* Toujours Provence, *from which this story was excerpted. He is also the author of the novel* Hotel Pastis, *and* A Dog's Life, *with drawings by Edward Koren. He lives with his wife in Provence.*

★

The doctor appears to be France's modern father confessor. The nation seems to have placed its faith in him: more is spent on health than on either education or defence. The present generation has used its new prosperity to quadruple the number of doctors. But it is now well established that however well doctors do their job, they never eliminate disease: the more of them there are to consult, the more leisure people have to consult them, the more they will be needed.

—Theodore Zeldin, *The French*

The Cave Where It Lives

There's nothing more French than cheese.

EVER SINCE I WAS A SMALL BOY STEALING SNACKS FROM MY mother's refrigerator, Roquefort has been one of the blue cheeses I have loved best. I never knew what was so special and unique about it, however, until the day I had breakfast in New York with a vivacious Frenchman called Jean-Paul Mittaine. I learned from him, after having eaten this noble cheese for 50 years, the extraordinary story of Roquefort, which has been called "the king of cheeses and the cheese of kings." It can be made—because of a fantastic set of geological factors—in only one place on earth, in certain caves in the mountains of south-central France, near the village of Roquefort-sur-Soulzon. There are hundreds of blue-veined cheeses, but there is only one Roquefort, and its name is legally protected throughout the world.

While this story was written some years ago, the principles of the cheese production it describes remain the same. M. Mittaine is no longer the director general of the Fédération Roquefort; he has been succeeded by M. Guy Soragna.

—JO'R, LH, and SO'R

As I sipped my mundane coffee and orange juice, Monsieur

Mittaine, an official of the Fédération Roquefort and president of the French national committee for controlled-appellation cheeses, told me a story that might have been the plot of an historical novel.

For more than 2,000 years sheep have grazed on the hills over-looking the Mediterranean coast of southern France. But the shepherds came to realize that in high summer the flaming heat of the southern sun was too great for the sheep, so each spring they would drive their flocks north about 75 miles to the mountains, now called the Cévennes, of the region of Aveyron. Here the land had been pushed up by volcanic action into high, arid mesas very much like those of Arizona and New Mexico. In French, these tablelands are called *les Causses,* "the barrens" or "the wastelands." On the mesas, where the supply of water was limited, the milk given by the ewes was especially rich and thick, excellent for making into sheep's milk cheese.

Then one summer—about twenty centuries ago, according to the legend woven into the stories and folk songs of the region—a young shepherd, high on *les Causses,* made the accidental discovery that changed the course of local history. A fiery sun was beating down and the young man was worried about the lunch in his leather shoulder bag—a large crust of rye bread, a piece of white sheep's milk cheese, and two apples. Along one side of this mesa was a high mass of rock, known today as Mount Combalou, tunneled with many dark caves. The young shepherd climbed up and set his lunch on a cool ledge in the deep shade of one of the caves, where the sun could not penetrate.

Soon after he descended to his flock, the sheep were attacked by a wolf and in the fray he forgot all about his lunch. Next day, because of the continuing wolf danger, he grazed his sheep on a different mesa. In fact, he didn't get back to the original place for about three months. Then, idly, he climbed back into the cave. He was not surprised to find the bread moldy and inedible, but the white cheese was interestingly shot through with jagged blue-green veins.

The young man was not afraid to taste it; he was used to eating up bits of old cheese. But this piece was quite different. It had remained perfectly soft. It had an interesting aroma and a faintly nutty, definitely tangy flavor. He took some home. All his family liked it too. His father decided that they would put some of their cheeses into the cave to develop the mold. The new cheese was an immediate success. Roquefort was born.

As increasing numbers of sheep farmers jumped in on this good thing, more and more caves above the mesa were used and were penetrated more deeply. It was found through trial and error that only the caves of one particular rock formation—Mount Combalou—had the power to cause the blue-green veins to appear in the cheese. Other caves, some only a mile away, produced no effect. For some 1,800 years thereafter the "magic" caves made the marvelous cheeses enjoyed by Roman Caesars, emperors, kings and princes, without anyone's understanding the magic process in the least. Since the cheese came from a fortress-like rock it was called, simply, "Roc Fort," and the same name was given to the hamlet where the cheese workers lived around the base of the huge "strong rock." Only in the 19th century did bacteriologists, geologists, and other scientists unravel the secret of why nature allows Roquefort to be made only in one tiny spot on earth.

Millions of years ago, when the earth's crust was cooling and shrinking, the solid limestone that was to become Mount Combalou was subjected to enormous cross-pressures that broke the mass up into huge blocks, tumbled together higgledy-piggledy. The spaces that lay between them varied in shape and ranged in size from the equivalent of an intimate den up to a cathedral with a vaulted roof. These are the many-leveled caves of Roquefort, rather like a cross between an apartment building more than a mile long and a deep coal mine. Geologists burrowing down to the lowest depths have discovered that, as Mittaine says, "broken old Mount Combalou has his feet forever standing in a lake." Under the rock a deep bed of clay holds all the waters that seep down after rainfall in the surrounding region. The lake water is constantly evaporating, and the vapors rise through the interconnecting caves above. The result is that, summer and winter, there is a strong draft of air through every cave, keeping the temperature always at around 45 degrees Fahrenheit and the humidity always at around 90 to 95 percent. When you go into these caves, you find them so icy-cold that you are glad to have a blanket to wear over your shoulders, and so damp that the air on your face feels like a sea-born mist. These are ideal conditions for the "benign and noble" mold microorganisms, existing in the caves for untold ages, which have now been dignified with an official Latin name, *Penicillium roqueforti.* Floating invisibly in the air, growing on every square inch of the walls, in every crevice of the rocks, and in every cheese that is placed in the caves for the blue-green veins to develop, this microorganism is found nowhere else in the world. It is the secret of Roquefort.

Roquefort is almost certainly the oldest fine cheese in the world, predating the Christian era. During the Roman Empire, Pliny the Elder wrote of this marvelous ewe's-milk cheese from Gaul, which was served at the banquets of the Caesars. From the time of the Emperor Charlemagne (when the name Roquefort first appeared on a document) to the present, Roquefort has received official recognition and legal protection of its identity.

Roquefort is one of the eighteen basic controlled-appellation cheeses of France, and the government will not allow any change in its production that might in any way alter its character. For instance, milk from a different breed of sheep may not be used—it would have a different taste and texture. Only fresh milk may be used; dried milk is forbidden. Not one drop of cow's milk is allowed. No artificial enzymes may be used for transforming the milk into curds; natural rennet from lambs' stomachs only is allowed. No additives of any kind are permitted. Finally, the blue-green veining must be induced naturally and only in the caves of Roquefort.

> *There are now 36 controlled-appellation cheeses in France, testament not just to the amazing variety of cheeses in France but to their commercial value.*
>
> —JO'R, LH, and SO'R

As outlined by M. Mittaine, this story sounded almost too perfect to be true, and I felt the strongest desire to visit the caves of Roquefort. At the end of our breakfast together in New York, he invited me to come to the village of Roquefort-sur-Soulzon. Before too long, I went.

We drove to Roquefort over the mountain road from the south and, over the last rise, we saw, in the valley below, the village with its huddle of blue and red tile roofs. Facing us across the valley was the rock "fortress" sharply outlined against the sky—Mount Combalou.

Later, as I walked with our host, Jean Bonnefous, a technical expert involved in Roquefort production research, across the village square toward the entrance to the caves, he told me that, while the magic of the microorganisms remains the same as it has been for twenty centuries, the caves now house a highly modernized production operation, in a subterranean city of eleven stories covering twenty-five acres—a labyrinth within a mountain, with nearly four miles of passageways. The main entrance is, quite unromantically, a huge ramp for the trailer trucks that bring the thousands of plain white cheeses for transformation in the caves and carry away the finished cheeses.

In the visitors' reception room I was handed a thick blanket to hang over my shoulders against the cold and the damp. We went down a long flight of stone steps and through a fairly steeply inclined tunnel to the space called "the first grotto." It was about the size of a church. The concrete floor was level but the walls, rising perhaps 30 feet to an apex, were jagged, raw limestone, broken by hundreds of cracks, crevices, fissures, holes, from which came gentle blasts of cold, damp air. It was air-conditioning on a fantastic scale; at each crack, the air jet was strong enough to blow out the flame of a cigarette lighter.

Then, down another long flight of steps, another steeply sloping tunnel, and I began to feel like the hero of Jules Verne's *Journey to the Center of the Earth*. We entered a huge workshop cave, which somehow reminded me of the chapter house of a monastery. The young dairymaids working here, with white coats over their warm clothes and woolen stockings, are traditionally called *cabanières,* a word of the region meaning "cave women." We watched them salting the cheeses, brushing them and perforating each with the 32 holes that allow the mold-laden air to reach the center and begin the development of the veins.

But the main work in the caves of Roquefort is the silent and timeless operation of nature. In one enormous cavern, 300 feet long and almost 100 feet high, oak shelves from floor to roof hold thousands of cheeses, resting on their sides and slowly developing. Each cheese is regularly turned by hand. After about three months, each is tested by an expert with a probe, which draws out a sample from the center. On the appearance, smell, and taste of this sample the decision is made as to how near the cheese is to perfection. Some cheeses continue to age for as long as a year.

The day after the cave visit Jean Bonnefous took me to one of the *fromageries,* the smallish, mostly very modern dairies where the white cheeses are made. The milk from more than 7,000 sheep farms is delivered every morning and evening to these *fromageries,* which are scattered in the various valleys and villages of the mesa region. In the village of Fondamente we went to the dairy, an extremely modern, two-story building, its interior bright with stainless steel, white with tiles, as clean and scrubbed as a hospital operating room—a perfect place for a cheese to be born. This dairy is run by a husband-and-wife team, very suitably named Monsieur and Madame Roc. He is the cheesemaker; she is a biochemist who, in her laboratory upstairs, with her thermometers and acidometers, graduated glasses and microscopes and test tubes, carries out many of the 263 tests made on the fresh milk and on every cheese during the process of production and aging.

The fresh milk brought by the refrigerated tank truck is pumped into open stainless-steel vats about six feet across and four feet deep, holding roughly 1,000 liters. Each vat is surrounded by a steam jacket that heats the milk gently to 86 degrees Fahrenheit. A measured amount of natural rennet is added to solidify the milk into curd—the first step in making most cheese. After the curd forms, it is "cut up" by a worker using a tool with strung wires that looks a bit like a small harp. As the curd is cut into cubes about the size of lumps of sugar, the watery whey is released and most of it is drained off. After a few hours the curds are ladled into stainless-steel molds with perforated bottoms. The molds are ranged in long lines on ribbed stainless-steel tables where the draining continues for three days. Then the cheeses are unmolded and salted and placed, well apart, on drying shelves in a room kept at a fairly low temperature. After about six to eight more days they are firm enough to be packed and transported by truck to the caves for "refining," as the process of transformation is called.

S adly, the process of making Roquefort cheese by hand has been abandoned, and all producers are now using machines.

—JO'R, LH, and SO'R

We spent one lovely, refreshing day with the sheep on top of a high, windswept mesa of *les Causses*. Our car snaked uphill over a narrow road bordered with limestone boulders, past flowering plants, bright-green young oaks and hazel bushes. The road led onto a flat tableland where the wind slapped at our faces. The arid earth was covered with stones and punctuated by clumps of dry grass and blue-flowered thistles. Locusts buzzed through the air. The arc of the blue sky was immense.

Above the sighing of the wind, sheep bells tapped out the song of the mesa. The sheep were at home here. They searched out the delicacies among the dry grasses—the wild sweet clover, the sage and thyme, the verbena. They drank the clear water pumped up for them into round stone ponds. We followed one of the flocks of ewes to a group of stone buildings, low under roofs of curved red tiles.

Inside, the bleating of sheep and the smell of oily wool combined with the purring of electric motors. The ewes were crowding around the latest type of milking carousel. On the revolving platform were 24 wedge-shaped pens with, at the head of each, a feeder filled with wheat, which is caviar to sheep. Each ewe fairly jumped into the pen and stuck her head into the feeder, immobilized in total concentration while the strong young shepherd fitted the udder into the milking cup. After the carousel had made one slow revolution, the job was done. The milk was at once cooled and pumped into the storage tank.

I tasted a glass of the fresh milk. It was creamy and thick—the first impression was one of richness on my lips and tongue. Then, it seemed to me to have the brightness, the cleanness, the purity of these wide and windswept spaces. There was also, I thought, a faint sense of those wild herbs cropped so eagerly by the sheep. At that moment I believe I knew why, all my life, I had so much loved the cheese of Roquefort.

Roy Andries de Groot was a celebrated food and wine critic who died in 1983 at the age of 73. He was born in London and was injured during the blitz of London in 1940, losing his sight as a result. He became an American citizen in 1945 and lived in New York, where he wrote several books and articles on food, wine, cooking, and restaurants for major American magazines.

✦

The action takes place in a Food for Less supermarket down on Fourteenth and Folsom [in San Francisco]. I'm going to the aisle where they display the cheese, to indulge in the last remnant of my French self. America has taken my language, America has taken my self-confidence, America has taken my identity, but America has not yet taken Brie cheese away from me.

As soon as I reach the refrigerated display stand, I grab a wedge of "Tradition de Belmont," a soft ripened Brie, and expertly press it between my thumb and my index finger, to check its consistency. "Tradition de Belmont" is the only American cheese that comes close to the real thing and still fits within my budget. Shamelessly, just as I used to do in the open markets in the south of France during the summer, I bring the cheese to my nose and sniff it like a maniac, trying to judge by its scent if it's old enough.

Seeing my trouble, a woman comes to my rescue and tells me with a strange accent, "It's not very good cheese. You know, it always tastes a bit like plastic."

Who is this woman who dares to think she might tell a Frenchman what a good cheese tastes like? Still, her accent intrigues me.

"Where are you from?" I ask her.

"I'm from France," she replies. I start to laugh. It is so unrealistic, and at the same time it makes sense. Where else but in a supermarket cheese section would I meet a French person? I switch to French and ask her name; it is Marie-Ange.

"How long have *you* been here? Oh! You're a bike messenger!" she says enthusiastically. Right away, it's getting too heavy for me to talk with her; speaking French unearths things, reaches too deep within, and the muse of her voice—something about her is so French and calls me, calls me, calls me. It hurts.

I'm trying to back off from being so emotionally involved. I say in English, "I'm sorry, I'm not used to speaking French."

But even in that retreat she pursues me: she answers in English; I switch back to French. I say something banal. We don't say anything. A minute passes.

She grabs a slice of Danish blue cheese and asks me, "Is this good? I've never had this."

I answer in French, "Oh, yes, it's kind of like Bleu d'Auvergne except it's made in Denmark."

"Oh, really? You're sure it's not like a Roquefort? Because I don't like Roquefort. It's so strong."

Oh, my God! She hasn't said it, but it's understood between us that she knows what a Bleu d'Auvergne is. It's been so long since I've had a casual discussion about cheese. She has stabbed me. She's gone right to the core of my French being with that Roquefort. She has done no less than rip my heart out of my chest. All those emotions suppressed for so long—I'm surprised I can still feel them. She looks at me now. She looks at me as only French women do. We talk about cheese, but it's only on the surface; beneath we talk about everything else. I'm having a communion of soul with her, I love her, I'm heartbroken. My French soul is screaming, reacting like dry soil thirsting for water for years and finally given a drink. She makes me feel like a man who could love, not like the emotional cripple I've become in my time here. I had forgotten that it can be simple and beautiful to be attracted to a woman.

But this is forbidden territory, those are taboo feelings. If I want to survive in the USA, I can't afford to be French. Don't look at me, Marie-

Ange. I turn my eyes away from her, I turn my body away. I turn my heart away. I go to the aisle where they sell ten-cent packages of noodles, to hide.

—Bruno Gheerbrant, *Tales of a Greasy-Spoon*

PART TWO

SOME THINGS TO DO

JAMES O'REILLY

Road Scholars

Eight thousand miles in France with three kids,
a van, and no hotel reservations.

OUR PLAN WAS TO SHIP OUR VW VAN—STUFFED AS THOUGH IT
were an indecently large suitcase—to France, drive around for six
weeks, find a town to our liking, and settle down for two years so
our three girls, aged three, five, and seven, could learn French while
I finished a book. Not exactly *A Year in Provence,* but maybe a year
or two in Montpellier, Pont-Aven, or Grenoble. Of course, it didn't
work out quite like that. Well, to be honest, it didn't work out like
that at all.

To begin with, there was the obligatory French dock strike. Our
van would be two weeks late, we were told, and it wasn't going to
arrive in France after all. Maybe Belgium, perhaps the
Netherlands. *Normalement* the boat would head for Antwerp after
bypassing Le Havre (where it was supposed to go), but for obscure
reasons it might have to unload in Rotterdam. Sitting on lumpy
mattresses in an atmospheric but squalid Left Bank hotel, Wenda
and I took a deep breath and decided to enjoy our fate while matters maritime sorted themselves out.

We explored Paris, bitterly cold in early January but devoid of
tourists. There were no lines anywhere. The Eiffel Tower in a rainstorm was ours. So too the Musée d'Orsay, the Louvre, and Notre-

Dame. There was nobody waiting for ice cream cones outside
Berthillon on l'Isle St-Louis. We were cheated by cab drivers and
snubbed by waiters. We rode boats on the Seine, wandered the
streets, visited Jacques Cousteau's Parc Océanique under Les
Halles, spent exorbitant sums on mediocre snacks, and in general
had a wonderful time. We decided Paris was indeed extraordinary,
oozing history and beauty like no other place, but that Parisians
who deal with tourists bear a distinct behavioral resemblance to
New Yorkers, Paris not being France the same way New York is
not America. Or is it? The question had too many layers to sort
out when a three-year-old wants to be carried through all six million miles of the Louvre.

We rented a little red Peugeot, stuffed dolls, bears, and children
into it and set off to find the real France, where we would set up
shop. No sooner had we left Paris than one of the girls threw up
all over the back seat. We pulled off the road next to a nice-look-
ing *auberge* by the Seine and cleaned the car. By then everyone was
hungry and cold, so we trotted past ducks and up stone steps and
inquired if the establishment was open. It was, *bien sûr.* We were
warmly welcomed, served great food at a reasonable price, and left
feeling that perhaps we had not made a mistake after all, that in fact
Parisians were only as good ambassadors as New Yorkers.

We headed for Normandy, where we stayed with friends in a
farmhouse near Caen. We visited the Peace Museum, walked
Sword Beach, and told the girls about World War II and the approaching fleet had this been D-Day so many years ago. One
evening I achieved *satori,* or, as Spalding Gray might have it, a perfect moment, sharing wine and camembert with our friends. I am
by no means a food-oriented person, but the French do indeed
have a remarkable and communicable way with food. The next
evening I made the mistake of expressing too much enthusiasm for
tripe à la mode de Caen and needed to eat a lot to convince our
hosts. In the morning my daughters entertained me with a dance
they called "Let's Do the Cow Stomach."

In Villedieu-les-Poêles we visited a foundry where the church
bells of France and other countries are made. We explored an

empty, windswept Mont St-Michel and listened to organ practice in a chapel. One of the girls fell down a flight of stairs. A Mirage fighter roared overhead. The bay was magnificent, the solitude extraordinary.

We drove to Blois, on the Loire River, arriving late in the evening. By now the children had become night owls, but if we didn't feed them by eight, rebellion was at hand. We staggered into a full and too-expensive restaurant and asked if the chef could produce something for the children. He presented exquisite little steaks at a fraction of the cost of a Paris snack. Wenda and I ruefully settled for shallow bowls of seafood soup, but after one mouthful it was apparent this was no ordinary soup. Many months later, on the Alaska Railroad, I struck up a conversation with one of the dining car waiters—he was French, from Blois— where he said there was a restaurant with this soup…How could soup be that good? I still wonder. But somehow it was.

French childhood is an apprenticeship, during which one learns the rules and acquires "good habits;" it is a time of discipline, of imitation of models, of preparation for the role of adult. As one French informant told me, "We had a lot of homework to do and little time to play." American childhood is, on the contrary, a period of great freedom, of games, of experimentation and exploration, during which restrictions are only imposed when there is a serious threat of danger.

—Raymonde Carroll, *Cultural Misunderstandings: The French-American Experience*

We stayed in a hotel next to Château de Chambord, where we were fawned over by a staff who acted as though they hadn't had guests in years. In fact, we were the only guests. It had become clear to us that one of the merits of traveling in winter with children was that hotel and restaurant staffs were more indulgent— and forgiving—than they might have been at peak season. But apart from the pros and cons of winter travel, we found people all over France to be warm and caring, especially toward children. Wherever we went, people seemed to look out for our daughters. It felt safe to let them out of our sight in a way that it doesn't in America.

In the morning, we explored the Château and its extraordinary ramparts and double-helix staircase. Huge fires blazed in the fireplaces, but couldn't chase the chill. I scattered a friend's ashes on the frozen Cosson River nearby; when spring came, he'd be carried into the Loire.

As our journey progressed we began to learn more about the peculiar attitude of the French to travellers, particularly towards eccentric ones like us. I don't think there is any society in the world where the art of putting down a stranger has been refined to a greater degree. They greet one with an abrupt, dismissive manner. If they are unable or unwilling to provide the service or merchandise being sought, they seem to take a delight in saying so. I have come to the conclusion that it is all a pose to conceal their innate shyness and insecurity. As soon as the ice was broken, we found that without exception they were on our side and became eager to help far more than natural courtesy and politeness would demand.

—Robin Hanbury-Tenison,
*White Horses Over France:
From the Camargue to Cornwall*

That night we walked the perimeter of Chambord, vast, dark, mysterious, Orion bright and hard in the January sky. We heard the laughter of the Château's guardians floating from their living quarters, mocking the excess of the dead.

We headed south, past the sprawl of Lyon, to a walled farmhouse high over vineyards near Orange in northern Provence. The mistral howled all night but we slept well, aided by our hosts' own wine.

By now we had seen dozens of towns and were adept at squeezing the car late at night down alleys meant for people and horses, in search of shelter. But a disturbing theme began to appear—we liked many places, but we couldn't see ourselves living in them. "Let's check out the next town," became our theme. The girls protested, but by now they were beginning to qualify as Road Warriors, if not Road Scholars yet. When they tired of history lessons, we reminded them they could be at school back in the States instead of eating chocolate for lunch and driving around France. Life could be worse. We told ourselves the same thing, but the fact is, we were getting worried. Little did we know we would be doing the same thing four months and thousands of miles later.

We thought we'd like Aix-en-Provence, but there were an alarming number of tollbooths straddling the *autoroute* outside of town warning of the hordes to come once the weather turned warm. We drove around for an hour before finding a parking spot and then stepped out into a pile of dog *merde,* and were immediately panhandled. These incidents, we decided, did not constitute good omens, and after looking around the admittedly lovely city, we decided it would be a great place to live in as a student, but that it was too crowded for us. So it was back to the road.

Near Bordeaux, we stayed on a farm where the girls saw hours-old baby goats and drank fresh warm goat's milk. Later, on another farm, they made butter with the farmer's wife and mother and saw a calf still steaming from birth. These farm experiences came to be an important part of the Road Scholar Curriculum, along with almost daily tutoring from Wenda.

We hastened on, for it was time to pick up our van, which we had been told was in Belgium. We dropped by our friends' Normandy home to recuperate, and then headed back to Paris. We stayed in a miserable hotel and took the train to Antwerp the following misty grey morning.

On the way to the shipping office, we had a cab driver who spoke French, Dutch, Flemish, German, and English. By now I think the utility of multilingualism was beginning to sink into the girls' minds and their games had a mixture of French and pretend French. They could see how ineffective I was with only minimal French, but how well their mother—fluent in French and Italian—could communicate. To be monolingual is to be socially hobbled, no matter how much of the world speaks English. The next morning, Wenda asked them if they wanted to wash their hair, and the three responses were, *"Oui, bien sûr," "Weird, bien sûr,"* and *"Oui, bien sure."*

We drove through stack after towering stack of sea-freight containers until we arrived at one which mercifully contained our van and manifold contents. The children were delighted to renew acquaintance with toys and clothes; we were astounded at the quantity of stuff we'd thrown at the last minute into our capacious van, so full that if we parked on an incline and opened the door, goods to stock a Wal-Mart tumbled out.

We sallied forth again, crossing Belgium and Luxembourg to the Alps and Chamonix, where we were to meet friends for a week of skiing near Mt. Blanc. Our often-prescient oldest daughter suggested that this was the town we should live in. The people were friendly, it was the right size, and even though there were tourists, the outlying villages were appealing. But adults are a thick-headed lot, and we said no, there were other places more appropriate (sniff) than a ski town. We crossed the Massif Central, visited Lourdes in its exquisite Pyrenean setting, congratulating ourselves that we didn't buy even one ashtray of the Virgin, saw vineyards covered in snow, drove through innumerable hamlets that charmed but didn't hold us.

The fact is, we were on a driving jag. The *autoroutes* were empty, the hotels still empty, the prices off-season low, and the children were seeing more of France than many French do in a lifetime. We completed our second circuit of the country and drove into Switzerland. In Geneva, the girls watched a friend work the floor of the U.N., lobbying for a human rights resolution on behalf of Tibet. We drove to Lausanne with its Transport Museum, Vevey and its Alimentarium, Interlaken, Zurich, and into Austria. But much as we enjoyed everything, we were happy to leave highway *ausfahrts* behind and return to French *sorties*. At least we were in the right country, learning about France and the French if not much French itself.

By now we had hit upon our best tactic for ensuring the girls' cooperation in exploring historic and religious sites—we bought postcards before entering and had the kids look for what was on the cards. It was also becoming clear to us, the more we roamed, that parents too routinely surrender the job of teaching to schools. There is great joy in seeing how your children learn, in a way you can't when you just help with homework at night. We also gained renewed respect for the work teachers do.

Heading south again, we committed cultural heresy by visiting EuroDisney, feeling it was small payback for months of good behavior in the back of the van. Nonetheless, to make up for our sins we hastened to Versailles. In the vast cobbled courtyard, my oldest daughter took me aback by pointing at the palace and asking "Daddy, can we buy one of those?" Their favored mode of viewing the Sun King's treasures was to lie on the floor and study the splendid, intricate ceilings.

On our third Tour de France now, we thought seriously about settling in Pont-Aven, the lovely town in Brittany where Paul Gauguin once lived, but a bizarre April Fool's day encounter with an emotionally disturbed potential landlord, replete with symbolism that would have us laughing later—a huge spider in a closet, mold, a rainy funeral, a dead horse, *deviation* road signs, and the fact that I was reading Stephen King's *Dead Zone*—sent us back to the *autoroute* with a sigh of relief.

But by now we had been driving for more than four months with only a week's letup here and there in a *gîte* (a country place for rent), and everyone's nerves were fraying. One night our three-year old shouted in a restaurant at the top of her lungs, "I hate menus! Just bring me food!" We, slow-to-learn grownups, began to wonder—perhaps we were overdoing this.

We went back to Normandy and left our van in a barn surrounded by chickens and bales of hay, and took the train to Paris. We rented an apartment for a week (through Chez Vous of Sausalito, California), an expensive proposition at first blush, but cost-effective for a family when you consider meals not eaten in restaurants. Our place was directly across the Seine from Notre-Dame Cathedral, which filled our living room windows, and around the corner from Mitterand's Left Bank home.

One night, *Vertigo,* Hitchcock's evocative San Francisco masterpiece, was on TV, and I discovered I could watch it in the dining room mirror with Notre-Dame also reflected there. A heady com-

bination of wonders sent my head spinning, places and names
scrolling before my eyes: Pont Neuf, North Beach, Pont-Aven,
Mission San Juan Bautista, Pont d'Avignon, and Jimmy Stewart
and Kim Novak struggling under the Golden Gate Bridge!
It was time to go.

Although we never did find a home on that first trip, we've
since returned to France. And of course, my daughter was right.
We returned to a village in the Haute-Savoie a few kilometers
from Chamonix, where she and her sisters are in a public school.
PE includes instruction in downhill and cross-country skiing and
they are now correcting their mother's pronunciation. Mine, they
just laugh at.

*James O'Reilly, president and co-publisher of Travelers' Tales, wrote mystery
serials before becoming a travel writer in the early 1980s. He's visited more
than forty countries, along the way meditating with monks in Tibet, participating in West African voodoo rituals, and hanging out the laundry with
nuns in Florence. He travels extensively with his wife Wenda and their
three daughters.*

✻

The French often refer to their country as the *hexagone,* which is more
than a mere description of its roughly six-sided shape. It reflects the perverse satisfaction, suggested by the character in the Claudel play, in being
incomprehensible to the rest of the world. The term *hexagone* suggests a
spiritual condition, usually an exclusive one, meaning that only the
French can really understand the French, that they are, in their difference
and in their exoticism, unbridgeably apart from the rest of the world.
Another expression suggesting the same sort of impenetrability is *franco-
français,* Franco-French, which refers to something so determinedly and
peculiarly French in nature as to be not merely mysterious but uninter-
esting to all other peoples. When a book published here is called Franco-
French, it means that it is unpublishable, virtually unreadable, outside the
hexagone, even if it was a major best-seller inside it.
    —Richard Bernstein, *Fragile Glory: A Portrait of France and the French*

JO BROYLES YOHAY

Loving the Middle Ages

Signing on for a working holiday
brings rich rewards.

I STOOD UP TO STRETCH MY BACK, WITH LEGS ACHING AND JEANS
covered in grime. All morning, four fellow workers and I had been
on hands and knees laying ancient clay floor tiles in a medieval
dovecote of a Provençal hill town. The building was a tall, cylindrical tower lined with dozens of perfectly round nest holes; no
doubt some wealthy villager had once kept sporting birds inside as
a sign of his prosperity. Here and there, sprigs of straw still hung
from the abandoned nests. The late morning sun filtered through
clerestory openings and fell in a soft half-light on our slowly pro-
gressing floor.

In the midst of one of our most gorgeous spots on earth—
hadn't the Impressionists thought so?—I was paying $250 a week
to crawl around in the semidarkness of a pigeon coop. Nearby lay
graceful La Roque-sur-Cèze with its cobbled streets, stone houses
under red-tiled roofs, gardens pungent with blooming lavender. I
could have been lingering under chestnut trees or strolling sweat-
free through a museum. Had I *really traveled* all the way from my
Manhattan apartment to swelter in the hot June of southern
France—to mix mortar with shovels, to haul great loads of cracked

149

tiles up a treacherous plank ramp into the second-story opening of a pigeon coop?

Yes. And my husband, Victor, had too. We were on vacation—part of an international team of volunteers convened to help a French organization, La Sabranenque, restore abandoned medieval sites in the villages of Provence.

We were tired of conventional trips: wrestling with road maps in a rental car, grumbling—starved and exhausted—while we hunted for the perfect, small, full-of-local-color hotel at the right price. Two weeks in one spot sounded just right.

As a veteran of one other volunteer vacation—a botanical expedition to the jungles of French Guiana—I had a pretty good idea that we were in for some serious work, a certain amount of discomfort and, most likely, a rich personal experience that would stay with us forever. And that we would come to know a place in a way that standard touring doesn't allow.

Victor, an architect, was game, delighted by the prospect of hands-on medieval construction. I had no particular qualifications outside of a keen interest in the history of building, a strong back from summers of gardening, a passion for France, and a willingness to roll up my sleeves. But I had long harbored a possibly romantic vision about groups of like-minded people working together in fellowship, as I imagined some had in the rural Alabama of my grandmother. I liked the idea of neighbors gathering for cotton picking, for quilting bees, or for births. Was it a chimera? What manner of traveler, besides us, would choose a vacation of hard labor? So we signed on.

When we got off the fast train from Paris in Avignon, Marc Simon met us at the station for the 25-minute ride to St-Victor-la-Coste, headquarters of La Sabranenque. We drove along a back road, past field after field of gnarled grapevines clutching tiny green clusters of developing fruit; past wineries whose signs invited us to come in and taste. Great bushes of broom grew wild, bordering the vineyards with brilliant yellow flowers on branching stems, long used to sweep French streets. On the way, we talked. American-born Marc told us he had volunteered for La

Sabranenque thirteen years before, and had loved it so much he stayed on, eventually becoming one of the three directors. That sounded promising. In tiny St-Victor-la-Coste, we passed a bakery, a butcher shop, a *tabac,* and two cafés with umbrellaed tables, cool under the spreading trees of the village square. Climbing farther, past houses bright with backyard gardens, we twisted up tight, narrow streets toward the ruined hilltop castle of the Count of Sabran—a beacon for travelers approaching from far across the plains. Below the castle, we stopped at one of the houses for volunteers.

The first sight of our room delighted me. Clearly, we had entered another time zone. Built entirely of local materials— stone, wood, clay tiles—the room opened onto the country-side, inviting in the lush light and rich colors of Provence. Elegantly spartan, it was furnished with two narrow iron-frame beds, a French country armoire for our clothes, a small hardwood table that became my desk, and a straight-backed chair. One large window looked onto a sunny, walled yard below. The ceiling, with huge exposed beams, pitched steeply, as in an attic, drawing attention to two small windows near the terra-cotta floor. The first framed the view over village rooftops to fields red with poppies, and miles of vineyards beyond. The other bordered a fig tree holding the first green fruits of early summer.

A wooden door on creaking iron hinges gave onto a little stone terrace overlooking the Rhône Valley. Well-worn limestone steps crawled up the sharp hill toward the accommodations of our co-

My watch broke the day I arrived in St-Victor-la-Coste. Living for two weeks in a medieval hamlet with 30 volunteers from around the world, I learned to tell time in a rustic language: donkey at seven, breakfast at eight. We all worked together every morning from nine until we heard what became a familiar cry: "Plus de mortier!" Even those who spoke no French knew it was time to put down their trowels, rinse the dust off their faces, and climb down from their 11th-century perch on the Côtes du Rhône hills. "No more mortar!" meant the day's work was done.

—Catherine Barnett, "Rebuilding French History," *House and Garden*

workers. Over the years, volunteers had restored all of this—by hand—using the same techniques we would learn. The total effect was a merging of indoors and outdoors. Somewhere in the distance a donkey brayed. The sound of a late afternoon *pétanque* game rose from the square.

By dinner, everyone had arrived. Two architects, an art teacher, a lawyer, a social worker, two interior designers, a librarian, a child psychologist, a financial manager—ten men, ten women—sat down at a huge table under the trees, surrounded by reclaimed stone buildings. The meal was simple: bread, freshly baked by the local *boulangerie;* a generous selection of cheeses on a huge wooden plate; Côtes du Rhône, bought in bulk from a winery in the town; a crisp green salad. The main dish—as on days to follow—was filling: at this dinner, a grand soufflé made with eggs laid the same day by neighborhood chickens. An enormous handmade basket brimming with cherries, just picked from nearby trees, was passed around for dessert. Two large affectionate dogs lounged near the table; a cat waited for her chance to inch closer and cadge some food.

Our first conversations consisted of the usual self-conscious "Where do you live?" and "What do you do for a living?" The group profile began to unfold: half North American, half European, ages ranging from around twenty to recent retirement. Two honeymooners, a couple married 23 years, two married people without their spouses, a majority of singles.

Founding directors Simone and "Ginou" Gignoux welcomed us. Soft-spoken and eloquent, Simone has lived in St-Victor all her life. She has the haunting, expressive beauty of a dark-haired Modigliani figure. Ginou, spirited and robust from years of physical work, is the more vocal. His reddish beard and bushy eyebrows frame transparent blue eyes that reveal as much as his voice does. That evening he spoke ardently, in French, about the work and the region—laughing, gesturing, garnishing his stories with personal passion.

With Marc on hand to translate when necessary, we learned that in the early '60s, Simone and Ginou had begun to restore the house they live in, once the property of Simone's grandfather. Successful, they kept on, organizing a volunteer project to preserve the 45-foot high castle wall. That project took two summers to complete. The volunteers' enthusiasm led Simone and Ginou to form La Sabranenque, with the aim of rebuilding the entire medieval portion of the village, which had been deserted in the early 1900s.

As word spread, neighboring villages asked for help to reclaim other historic sites. La Sabranenque committed itself to restoration for public use: chapels, monuments, portions of castles. Several times the French government has recognized the groups for projects well done, especially noting the integrity of the work and the value of the contribution.

The next morning set our daily routine. We ate the traditional *petit déjeuner:* coffee, cocoa, and hot milk from steaming caldrons on the stove; fresh-baked bread, butter, and homemade jam. By eight thirty we were ready to pile into vans and drive to the day's work site, where we stayed until twelve thirty or one before returning for lunch. Most afternoons were left free for relaxation or exploring.

During the two-week session, we worked at two locations. The first, a complex of abandoned buildings in La Roque-sur-Cèze, will eventually house the town's community center. Work assignments were general—and congenial—consensus. While four of us tiled the pigeon coop, others cut limestone for window and door openings. Victor, familiar with the unyielding granite of Massachusetts, was thrilled to chisel and saw limestone into rectangular blocks. Some volunteers tore out unsafe beams to prepare for new beams; others dug a drainage ditch and lined it artfully with stones.

The second site, a half-hour drive from St-Victor, was the Château de Gicon, a deserted hilltop ruin whose villagers had solicited La Sabranenque's help. There, one volunteer group repaired a steep stone pathway, another shored up a castle vault, still another shoveled earth aside to uncover a fortification wall.

La Sabranenque's able directors worked alongside us. They gave expert instruction at the beginning of each session and cheerfully supervised our progress. The more we labored together, the more I came to understand their intentions. Every detail reflected their tastes and values and respect for history.

The Sabranenque methods of working—with simple regional raw materials and rigorous, manual techniques of stone masonry, stone cutting, and vault construction—are fast-disappearing crafts. Simone and Ginou hope to do more than restore the actual sites; they also want to preserve a rural way of life. They speak of the industrial world that threatens to homogenize us, that swamps us with "produced" things yet robs us of basic process. Ginou feels that volunteers, even those who work for only a short time, take something valuable back with them into the mechanized world. A Provençal farmer once would pick up rocks from his field to build his house; he located it on a hilltop to save arable land for crops; he placed his roof tiles at a certain slant to minimize erosion. The process was direct—firmly rooted in human need, in the topography and climate. Simone told me: "The spaces we use mold us. In these rural places, where there is no separation between the inside and the outside, people walk differently." I thought of myself, apartment-bound, in the damp, gray winters of Manhattan. True, by February, I too felt damp and gray and yearned for places pastoral.

With each day, as our connection to the work developed, the group relationship deepened. We lingered over meals. We gathered in the evenings at local cafés to mingle with villagers; on free afternoons and a Sunday off, we explored the countryside in small groups. One Saturday, La Sabranenque vans took everyone on a day's outing to the lively market of Uzès and a picnic at the Roman Pont du Gard. Personalities emerged: Two stand-up comedians found their audience; a couple of serious snorers caused roommate problems; a woman, on vacation from her husband, committed indiscretions. But stronger than anything else, the work bonded us and gave us a depth of purpose. And it was sharing the work that finally left us with the empty-stomach feeling of loss when, at the end of the two weeks, we hugged goodbye.

Performing physical labor side by side left plenty of time for conversation. We advanced into the stuff of friendship. We talked about architecture and books and travel and boyfriends and families and dreams and feelings. And always the work.

One morning, for example, six of us were clearing rubble before we could shore up a castle wall. The conversation moved from movie preferences, through a few bawdy jokes, to a recitation of knock-knock jokes way beyond the usual third-grade level (plays on "Euripides trousers" and "Odoriferous rising"). Hilarity was what rose. When we had recited all the limericks we could remember, a Canadian barrister, all the while shoveling dirt, quoted verbatim a segment from Monty Python. The pace quickened. Still working, Carrie unselfconsciously began to quote E. E. Cummings: "O sweet spontaneous / earth how often have / the / doting / fingers of prurient philosophers pinched / and / poked / thee..." The instant she was done, Brendan recited, "Whose woods these are I think I know..." Birgitte followed with *"Frühling ist wiedergekommen, Die Erde / ist wie ein Kind, das Gedichte weiss...."* ("Spring has returned. The earth is like a child who knows poems.") As if the morning had opened up something fresh inside our hearts, we went on and on, one beginning when the other finished, quoting poetry drawn from deep within our memories. So, I thought, my notion of people working together was not just romantic after all.

Another day, at the end of an especially hot work session, we were all gathered around two huge barrels of water, cleaning mortar off tools and buckets before putting them away. One playful comment led to another,

> *It is enough. For me,
> upon the sea of history,
> Thou wast, Provence, a pure
>   symbol
> A mirage of glory and victory,
> That in the dusky flight
>   of centuries,
> Grants us a gleam of the
>   Beautiful....*
>
> —Frederic Mistral,
> as quoted by Laura Raison,
> *The South of France: An Anthology*

a splash of water led to a splash back, and a full-fledged water fight broke out. We all shrieked like children at the beach, exuberant. I felt pure joy: in the people, in the ability of my body to perform hard work, in the act of doing something satisfying and enduring, in the pleasure of being alive.

The work *was* hard. Stones, inevitably are heavy and must be moved from here to there to build paths and walls. Summers in Provence were hot. The mistral sometimes whirled dust into our eyes and mouths as we worked. But it was worth every callus.

One morning Victor and I worked side by side with five other people, scraping centuries of accumulated earth and vegetation from a pile of rocks that formed a crumbling fortress wall around the 11th-century Château de Gicon. We were the first volunteer team to work at this site. Early that morning when we started, the wall had barely been visible—a pile of rubble, silent for centuries beneath the plants and soil that had claimed it. Several hours later, tired and drenched in sweat, I put down my trowel and looked out. Beyond our hilltop, 360 degrees of Provençal valley stretched over miles of vineyards, ancient olive groves, and cherry trees—branches drooping with ripe, scarlet fruit—to the roofs of the farm town Bagnols-sur-Cèze on the horizon.

I said to Victor, "Let's stop and see how it looks." Stepping back, we were astonished to see that where there had been nothing, now there was something. While we worked, stone after stone had come to life, revealing an imposing fortification wall. Massive rectangular stones at its base indicated that the wall was older than suspected—Roman, perhaps even pre-Roman. It started at what was once a castle's edge and marched across the hillside, stopping only when the hill dropped into the valley below.

For the first time, I fully understood the addiction of an archeologist's search, the exhilaration of uncovering something that no one now alive on earth had ever seen.

None of us would ever again look at stonework casually. I knew that whenever I could, I would return to this spot. Because in some indelible way, this wall—which would now give pleasure to people for ages to come—belonged to me.

Jo Broyles Yohay—wife, mother, adventurer—lives in New York.

✳

The first man who, having fenced in a piece of land, said, "This is mine," and found people naïve enough to believe him, that man was the true founder of civil society.

—Jean Jacques Rousseau, Speech on the Origin and the Foundation of Inequity Among Men, 1754

* * *

Bovary Country

The author becomes a literary detective for a day,
hot on the trail of Flaubert.

FOUR WIDE BLOCKS UP FROM THE RIVER BY HÔTEL-DIEU
Hospital, is a white stone domed mansion around a courtyard
where Gustave Flaubert spent all of his early years. He was born
on the second floor of his family's apartments in the building. His
father was chief surgeon, and the Flauberts' garden overlooked a
ward where bodies were dissected for autopsy. Now the rooms are
a museum, with Flaubert's books and letters.

Young Gustave was not on the Rouen tourist board. At nineteen, he wrote to a friend, "Confined in this oyster of Rouen...I
believe that I have been transported by the winds to this land of
mud, and that I was born somewhere else, because I have always
had memories, or instincts, of balmy shores, of blue seas. I was born
to be emperor of Cochin China." Rather than his due of six thousand women and pipes of pleasures, he said, "I have nothing but
immense and insatiable desires, and atrocious boredom, unending
yawns."

Three years later, Flaubert excoriated his native city. "It has
beautiful churches and stupid people," he wrote. "I hate it...Oh,
Attila, when will you return, great humanitarian, with 400,000
horsemen, to burn this beautiful France, this nation of doormats

and suspenders? And start, I beg you, with Paris first and with Rouen at the same time."

Flaubert might have enjoyed the Allied bombing. He died 62 years too early, eaten with syphilis at the age of 58, never having spent much time beyond an easy stroll from the Seine. Where his villa stood at Croisset, just downstream from Rouen, is an ugly red-brick paper factory, with corroding iron gates. The Seinescape out front is a back end of the Rouen port, nothing to write George Sand about.

A tiny museum squats in the corner of the villa's gardens, a room where Flaubert and his last few pals sat and sipped. There are some photocopies of manuscript pages; a few of the goose-quill pens he insisted on using when fountain pens got to be the rage; the unremarkable Amazon parrot that Julian Barnes made famous; Flaubert's favorite kind of small varnished clay pipe with a tobacco jar; and busts, photos and assorted whatnot. The writer would not have been pleased to know entrance was only two francs.

A helpful curator answered questions without a lot of false cheerleading. When I asked whether disputes continued among nearby villages over which was the real Yonville-l'Abbaye, Bovary's hometown, she shrugged. "Normans," she said, "are rather indifferent on the subject of Flaubert."

Not in Ry. In that little village on the way to nowhere, a mute Flaubert makes up the better part of the gross municipal

*R*ouen is where Joan of Arc was judged, con-demned, and burned at the stake, and where her heart, unconsumed by fire, was thrown into the Seine.

—Richard De Combray,
"A Current Affair,"
European Travel & Life

product. If it is not the place, no one can make a better case for anyplace else, and the author is not talking. Late in the afternoon, I rolled into Ry, past La Bovary restaurant and Le Flaubert bar, and headed toward something called the Madame Bovary Automat Museum. It promised 500 animated puppets depicting 300 scenes from the novel. But it was closed.

I found the doctors' offices, in the old red schoolhouse. Emma's husband was the local physician, and that seemed like a good place to start. The waiting room was filled with sick people whose minds were not on literature. At Le Flaubert, none of the beefy-armed workmen staring at their beer looked like readers. The bar lady said, yes, Bovary attracted a lot of saps such as myself and was great for business; what would I have?

The Bovary house is reputed to have been what is now a drug-store, clean, well lighted, and computerized. The alleged textile shop where a conniving old lech played on Emma's vanities to draw her into ruinous debt now sells toy airplanes and spools of thread. And so on. I went back to the museum, where it looked like some other crafty citizen had found a way to profit from the woman's torment. Then someone directed me to Michel Burgaud, the jeweler—the crafty citizen in question.

"All right," he said, with some reluctance. "But just for a minute. I have an appointment and then I've got to be somewhere else." We returned to the museum, a converted cider mill, which he opened with a foot-long iron key. With a flipped switch, he lit up Bovaryland. Hundreds of stiffly moving little characters brought Emma back to life.

We saw a dullard medical student helped through school by connections. We watched his first wife die, old and ugly, without leaving him a franc of the fortune he thought he'd inherit. A sev-enteen-year-old, not bad looking but for her chipmunk cheeks, married the widower; all of the 43 guests Flaubert put at the wed-ding dinner were around Burgaud's table. Then there was the splendid ball where Emma fell in love. Doc Bovary snored as Emma primped despondently at her vanity mirror. The tax man popped out of a barrel (can't help you here). It's all there.

In one scene, a little lace-cuffed white hand shoots in and out of a closed coach window. This is Emma, being ravaged inside and tossing away a *billet-doux* she decided not to deliver. In another, at the Hôtel de la Croix Rouge with Léon, she pops her corset ties, exposing crimson nipples. She buys more fripperies she can't afford, and the cops close in. Finally, she raids the chemist's poison cabinet.

"I've done these over twenty years," explained Burgaud, a man of genuine passion. "I had trained in *beaux-arts,* I was a jeweler, and I repaired television sets. All the skills were there. I thought, why not this?" It was original, all right. He acquired the old chemist's paraphernalia and reproduced the shop down to its door half covered with the owner's pretentious titles, ending in *etc.* A separate room displayed Flaubert memorabilia and item after item that showed Ry was the place.

First, there was circumstantial evidence. Flaubert mentioned a town with a single street as long as a rifle shot, a church and market set off to the side, and a fair complement of loutish people. So far, so good. But there was much more.

Just before Flaubert started the book, a Doctor Delamare died in Ry. He had studied under Flaubert's father. His wife, Delphine Couturier, led an Emma-like life. Delamare borrowed money from the Flauberts that he could not pay back. Old files showed that the doctor sued his former mother-in-law for lack of inheritance, as Bovary did in the book. A letter to the author from a friend asked how he was doing on the Delamare saga.

The clincher was the wordplay. *Boeuf* means "steer" or, if you want it to, "cuckold." "*Boeuf à Ry,* Bovary, get it?" Burgaud said. "There are so many more connections, I could go on until tomorrow morning." He tried his best to do just that. Our few minutes had gone to well over an hour, and I was grateful. Less of an opportunist, he was a man with a mission. At least someone in Normandy remembered Flaubert warmly.

Mort Rosenblum also contributed "River of Light" in Part I. Both stories were excerpted from his book The Secret Life of the Seine.

※

Yet the "Hermit of Croisset," as [Flaubert] came to be called, should not be looked on as a musty anchorite. He was a strapping, strikingly handsome, six-foot-tall *bon vivant,* a dazzling, salty conversationalist with a trumpeting voice and a booming laugh. He was also said to be an exceptionally gifted lover. ("Life! Life! To have erections!" he wrote in a letter.)

—Francine du Plessix Gray, "Sex in the Grass," *Condé Nast Traveler*

CARLA S. KING

* * *

Fêtes de la Musique:
A Memory in Three Parts

The author discovers a melody line in her visits to France.

IT WAS LATE JUNE WHEN I SAW PARIS FOR THE FIRST TIME, HAVING
arrived by motorcycle after a camping tour of the countryside. I
was tired and dirty and in shock from trying to find my hotel in
the insane traffic after experiencing the calm country roads of rural
France. But I was looking forward to seeing the famous city, and
after a shower and a change of clothes, I set off on foot to the Latin
Quarter.

The evening was warm and clear and I was glad to give my legs
a stretch after so many hours of riding. I strolled, wide-eyed as only
a first-time traveler can be, walking the cobblestoned streets of the
Left Bank, in awe of the city's beauty and spirit. I had never imagined there would be so many cafés, so many people, and so much
music in the air! There was a string quartet on one street corner,
a saxophone soloist on the next. In this square there was a rock
band, in another an orchestra.

I wandered for an hour, darting down side streets and alleyways,
attracted by the golden glint of a horn, or the strains of a violin
echoing off ancient stone walls. The music wafted almost visibly,
like cartoon character notes, dancing over the heads of statues, circling round splashing fountains and darting under the legs of tables

and chairs of sidewalk cafés. I followed the black threads that carried the sharps and the flats through the air. I wandered, floating through the afternoon, smiling at Parisians who, contrary to what I had been told about Parisians, smiled back.

I walked past a church, its huge wooden doors thrown wide so that outside we could listen to the symphony orchestra performing inside. From each public building spilled a chorus, a ballad, an anthem. Behind it all was the constant rhythm of people moving about, being pulled in every direction by the music.

All the walking made me hungry, and I found a table just inside the door of a café on the rue Mouffetard, where I ate a thick slice of layered terrine and half a baguette, and drank perhaps too much from a rough earthen pitcher of red wine. My table looked onto the street where Parisians, schooled in the fine art of strolling, maneuvered elegantly through throngs of manic tourists who ran from one square to another, because, like me, they were afraid to miss one magic moment. I sighed, thinking that the only thing missing was someone to share this with. As though they read my mind, a group of people at the next table invited me to join them for coffee.

"How do you like the festival so far?" they asked.

"You mean Paris isn't like this every day?"

It was only then that I learned I had inadvertently stumbled onto France's *Fête de la Musique*. On this one day, professional and amateur musicians come out to play all over the city, in the streets and in the concert halls. And price is no object, because all performances are free.

Night finally fell on this longest day of the year, the summer solstice, but the celebration continued, and my *gentil* Parisian companions made a toast to health and a toast to the day. We clacked our china cups of cappuccino as the sound of a big band tuning up reached our ears, and giggled when the baritone of a tuba blasted rudely through the thin trill of a flute.

We finished our coffee and went dancing in the neighboring square. A big band was in full swing, and I danced, whirling through the other couples around the fountain in the center of the square. It was my first night in Paris, and I felt in harmony with everyone, with the city, with the earth, and the universe. The tiny white lights strung through the trees and the hedges seemed heavenly gifts of fallen stars to me, an earth-bound creature drunk with music and wine and the magic of Paris.

I didn't expect to experience another French *Fête de la Musique*, but a year later I was working for an electronics company in Lyon, and on the day of the festival, a group of us sneaked out of work early to go to the old town.

On our way there we were distracted by the musicians who played on the banks of the Saône, and by the bands that played in each of the little parks we passed. Residents picnicked on baguettes and *saucisson*, Lyon's special smoked sausage, and plenty of red Rhône wine. Where there was a café, all the tables were pulled out onto the street, the patrons serenaded on all sides. It was hours before we reached our destination.

In the old town, I heard once again the chorus of string quartets, saxophones, jazz, blues, rock and entire orchestras that competed for attention in every corner, spilling from churches and tumbling from street-front balconies. My friends and I squeezed our way, single file, through the cacophony that reverberated through the narrow streets, to see the symphony orchestra.

The cathedral was impossibly crowded, so we wandered until evening, when we found a table big enough for six outside on a cobblestoned square. I remember sitting under the awnings of the restaurant. It rained lightly off and on all night, which, far from deterring anyone's enthusiasm for the celebration, only added to the romance.

We sipped Champagne cocktails before eating a typically magnificent Lyonnaise dinner, expertly prepared and exquisitely served at our alfresco table. The tinkle of silver on china plates and the trill of crystal wine glasses, raised in never-ending toasts to friendship, health and love, created a melody of *gastronomie*, while we were serenaded by five different kinds of music playing at once.

After dinner I relaxed with my coffee and realized that I had truly achieved inner harmony. The night air was warm, the rain pattered on the awning, and my friends chatted amicably. Soft lights glowed through the drizzle onto the first levels of the aged stone buildings that surrounded us. It was quieter now, and the contented guttural grumblings of pigeons settling into their nests for the night could be heard from every curlicued edifice. An upper window across the square was illuminated for a moment by the flare of a match. Then there was darkness again, and the orange glow of the tip of a cigarette.

A string trio played some ancient romantic tune. As I listened, a dove coasted to the ground from its perch on a balcony, pecked a crumb from a momentarily empty patch of sidewalk, and fluttered away. Its wings became transparent, underlit by the streetlamps which seemed to buoy it upward. It soared past the balconies and the gray stone gargoyles, past the gutters and the roof tiles, and I imagined that its wings moved to the strains of the violin as it disappeared, as if by magic, into the misty black sky.

On each visit to France I seem to land farther and farther south. Last year I spent six months in Nice, where everything seems light: the crisp dry rosé wine served ice cold, the cuisine, which is more northern Italian than French, the summer sun glittering on the Mediterranean, and the moon shining from a cloudless sky. The mood is light, too, among its residents, who are more *sportif* than sophisticated.

In Nice, the festival has a different atmosphere, perhaps because the city is full of young tourists in summer, their main objectives to tan and to dance.

The morning of the festival I attempted to go jogging on the Promenade des Anglais, the wide pedestrian walkway that separates the rocky beaches of the Mediterranean from the street. Normally at seven a.m. it is a peaceful place, populated by sea gulls, joggers and locals led by poodles on their morning walk. But today the screech of the gulls and the yap of the poodles was punctuated by the staccato of workers hammering together bandstands, the squeal of feedback and the effervescence of electric white noise. It was evident that an auditory assault was being planned, and that I had better stay far away from there if I didn't want to rock and roll.

But rock and roll I did, that apparently being the program in Nice. My friends from language school and I walked along the promenade that afternoon. Many people had staked claim on a section of beach below, sandwiched between the surf and the stage. They happily picnicked on rosé and pizza-by-the-slice, entertained by the performance of the moment. The program changed hourly, but seemed limited to new English rock, new American rock, old English rock and old American rock. So we made our way to the old town. It being the height of the tourist season, the streets were jammed with people of all nationalities, many of them very sunburned.

ieux Nice, the old part of town, is a walker's dream. On a brilliant morning we walked along the Promenade des Anglais, under towering palm trees, past dogs accompanying masters and mothers pushing baby carriages, until we reached the Quai des Etats-Unis and stepped through a portal in an old stone wall into the 18th century. We were in a narrow plaza lined with shuttered pastel buildings, the Cours Saleya, site of the Sunday flower market and an antique bazaar the rest of the week. The place was a haven from cars and an oasis of sidewalk cafés crowded with people enjoying the fine spring sunshine. We were seduced to stop for coffee and pastry, and spent an easy hour watching people come and go.

—Larry Habegger, "Springtime in Nice and the Côte d'Azur," *Relax*

We gave up waiting for a table in the main square and bought a bottle of wine at a store to drink from emptied glass yogurt cups. We stood a while in front of a particularly bad garage band attempting to emulate the loudest '70s rock groups. A group of college students loudly chanted "Rock and roll!" and sprayed each other with beer. I took a sip of warm rosé and, from a safe distance, reflected on the day when I would have run over to participate in their antics.

We lost a couple of our younger companions to the beer-spraying group, and the rest of us moved on to areas where jazz and blues were playing to more subdued but equally enthusiastic crowds. Then we entered the maze of alleyways where unamplified horns, wind, and string instruments sent their echoing notes along the cobblestones and up the narrow corridors to the balconies hung with drying laundry.

We stopped to watch a marionette artist performing to the tune of a clarinet. Everyone began clapping to the dance of the puppet until an old lady shouted *"Silence!"* from a fifth-floor window, and threatened to empty the *poubelle* onto our heads. This kind of reaction I definitely remembered from younger days.

It was four a.m. when we started home. We retraced our steps of that afternoon, passing through deserted squares and streets. The scent of baking bread replaced the strains of music wafting through the air, and we followed it to the screened back door of a *boulangerie*. The smell made me hungry and sleepy at once, and suddenly I couldn't wait to get home.

Re-energized by chocolate croissants, I decided to take the long way home, and after saying goodbye to my friends, I walked slowly along the promenade past the stages that were now just large empty boxes facing seaward. In the silence the water lapped at the rocky shore, and the light of the moon showed the sky to be that deep navy blue color I've only seen at night on the Mediterranean.

Ahead of me on the promenade a man in a tuxedo kicked rocks at the balustrade, ignoring the car that sped by, its still-enthusiastic occupants shouting from the windows. A bedraggled group with a mangy dog sat on sleeping bags on the beach; a girl sang softly while someone played the bongos along with the background rhythm of the waves. As I walked I thought of Paris and Lyon in the years before and wondered where I'd be in future years. I sat on the balustrade, my feet dangling over the edge, to listen to the sea, the song, and the soft staccato of the drum, and noticed that the stars had disappeared into morning's first light.

Carla King started writing about travel in 1988 during a technical writing job in Lyon, France. In 1993 she penned a mountain-biking guide to the Alpes-Maritimes, then left for a four-month bicycle trip through West Africa. Since then, she's published stories about motorcycling, bicycling, kayaking, scuba diving, and travel technology in newspapers, magazines, and anthologies, including the San Francisco Examiner, Rider, Dive Travel, Rough Guides' Women Travel, In Search of Adventure, *and* Travelers' Tales. *In 1995 Carla pioneered the art of the real-time Internet travelogue with the popular* American Borders *dispatches, followed up by* China Road, *and* Indian Sunset, *on each trip riding a different vintage motorcycle.*

★

Anyone with fantasies of listening to Edith Piaf in French cafés will quickly be disabused of such notions. Rock and roll, American and British, is the standard fare.

—JO'R, LH, and SO'R

ROB BUCHANAN

Carve Every Mountain

*The perfect "all you can eat" analog for skiing
lies in the French Alps.*

IT'S A BIT OF A GRUNT, CLIMBING FROM THE TOP OF THE LAST chair up to the ridge, but no one complains. Les Arcs is young and chic and less of an eyesore than most French ski resorts. On a sunny day in late March, midway through school vacations, it's also a madhouse. One doesn't mind getting out of earshot.

At the top, as we snap on our skis, our guide, Jean-Pierre Soubayrols, points out the landmarks. To the north, the massive fin of Mont Blanc and the jagged ramparts of the Grandes Jorasses. East, the Petit St-Bernard pass, said to have been crossed in 217 B.C. by the Carthaginian general Hannibal and his famed elephants en route to attack Rome. South, Val d'Isère, where we'll be skiing tomorrow...

Nobody is listening. Instead, we're staring down between our ski tips at Les Lanchettes, a classic off-piste *itinéraire*. It drops away in a sickening plunge to the north, nosing out over itself almost vertically before curving away to the east and briefly flattening out. Then comes another pitch, slightly less severe, and a third that leads into the forest above Villaroger. From our vantage point we see the little village virtually in plan. It's 4,000 feet below.

"Remember, we are in the no-fall zone." Jean-Pierre says. "If you fall, *boum,* you are all the way to the bottom. *D'accord?*" The seven of us, his trusting clients, look at him blankly.

"*Allez!*" he says, dropping off the edge of the world.

Wherever there are big resorts in close proximity, skiers fantasize about long, continuous runs linking one mountain to the next. Nowhere has the dream come closer to being realized than in the Tarentaise region of the French Alps. Thanks in large part to the massive construction boom that preceded the 1992 Winter Olympics, each of the Tarentaise's seven biggest ski stations, giant networks in and of themselves, have been knit together in one immense network of some 500 lifts and 275,000 beds. In other words, it is now possible to ski all the way around the 50-mile breadth of the Tarentaise on one lift ticket, practically without taking off your skis.

Hence the circuit know as Les 12 Vallées. In the space of seven days, a guide leads a group of tourists, often of middling ability, in a great clockwise circle from La Plagne to Les Arcs to Val d'Isère to Tignes, and finally to the Trois Vallées: Courchevel, Méribel, and Les Menuires-Val Thorens. Accommodations range from rustic hostels to semideluxe hotels; a van brings your bags around at night.

You could call the 12 Vallées a lazy man's Haute Route, since it offers the same kind of backcountry descents that the famed Chamonix-to-Saas Fee trek does, without any of the tedious uphill slogging. Or you might look on it as a poor man's heli-ski vacation. After all, you get the same camaraderie, the same avalanche transceiver, and better food than you do in the Canadian Rockies, for about a quarter of the price. You don't get the helicopter, of course, but since your guide is a member of the French national ski school, he can snark you to the front of any lift line. Status-wise, it's just about as satisfying.

But what the 12 Vallées circuit really offers is a good look at one of skiing's possible futures. The French have taken the hard path. They've run lifts up every peak and built huge concrete "hamlets" far above timberline. In a practical, European way they've democratized the sport. It's all very exhilarating to witness. But after a while, cresting a new rise only to find another megaresort, you find yourself wondering whether endless interconnectability doesn't obliterate the wilderness it's supposed to open up. Would we really want to see lifts running from Vail to Aspen, or all the way around Lake Tahoe? Or is this one French idea we'd rather not import?

An important thing to consider when skiing the French Alps is the schedule of French children's winter vacation (vacance scolaire), when ski towns and slopes are crowded with families on holiday and school groups taking children on ski weeks. All French school children have a two-week vacation, scheduled sometime between early February and mid-March. For the first and last weeks of this four-week period, one third of the French children are on vacation. The most important period to avoid is the middle two weeks when two thirds of the country are on holiday.

—JO'R, LH, and SO'R

The first turn is a cautious, scraping, unhandsome thing. Weight too far forward, knees overflexed, pole-plant too hard. But underfoot, the snow feels pretty good. The sun's been on it awhile now, and it's softening up. Gradually, turn by turn, confidence floods back into my limbs. Soon I'm no longer throwing myself back and forth across the fall line; I'm ratcheting off huge giant-slalom sweepers, falling through space.

No one loses it. Not Mr. Okiawa, the lithe Japanese tycoon in the Canadian Mountain Holidays ski suit, the kind you get free when you've accumulated a million vertical heli-feet, nor Robert, the hard-nosed German publishing executive, nor even Marie-Claude, the sturdy, stem-christying midwife from Mulhouse. Jean-Pierre seems most worried about the lock-kneed Italian contingent, Roberto, Giovanni, and GianFranco—a harbor pilot, an engineer, and a lawyer, respectively. He needn't be. By keeping up a constant flow of chatter, they talk one another down.

The second pitch goes better, and by the third everyone is a pro, off on his or her own line, ignoring Jean-Pierre's sensible lead down the middle. Toward the bottom, the snow grows noticeably heavier and sloppier. By the time we arrive in Villaroger, we're poling through slush. It's spring down here.

Lunch is on the terrace of a restaurant with gray stone walls encrusted in lichen. Smoke from the grill blows across the deck. There are flowers on the table, and carafes of tart Savoyard wine. We dine on a bacony country salad and great slabs of roast lamb with rosemary. After coffee, Annie, the restaurateur, proposes a *genepy,* a local liqueur, and Mr. Okiawa beamingly orders one for each of us. We toast his homeland and tip our heads back into the sun, too sated to talk.

Four o'clock finds us climbing to Grand Col, the saddle between the Aiguille Rouge and Mont Pourri. From here we'll ski to Le Planay, then hop into a van for the short ride up to Val d'Isère. The back side of the Col is much more intimidating than Les Lanchettes: a steep couloir that funnels to a choke point not much more than 30 feet across. Worse, the snow is now beginning to ice up in the shade. But that's the way it is on the 12 Vallées circuit: the most dramatic descents come at the end of the day, when you realize that your legs are shot and a full-blown lunch hangover is beginning to kick in.

Robert is the last person I expect to see fall in the no-fall zone. He's in his mid-fifties but is one of the better stylists in the group, and strong. After missing a turn in the slot, however, he gets out into the deep crud on the edge of the couloir and compounds his mistake by trying to force his skis around. Suddenly he's down on his back and accelerating fast, thanks to a perfectly slick one-piece microfiber ski suit. Then he's cartwheeling, bouncing once, twice, and hitting with a shattering impact that leaves one ski shivering in the snow like a tuning fork.

A couple of us speed over to him, nearly spearing him in our haste. He's lying on his back, calmly looking at the sky.

"Is everything OK?"

"No, it is not," he replies. "I believe my leg is broken."

The guides, upon hearing this, roll their eyes. But when we pull Robert up into a sitting position, his boot swings free in the breeze, as if only the skin and a few muscles and tendons are holding the foot to the rest of the leg. It is indeed a classic double break, the boot-top tib-fib.

"*Putain de merde,*" whistles Jean-Pierre. Holy shit. Robert just stares off at the mountains, turning pink now in the late afternoon sun.

It's nice not to have to deal with the hysterical self-importance of American ski patrollers, but the twelve guides take it to the opposite extreme. Their idea of first aid consists of wrapping Robert in a foil emergency blanket, thin as a candy wrapper. Marie-Claude, the midwife, suggests a splint, and we fashion one from Robert's ski poles. Jean-Pierre lazily radios for a helicopter, and lazily, 50 minutes later, it arrives. It can't land anywhere near us— too steep—so we have to drag Robert down the slope to a flat spot far below, his booted foot rocking in the clumsy splint. He takes the whole thing stoically—the composure of a European with good insurance.

After the hypersprawl of La Plagne (112 lifts, 45,000 beds) and Les Arcs (79 lifts, 24,000 beds), it's a relief to get to Val d'Isère. The place is just as big as the preceding two—bigger, in fact, if you count Tignes, with which Val is linked in the gargantuan grid known as L'Espace Killy—but it's more of a real ski town. Deep in its core are old stone barns and even a chapel dating from the 11th century, when the place was advance base camp for shepherds and hunters. Most of the quaintness has since been swallowed up by midrise condominiums, but the town still huddles in on itself cozily.

A dozen years ago, when I was seriously pursuing studies at the University of Grenoble, I spent a few weeks here sharing a condo with five to six other college kids. The town hasn't changed all that much; it's still the address of choice in the French Alps for anglophone ski bums. It's more prosperous than I remember. Now, at night, giant floodlights are trained on the mountains that enfold the town, in particular on the Bellevarde, site of the designer downhill run created by Bernhard Russi and Jean-Claude Killy for the 1992 Olympics. Killy is still the local hero, even though for tax reasons he now lives in Switzerland. As a teenager, he used to race the tram as it came humming down the Solaise, the epic mogul run opposite the Bellevarde—until the day his knee came up off a bump and broke his jaw. Times are changing. With detachable chairs running up every ridge now, the slopes are more crowded and wild stunts less appreciated. A few weeks before we arrived in Val d'Isère, a little girl was hit and killed by a speeding skier. In response, the town council voted to deputize all ski instructors, patrollers, and guides to yank the tickets of anyone judged to be skiing too fast.

Jean-Pierre is having nothing to do with this experiment. When someone goes rocketing by, he just smiles. "This isn't America," he says. "I'm not a cop." In any case, we're headed away from the crowds on two long off-*piste* exploratories, one before lunch, one after. Only on the north-facing slopes below the Col Perse do we find a few pitches with decent powder; otherwise it's crud. But that's to be expected. It's late March, crud season.

People often rank Val d'Isère as the ultimate French ski resort, but it may be Tignes that deserves the title. Tignes is not a pretty place, but it's a place where technology has finally and forever triumphed over the elements. You can ski longer (365 days a year) and higher (11,500 feet) here than anywhere else in Tarentaise. Just keep an eye out for lift pylons. Chairs are staked out three and, in one instance, four abreast. Gondolas run side by side. Countless pomas wander off into the hills like stapled Frankenstein scars on the landscape.

To be fair, unsightly lift towers aren't a uniquely French phenomenon. The problem is geographic. Since tree line in the Alps is at about 6,000 feet, 5,000 feet lower than in the Rockies, there's nowhere to hide a lift. The powers that be at L'Espace Killy have a grand scheme to remedy this situation: underground ski lifts. I laughed when I heard about it, but there's one in service at Val d'Isère—the Funival, a subterranean monorail funicular that speeds 200 skiers at a time from La Dailee to the Bellevard, 3,500 vertical feet, in less than four minutes. They've installed one at Tignes, too—the Funiculaire Grande Motte, which takes skiers up to the base of the glacier of the same name.

About the only place the lifts don't run in Tignes is the original village. Old Tignes was evacuated in 1953 to make way for a hydroelectric project, and now it's buried by a reservoir 300 feet deep. It's tempting to see old Tignes as a symbol for what's happened to the Tarentaise as a whole, particularly in the wake of the Olympics—a montagnard culture that had lived for centuries in harmony with the earth rushing to obliterate itself in four short decades of development. But, of course, that's only one way of looking at it. One has also to remember what life was really like up here in the days before the ski industry arrived.

A Hemingway story called "An Alpine Idyll" comes to mind when I think about Tignes. In it, the narrator hears the story of a mountain peasant whose wife dies early in the winter. Since the ground is frozen and his farm snowbound, he lays her body atop a pile of logs in the woodshed. When he eventually needs to cut some wood, he stands her stiffened body up against the wall and, for want of a peg, uses her frozen, gaping mouth as a place to hang his lantern. In the spring, he finally hauls the disfigured corpse down to the village for burial.

> *Over 200 million years ago dinosaurs lived out their last days in a temperate region by the edge of an ocean known as Tethys, which covered the area where the Alps now stand. The movement of giant continental plates on the surface of the earth spelt the end for this ancient sun trap, and the dinosaurs. The land mass south of Tethys pushed north, causing the sea to dry up as it went. Where continental plates clashed, the Alps heaved high into the air.*
>
> —Douglas Botting, *Wild France*

"It was very wrong," the priest tells him. "Did you love your wife?"

"Ja, I loved her," the peasant answers. "I loved her fine."

The romantic impulse that aestheticized the alpine landscape, making mountains into objects of beauty instead of terror, is a relatively recent arrival. Before that, the place struck most people as a desert. Winters were long and hard, and spending them locked in the insular fastness of a small village could have monstrous results. Cretinism. Goiters. Lantern-jawed corpses. Who could blame the Savoyard communes for wanting to trade in their cheese barns for ski lodges and bung ski lifts up the side of every mountain? Wasn't it ultimately a healthy thing, this desire to interconnect?

"Oat tub?"

The three Italians are team-flirting with Nathalie, the receptionist at the Grand Hotel des Thermes in Brides-les-Bains, and she looks a little confused when I break in with my request.

"A hot tub," I say. "You know, like a Jacuzzi."

"Ah, Jacu-zee," says Nathalie.

"Jacu-zee" chime the Italians, immediately warming to the idea.

"Jacu-zee." I repeat.

Brides is a spa of international repute. Stinking, steaming water bubbles out of the cliff behind the hotel. Considering the long passage from Tignes to Champagny that we've made that morning, it seems like something we ought to take advantage of. Unfortunately, Nathalie tells us, the hotel, despite its name, does not have any official connection to the spa. The spa is a private establishment, whereas the hotel is owned by the municipality.

"So you see," says Nathalie, "you cannot use the spa without paying."

"Well, how much is it?"

"One hundred and twenty francs." About twenty-five dollars.

Nathalie takes advantage of our visit to hone her already sharp English. "Brides is known as the Slimming Capital of Europe," she says, with the tiniest hint of a smirk. "That means the water has laxative properties. You should see the place in the summer. We're invaded by pachyderms of 120 kilos, like the kind you get in American malls."

Once inside the spa, we're issued terrycloth robes and directed to an immense tile *hammam,* or steam room, where a tableau of Rubenesque maidens eyes our scrawny frames with what looks more like pity than envy. Then comes the Jacuzzi. Finally, a session in the solarium on vibrating dentist chairs called *fauteuils schiatsus,* "shiatsu chairs," where a woman in a white lab jacket serves us tisane. Most of the clients seem to be just plump, not obese, though we do catch a riveting glance, through the open door of the tanning salon, of a massive blue breast baking away under the UV.

The machinery is all a little much: extravagant and technology-heavy and likely, it seems to me, to be out of fashion within five or ten years. What then? It's like the $47 million white elephant of a bobsled run at La Plagne, and the Funival, and all the still-brewing schemes to interconnect every last ski station in the Tarentaise, once and for all. What this place needs is a little slimming down.

Afterward I try to explain my reaction to Nathalie. All we really wanted, I say, was to sit in a tub outdoors with a view of the mountains and a cold beer within arm's reach.

"Wow," she replies. "How vulgar!"

The last three days pass in a blur. They're given over to exploring the Trois Vallées of Méribel, Courchevel, and Les Menuires-Val Thorens. Taken together the three form what is billed as the world's largest "skiable domain": 200 lifts, 65,000 acres, 100,000 beds. But each has it own distinct ambiance.

People always say that Méribel, with its individual chalets and steeply pitched roofs, looks the way a French ski resort should look. No doubt that's why CBS used it as a backdrop during the 1992 Games. But in fact, Méribel is hardly French at all. It was founded in the late 1930s by British sportsmen on the run from Nazi-dominated Tyrol, and even today you hear as much English as French.

Courchevel lies just over the hill. Its setting is the finest in Les Trois Vallées, and perhaps in all of the Tarentaise: a dramatic shelf jutting out north into space, with the fantastic rock formations of the Saulire and the Aiguille du Fruit forming its southern periphery. Architecturally, it's uneven: there are old socialist-era apartment blocks and 50s-style flat-roofed chalets, though lately some of the town burghers have taken to refitting them with Méribel-style peaked roofs. But the chaos is part of the charm. On a sunny day, Courchevel becomes a Brueghelesque scene with multihued hang gliders and *parapentistes* flinging themselves into space; fat jowled Venezuelan and Saudi oilmen treating their bronze-faced French ski instructors to lunch at *restaurants d'altitude,* bunnies up from St-Tropez, shopping in poodle boots or sunning *à poil*—literally, "in the hair."

> *S*omething every diehard (and strong intermediate) skier should do before turning to lawn bowling is experience the Vallée Blanche in Chamonix, a stunning high mountain route one begins by hiring a guide and taking the Aiguille du Midi tram up 9,000 vertical feet to the shoulder of Mt. Blanc. You walk out of an ice cave with the Matterhorn in view on the horizon, rope up with your ski partners, descend a snow staircase with hair-raising drops on either side (not for the agoraphobic), and commence to ski for hours and hours across snow fields, crevasses, ice bridges, weird ice formations, and a 1,200 foot thick glacier, the Mer de Glace, before skiing back down to town. At one point, you come upon a vision from a modern-day Inferno: tiny black specks of skiers winding down, down, down a long ice and snow spiral track beneath huge seracs.
>
> —James O'Reilly,
> "On and Off the *Autoroute*"

"*Bof,*" is Jean-Pierre's entire reaction to Courchevel. He's anxious to get on to Val Thorens, his hometown and the highest of the Trois Vallées. So on we speed, lift to lift, valley to valley, flying through pinched Méribel and nightmarish Les Menuires, where the French Alps meet *Eraserhead,* and on to futuristic Val Thorens, at 7,000 feet the highest resort in Europe. If the snow's not good here, Jean-Pierre says, it's not good anywhere.

It's been good—too good. In December 1992 there was so much that a normally stable mountainside above Val Thorens avalanched, killing seven tourists who happened to be standing underneath it in the middle of a *piste*. Now the ski patrol is bracing for a wave of lawsuits, a relatively new phenomenon in France, and the merchants and hoteliers are worried about long-term damage to their resort's image. Everyone insists it was a freak accident that will never recur. Yet with new lifts and interconnects opening every year, how can it not?

That's the substance of our dinner conversation. By day we just ski, racing around the giant north facing cirque that comprises Val Thorens. As Jean-Pierre has promised, we find the best snow of the week: cold powder on the Aiguile de Péclet, and then, above the Lac de Lou, that most improbable stuff of all: perfect 35-mile-per-hour corn. For one shining moment we are all Ingemar Stenmarks carving the Platonic turn.

On the last afternoon we tram to the Cime de Caron, the summit of Val Thorens, and catch the big view south. Beyond the rugged Massif des Ecrins the ranges roll away like waves, each, as in a watercolor, a shade lighter than the one in front. You can almost smell the lavender and the jasmine blowing up from Provence. There are dozens of ski areas out there. With a few judiciously placed chairlifts, it occurs to me, one might conceivably ski to the Mediterranean itself.

Rob Buchanan spent a year in the French Alps between his second and third years in college, and has returned at least once a year ever since. He is a contributing editor at Outside, *and has written about extreme sports, the advertising business, and civil rights.*

*

The barometer, nailed onto the outside of the chalet, is still there. It has survived the winter. We put it up four years ago. It's not the sort of barometer you can buy in a shop, down below on the plain, where the rivers flow calmly to the sea; it consists of a small branch of a fir tree, stripped of its bark, and is used up here on the *alpage,* an alpine plateau at an altitude of 5,250 feet where, each summer, men and women from the village below come to graze their cows in the mountain pastures. Nailed upside down, the *alpage*-variety barometer has more or less the form of the letter Y, and when it's going to rain or snow the little branch moves closer to the larger one, reducing the angle between them. One quickly learns to read the angle—as with the hands of a clock. The farther apart they are, the finer it's going to be.

The underlying mechanism is simple. When it's going to snow, fir trees retract their branches, so that the weight of the snow they'll have to bear is reduced. And this reaction is programmed in the wood of every branch, even in those smaller than a little finger. More surprising is the fact that the wood is now so dry that it's apparently dead. Yet it still works, and we still look at it every morning.

—John Berger, "The Named and the Celestial," *Harper's Magazine*

KATHERINE GIBBS

Merlin's Forest

A family finds magic and rejuvenation
in the wizard's lair.

THERE WE WERE, THE FOUR OF US STUFFED INTO A BORROWED
VW GTI with extra-wide racing tires and fake lambswool seat
covers. The kids (ages seven and nine) sat in the backseat, awash in
a sea of cassette tapes, candy wrappers, and Barbie pieces. My husband and I were tucked into the front bucket seats with maps and
tour books churning around our ankles. We were speeding down
French highways from Mont-St-Michel to the ancient Breton
capital of Rennes. We'd been traveling for ten days, and we needed
to get out of our tiny moving box.

We arrived in Rennes in the late afternoon, desperate for a
break. Up to this point we had spent every night in a different
town. We had done well, but the days spent folded into our car,
punctuated by the daily adventure of hotel-hunting, and accented
here and there with the less-than-amiable interactions of the kids
had taken their toll. As we circled Rennes, the kids bickering, the
evening traffic snarling, and the direction signs pointing to some
mythical *"centre-ville,"* the lure of the road distinctly lost its romantic charm. We needed an easy motel and a day out of the car.

Heading back out of town, we prowled the motel parking lots,
knowing instantly which one was for us: the Buffal-Otel. The

place had a great price and, of course, a great name. We decided to stay for two nights and moved in, basking in our permanence.

So many impressions from travel have no "meaning," they are simply shooting stars that once in a while light up the mental sky. I have a vivid memory, for instance, of a storm-tossed night on the Normandy coast. A little beach town, ugly, deserted in late winter, but on a gloomy square less than fifty meters from the crashing surf, we found a restaurant that was open. The food, the decor, nothing special there. But the waitress: she was young, very pretty—and she had a huge scar across her face. A dog had bitten her when she was a little girl.

Another time, shortly after Spielberg's film Hook (Capitaine Crochet *in French) had appeared in France and we had taken our children to see it, we stayed in a dusty inn where the host mysteriously served us dinner with one arm behind his back. Until the main course, that is, when the serving platter was too heavy, and he had to use both arms, revealing a gleaming metal hook in place of his right hand. The children were astounded, as were we.*

—James O'Reilly,
"Troglodytes in Gaul"

We even had a plan—to explore the magical forest of Paimpont, about twenty miles west of Rennes. According to the legends of Brittany, Paimpont—once part of an immense forest known as Brocéliande that covered all of central Brittany—is rife with Arthurian spirits, including those of Merlin, the magician and seer of King Arthur's court, and his beloved enchantress, Viviane. The next morning we headed west on the N24 in search of Merlin, fresh air and a few hours free of the confines of the car.

A designated 40-mile driving route passes by seventeen points of interest in the forest, and we set out to explore them all—but soon realized that would take much longer than the single day we'd allotted. Instead, we used our map as a rough outline, and then we simply followed the other cars.

By the end of the day, a silent camaraderie had developed among us and about seven other carloads of tourists. As we spotted one another speeding in opposite directions or disappearing down forest roads, we would wave cheerfully and, depending on our current state, drive confidently on or slam on our brakes, make a U-turn and speed off in pursuit. During the course of our day, we repeatedly crossed paths with families from Germany, Holland, Northern Ireland, and France.

Despite intermittent rain and confusing directions, we visited every site that we were interested in. Some stops involved a short walk from the car; others involved relatively long hikes. By the end of the day we were exhausted, refreshed, and enlightened.

It was shortly before lunch when we finally found Merlin's tomb, the high point of the tour for us. The prehistoric grave is marked with standing stones about a quarter-mile from the road. In the centuries since its discovery, the grave has become a spot for Arthurian pilgrims; it was elaborately decorated with woven grasses, branches and flowers, and tiny papers covered with messages for the sorcerer were tucked in the cracks of the rocks. The dark boughs of an ancient holly tree bent and twisted over the site. If this wasn't Merlin's tomb, it certainly should have been. A short distance past the tomb was La Fontaine de Jouvence (the Fountain of Youth), a small spring with all the rejuvenating powers of any such fountain.

Soon we were off in search of our next site. Only a few wrong turns later, we found the trailhead for the Fontaine de Barenton, where Merlin met his beloved Viviane—and where you can supposedly conjure up a spell or two of your own.

To get to this spring, we walked about a mile and a half, during which time we were treated to a monologue by the seven-year-old on the relative merits of the long uphill climb. However, once we arrived, she seemed instantly refreshed, and took particular interest in knowing that this was the exact spot where Merlin met Viviane. Also of interest to our kids, and the other children milling around, were seemingly limitless possibilities for creek damming and sibling splashing.

Surrounded by the deep green of the forests and the splashing of water down timeless rocks, we were alone with ancient spirits and our tourist comrades. The kids slowly followed the water's path, dropping everything they could find into the small current.

The forest was working its magic. We were definitely free of our doldrums from the evening before.

Our next stop on what had now become the Merlin-and-Viviane tour was the Val Sans Retour (the Valley of No Return). On the longest hike of the day, we walked about two and a half miles to a ridge where we could look down on the valley. By our tenuous calculations, we were standing on the Rock of False Lovers, where the sorceress Morgana was said to have captured men who had been unfaithful to their wives.

From this imposing ridge, we could gaze down to the mystical Fairy's Mirror, the lake where Viviane, afraid of losing Merlin, held him in a prison of air. According to legend, Merlin was so powerful that he could have escaped at any time. He knew, though, that he'd have been a fool to leave Viviane. We made our way silently from the ridge to the banks of the Fairy's Mirror. The lake was still and green as we walked by its side.

We returned to our car and sank gratefully onto the fake lambswool seats. What had begun as a much-needed day of fresh air, space, and exercise ended leaving us feeling like time travelers. We had passed out of our modern century into a world of enchantresses, spells, magical waters, and deep green forests. We had touched on the legends of Merlin, and we were refreshed with our restored knowledge of the magic of travel. As we drove back to the Buffal-Otel, the long ribbon of road glinted in a ray of evening sun. The romantic sheen was back.

Katherine Gibbs is a freelance writer who lives with her family in Riverside, California. She has a Ph.D. in psychology and teaches part time at the University of California, Riverside.

✴

We were in Merlin's forest. And the girl's first name was Soizic. Truly. She'd been standing in the mist with her thumb out. Only the hitchhiker's pose and her jeans placed her in our own real time. For the rest, she could have been an Aubrey Beardsley illustration of Sir Thomas Malory's *Le Morte d'Arthur* or some knights of the Round Table comic book figure. She had long, thick red hair and wore a loose white smock and thonged

shoes. She had the high, chiseled features and long narrow eyes that belong most precisely not in this part of Brittany but amongst the Celtic
subgroup of Bigoudens on the Cornouaille coast to the southwest. That
was where she was heading. Did we believe in magic, she asked in the car,
and if not, what were we doing driving around in Merlin's forest?

She believed in magic. Not in the tarot and whatever other pop cults
kids prone to thonged sandals pick up in college. But in her own time-
honored Breton magic. In the Ankou, the grim reaper with his tumbrel,
who prowls the whole peninsula, in charge of transporting souls between
here and now and eternity. In the washwomen of the night, who can en-
tice you, if you're out late, into helping to wring out the burial sheets they
wash at the country *lavoirs,* and who'll twist all your bones as they wind
the sheets, unless you twist the opposite way. In Merlin? Well, yes, she said,
he did live here in this forest. You can see the fountain where Merlin created thunder by splashing water on a rock, and the Valley of No Return,
where Lancelot freed all the imprisoned faithless lovers enchanted by
Morgane, the water goddess....

—G. Y. Dryansky, "Merlin's Magic Shore," *Condé Nast Traveler*

CHERYL MACLACHLAN

Footsteps of the Impressionists

Escaping Paris for a run in the French countryside,
the author encounters the spirit
of Vincent van Gogh.

IT HAPPENED THIS WAY. I WAS IN PARIS LAST FALL RESEARCHING A book and feeling the need for a good run. Paris is a highly livable city with gorgeous light, stunning architecture, and incomparable food. But when it comes to running, the choices are limited. The parks of Paris—unlike other great urban oases such as Central Park, Golden Gate Park, and Hyde Park—offer little in the way of multimile runs.

One day I complained about this to some of my Parisian friends and asked for suggestions. They told me about a wonderful running trail in Auvers-sur-Oise, a little village just 30 minutes north of Paris. Auvers is perhaps best known as the village where Vincent van Gogh spent the last months of his life and painted some of his most famous works.

Van Gogh is one of the artists I most appreciate. Seven or eight years ago, when I saw the "Van Gogh in Arles" exhibit at the Metropolitan Museum of Art, I was struck by the beauty of *The Starry Night, Irises, Café Terrace at Night,* and many of his other paintings. It was such a powerful experience. Some quality in van Gogh's work captivated me. I willingly endured the mad crush of the crowd around me just to stand in the presence of so much mystery and energy.

Needless to say, I couldn't resist the opportunity to visit Auvers-sur-Oise. I grabbed a train schedule, put on my running clothes and headed to the Gare du Nord, the train station with departures to the suburbs north of Paris.

When the train pulled into Auvers, I set my running shoes onto the same platform that a penniless van Gogh had stepped onto in 1890. The village seemed unaffected by time, with its narrow streets, quaint stone houses, and bright flowers tumbling from every window ledge. It looked like a vision from a storybook you might read to your children at night.

I finished my stretching and began running up a small hill toward a massive stone church. It turned out to be the Gothic-Romanesque church van Gogh animated under a sky of dancing indigo in his painting, *Church at Auvers-sur-Oise,* which I had seen several times at the Musée d'Orsay in Paris. As I passed by the north side of the church, I became aware of a sensation that did not so much resemble running as it did floating. Everything was soft—the air, the light, the colors. I felt as though I were leaving behind footprints in muted gray, blue and green oil.

I later learned that Auvers-sur-Oise, with its strikingly textured skies and landscapes, was the site of van Gogh's last desperate attempt to escape the ravages of depression and hallucination. During the previous two years, he had lived and worked in the southern French villages of Arles and Saint-Remy-de-Provence. His episodes of delirium included the evening he severed part of his right ear.

Concerned for van Gogh's welfare and believing a change of scenery might restore his mental health, the painter Camille Pissarro suggested to Vincent's brother Theo that Vincent seek out a Dr. Paul Gachet, who lived in Auvers. Pissarro said that Gachet, a physician, amateur painter, and generous patron of the Impressionists, would be willing to take van Gogh under his wing.

S uppose you came upon a village where the only artist in history yet to produce a painting valued at more than $50 million had lived and worked. And suppose the little inn where he had taken a room, and where he had died dramatically, was still there, looking out on the picturesque city hall he had painted. Suppose, further, that the artist was now buried, beside his brother, in a simple cemetery at the edge of the village, set among the wheat fields he made familiar to the world, and a short walk up the hill from the town church that appears in one of his best-known masterpieces. And if that village could be found, by a riverbank, less than 25 miles from one of the most visited cities in the world, and if it still appeared much as it did a hundred years ago, when this artist, and others, recorded it as they thought they saw it....

In California that would be enough for a theme park. In Auvers-sur-Oise, in France, it is a day in the country, spent virtually alone. "Here one is far enough from Paris for it to be the real country," Vincent van Gogh wrote a few days after settling in Auvers, in May of 1890.

—Les Daly,
"The Artistry of Auvers,"
The Atlantic Monthly

Following Dr. Gachet's advice to paint, paint, and paint some more, van Gogh in Auvers displayed the endurance of a long-distance runner who tirelessly logs mile after mile, day after day. In his case, he walked and walked and walked, seeking out every part of the village and surrounding fields. The beauty of what he saw so entranced van Gogh that he worked himself into a frantic state trying to put it all down on canvas. He painted an astounding 70 canvases in 70 days.

After running just a few kilometers from the train station, I found myself moving beyond the town and into a more pastoral setting. Before long, I reached the exact spot where van Gogh stood to paint *Fields Under the Rain*. In the warm afternoon light, I looked onto undulating folds of green, punctuated by the terra-cotta roof tiles of homes on the banks of the river Oise.

How did I know this was the spot where van Gogh painted? The townspeople have placed illustrated signs marking the sites of several of van Gogh's works.

Next I turned left onto a dirt path that farmers use to gain access to the fields. The wide open space here gave me a particularly striking perspective on the skies over Auvers. They are often the stage for a brilliant choreography of cumulus clouds that billow upward for thousands of meters and then glide along with the prevailing winds. These striking clouds clearly made an impression on van Gogh and challenged him to achieve one of his greatest accomplishments as a painter: developing a style that captured the energy and movement of these clouds.

Along the right edge of this path still moist and soft from the previous evening's rain, I passed a poster marking the spot where van Gogh painted *Wheat Fields with Crows*. On this particular day the crows were out in force. They circled, swept, dove, and cawed above my head. I slowed to a jog, letting myself soak up the diverse elements that inspired van Gogh's brilliant and moody masterpiece.

I had always thought I fully appreciated great works of art. But I never had experienced so many senses converging at the same moment. Sight, sound, motion. The perspiration on my skin, the smell of the ground, the touch of a few raindrops that started to fall.

I came to a completely new understanding of *Wheat Fields*. When I remembered that it was

> *Painting is only a bridge linking the painter's mind with that of the viewer.*
>
> —Eugène Delacroix,
> *Journal, 1893–1895*

van Gogh's last painting, it seemed only natural that I should have had such a strong reaction to it. *Wheat Fields* represented the crescendo of van Gogh's career, an odyssey during which he evolved from sketching forlorn figures in charcoal to rendering emotions in brilliant color.

It caused me to reflect on the evolution of my own "odyssey," the ebb and flow of more than ten years as a runner. I realized that like van Gogh, I have passed through some very distinct phases. I always loved distance running and spent most of my twenties somewhat obsessed with marathons and new PRs [personal records]. But as the years went by and my career took me to Manhattan, my emphasis shifted. My primary goal became simply staying in shape. Ten years flew past, filled with frequent business travel, few leisure hours, and a frustrating lack of quality time in which to enjoy my running.

Then came a change. Not long ago, I moved to Marin County, California, where my husband and I often run on mountain trails. There, I discovered a new dimension to my running. I find myself concentrating more on the quality of the sensory experience. I focus on my surroundings—the trees, the fields, the ocean. You might say, I suppose, that I run as a painter would run, trying to drink in every little nuance of the surrounding environment.

Just beyond the wheat field, the path flowed into a deciduous wood. The trees formed a canopy overhead, while the chestnuts crunched underfoot. The sunlight filtered through the leaves in a most extraordinary way, forming a shimmering mosaic of pale green.

I had always imagined that van Gogh must have painted from his hallucinations. How else could one explain paisley leaves or yellow stars radiating green streaks? But running in his footsteps, seeing and feeling what he saw and felt, I understood the simplicity and power of his genius: he could truly capture the essence of a place.

It has been said that facts are facts, but reality is what we, as individuals, experience. Van Gogh's reality allowed solid rock to ripple in waves of red, clouds to form chain links, and pastures and skies to lick each other in paisley curls.

I have also felt a private reality—in my running. My watch says I've been out on the trail for over an hour, but my conscious mind seems to believe that only a few minutes have elapsed. The facts of physics say that I must propel my body forward, but my experience is of being pulled by some force that I've allowed myself to encounter.

As I ran in van Gogh's footsteps, I began to understand his struggle to integrate all the conflicting realities he experienced—the dance of opposites that commandeered his body and mind. Sadly, he couldn't maintain an equilibrium. On July 29, 1890, he died in Auvers-sur-Oise of a self-inflicted gunshot wound.

On the train back to Paris, I couldn't help but reflect on the differences between van Gogh and myself. As a runner, my emotions were allowed to play out in the privacy of my run. Van Gogh had no such luxury. His genius forced him to work out his conflicting realities on canvas, preserved for all the world to see.

Cheryl MacLachlan is a former associate publisher of Esquire *magazine and holds personal records of 3:15 in the marathon and 41 minutes in the 10-K.*

✦

Painting isn't an aesthetic operation; it's a form of magic designed as a mediator between this strange hostile world and us, a way of seizing the power by giving form to our terrors as well as our desires.

—Pablo Picasso

STEVE FISHMAN

✳ ✳ ✳

A Lovely Day for a Miracle

Lourdes is the world's most popular pilgrimage site,
but does it still produce miracles?

THE WEATHER IS GLORIOUS, AND LOURDES, THE CITY OF MIRACLES in the French Pyrenees, is in high season. May to October—during those 184 days, you get the bulk of your miracle cures.

And what bulk! The Catholic Church has authenticated 65 Lourdes miracles, each nicely listed on a handout with the cureds' hometowns so that, if you like, you can get their numbers from an operator and call them on the phone. And these are just the Church-verified miracles. Everyone knows that this 137-year-old holy site in southern France fetches up cures—not sanctioned miracles but medically unexplainable nevertheless—by the thousands. *Thousands.* Has everyone who's been here seen one? "My mother," says J.L. Armand-Laroche, an aristocratic Paris psychiatrist whose family has been going to Lourdes for generations, "saw a woman's swollen hand deflate like that. *Pffft.*"

This is a strange time to go on a miracle hunt. Indeed, it's a strange time for the "land of miracles," as Lourdes is sometimes called. When someone today says, "We live in an age of miracles," what's meant is that we live in an age of artificial hearts and gene transplants. What's more, one is led to believe that when medicine comes up short, in just a matter of time—months maybe—it will meet the challenge. Yet more people than ever jam Lourdes. And, says pollster George Gallup, eight in ten Americans believe God does miracles.

Can we have it both ways? Can we see the world as doctors do, as a place that heels to biological explanation (and manipulation), and also as true believers do, as a magical place where natural laws are transgressed? Can medicine accept miracles?

Lourdes is just the place to take up this matter. Not only is it the most popular pilgrimage site in the world—more popular than Rome or Mecca or Jerusalem—but also at Lourdes the Church long ago struck a deal with medicine. Unlike any other pilgrimage site, Lourdes has an international committee of doctors who judge, even before the Church does, whether a cure ought to be considered a miracle. At Lourdes they hunt miracles, Lord of Lords, with CAT scans.

In 1858, the teenager Bernadette Soubirous went out to gather wood and returned instead with reports of an apparition. In a lovely grotto near her house in Lourdes, she'd seen a beautiful lady in white with a yellow rose on each foot. Her mother thought Bernadette was crazy and warned her never to go there again. But Bernadette would see the Lady eighteen times—though no one else could. One time, the Lady, who priests figured out was the Virgin Mary [after she identified herself, in provincial French, as *"Que soy l'immaculada concepciou"*], showed Bernadette a spring in the grotto's floor. Soon people were dipping their clawed hands, blind

> *The Catholic Church became the great unifying force of the High Middle Ages (1000 to 1300 A.D.) for many reasons.*
>
> *The greatest single cause of the Church's rise was society's dramatic economic progress after the millennium, much of it itself due to the Church. Archbishops and bishops of the cathedrals and abbots of the monasteries had for centuries bought, inherited, and reclaimed vast tracts of arable land. On this land, they fostered every kind of agricultural improvement, even more purposefully than did the secular noblemen on their own estates.*
>
> —Henry S. Reuss and Margaret M. Reuss, *The Unknown South of France: A History Buff's Guide*

eyes, and sick infants into the chilly water and reporting cures, miraculous cures.

Today the city's narrow, hilly streets hold more hotel rooms than any city in France except Paris. (As if it were a theme park, the hotels have names like Hotel Madonna, Hotel Vatican, Hotel Christ Roi.) These days every room is needed. During the six-month season, Lourdes, a city of 18,000, accommodates five million, almost twice the population of Los Angeles.

"Since I've been coming to Lourdes I've started to reflect," says José da Silva, a paraplegic since a moped accident a few years ago. "I tell myself, I have my hands, I can get around in my wheelchair. There are others who can't do as much as I can. It's been like a click in my head." At home in a small town near Lyon, da Silva is isolated—he can't even go to Mass because the local church has steps. At Lourdes, volunteers wait on him; he is part of a community. Da Silva appreciates these things. Yet he also says, "If God could make me feel my legs...you know, half my body. There is always a hope."

Da Silva, like many, spends his days at Lourdes being wheeled around the sanctuary, the 74 acres fenced off from the tourist city. In the sanctuary are the holiest places in Lourdes: the grotto, the spring, and the baths it now supplies, six churches, and all the other places where, history says, miracles are most likely to occur.

One sunny afternoon, when the sky is spotless enough to have been poured from a paint can, I tag along behind another wheelchair, a tiny one holding a small boy whose hands begin at his elbows. Pushed by his mother, he makes his way to the huge Rosary Square—almost the length of one and a half football fields—in front of Rosary Church where, at the height of the season, 50,000 gather every afternoon for the Blessed Sacrament procession. The boy's mother confides, "Miracles happen here," and lines her son up in an area that fills with eight, then ten, then twenty rows of disabled people. As a priest winds through the square, blessing individual cases, the boy calls, "Jesus, cure me."

Cures have happened in the square. In 1947, tuberculosis patient Marie-Thérèse Canin, 50th miracle, got up for the first time in years right after the procession. In 1950, Leo Schwager, 57th miracle, unable to move because of multiple sclerosis, reported his symptoms vanished during the procession. Doctors still position themselves toward the front of the crowd to scout for people who suddenly toss away their crutches or rise from their wheelchairs. This idea—that cures are so frequent all you have to do is wait for them—thrills me.

I go to the grotto, a dent at the base of a cliff, which is a five minute walk from Rosary Square. The grotto, beside the bottle-green River Gave, is the loveliest place at Lourdes and another site of miracles. In 1908, Marie Bire, 37th miracle, was cured of blindness here. And in 1948, Jeanne Fretel, 52nd miracle, felt the first signs of her TB cure after a visit. People file through this shallow cave in a silent devotional trudge, running their hands along the cliff, now smoothed by so many touches. They deposit long-stemmed roses on the tiled floor, which is marked with the places where Bernadette first kneeled to Mary. With out-of-date Instamatics they take snapshots of the banal statue of the lady with the roses on her feet, a statue Bernadette never liked. On a metal line overhead hang a few of the crutches, black with age, that the once-lame are said to have tossed away after a visit. I dawdle, eagle-eyed.

A woman from Liverpool, England, passes through with her infant son, who has a plum-sized growth over his right eye. She has come to pray for the growth's disappearance and to replenish her stock of

The grotto

Lourdes water, which she dabs on his eye every day.

"My mother has jerry cans full," she says. "When we run short we make an emergency trip."

Next to the grotto are the miraculous baths, filled with water from the spring that Mary showed Bernadette. The spring begins in a limestone reservoir, now two-thirds empty, and is piped into eleven gray marble baths for women and six for men—women bathe more than men.

As they do everywhere in Lourdes, at the baths the sick and infirm go first. Behind a curtain, volunteers help them undress, wrap them in a wet towel. Two steps lead into the slate-gray water. A volunteer hands a small statue of Mary to the sick one. There is a moment for prayer. Then strong arms grip the supplicant. He or she is dipped backward into the 52-degree water.

Since the water, which has no medicinal value, is emptied only twice a day, dunking the sick first may not be the healthiest ordering. Consider for instance that the ninth miracle had a twelve-inch long ulcer of the leg. Some of the devout are even known to drink the water. "The water is totally septic," says psychiatrist Armand-Laroche. "It's a miracle that people don't fall sick."

That discourages hardly anyone. One Italian woman doused snapshots of her family, since they couldn't be at Lourdes. Pravin Mandalin, Hindu dressmaker, drove his paralyzed father and seven other family members 1,000 miles from England to bathe. "I'm praying whatever I believe in, but I'm praying to the Lady too," he says. Mandalin's father, who has had a stroke, wheels around in his chair gaining strength, not all of it physical. "When you're ill, if others are more ill, you forget. You think you are better off," says Mandalin. Still, he and his father wouldn't mind a miracle, even a little one. "If my father could get from his bed to his wheelchair by himself that would help," Mandalin says.

I head to a place where I know cures abound. In an office off Rosary Square is a photo gallery, which must be unlike any other in the world. "Some of the 2,000 cures recognized as inexplicable after a medical inquiry," reads one title. Every one of these cases has been examined by at least one doctor who found that medicine couldn't explain it. It is from these 2,000 inexplicable cures that the Church has chosen the 65 official miracles of Lourdes. The quantity of cures is impressive: the equivalent of one every twelve days of the six-month season for the past 137 years.

I phone the office of Lourdes's medical director, through which all miracles must pass.

Any today? I ask, as I have every day of the week.

Not yet, I'm told.

So I hadn't come up with a miracle in the land of miracles. People want and don't always get. That's the way it is with miracles. I still have the list of 65 verified Lourdes miracles. These are miracles I can talk to. The most recent *miraculé,* as the French call them, is Delizia Cirolli, a Sicilian whose cure was authenticated by the Church in 1989, evidence that Lourdes still pumps them out.

Delizia's family had been too poor to afford medical help, so she'd gotten the first X-ray of her aching knee under the name of an insured neighbor. *"Bruto,"* pronounced the doctor, cancer of the bone. Specialists verified the prognosis. She would soon die. Radiation was proposed, though little hope offered. Amputation was mentioned—it might prolong her life a few months. Her father refused. "When she dies, she dies," he said. Instead she went to Lourdes.

"I did not even know where Lourdes was," says Delizia's mother, Gaetana. "Nor did I go because I believed. The girl was hopeless. I just went because they told me to go." "They" was one of Delizia's teachers, who raised the money for the girl's pilgrimage from other teachers.

At Lourdes, nothing happened. Back home, Delizia quickly dropped more than 25 pounds and couldn't even pull herself out of her bed. She asked for a knife to kill herself. A few months later her uncle was going out for Christmas bread. "I want to go, too," she said. And she did.

"Even now I don't understand what happened," says her mother.

To be considered for miracle status, you need not be religious, but you must nominate yourself. You do that by making your way to the Medical Bureau at Lourdes and telling your story. Delizia appeared before the bureau the year after her cure. Her recovery was due to prayers to the Virgin of Lourdes, she said. As is the rule, medical director Theodor Mangiapan summoned the doctors then visiting Lourdes, most of whom were accompanying pilgrimages.

The 30 doctors assembled were, it's fair to say, perplexed. Delizia had been X-rayed under a fake name, consulted specialists, and then refused their advice. "Delizia's story," says Mangiapan, "was completely crazy." Then she produced the X-rays. In one, bone was breaking apart; in another, thirteen months later, the bone was clearly filling. The doctors voted. They decided that Mangiapan should prepare a report for the International Medical Committee. The process by which someone becomes a *miraculé* had begun.

Because Europeans tend to feel every person is hierarchically in his right place, they also tend to believe in the "rightness" or "wrongness" of many things. Accordingly, a greater intellectual certainty and a drive toward ever more certainty will often erupt in Europeans, aspects of intellectual style that go far beyond any American hankering after consensus. The mass movements of fascism and communism are only the most extreme and destructive examples of how this yearning for rightness and simple organization can surface from the depths of a culture which has known, for long centuries, such clarity.

—Stuart Miller,
Understanding Europeans

At Lourdes, six cures were reported in the first few months after Bernadette saw the Lady. Just as soon, the Bishop of Lourdes heard from skeptics denouncing the cures as hysteria or, worse, frauds. He needed help. In 1883, he hired a doctor, the first medical director of Lourdes (or of any shrine, for that matter). In 1947, the Church organized a second level of medical review, a committee of French doctors. Today the committee includes 25 Catholic doctors from seven European countries who meet once a year. Their job has always been to sort out from among the alleged cures, as the doctors call the candidate pool, those that are truly medically unexplainable.

An inexplicable cure, says the Church, must be sudden, complete, and obtained without effective treatment.

If the doctors find a cure inexplicable, it is passed to the bishop of the candidate's home diocese. It is he who finally decides whether the inexplicable is a genuine miracle or just...inexplicable. That Lourdes has 2,000 cures but only 65 miracles speaks to the bishops' enormous prerogative. Some bishops are suspicious of miracles, believing faith should have another basis. At times, they don't respond at all. Other times, they conduct their own medical review. One bishop, for instance, rejected a case of cured blindness—a case the doctors found unexplainable—because the recovery of sight wasn't perfect. The would-be *miraculé* needed glasses.

Once the International Medical Committee received Delizia's case from Mangiapan, it assigned two of its members, a French professor of orthopedic surgery and a Scottish fellow of the Royal College of Surgeons of Edinburgh, to investigate. First, the two doctors established that Delizia had been cured. (It wasn't sudden—her knee took several months to heal. And it wasn't complete. She was left knock-kneed. But the committee has decided to "nuance" the Church's guidelines.) Then they established that she hadn't gotten any treatment that could account for her cure. Delizia, in fact, hadn't gotten any treatment at all. This was important. "We can always tell ourselves that a treatment could possibly have had *some* effect," says committee member Charles Chassagnon, former chief of medicine at a Lyon hospital. Indeed, says committee member Jean Rousseau, former assistant director of the Curie Institute in Paris. "The miracle of Delizia is that she qualified to be a miracle."

In Delizia's case the principal medical controversy was the diagnosis. What kind of tumor had it been? One Italian pathologist diagnosed a metastasis, or an offshoot, of a neuroblastoma, a tumor of immature nerve cells. Three French pathologists favored Ewing's tumor, a type of bone cancer. (In such terms are miracles discussed nowadays.)

In particular, the investigators worried about the different rates of spontaneous remission, or sudden disappearance of disease without effective treatment. Spontaneous remission is a tricky issue for miracle hunters. A miracle is a spontaneous remission. And yet, if a disease is known to have spontaneous remissions then a spontaneous remission can't be considered an act of God.

The investigators searched the literature. Spontaneous remission had never been reported for Ewing's tumor. But neuroblastomas, the investigators said, "are susceptible, in some conditions, to spontaneous cure." Spontaneous cures of neuroblastomas have been reported only in children up to age two.

In either case, Ewing's tumor or neuroblastoma, the doctors seemed safe. For at the time of her cure Delizia was well past age two. Yet the committee pushed the point. They wanted to be precise. They studied the slides, the X-rays, the reports. Then, for an afternoon and part of an evening, they debated the diagnosis. "We are for extreme scientific rigor," says Rousseau.

In the end, heaven's hand was affirmed by majority. The diagnosis? Of fifteen doctors present, ten were for Ewing's tumor; four would say nothing more than malignant tumor; one abstained. Did it constitute a phenomenon contrary to the expectations of medical experience? All fifteen said yes. Was it unexplainable? All but one said it was. The case of Delizia Cirolli was passed to the bishop of her diocese.

I wanted to know if Delizia was happy when the committee pronounced her cure inexplicable, clearing a major hurdle toward becoming a miracle. Half-smile in place, Delizia was impassive. "It all happened so long ago," she said.

Long ago? Was there some mistake? The Church just declared this a miracle in 1989. Delizia said, "I could not realize how ill I was. I was only eleven." Despite her gamine looks, she was now 27, working as a maternity nurse. She hadn't been acting blasé. She'd moved on. I had expected someone hopped up with the extraordinary; she was tired of dwelling on the past.

That the 65th miracle *seems* current, it turns out, is principally an artifact of the process. It took two years to prepare her dossier, another three years to find the cure inexplicable. The medical committee passed Delizia's case to her diocese in 1982. Her bishop, a man referred to as "prudent," made no decision for a vexing seven years, then retired. It fell to his successor to proclaim, a few months after taking office, "Such a miracle seems to be a harbinger of good times."

The miracle of 1989 is really the miracle of 1976! The land of miracles has not offered up a miracle in sixteen years. In fact, some checking reveals that since Delizia's case, the medical committee has not had a single case to consider.

Once I had shuttled around Lourdes wondering which was the best place to wait for a miracle. Now I had something else in mind: is Lourdes a place without miracles?

Theodor Mangiapan, the former medical director of Lourdes who presided over Delizia's case, a pediatrician described as "the militant Christian," is shouting. As if I can't hear. As if anyone couldn't hear.

"I passed my life at Lourdes saying that we are facing a penury!" he shouts.

A penury?

"A total penury of inexplicable cures!"

But this is Lourdes, land of miracles. What's going on?

Look at the history, Mangiapan urges. At the turn of the century when medicine couldn't explain anything, then medical director G. Boissarie was able to produce a mind-blurring 1,536 inexplicable cures in 26 years. By mid-century, however, doctors could explain a few things. By the 1940's, for instance, they had learned about the bacillus that causes tuberculosis. That meant trouble for the miracle business. TB is the disease cured in 27 of the 65 miracles—40 percent. TB can now be eliminated with antibiotics.

Mangiapan didn't see a single case of TB. In fact he didn't see much of anything. Mangiapan, who served from 1972 (the year the CAT scan was introduced) until 1990, presented the committee with the full fruit of his labor and it amounted to three inexplicable cures. Delizia's and two inherited from his predecessor. Without inexplicable cures, there could be no miracles. "Who would accept this as the expression of a loving God?" asks Mangiapan.

Not that Mangiapan gave up. Over the years, he'd asked many of the committee's doctors to take a preliminary look at an alleged cure. Mangiapan shipped them dossiers thick with X-rays and histology reports and hope, yes, hope that they could pluck out a case that would defy medical circumspection and, in a sense, medical progress. But time and again they examined and they dismissed. It was as if, illuminated by the pale light of X-ray viewing screens, they had to give case after case a backhand swipe and say, "This, this can't possibly be a miracle." Says committee member Bernard Smits, a gastroenterologist at Walsgrave Hospital in Coventry, England, "People are saying 'I'm cured,' and we're going out of our way to pull apart the case and say, 'No, rubbish, it's not true.' We almost go to extreme lengths. I'm aware sometimes of almost a sense of guilt in being too powerful."

Some elements of the Catholic Church have let the doctors know they're nervous. "The French clergy says, 'The people of God need miracles,'" reports committee member St. John Dowling, an English general practitioner. "They say it to us."

I say it, too. Mangiapan, I say, this is a crisis.

"I went all the way to Rome!" he thunders back.

He went to the Vatican's Consulta Medica, which investigates medical miracles performed anywhere in the world, anytime in history by candidates for sainthood. Mangiapan maintained that God hadn't disappeared but that His works could no longer be detected. The Church's guidelines for a miracle cure, unchanged in 250 years, require that no effective treatments have been given. But today anyone who gets diagnosed gets some treatment, and every treatment has some chance of being effective. The Church, Mangiapan argued, had to loosen its rules to meet the changed state of medicine.

What did the Vatican respond?

The militant Christian shakes his head. "The Vatican doesn't care," Mangiapan says. "It doesn't care." Mangiapan was told this:

"Lourdes should do what it must so that there are miraculous cures."

But how can the Vatican not care that miracles aren't found at Lourdes?

"Because at the Vatican there are still miracles!" In the last decade, the Consulta Medica has recognized 80 inexplicable cures, according to Mangiapan. The Consulta Medica uses the same guidelines as the medical committee of Lourdes. But it seems to the doctors at Lourdes that the Consulta Medica applies them differently. "They get reports from Chile and Papua-New Guinea with documentation that may be inadequate, but make a decision anyway," says Smits. "Whereas we have to look at slides and X-rays."

If anything, instead of pumping out new miracle candidates, these rigorous doctors seem to undermine the miracles already established. In 1984, Dowling reviewed the past fifteen miracles for the *Journal of the Royal Society of Medicine,* and he uncovered a recurrence. Ginette Nouvel of Carmaux, France, the 60th miracle had supposedly been cured of Budd-Chiari disease, a circulatory problem. But she died of complications of the disease. "At the time no one knew it had a long course of remission," says Dowling. "The committee recognized its error." The Church still counts her a miracle. Says Dowling, "There's no mechanism for de-miracle-izing people."

In a 1988 review of some Lourdes miracles in the French journal *Psychologie Médicale,* Chassagnon contended that in three miracles—number 38, chronic inflammatory bowel disease; number 42, rheumatic spondylosis; and number 48, adhesive peritonitis—the diagnoses might well have been in error and thus rapid recovery shouldn't have been surprising.

(Even I stumbled onto an inexplicable cure that turned out to be in error. At Lourdes, eight-year-old Gérard Baillie, blind since age two, said to his mother, "Oh *Maman,* how beautiful you are." When I caught up with Baillie 44 years later, he was visiting Paris, traveling up the Seine in a chartered boat. The guide announced.

"On the right is the residence of Pierre Cardin: on the left is the Louvre." Baillie's eyes were aimed at a dull plastic tabletop. By sixteen his sight had receded. By twenty, he was blind again.)

Chassagnon, president of the medical committee, says, "In fact it's difficult to affirm that any cure is medically inexplicable." In that case no one could ever become a miracle! Is it possible that in the heart of the miracle-hunting committee some doctors don't believe in miracles?

At first, Chassagnon will not address the question directly. He will say only this: either you believe in the explanatory power of science or you believe in the explanatory power of religion. Then he indicates his choice. "A doctor," he says, "is by definition a scientist."

The miraculous has always existed just beyond the limits of scientific explanation. And what happens when science pushes out those limits? Miracles are squeezed, sometimes out of existence, so that even when a cure is inexplicable, and thus potentially miraculous, explanation seems only temporarily out of reach, a phenomenon we don't yet understand but, as Chassagnon says to me, soon will.

The truth is, you can't just hand a scientist a CAT scanner and tell him or her to go find miracles. Introduce CAT scans and you introduce the beliefs CAT scans grew out of: that through science—and not through prayer or faith or miracles—the invisible world will be made visible; that through science the unexplainable will yield explanation.

Finally, committee president Chassagnon, who considers himself a good Catholic, comes out with it: "The miracles of Lourdes are, in the strict sense, a little old-fashioned."

So Delizia Cirolli represents the last generation of Lourdes *miraculés?*

Mangiapan, who once hurried to afternoon prayers to scout for miracle cures, says, "*Voilà,* I subscribe to that."

What seems most astounding to me now is who else subscribes

to that. Father Barraqué, the secretary-general of Lourdes, an excitable, genial man in a Lacoste shirt, has a sign on his desk. Do It Yourself, it says. God Can't Be Everywhere. It's cute, and what's more, it's policy.

People may still long for miracles at Lourdes. But the official message of Lourdes is now this: don't long for a perfectable world. That's an impossible world. Hunt miracles, but other kinds of miracles. The miracles at Lourdes, says Barraqué, will be personal and unverifiable, miracles of understanding, comfort, strength. Like the strength that Jose da Silva sitting in his wheelchair took when he saw others and thought, "Look at all I can do." Or the miracle of Pravin Mandalin's father, who found Lourdes a place to feel happy and not so alone, and perhaps, as a result, was more eager to undertake the long trip from bed to wheelchair.

"Miracle cures are not the big interest," says Barraqué. Unofficially miracle cures may be real at Lourdes, as real as our desire for them, which is huge; officially they are downplayed or denied. Officially, you might say, Lourdes prepares for a scientific world.

"The majority of people come trying to find out what their suffering serves for. They look as much for meaning as for cure," says Barraqué, and swallows a pill for his diabetes.

Steve Fishman is a contributing editor for Vogue *and* Details *magazines. Three times he has won the Best Magazine Story award from the American Society of Journalists and Authors. He is the author of* A Bomb in the Brain: A Heroic Tale of Science, Surgery, and Survival. *He lives in New York.*

✳

Neither crypt nor upper basilica [at Lourdes] can be called a chapel. The bottom basilica, which is bigger still—it can hold 4,000 persons—was finished in 1889. A huge mosaic of the Virgin surrounded by angels fills almost the entire apse. At Easter, concerts of sacred music are held in this lower basilica to get the season off to a good start, so to speak. The area under the mosaic serves as the stage. The musicians, who are of international stature, draw big crowds, and the acoustics of the church are said to be splendid.

Even the lower basilica was far from the end of it, and new construction has rarely slowed down since: outbuildings, chapels, conference rooms and press rooms, three hospitals, the fourteen baths fed by the miraculous spring into which hundreds of hopeful or desperate people are plunged every day (in season), life-size bronze stations of the cross climbing the hillside for almost a mile, parking lots. The river was confined to its concrete trench and the bridges rearranged. In 1958 still another "basilica" was ready—the meaning of words was being rearranged too, for this basilica was entirely underground. It was 200 yards long and could hold almost 30,000 people during celebrations, liturgical processions, and the like.

—Robert Daley, *Portraits of France*

PAM HOUSTON

★ ★ ★

The Hidden Ardèche

An American outdoorswoman explores
France's "Wild West."

I SHOULD HAVE KNOWN I WOULD FALL IN LOVE WITH THE ARDÈCHE, with its green craggy hills and amber wine lands, with the crystal rivers that bubble and spill past tile-roofed villages. I should have known I would fall in love if only because I was going in September and there's no way I can keep myself from loving a place where I get to witness the sweetness of summer's end.

This little-known region of France is a long drive from anywhere and always at the mercy of the weather. Nestled between the region of the Loire to the north and Provence to the south, between the banks of the Rhône to the east and the Cévennes Mountains to the west, the Ardèche is among the least talked about, least expensive, and least touristed parts of France.

At first glance it seems without superlatives: a land of moderately high mountains and somewhat deep gorges, of medium-sized villages full of basically friendly people who produce reasonably good wine and goat cheese and sausage so fat and salty that you can feel the years slip off your life as you chew. Its endlessly receding valleys are filled with goats and cows and the occasional farmhouse; its roads were built by people who think driving should be a full body workout.

Although the mountains and high villages in the Ardèche draw the eye skyward, it is the rivers that dominate the landscape, shaping the land and the lives of the people, dictating where the wildly curving roads will go. The green Ardèche River rises in limestone, the slightly bluer Eyrieux in granite, the mighty Loire in volcanic basalt. All three major waterways are fed by a dozen smaller rivers, each of which in turn is fed by even more streams.

The Ardèche may seem without superlatives, but that's only until the sun comes out to shine on those river valleys, to light the orange roofs and make the green fields glisten between walls of clean white stone. Then you realize you are as close as you have ever been to discovering some authentic unpretentious heart of France. For the Ardèche is where the French go to get back to nature, when they want to float in a kayak down unspeakably beautiful canyons or put on a backpack and walk through rugged mountains. Over the past ten years I've rowed boats on America's wild rivers and led hiking trips in the Rockies. Now, as I arrive in the Ardèche, I want to see if the "Wild West of France" lives up to its title—and to see what kinds of adventure I will find.

My visit begins in the town of Vals-les-Bains. I choose to shed my jet lag at the Hôtel de l'Europe, which is simple, clean, and moderately priced. The proprietors, Renée and Albert Mazet, couldn't be friendlier or more helpful to an unaccompanied female tourist speaking sleepy and halting French. The town is lively, especially on market day, Saturday, when the streets are closed to traffic so vendors can set up stalls selling fruits, vegetables, and an infinite variety of sausages, cheeses, handwoven scarves, cassette tapes, honey, fruit juices, jeans, and grapes of every color.

A kind of Mason-Dixon Line in the Ardèche, Vals-les-Bains marks the place where the region divides itself in half, geographically, climatically, philosophically, and spiritually. To the north, winding rivers cut narrow valleys; towns are roughly hewn out of the steep dark walls. The threat of winter seems ever-present here, where ridgetop winds are sharp and unforgiving. Catholic churches dominate every village, and crucifixes, each one depicting a more agonized Jesus, punctuate the hillsides.

In the southern Ardèche there are no crucifixes, and you can barely find the churches (which are Protestant) among all the vineyards and cafés. From Vals-les-Bains the land rolls off the south in waves every color of harvest. Chubby farmers slow traffic almost to a standstill with tractor carts full of grapes, and the smells of garlic and olive oil hang heavy in the village air. In the late afternoon sun, winter feels a lifetime away.

Because wine and garlic appeal to me more than damnation and sudden snowstorms, I decide to explore the southern villages first. Les Vans and Joyeuse, both centuries old, are poised between haphazard restoration and the simple luxuriousness of decay. The quiet beauty of these villages is startling to my American eye: a flower box full of red blossoms, the creamy tan of a windowpane against a blond stone wall, a line of laundry, each item either black or white, hanging in front of purple weeds.

The sign before the village of Largentière says, "1,000 Years of History," and a white-haired woman walking an albino Afghan hound at the town's entrance looks as if she's old enough to have seen all ten centuries. As in every Ardèchois town, a clear cold river tumbles through the center, imparting a vitality that the quiet narrow streets belie.

In spite of Largentière's age and sleepiness, I get the feeling that young people lurk behind these walls. Maybe it's the black dog wearing the red bandanna, the psychedelic tights hanging on a line. Sure enough, I round a corner to hear Van Morrison coming out of an open window. When I try to sneak a look inside, a thirtysomething Frenchman with crazy black hair and a single dreadlock hands me a stem of purple grapes through the window's iron bars.

The major tourist destination in this part of the region is the Ardèche Gorge, 1,000-foot-high white walls of granite that wrap themselves around the riverbanks for 30 miles. The river road climbs sharply up the first granite fin and stays there, allowing drivers only glimpses of the tiny green river far below—and leaving the gorge itself wild for the hundreds of hikers and kayakers that visit every year.

The access town for the gorge is Vallon-Pont-d'Arc. After the quiet 15th-century villages I've been exploring, it feels a little like honky-tonk Gatlinburg, Tennessee. There are no quality hotels in the town, but there are plenty of inexpensive beds. You can camp at countless places along the river and rent anything you want— mountain bikes, kayaks, canoes, horses—from any one of at least three dozen locations.

On the morning I arrive at the gorge there's a September nip in the air. A low clinging fog makes the idea of sitting in a plastic boat just below the waterline unappealing, so I reach for my hiking boots instead. The French build their trails the way they build their roads: why bother with switchbacks when it's shorter to go straight up? Such an attitude has some charm, but it gives little consideration to things like flash floods and erosion. In the river bends, piles of debris—fallen trees, broken canoes, lost water bottles—tell me that this quiet little river must be wild in the spring.

I climb to a point overlooking a deep meander and watch the morning mist slowly lift. One hundred feet below me, a fish jumps, and near the shore I can see water tumbling over a rock. As three kayakers paddle silently by, one opens his jacket to the sun.

Later, at a riverside café near Vallon-Pont-d'Arc, a Frenchman in a battered paddling jacket takes pains to explain to me that while the Ardèche Gorge is thought of as the Grand Canyon of the Ardèche, the Tarn Gorges in the neighboring province of Lozère are considered the Grand Canyon of all France. How could I think of coming to France without seeing its Grand Canyon?

How, indeed, I say. Bidding him farewell, I drive through the wine lands, then climb higher and higher into the ferny forests of the Cévennes. As I pass through the villages of Villefort and Pont-de-Montvert I am tempted by the warm-windowed cafés with mountain bikes parked outside, but I continue on. As the road leads out of Pont-de-Montvert and winds along the Tarn River (still just a trout stream here), I get behind a Land Cruiser that can't seem to stay on its side of the road. The driver has his whole upper torso out the window; he's leaning over, trying to see down into the gorge. The passenger has one hand on the wheel, but he can't resist looking either. Every time they meet another car the blare of a horn and French curses force them into a deep swerve.

Even before I notice the two kayaks stuffed into the vehicle's open back, I recognize this as river-rat behavior. When the road bends away from the river, I take the opportunity to pass. As I do I give them the "everything's okay" sign in kayaker language (two thumbs up) and they honk the horn and wave.

I turn away from the Tarn River onto a road that climbs ever higher, around Mont Lozère to a waterfall, Cascade de Runes. The west side of Mont Lozère was deforested long ago, leaving golden terraces of field grasses, outcroppings of white stone,

escribing the wonders of the Gorges du Verdon [located in Provence, 60 miles northwest of Cannes] in 1928, the French explorer E. A. Martel wrote: "You have to visit the Canyon at least twenty times before you can dare say that you have seen it. It is a marvel without equal in Europe, the largest, the wildest, and the most varied of the great faults in the Old World." Today you can drive along the top road with relative ease and peer over the sometimes less than substantial safety barriers, into the gaping chasm beneath. Even better for exploring the gorge is the footpath along the bottom. Beware, though: once committed there is no way out until you reach the end (about 25km/15 miles) unless you retrace your steps.

—Douglas Botting, *Wild France*

big-eyed dairy cows with bells around their necks, and endless fields of purple heather. An old woman walks up the road carrying a huge tree branch in one hand, a gold-tipped cane in the other. She screams at me as I pass, and around the corner I see why: goats, at least 50 of them, strewn about the road. I slow the car and try to inch around them, but they are as stubborn as goats can be. The woman, suddenly looking ten years younger, sprints up to my car, raises her branch high in the air, and shrieks at the goats until they part in front of me. Then she raps her cane on the hood of my car and offers a loud *"Merci."* I can see by the enthusiasm in her toothless smile that people sometimes run over her goats, or at least use their fenders to bump them out of the way.

Surrounding the area's farms and villages is the Parc National des Cévennes. Signs indicating hiking trails point into the forest, up toward the ridge lines, or between stone walls marking fields. I choose a forest path and, after a few hundred yards, I am surrounded by the softness of and utter silence of ferns and hemlocks. In three hours of walking, the quiet is broken only twice, once by a German couple and their border collie and once by a farmer and his donkey looking for all the world like Robert Louis Stevenson returning from his travels in the Cévennes.

Back in the car I wind down toward the Tarn on a road that is little more than a farmer's lane. Before long I see the multicolored sandstone and granite walls that form the Tarn Gorges. The fact is that neither the Ardèche Gorge nor the Tarn Gorges look anything like the Grand Canyon. I admit to feeling a Grand Canyon-size wonder, however, as I stand on the edge of the Tarn— the same heart stopping astonishment that arises whenever the human eye gazes into more vertical space than it can at one time comprehend. The French have given us a word for that step

I could not claim to tell you all about the Cévennes. It takes more than one trip in a car to pry into the secrets of this shy region with its reputation of witchcraft. If you stay out of the valleys and the spectacular Corniche des Cévennes, you can be overcome by loneliness on roads that dead-end in wilderness at farmhouses with the air of fortresses, many of them abandoned. There are many dirt tracks; the best way to get to know the Cévennes is on foot, or with a four-wheel-drive vehicle, or on assback, the way Robert Louis Stevenson explored the region a century and a quarter ago. It has changed little since then, or for that matter since the Protestants took refuge in its wilds after the revocation of the Edict of Nantes in 1685. They stayed. In contrast with the rest of France, you see far more of their simple temples, as they are called in French, than of Catholic churches.

—G. Y. Dryansky, "The Summer of the Cream," *Condé Nast Traveler* beyond beauty: sublime. And Point Sublime is the best place from which to grasp the majesty of the Tarn Gorges.

It is also possible to drive down into the gorge, to wind around the sides of the gray-streaked cliffs covered with weeping pines and hemlocks. The stone houses built into the cliff sides are so old and permanent it is hard to tell where the rock ends and the walls of houses begin.

I stay that evening in the canyon at the Château de la Caze, a fairy-tale castle beyond my wildest imagination, converted into a four-star hostelry (but due to close). The rooms have names, not numbers, and the woman in charge does not take too kindly to my arriving alone, after dark, and wearing sneakers. You pay a price for a stay in a fairy tale, not only with money (the château was my most expensive hotel on this trip) but also with having to bear the snootiness of Madame and her sidekick, the mangiest German shepherd I've ever seen. However, it is worth both the money and the snootiness to tread stone passageways worn smooth by 500 years of secrets, to throw open the doors on a turreted balcony and imagine armored suitors on the lawn, to climb into a canopy bed wrapped in lace older than I am, to pretend across cultures and centuries.

The next morning I head back toward the Ardèche via the high road, which travels along the Corniche des Cévennes and affords a beautiful view of the entire region. Stopping at an overlook, I walk out to a point. The altitude is nearly 5,000 feet and the bite in the air carries more than a hint of winter. A man in a tweed jacket with heather gathered in his arms meets me on the trail.

"*Bonjour, madame,*" he says. "*Il fait froid ici.*"

"*Oui,*" I say, "*Il fois.*"

He smiles and walks on. Later, I return to my car to find a small bunch of heather stuck under my windshield wiper. This is what's so beguiling about the French: one minute they're disapproving of your sneakers, the next they're offering you grapes or heather.

Back in the Ardèche Valley, cold weather has brought on a flurry of activity. Farmers and their dogs are moving sheep down the hillsides; men hauling loads of grapes seem to have shifted into a higher tractor gear. I spend the afternoon moving from wine cave to wine cave, sampling what the local vineyards have to offer (some reasonable Cabernets, at least one excellent Merlot). Then I leave the wine country behind to climb, for what feels like hours, into the northern Ardèche.

It is dark by the time I arrive at the Hôtel du Midi in Lamastre, and I'm tired and road-weary, ready to stay put for a few days, to be taken care of. The Hôtel du Midi has bright window boxes and cheery yellow paint, and a chef, Bernard Perrier, described as the region's best. But it is Bernard's wife, Marie-George, with her instant warmth and generosity, who lets me know I've come to spend these last few days in France at the right place.

"Have you an elevator?" I ask Pascal, one of the two handsome waiter/bellhops.

"No," he says, grinning, "you have me, and I am very strong."

"Very well," I say. *"Allons-y."*

The room is elegant and rustic at once, sparsely furnished with antiques: a cherrywood desk with curved legs, a handworked lace bedspread, a shiny brass lamp. The bathroom is bigger than any hotel room I've had so far; in the center is the largest tub I've ever seen. In my mind, I'm already in it. Then Pascal asks if I would like a table at eight.

"Eight-thirty, please."

"Merci," he says, and then, in heavily accented English with a faint California twang, "See ya later."

I am charmed beyond responding. It is the first English I've heard in seven days.

Bernard Perrier's cuisine is, quite simply, the best I've had in my life. After the first evening I don't even look at the menu. Marie-George chooses my course, explaining everything in a combination of French and sign language that includes buzzing slender hands around her head to indicate honey and making horns or floppy ears to differentiate between beef and lamb.

I spend four of the most wonderful days of my life in Marie-George's care. At breakfast she teaches me the French names of the flowers she's arranging for my room; when I take my after-dinner walks she won't let me go without an umbrella.

Every morning I set out into the wild countryside that surrounds Lamastre. I hike trails that follow along the ridgelines and rivers, that connect the villages and peaks. Banks of sunshine and clouds move quickly through these mountains, and there is nearly always a rainbow. In the summer, they tell me, it's hard to find a cloud in the sky, but these days the fog pours over the mountains like running water. I gleefully get wet and cold and dirty, knowing that what awaits me at dusk is Bernard's cooking, an hour-long soak in my tub, and Marie-George's feather pillows. I feel as if I am approaching some ultimate definition of the word "vacation."

On my last full day in the Ardèche, I decide to climb Mont Mézenc, the highest peak in the region. From its summit I can see a hillside of sub-alpine firs stretching down to the terraced tablelands, then the scattered villages of the Haut Vivarais, and beyond that the river gorges of the Eysse, the Dorne, and the Eyrieux, and the town of St-

We stayed in a nice little inn next to a mill in Vannes. The inn was made up of two buildings separated by a road, with the office in one, and rooms and dining area in the other. When we checked in, the proprietress struck us as a bit odd, as though she had to work hard at being hospitable.

Our feelings were confirmed the next morning when we walked into the dining room and she barked "What do you want?" I began to bristle, but Wenda, of better temperament, simply said, "Good morning." Our hostess was immediately chagrined, blushing and apologetic, and we started the morning afresh. Dressed in a business outfit, she took our orders, then put on an apron, and proceeded to make breakfast. The phone rang, and off flew the apron, and she ran across the street, pulling on a jacket as she went into the office. Out she came again to put on the apron and serve breakfast, back she dashed to be behind her desk when a car pulled into the parking lot.

Later, when we found her on hands and knees cleaning our rooms, we realized that she was simply unsuited to wearing so many hats in one day. We left feeling quite fond of her.

—James O'Reilly,
"On and Off the *Autoroute*"

Agrève on the horizon. To the south the Cévennes stretch end-lessly: Mont Lozère, where I was only a few days ago, forested hills and pastured valleys, stone farmhouses clinging here and there to hillsides that catch the intermittent sun. Far to the east lies the edge of the high plateau that is the wine country of the Rhône. Beyond the Rhône rise the foothills of the Alps, and beyond them is Mont Blanc, almost three times higher than where I am standing now. Since the clouds have it surrounded, I can only see its base.

They say one goes to France to fall in love, and I did, first with Pascal's devilish wit, then with Bernard Perrier's food, and finally with the kindness of Marie-George, a kindness that broke the language barrier without compromising her professionalism, that made me feel more at home than I ever had abroad. By the time I had fallen in love with the Hôtel du Midi, I also loved Lamastre, the way it clings to the hillside like a sad and intelligent child.

As I climbed those craggy hills for the last time, past the dying vegetable gardens and herds of goats that had so quickly become familiar, I was flooded by a melancholy way out of proportion for a ten-day holiday. Shortly after that, I got in my car and crested the hill that would take me out of the Ardèche, down to the flatland, the highway, the airport, and eventually home. I realized that in the time I'd been in the Ardèche the leaves on the trees had gone completely yellow; summer had turned to fall. I pulled over for a last look across the green valleys. Only when the sun went behind a cloud and the rain began was I able to leave.

Pam Houston is an outdoorswoman and writer who lives in Oakland, California. Her work appears in major American magazines and she is the author of Cowboys Are My Weakness, Waltzing the Cat, *and* A Little More About Me.

✳

The entire region [the Cévennes] is in what was known historically as the Languedoc, whose local dialect, similar to Provençal, produced its own considerable literature—analyzed in a fascinating book by Emmanuel Le Roy Ladurie called *Love, Death, and Money in the Pays D'Oc.* It is the kind of place that has no flat land at all. Village after village is located underneath some steep valley floor next to a fast-flowing stream, surrounded by profuse vegetation. Grapes and wisteria vines overflow their trellises. It is a damp and, in the summer even steamy place, a haven for butterflies, dragonflies, lizards, centipedes, grasshoppers, flies, and small scorpions that, I was told, are relatively harmless. The sound of water flowing is never far off, behind a row of houses, alongside the road, trickling through the rocky meadows. Roads all curve crazily as they make their way up and down the hills, running past narrow, semicircular terraces that are buttressed by millions of stone ramparts, a testimony to the hard labor of years past. Everywhere there are views of valleys flowing between successions of green hills, and in the early morning and evening, they are shrouded in mysterious blue mists. Many of the village houses are large and square and imposing but show signs of dilapidation, suggesting that the families living inside them had once been wealthy but have since fallen on harder times, or moved away altogether, leaving the old homestead of the valleys to the mercy of the rain and the wind.

—Richard Bernstein, *Fragile Glory: A Portrait of France and the French*

Confessions in
Fractured French

*The unspeakable suffering of the inarticulate
is showcased in Paris.*

As we approach Orly airport on my first visit to Paris, I look out the window at all the little houses and cars filled with people and am struck by a sobering reality.

All those people speak French.

And I don't.

In fact, except for a few trips to Mexican resort areas—where it's easy to get by with no more Spanish than *margarita* and *gracias*—this is to be my first time in a place where I have no language.

I did my best to bone up before leaving home. I practiced the basics of courtesy: *merci, s'il vous plaît, bonjour.* I bought a Berlitz phrase book and a lively little workbook titled *Survival French,* published by Langenscheidt. The premise of the latter is that the TV generation needs more than words to learn a language. It needs cartoons, fill-in-the-blanks, and crossword puzzles.

A reasonable premise. And I did learn something from the book. The night before the trip, I awakened in the middle of the night.

"Le beurre!" I thought. *"Le beurre, le beurre, le beurre, le beurre, le beurre."*

That's, "The butter! The butter, the butter, the butter, the butter."

That should prove useful.

But now there is no more time for preparation. I've checked into my Paris hotel, and my first opportunity to experiment with the language arrives when a bellman brings a package to my room.

"*Gracias*," I say.

Then I shut the door and beat myself about the head and shoulders.

I have a tremendous inferiority complex about my lack of a second language. The French, I think, encourage that. Personally, I think they're just mad because English has eclipsed French as the international language.

Why is it that when a French person speaks English with a French accent, we find it charming, but when an American speaks French with an American accent, they sneer?

After all, we don't have television shows teaching us French, as they do English. On my first morning in Paris, I see one produced by the British Broadcasting Co. Sentence of the day is, "I have a new jacket."

Surely all over the city that day, people were exchanging those friendly words.

"*Bonjour, François.* I have a new jacket."

"*Bonjour Françoise et Gabrielle. Le beurre.*"

She suggested we watch TV and go to the movies to help our comprehension, but for me, one of the best places to practice was at a playground. The imperatives called out by mothers to young children, the simple explanations, often repeated like instant replay, the basic vocabularies of eating and the temperature and the time and coming and going— all these gave me an exaggerated sense of being able to understand.

—Kay Eldredge,
"How to Make the Most of Your Speaking Engagements,"
European Travel & Life

Phrase book tucked in my purse (it wouldn't do to be seen with it), I venture into the streets of Paris where the first order of business is changing money. I carefully memorized the appropriate phrase.

But while the Berlitz phrase book is extremely helpful, it can only tell you what to say, not what other people say in response.

I have an additional issue: my parents, having lived in Paris at one time, spoke French to one another throughout my childhood. While I did not learn the language, it is my good or poor fortune to have picked up a fairly convincing accent.

This does not work to my benefit when I approach a bank teller and carefully pronounce my memorized sentence. Instead of producing francs for my traveler's checks, she answers with a barrage of French.

When I make the teller understand that I don't really speak French, she very helpfully continues speaking French, only louder and slower.

Finally, with gestures, she directs me upstairs to speak with someone else. For reasons that remain obscure, I am sent to a very cluttered desk behind which a man is barking French into a telephone.

It's funny about French—no matter what the subject matter, the language sounds like poetry. It almost makes me want to stay French illiterate. As it is, I can walk down the street and it sounds as though everyone is cooing words of love to each other. Behind all the rich vowels and rolled Rs, though, they're probably saying, "My feet hurt" and "Liver, again?"

At any rate, the man on the phone is obviously having a love affair too tempestuous to interrupt, and I finally give up on him and move on to another bank where my little phrase brings the desired results. Then I do the tourist thing—the Arc de Triomphe, the Champs-Elysées. You know.

I enjoy the fact that in my wanderings a couple of people approach me and speak Italian. I don't understand a word, but it makes me feel European.

Stopping at a café on the ritzy boulevard Saint Germain, I am pegged as an American by the waiter after I respond to his welcoming French with an uncomprehending blush. *"Anglaise?"* he asks.

When it is time to take my order, respectful of my deficiency, he puts his ear close to my mouth and, in the most gentle way he can manage, says, "Tell me."

I have been silently rehearsing and manage to say *"Croque-monsieur et café au lait, s'il vous plaît."* (That's a ham and cheese sandwich and coffee with milk, please—but it sounds better the other way, doesn't it?)

I was doing my usual shuffle, trying to convey something in French to a horrified merchant, when my daughter Anna, then eight years old, took me aside and advised, "Daddy, you need a lot of spit in your mouth to speak French." Alas, my drooling has only caused more problems.

—James O'Reilly,
"Troglodytes in Gaul"

Of course, it's considered gauche to drink *café au lait* in the afternoon, but I don't learn that until later.

As I eat, a delivery man comes in and tries to pick me up in Italian—geez, are all dark-haired people immediately assumed to be Italian?—which makes me feel much less a clumsy American for a minute.

While for much of the trip I am with friends who are more adept at the language than I am, I also find little ways of avoiding run-ins with French. Limiting, perhaps, but face-saving.

I don't order anything in a restaurant unless I already know what it is. (Menu translator books are useful.) I don't ask many questions.

Riding the Métro, I give the stations nicknames that I can easily remember. Pigalle, for example, becomes Pighead to me and Simplon becomes Simpleton. Not pretty, but they serve a purpose.

And though my phrase book contains an English-to-French dictionary, next time I will bring a French-to-English dictionary, which I think would prove equally, if not more, useful.

Eventually, I take a train to Spain, leaving my troubles with French behind. When the Spanish conductor checks my ticket, I know my manners.

"*Gracias,*" I say.

"*Merci,*" he responds.

Sophia Dembling was born and raised in New York City, but at age nine-teen discovered life west of the Hudson. She is a freelance writer who lives in Dallas and is the former assistant travel editor of The Dallas Morning News.

★

As a student in Paris some time ago, I found myself late one afternoon in the middle of a bemused crowd of Parisians at the information counter of the big department store B.H.V. I was asking where I could buy an item that I was calling a "*port-FOY,*" by which I meant a wallet—not that I had much money in those days to put into it.

"*Port-FOY? Port-FOY?*" the woman at the counter repeated with dis-taste. "*Oui, madame,*" I said shyly. "*Ou sont les port-FOY?*" The woman re-fused to understand. The room seemed to grow dark, the snickering crowd to deepen.

Finally, the hateful creature brightened and turned to the assembled native French speakers. "*Et bien,* he means *port-e-FOY,*" she said, inserting a hitherto undiscovered syllable into the middle of the word. "Third floor, monsieur."

A writer friend in Paris tells me that the most humiliating thing in the world for an adult is to take up a new sport. No, I reply, nothing can be more humiliating than being a beginner in French in Paris.

—Richard Bernstein, "Gallic Gall," *New York Times*

The Loire on Wheels

The best way to see France may be on a bicycle.

TO MY MIND, THERE ARE TWO KINDS OF ADVENTURER: THE ONE who jumps at the chance to save a rain forest, happily sweating it out for weeks in a flea-infested tent; and the one who goes on cushier safaris. The first scales K2; the second scrambles up the Spanish steps. One thrives on Indiana Jones-style survival tests; the other prefers to have his or her danger meted out in daily self-prescribed doses.

Adventure is, after all, where you find it, an attitude as much as an experience. And for adventures of the gentler sort—the kind where you come eye to eye with moo-cows instead of cobras—the back roads of France's Loire Valley are unparalleled. Twists of fate come about as often as twists in the road; potential disasters have a way of turning into happy accidents. The middle ground here between leaky tents and over-upholstered tour buses is a bicycle: on it you're a kid with all the advantages of being grown-up.

The Tour de France wasn't invented for nothing. The French love bikes—and you, if you're on one. Our tour guide found herself screeching to a halt one day because an old lady, arms thrown out, stepped into her path. The woman didn't want to chide her

223

for going too fast or for riding on a private road; she wanted to kiss her on both cheeks. (What is adventure if not almost running down an old lady, only to discover that she loves you?)

Within the realms of cycling, there are various levels of comfort. If you are hardy, you can pack your own gear on your own bike and chart your own course. But if you are savvy, you will let someone else do all that for you, couching adventure in comfort, which is what I did.

Our group—a healthy-looking lot whose ages range from early twenties to late fifties—is friendly and only slightly shy. The majority seems to be from California, Colorado, and Canada, and professional: doctors, lawyers, financial analysts and such. Two couples are traveling together, a mother and daughter are celebrating the latter's college graduation and, along with several other couples, there is a healthy single contingent, mainly women.

Shaking hands and starting conversations, we file out to the bus that will take us to our first hotel. An hour later, the bus turns into the long, tree-fringed drive of the Château de la' Menaudière, which comes complete with moat, gatehouse, tower-climbing roses and a history that dates to 1443. The trip is scheduled so that we stay in four different château-hotels for two nights each, cycling out from and back to one on the first day. In our wake runs a van, which transports luggage from hotel to hotel—and occasionally people, too.

Some of the group adopt the cyclist mentality immediately: they show up for orientation in sleek long biking shorts and jerseys, helmets in hand. Others dress more tentatively, in regular shorts or sweatpants, padded fingerless

The Loire Valley, beginning near Orléans and extending roughly to the Loire's mouth on the Atlantic, is a magical world unto itself. It is saturated with history and consequently overloaded with the machinery of tourism, but that shouldn't dissuade you from venturing there. Whether you drive, walk, balloon, or cycle, a meander through the Loire Valley and its treasures will only disappoint someone who shouldn't be traveling in the first place.

—James O'Reilly,
"On and Off the Autoroute*"*

gloves tucked discreetly in pockets. Our guide Heather—thirtysomething, blond, Canadian—gives everyone maps and route instructions, along with water bottles. She speaks some French, but cycling is her expertise; she used to race. Now she spends summers as a guide and in the winter puts her Ph.D. to use teaching Gaelic literature at the University of Toronto. Then we all go down to the stables-cum-garage, where our bikes stand shining in a row, bearing bright red name tags. I find mine, a silver 12-speed racer, and get my first lesson in putting air in tires from David, our other guide. He, also Canadian, is the language expert, although he looks at home on a cycle as well. As other people adjust their seats and try on their helmets, my impatience grows—it's a beautiful afternoon, and I don't want to waste a minute. Seeing a couple of people take off for the short test run that's been charted for the remainder of the day, I cautiously slip my foot into the toe clip and push off after them.

The "gentle incline" up the long driveway of the Menaudière is not so gentle. As I catch up with the upstarts, I am happy to see that I am not the only one huffing and puffing. But turning onto the road is a reward. The terrain is fairly flat, there's little traffic, and flowers I usually see only in the florist's shop nod in the breeze along the roadside. I had worried that the aerobics classes and miles logged on the stationary bike at my health club wouldn't be enough preparation for this trip. But the four of us manage to pedal at about the same pace, and I decide I am where I belong, in the ranks of the semi-fit. A couple of miles out, we begin to exchange bits of conversation, and it doesn't take long to discover a fact that sends us wobbling in fits of giggles. Every member of this, the jump-start club, is from New York. Typically impatient, we all shoved off according to some instinctive make-haste mechanism and wound up together. The next discovery halts our progress entirely: two of the women learn that they are not only both from New York, they live *across the street* from each other. Their daughters are close to the same ages, went to the same prep school and even the same college; they have friends in common. Never once at the greengrocer's or the dry cleaner's or parent-teacher meetings

have they encountered one another. Only here, on a deserted back
road in France.

On Thursday, our first full day of cycling, a private guide meets
us after we bike the two hours from the Menaudière to Amboise,
a town on the Loire with a château where Leonardo da Vinci is
buried. Isabelle, our guide, is an art historian with a pretty accent
and a fondness for quirks of language. In the course of describing
the château's architecture and furnishings, she makes quick and
colorful departures to explain the curious origins of words like
"tennis" and "budget," and incorporates a mini lecture on the rise
and fall of the bath's popularity in France.

That afternoon, after two hours biking from Amboise, she
meets us at Chenonceau, a castle that straddles the Cher River.
This is perhaps the valley's most famous château, and certainly
one of its prettiest. Formal gardens of pink and crimson roses border the river and the castle, an almost perfect example of French
Renaissance architecture. It takes overhearing only snatches of
other tours for us to realize that we are getting a far more interesting, elaborate one. Others around us realize it, too: 20 minutes
into the tour, the size of our group has doubled. Curious listen-
ers discreetly tag along to hear the lovely Isabelle explain how
Catherine de Médicis got the upper hand of her husband's
mistress.

After this day of château-touring, activities are less structured
and the group tends to splinter. At least one of our guides is at
breakfast every morning to discuss the day's route, give alternatives
and help with any problems and questions about the bicycles. The
suggested activities are optional, and it soon becomes apparent that
you cannot see all the châteaus, visit all the wine *caves*, meander
through every charming town and take every detour to an interesting landmark. But a pattern quickly establishes itself—one that
runs, appropriately, in cycles. Simply put, it is: eat and bike, bike
and eat. And drink. Vintners large and small post roadside signs offering tours and tastings—*dégustations*—of the local goods. Some
of us bike from town to town, searching out tiny antique shops or
the café with the best *crème*, espresso laced with frothy steaming

milk. Others go from *cave* to *cave*, tasting their way through the valley and returning to the hotel most nights with bottles anchored by bungee cords to the backs of their bikes. Still others go from château to château, immersing themselves in architecture and history. The only requirement is to show up for dinner each evening.

Lunch we find on our own—mercifully, as it turns out, because dinners are so elaborate that a midday picnic or light café meal is all you want. On the second day out, I find myself biking with Katie, a nurse from Denver who has taken this trip to celebrate her 40th birthday. Second amazing coincidence: we discover that her grandparents lived for more than forty years in the tiny southern town where I grew up—a place at the top of the Truly Obscure list. There is just enough difference in our ages to have kept us from ever meeting, but our cast of characters is the same, and we swap stories all week long.

> *In all, François I [who built Chambord, the largest of the Loire châteaus] would spend 42 days here. Taking account of the time in residence of all of its owners, Chambord has been occupied no more than twenty of its 464 years.*
>
> —Gail Russell Chaddock, "Linger in the Châteaux of the Loire," *Christian Science Monitor*

We opt for an alternative route, slightly longer but more scenic. Eventually, it takes us up a series of hills that, under the noontime sun, are no easy climb. But when we get to the top, the road narrows to a paved path and we coast into vast stretches of vineyards. Under the June sun, the pale green leaves are deepening in hue and beginning to curl around their stubby black-brown vines. The sky is the saturated blue of cornflowers, ornamented only with wisps of cloud that feather across the sky from a single point on the horizon.

By the time we ride down into Vouvray, a little town famous for its white wine, we are famished. Steering through the narrow, cobbled streets, we head for a café in the middle of town that's doing a bustling business. What better recommendation than the patronage of the locals? And it seems casual enough for the biking shorts and t-shirts we are wearing.

Casual it is. Innocents abroad, we walk past the bar and into the café—clearly the point of no return—and the roar of conversation abruptly halts. For a full five seconds, there is absolute silence as we stare at fifty-odd French truck drivers, who look back at us as if we've fallen from Mars. The sinking feeling of knowing we are in absolutely the wrong place overcomes our gnawing hunger. How could we have known it was a truck stop?

There is nothing to do but smile politely and walk all the way to the back of the café, where a single table is unoccupied. As conversations slowly resume, our waitress—the only other woman in the place—explains that there is no menu; just the French equivalent of a blue-plate special. Fine, we nod, secretly pleased. Out comes a long basket of crusty bread. The meal that follows is soul food: after the salad, a big plate of mashed potatoes and a delicious pork cutlet come smothered in a light, creamy sauce. Then the cheese course arrives: chèvre, Port-Salut, Brie and several other unidentifiable but heavenly cheeses, all arranged on a huge plate passed from table to table. We eat everything. The waitress can't understand why we don't want dessert, since it's included. Simple, delicious, it is one of the best meals of the trip—certainly the cheapest, and the most fun. The truckers smile with barely concealed curiosity, but, if a little amused, they are studiously polite. (One ambitious fellow unbuttons his shirt a couple of buttons and glances over hopefully, but we are devoted to our mashed potatoes, and he takes the hint gracefully.) By the time we finish our meal and leave, it is clear that we have made their day, as they have ours: the episode is the hit story at dinner.

But there is a long way to go before dinner. This is one of the most demanding days on the bike, and after a couple of hours we begin to tire. By late afternoon, the promise of a swimming pool at our new hotel is beckoning.

Just outside Fondettes, coasting down a small hill, I hear a mysterious, slightly sinister *ssshhh*. With the trepidation of an inexperienced and untalented mechanic, I reason that if I ignore the sound, it will (please, God) go away. But all that goes is the air in my front tire. We wheel the bike over to a house on the roadside that, in the midst of the surrounding vineyards, is the only evidence of civilization and the only possible thing to lean the bike against. Katie knows about as much as I do about changing flats; after we work for ten minutes (mainly locating and identifying components of the tire-changing kit), a car pulls up to the house and a small, sandy-haired woman carrying a bag of groceries goes inside. A few minutes later she reappears, smiling sympathetically. "Do you need help, or would you like a glass of juice?" She asks in French. "My husband is a mechanic and he could easily fix the tire. I'll send my daughter for him at work."

But at this point, there is actually hope in sight. "No, no," we answer in our best fractured French, smiling cheerfully. "Please don't bother, it's almost done, and we're fine..." She smiles and nods, goes back inside, but reappears after five minutes, when we are pumping air into our project. "You must be hot and tired. At least come in to wash your hands and have some juice. I insist." Gratefully, we nod and follow her—we *are* hot and thirsty, and it seems rude to refuse.

Seating us in the kitchen, a small room in a modest house, she introduces herself and her daughter, who looks more like a younger sister. She pours our juice and, instead of filling the glasses with ice cubes, empties the ice trays into a delicate blue bowl that she carefully sets on the table with a silver spoon. It's a genuinely hospitable gesture, one that seems particularly sweet-spirited in a room where dishes are in the sink, groceries are on the counter and diapers dry on a portable clothesline. We talk, exchanging histories that seem equally exotic to one another. Then the five-and-a-half-month-old baby, Charlie, a charmer with big brown eyes and dimples, is brought in by his big sister, who shyly but proudly introduces him. He seems taken with the bright colors of our fingerless gloves and gurgles happily in my lap while we finish our juice.

Just as we're getting ready to leave, the husband arrives home from work and comes out with us to inspect the newly changed tire. We stare in dismay; it is now as flat as the first. The new inner tube, he surmises, must have been *pas bon*. The whole process is begun again, this time with Katie's spare and the master mechanic in charge. He changes the tire in a quarter the time it took us and then insists that we come back to the garage to see his bike, a single-gear one with sew-ups—expensive tires with silk inner tubes that are more resistant to flats. Of course, Frenchman that he is, he races bikes. After a serious discussion of gears, brakes, frames and—of course—tires, we all shake hands and part comrades. Charlie blows us a kiss and we ride away, yelling good-byes and thank-yous, turning around again and again to wave until they are pin-dot-size, then finally lost behind a hill.

On Sunday, several of us meet after lunch in Ussé, a town with the château that inspired Sleeping Beauty's castle. Coasting down the long, straight road that leads across the Indre River and right up to the château only increases its fairytale charm; cycling to it allows you time to just stare, pleased that there are things in real life that look like things in picture books. We catch a tour and then head out on the fifteen-mile stretch to Bourgueil, the town closest to our next hotel and famous for red wine.

Although we set out in a group of ten or twelve, several people press ahead, others fall behind. We decide to rendezvous in town to find a *cave* that will give a tasting. I wind up with Judy, an advertising executive, and when we finally reach Bourgueil there is no sign of David, the appointed tasting coordinator. But there does seem to be a lot of activity for a late Sunday afternoon in a country town. Streets are barricaded, and the lilting toot-toot music of carousels grows louder as we approach.

It is, we discover, the final hour of the *Festival International de la Musique Mécanique*, a weekend-long event that has brought 60 instruments—huge calliopes that once belonged to circuses, hand organs with singing operators, oversize music boxes and player-piano contraptions run by old couples dressed in vaudeville costumes. They line the steep streets, each playing a variant of the same merry-go-round music. Many spectators are costumed as well: two couples in Twenties attire do a modified Charleston in the street; children in haphazard getups stand transfixed before a calliope with a stage and wooden figures that dance a minuet to the music. We are transfixed, too. The pale, diffused sunlight reflects softly the vanilla-pudding color of the buildings, and church bells chime in dissonance.

Parents and grandparents stroll by, pushing carriages or carrying toddlers on their shoulders. Three elderly ladies, their cardigans buttoned at the neck, gather around a piece of sheet music held level with their bifocals and sing with the force and conviction of those who have had elocution lessons early in life. When the watery vibrato of their voices dies away with the music, the crowd that has amassed claps enthusiastically and they nod in acknowledgement, very dignified but pleased and suddenly a little embarrassed. Then the grand calliopes, large as tigers' cages, are disassembled. We hop on our bikes, humming, and head for the hotel.

C ycling is delightfully easy along the Loire and Loire valleys, and you probably won't lose any weight while you're riding here—the food and wine are just too good. Nearly every town offers its own wine, and several renowned regional wines accompany a wide variety of French dishes.

—Karen and Terry Whitehill,
France By Bike: 14 Tours Geared for Discovery

As we wheel down the gravel drive of the Château des Réaux, Florence de Bouillé, the resident *châtelaine,* walks out to greet us, holding her overfriendly, overlarge dog at bay. Although a little simpler than our other hotels, this place, with red-and-white checkerboard towers and a miniature moat, turns out to be my favorite. Florence runs the hotel in a brisk, friendly fashion with her husband, Jean-Luc. This château has been in her family for more than a century, passed daughter-to-daughter from her great-grandmother on down. Family portraits and photographs are grouped on the walls of the dining and drawing rooms. The guest rooms, each quite different from any other, are decorated with originality and charm.

The eating part of the car-and-bike mode reaches an all-time high here: dinner is a raucous affair fueled by delicious white asparagus, delicate medallions of poached *lotte,* and of course plenty of good Bourgueil and Sancerre. After five days together, friend-

ships nurtured by shared experience and odd coincidence are beginning to take root. Discussions get deeper, jokes get more
risqué—and funny—and we slip into a camaraderie that is as comfortable as a favorite old workshirt. After dinner, several of us
gather around the grand piano to play, sing and clown; downstairs,
a doctor-turned-pool-shark gives lessons in billiards.

On the day we push on to our new hotel, Le Prieuré, for the
last leg of the trip, several of us meet for lunch in Fontevraud, a
tiny village that holds one of the oldest monasteries in France. Our
destination is Saumur, a city stretching between the Loire and
Thouet Rivers, that will take an afternoon of serious cycling to
reach. After getting well-meant but incorrect directions from a
house painter, we breeze down the very steep, very long hill out of
town that we had climbed arduously to get to lunch. Finally, when
none of the map markings or route directions match up with what
we're cycling past, we realize that the road we want is behind us,
at the top of the hill. The decision is unanimous: no way are we
going back up, so instead we set off on a narrow road of gentle un-
dulations that looks as if it goes more or less to Saumur. An old
windmill marked on the map helps us get our bearings, and farmhouses with sprawling yards anchored at each corner by shade trees
soon give way to open fields. The terrain becomes very steep and
difficult to negotiate. It goes on and on, curve after curve, hill after
hill, each one harder to push up than the last.

Finally, sweat pouring off our faces, we reach level ground. Here,
up high, you can see for miles: faraway villages nestle in the crooks
of hills; thousands of vermillion poppies make exclamation points
against fields of pale green grass; newborn grapes peek from beneath leafy canopies in vineyards. It is the perfect country scene of
art naïf painting. We stop, gasping from the loveliness as well as from
our collapsed lungs, and silently agree: this place, this moment, is
why we came on the trip—to feel this removed from the hassles of
everyday life, to see something this beautiful, to find it where we
never intended to go in the first place. Cameras come out to commemorate the moment; heavy gray clouds roll in above us, inten-
sifying the colors and providing welcome relief from the sun.

Setting off again, a couple of us move ahead in our enthusiasm, while others cycle at a more leisurely pace, unwilling to leave the surroundings so quickly. After a while, the threat of the clouds is confirmed by claps of thunder. Kathy, my riding buddy, and I pedal harder, and after fifteen minutes the sky above appears lighter than the heavy charcoal-colored one behind us. "I think we beat it," she says proudly. I agree, and we continue at a less frantic pace, pleased with our prowess.

The joke is on us. Moments later, the first drops fall—huge, heavy raindrops that dot my face and arms, splash into my hair and after a few minutes run down it in rivulets. We begin to laugh from the sheer pleasure of the sensation and, with no one else around to hear, sing all the songs about rain we know, from "Itsy Bitsy Spider" to "Singin' in the Rain," loudly and off-key. After all, we haven't *really* gotten rained on yet. Isn't that a part of the adventure?

It is. Slowly the drizzle turns to downpour, and then the sky dumps its entire contents on us in such a rage that I can't even see Kathy's lemon-yellow shirt only twenty yards in front of me. The roar of the storm is deafening; I can barely hear her yelling, then I lose track of her entirely.

I did not know it could rain this hard—stinging needles that prick through your clothes to your skin and then pummel your muscles. There is nowhere to take cover (not that I can see, anyway), so I keep slogging on. Finally we find each other and take refuge beneath a big oak tree not far from the Saumur city limits. The storm slowly lets up to a mere downpour. We are soaked completely through—squishy shoes, puddles in the bike bags, the works. And we are shivering. There is so much water gushing down the sides of the road that there is no place to ride but the middle—not such a good idea, since our brakes are wet and all but useless. Soggily, we trudge toward town. It is cold, we are exhausted, but we can't stop laughing at the absurdity of the situation. We don't know where we are, we don't know what has hit us. We certainly don't know how to outrun a rainstorm. A phrase from a brochure that I had looked at askance several weeks earlier pops into my head, like the closing sentence of an Aesop fable: "Getting lost is part of the adventure." It is the happiest moment of the week.

Now, when people hear I've been on a bike trip through the Loire Valley, they almost always ask what my favorite part was, and usually guess at the answer before I can get a word out. Was it seeing all the châteaus? Staying in the great hotels? The incredible food? The wine? I assure them that it all was wonderful. But when I try to explain that my most cherished moments were walking into a truck stop by mistake, getting a flat tire in the middle of nowhere, and taking a wrong turn, only to get lost and drenched in a downpour, they look puzzled and a little put off.

But one friend understands exactly: she spent last summer sleeping in a flea-infested tent, saving a rain forest.

Rosemary Ellis is a former senior editor at Travel & Leisure *who lives in New York.*

★

Probably the most dangerous driver in the world is the hungry provincial Frenchman on his way home to lunch. They will scream past you with inches to spare and a hundred meters further on slam on the brakes, swerve into their driveway and stop. I try not to be on the roads during the half hour after the town siren sounds for lunch.

—Rex Grizell, *A White House in Gascony: Escape to the Old French South*

DAVID ROBERTS

Stones of Carnac

A neolithic site in southwestern Brittany
makes Stonehenge pale by comparison.

As I walked down the country lane toward the old château, cuckoos cried from the pine trees overhead. On either side thickets of gorse blazed yellow in their April bloom. I came to an unmanned guardhouse: inside, a hand-lettered sign asked me to drop three francs in the box and take key and flashlight. From the guardhouse I followed a path across a carpet of pine needles, coming to a clearing. No one else was around.

Before me loomed a grassy mound, in the side of which I found a portal framed by granite blocks, sealed with a makeshift wooden door. I turned the key in the lock, swung the door open and, stooping slightly, left the sunny warmth behind and moved into a dank tunnel. After I could see by the wan beam of the flashlight, I edged my way along a twenty-foot corridor of granite. Great slabs planted upright formed the walls, the gaps chinked with stones, while even-greater slabs laid flat overhead composed the ceiling. At the end of the tunnel, I entered a square chamber in which I could stand upright. My light played on a dim design engraved on one of the walls—a face, perhaps, or a figurine, or a shield?

It was a strange place, at once gloomy and serene. I felt the exultation of a pilgrim, for I was standing inside the passage grave of

Kercado, near the town of Carnac on the southwest coast of Brittany. (Those curious structures, long corridors leading to burial chambers and then mounded over, were forgotten for thousands of years.) My mind danced with a startling thought: *This is a structure that was almost 5,000 years old when Christ was born.*

The next day, a few miles to the east, I sat on a patch of heath and pondered the gigantic object in front of me. Shattered into four clean blocks by some enormous force, the wreckage of a giant pillar that once measured 67 feet and weighed close to 340 tons lay shrouded in the enigma of its collapse. The top three pieces rested neatly end-to-end, but the mammoth base had flipped and twisted so that it pointed at an angle. Had lightning struck this great monument, or an earthquake toppled it? Or did it fall and break as its builders struggled to lift it upright?

Whatever the case, the Grand Menhir Brisé—sometimes called the "Fairy Stone"—is by a considerable margin the largest stone ever quarried and moved in ancient Europe.

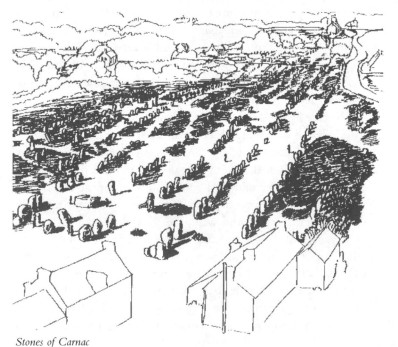

Stones of Carnac

When one speaks of megaliths—"great stones," from the Greek—most people think first and foremost of Stonehenge. Yet in that stunning edifice on the Salisbury Plain, the loftiest pillar is only 29 feet in height, the heaviest some 50 tons. The first scratchings at Stonehenge are younger than Kercado by more than 2,000 years. Some 80 stones make up that most famous megalithic monument in the world; in the vicinity of Carnac, there are more than 4,000.

To put it simply, Carnac's megaliths are the most impressive in the Western world. Two centuries of poking among the Breton fields and forests have unearthed a rich collection of facts and artifacts, but the conundrum of their meaning persists. In the words of Evan Hadingham, a British writer and archaeologist who has done research at Carnac, "It's one of archaeology's most enduring mysteries. I think it poses as many tantalizing unanswered questions as the pyramids."

Around Carnac lie scores of ancient tombs—some, such as Kercado, still buried in the mounds of earth and stone that were heaped up to enclose them, others denuded of cover so that their massive walls and capstones look like the playhouses of giant children whose building blocks were granite. Seemingly at random, the moors and woods are scattered with hundreds of isolated menhirs—in Breton, "long

The dolmens at Locmariaquer are tombs. It was a little jolting to find the principal ones fenced in, in the middle of town, and up an alley. But the Dolmen des Pierres Plates are out on the beach, nearly washed by waves. You can make your way inside, bent over with a flashlight, to see the inscriptions in the granite: a human face, a set of human ribs, the torso of the nine-breasted mother goddess. When I reached the burial room, I came upon a young guide holding a wooden pendulum, which kept twirling, to the astonishment of the two young women he'd guided there. He claimed that there were waves of energy in the radioactive granite that set the pendulum twirling. If you stood in the burial room naked, he added, you could profit more from the energy. "I do it all the time," he said.

—G. Y. Dryansky
"Merlin's Magic Shore,"
Condé Nast Traveler

stones"—up to 31 feet in height, some shaped and smoothed by prehistoric stone tools. But the most arresting sights in Carnac are the alignments.

If you take a small road north from the center of town, in half a mile you come to the tiny hamlet of Le Ménec. Suddenly an extraordinary sight opens before your eyes. From the edge of a few old farmhouses, a forest of menhirs stretches east across the undulating ground, almost as far as you can see. A glance reveals that the stones have been erected in rows—twelve of them.

On my first full day in Carnac, I took a magical three-mile walk among the alignments, starting at Le Ménec. The spacing between the stones is irregular, and the lines themselves curve slightly. The tallest stones (up to thirteen feet in height) stand at the west end, near the farmhouses, and they dwindle steadily in size as you move east. After two-thirds of a mile, the stones end in pine woods. Hiking farther eastward, I crested a small rise and found myself at the edge of Kermario, the second set of alignments.

These stretch even farther than Le Ménec's, though in seven rows instead of twelve. I stopped for a picnic of bread, cheese, sausage, and beer at a ruined windmill in the middle of the array. From atop the windmill I gazed at the rows of stones marching away on either side.

Another thin forest intervenes before the onset of the Kerlescan array. Here thirteen rows extend for a mere 400 yards, but it seems likely that there were once many more stones, for the alignments run smack into the old village of Kerlescan, whose very houses may have fragments of menhir all through their stonework. By the end of my walk, having strolled past 2,471 standing stones, I was in a happy trance. Never before had I seen anything like these rows of granite pillars.

It is hard to imagine that the alignments could ever have been taken for granted—yet, astoundingly, there is no written mention of them before the 18th century. Once travelers and antiquarians began, in the 1720s, to pay attention to those anomalous ranks of upright stones, a relentless parade of theories to explain them was launched.

The patron saint of Carnac—a very local one, unrecognized by the Vatican—is Cornély, to whom the village church is dedicated. Cornély's chief function is to protect cattle. We know that in 56 B.C., during his subjugation of Gaul, Julius Caesar won a great battle against the Veneti somewhere in the neighborhood of Carnac. When Parisian intellectuals began to descend on the region in the 18th century, locals offered their explanation of the alignments. Fleeing from a troop of Roman soldiers, they said, with only a pair of oxen to carry his gear, Cornély had climbed a hill just north of today's village. In a miracle, he turned the pursuing Romans to stone. They stand there today, no two alike, frozen in their steps, transformed into abstract granite.

While discounting the legend of Cornély, the Parisians made the natural assumption that the menhirs were contemporary with Caesar, who remains the chief classical source for our knowledge of the Gauls (Celts living in what is now France) and of their elite, the Druids. The alignments, then, thought the early investigators, must be Druid temples. Caesar had described gruesome human sacrifices carried out by the Druids. The intellectuals had no trouble finding recumbent stones, which they called *tables de sacrifices,* whose naturally eroded contours they mistook for sculpted hollows that perfectly fit the human body.

This was far from the wackiest theory propounded by earnest students of the alignments during the next two centuries. In the early 19th century, a new generation of savants saw serpent-worship everywhere: the alignments themselves, with their curving "sinuosities," imitated the very shape of snakes.

Other learned explanations over the years interpreted the alignments as fish-drying platforms, markets, hotels, routes to the stalls of prostitutes, and fields for ancient analogues of cricket or bowling or golf. One thinker deduced that the Romans had actually erected the stones as windbreaks for their tents. In the 20th century, it has been suggested—though certainly not by a scientist—that the alignments are the remains of ramps and landing pads used by extraterrestrials to visit Earth.

Although one shrewd investigator had suggested as early as

1764 that the megaliths might be pre-Celtic, it was only after the first responsible excavations, more than a century later, that this view prevailed. By the 1950s, archaeologists had studied thoroughly the artifacts of the megalith builders and had reached a conclusion about their age based on comparisons with the great literate civilizations of the Near East. They concluded that the megaliths spanned the years 2000–1400 B.C. The general outlines of the spread of cultural influence were clear to them also. From a Neolithic cradle in the eastern Mediterranean, ideas traveled north and west, by land and sea, over the centuries. Stonehenge bore the imprint of a Mycenaean prince; the art of Carnac was abstracted from goddesses of Crete and Egypt.

The experts were in for a great shock. The new technique of radiocarbon dating began to furnish a chronological precision that had eluded traditional archaeology. In 1959, the first tomb in Brittany to be carbon-dated seemed to give the impossibly early date of around 4300 B.C. It was no mistake. Site after site revealed origins in the fourth and fifth millennia before Christ. The oldest date yet established is Kercado's, with a carbon reading of 4650 B.C.—making the somber passage grave in the pines some 3,000 years older than experts had sworn it was.

All the early theories had to go out the window. The passage graves of Brittany were actually far older than the Mediterranean structures they supposedly imitated. Rather than being a distant, derivative ripple of Mycenaean or Egyptian glory, Carnac had to be considered as one of the world's greatest fonts of Neolithic culture.

The most redoubtable constructions, however, are the famous Carnac mounds. To the naïve eye, these do not look like much—symmetrical hills covered with vegetation. One of them lies very near the center of Carnac village; called the Tumulus St-Michel, it is topped today by a small church. Only when you realize that these mounds were amassed by the hand labor of people who never knew metal tools does the magnitude of the achievement dawn on you. Zacharie le Rouzic, the great local archaeologist who excavated the Tumulus St-Michel between 1900 and 1907, estimated its volume at 1,412,000 cubic feet. The Carnac mounds have proved the richest sites of all in terms of burial goods. From them scientists have retrieved hundreds of beautiful ornamental axheads made of jadeite, diorite, and fibrolite, polished to a sheen; scores of necklaces of turquoise-colored callais; countless beads of variscite; pendants and disks of jasper and serpentine; pottery and arrowheads; and the burned bones of animals, evidently funerary offerings.

What, then, are all these monuments about? What did the pre-Celtic civilization that built them intend to signify by all these prodigious and startling works of stone?

The question itself is flawed. The megalithic age in Brittany spanned a longer period—2,500 years—than has elapsed between Julius Caesar and François Mitterrand. In all likelihood, the stone structures of Carnac spring from a complex succession of cultures, each with its own myths and mores. There is evidence that some generations of megalith builders deliberately destroyed the monuments of their predecessors.

All this I was coming slowly to appreciate as I rambled on foot and by car to one prehistoric site after another. Mine was a labor of delight. Hedges of broom splashed the woods with yellow, pine sap sweetened the breeze, and the songs of a dozen unfamiliar species of birds accompanied my footsteps. Each summer Carnac turns into a crowded beach resort, but now, in April, half the hotels were closed and the seacoast was abandoned by all but fishermen. In quiet cafés night after night, I ate the best oysters I had ever tasted and drank good muscadet at a modest price.

One afternoon at the Bar de l'Océan, a smoky café hidden in an alley near Cornély's church, I struck up a conversation with three local octogenarians who were sipping the *vin rouge ordinaire.* They wore gray jackets, threadbare sweaters, and *casquettes*—short-billed cloth caps (as had 1920s golfers). Their square, weathered faces, long noses, and ruddy cheeks bespoke a region that as late as the 1960s was still so insulated from the rest of France as to seem to be almost a separate country.

After some chat about the weather, I asked the men, "And does Cornély continue to protect…" I was going to say *"les vaches"* (cows), but one of the old men interrupted: *"Les bêtes à corres? Oui."* The trio laughed hard at the hoary joke:"beasts with horns" was purposely ambiguous; as in English, the epithet covered sexually aroused men as well as cattle. I stood corrected.

It dawned on me that a deep truth might lie buried in the conventional witticism. Until quite recently, all over Brittany, the megaliths have figured in ancient folk rituals, many having to do with fertility. At Cruz-Moquen, women hoping to become pregnant used to raise their skirts to the dolmen at full moon. On the night of May 1, maidens from Locmariaquer would sneak out and slide, bare-bottomed, down the huge fallen stones of the Grand Menhir Brisé. Also at full moon, childless couples would visit the menhir called Le Vaisseau in the alignment of Le Ménec; both completely naked, the husband would chase the wife around the stone, while their parents, hiding behind another menhir, acted as lookouts.

The first 18th-century students of Carnac showed little interest in the numerous rituals and legends attached to the monuments, sneering at the superstitions of "peasants almost as rude and uneven as their stones." Yet we know now that old stories can carry truths that last over millennia. Names can also be loaded with ancient significance. In pondering the great alignments of Kermario and Ker-

> *Specific "warm stones" are reputed to have the power to find marriage partners for young women who choose to sit on them, but as the particular stones are not indicated in any way, the mate-hunting young ladies will have to discover which for themselves by trial and error. (The ruined dolmen of Croez-Moquen, not far away, gained a similar reputation so potent that the local priest wisely decided to conduct a procession to it every spring so that all the local spinsters could visit it together under the auspices of the Church rather than making solitary pagan pilgrimages to it on their own.)*
>
> —John Wilcock and Elizabeth Pepper DaCosta, *Magical and Mystical Sites: Europe and the British Isles*

lescan, what should we make of the fact that in Breton the first name means "place of the dead" and the second, "place of burning?"

The spiritual resonance of the Breton megaliths through 1,700 years of Christianity is revealed indirectly in church documents. Edicts from Tours and Nantes, not far east of Brittany, in the 6th and 7th centuries threatened *"les adorateurs de pierres"* (stone worshipers) with excommunication. In 769, Charlemagne officially anathematized any Frank who failed to observe his Christian duty to destroy all pagan stone monuments that he might find in his fields. Vandalism in the name of faith did not end with the Middle Ages. As recently as the turn of the century, the fanatic Abbé Jacques Cotteux ordered scores of ancient stones hauled from their sites to make a base for a calvary in Louisfert, southeast of Carnac. Atop a mound of ruined megaliths, he erected crosses, Christian statues, and plaques quoting his own poetry. Under the altar he had an explanatory footnote carved: "The debris of a bloody cult."

The very severity of the pious attack testifies to the power the stones continued to exert over long ages. By the time Christianity took hold in Brittany, early in the 4th century A.D., More than 2,000 years had elapsed since the last megalith had been erected. Today, you still can see Christianized menhirs and dolmens, their pagan spell subverted by the crucifixes that have been carved into them.

The depredations of 4,000 years of vandalism are incalculable. Pierre-Roland Giot, the leading French expert, estimates that among the Carnac alignments alone, where fewer than 3,000 stones now stand, there may once have been 10,000.

Neither national nor local authorities have done much to protect these priceless sites. Accustomed to our own national parks, I found it hard to get used to the indifference, even neglect, that hovers over the prodigies of Carnac. At first there's something refreshing about this state of affairs: you have to locate the monuments on your own, but you're allowed to putter about to your heart's content and no signs scold you with lists of "thou shalt nots." An age-old custom, and a harmless one so far as I could see, is to picnic among the alignments.

Yet at other times I was shocked by the consequences of this easygoing approach. The passage grave of Goerem, in Gavres, has a unique architecture and several haunting carved slabs. It was discovered only in 1963, when a bulldozer cleared dunes for a new subdivision. Because it had been undisturbed for 2,000 years, the tomb was of profound archaeological value. But it was hard for me to concentrate on Goerem's beauties as I tiptoed by flashlight around the plastic wrappers, broken glass, and even toilet paper and human excrement that lined the floor of the chamber tomb.

Toward the end of my trip, I took a boat from Larmor-Baden to Gavr'inis—"Island of Goats"—in the Gulf of Morbihan. On the south edge of the island, buried in a large mound, is the most dazzling display of Neolithic art in Brittany. On 23 of the 29 slabs that line the interior of the passage grave, some master of the fourth millennium B.C. carved a riot of concentric arcs, stylized axheads and serpents, and patterns that suggest shepherd's crooks, fir trees, and perhaps goddesses.

Gavr'inis was finally bought by the *département* of Morbihan in 1961, and today it is the best-protected monument in the Carnac area. Last year 30,000 tourists crawled into the tomb to marvel at its ornamented stones. The very homage of such visitors, as they brush past one another in the narrow passage, turning with backpacks and coats that rub the walls, has begun noticeably to degrade the carvings. In 1989 the number of tourists was being limited to ten people every fifteen minutes, mornings only. With a grim look on his face, the director admitted to me that in the future, to protect its irreplaceable art, it may be necessary to close Gavr'inis to all visitors, as Lascaux and many other Ice Age painted caves in southern France have had to be closed.

The passage grave inside the mound at Gavr'inis was first looked into in 1832. When the site was reexcavated from 1979 to 1984, the archaeological team under Charles-Tanguy Le Roux made two stunning discoveries. It had long been assumed that the mounds covering tombs were built by piling on dirt and stones at random. Le Roux's team found instead that the mound of Gavr'inis had a deliberate, visually dramatic structure based on concentric terraces of stone, roughly like bleachers in a stadium. And when Le Roux examined the top side of the great slab that caps the inner chamber, he found incomplete carvings of long-horned cattle and a hafted ax, and realized with a jolt that they segued perfectly into the designs on the capstone of another great tomb, La Table des Marchands, more than a mile away. The only explanation seemed to be that a huge, superbly decorated slab that had once been 46 feet long—possibly a giant menhir—had been deliberately broken so that the pieces could be reused in new monuments.

The very size of the largest menhirs, of the capstones in many Carnac tombs, makes it obvious that to move and erect them required extraordinary skill and large gangs of workers. The stones, most of local granite, may have been quarried by pounding wooden wedges into natural cracks, then soaking them with water so that they would expand and fracture the rock. Dozens of transport theories, involving inclined planes of earth, ropes, rollers, levers, pulleys and even boats, have been

In the mountains of southern France, where humans have habitually hunted, loved, and produced art, explorers have discovered an underground cave full of Stone Age paintings, so beautifully made and well preserved that experts are calling it one of the archeological finds of the century.

The enormous underground cavern, which was found on December 18, 1994, in a gorge near the town of Vallon-Pont-d'Arc in the Ardèche region, is studded with more than 300 vivid images of animals and human hands that experts believe were made some 20,000 years ago.

In this great parade of beasts appear woolly-haired rhinos, bears, mammoths, oxen, and other images from the end of the Paleolithic era, creatures large and small and variously drawn in yellow ocher, charcoal, and hematite.

Specialists say this ancient art gallery surpasses in size that of the famous caves of Lascaux, also in southern France, and Altamira, Spain, which are widely held to be Western Europe's finest collection of Stone Age art.

—Marlise Simons, "Prehistoric Art Treasure Is Found in French Cave," *New York Times* advanced. In 1979, at Bougon, a crew of hearty volunteers set out to move by Neolithic means alone a concrete slab weighing 32 tons. Two hundred people, pulling ropes and using wooden rollers, succeeded in moving the great burden across level ground. The capstone on the tomb of Mané Rutuel, however, weighed 50 tons, and the Grand Menhir Brisé that unthinkable 340. The latter stone was apparently transported two and a half miles from its probable quarry site to the spot where it lies shattered in four pieces today. Of such an effort by prehistoric work gangs, British archaeologist Aubrey Burl—whose guidebook *Megalithic Brittany* is the best single work on the monuments—writes, "this obsessive undertaking bewilders the modern mind."

The idea that the Carnac megaliths had an astronomical purpose was first advanced as early as 1874. In the 1970s, a tall, lanky, retired professor of engineering at Oxford, named Alexander Thom, crisscrossed the countryside, surveying every stone he could find. The toil was fiendish, as Thom, then in his 80s, dragged his triangulating chains through endless thickets of gorse, tearing his clothes, and raking his flesh on the thorns. The Oxford don had already spent three decades studying megaliths at home in the British Isles. In a series of papers and books loaded with mathematical formulas, Thom announced a startling new view of the intellectual capabilities of Stone Age peoples.

The farflung megaliths of Carnac, Thom claimed, amounted to a highly sophisticated lunar observatory. The crucial stone was the Grand Menhir Brisé, which he was convinced had been quarried, shaped, dragged to its site, and erected for that purpose. Thom thought that the ancient astronomers had used it as a sighting device; stationed at different locations all over the Carnac area, the observers lined up the distant tip of the Grand Menhir against the disk of the rising or setting moon. Then they marked their observing positions permanently by erecting smaller standing stones. In this fashion, the builders supposedly recorded their knowledge of the moon's cycle of declination and other phenomena. Moreover, according to Thom, the Neolithic observers had used their lore to predict eclipses of the moon. And they had also set out their stones in geometrical patterns based on a standard unit of length, which Thom called the megalithic yard.

These astonishing conclusions were not the work of a fanatic, but of a man who knew his science. An intricate professional debate ensued. In the 1980s, Evan Hadingham and Aubrey Burl returned to Carnac to reexamine the sites claimed by Thom to be part of his megalithic observatory. Their work, and that of other skeptics in England and France, cast serious doubt on the lunar thesis. The chief problem with Thom's theory is the multitude of stones that must originally have had clear sightlines to the Grand Menhir Brisé. Says Hadingham today, "Thom's work made archaeologists take the possibility of megalithic astronomy seriously. His achievement is that most of us now accept the notion that some imprecise level of prehistoric knowledge of the sun and moon is reflected in the layout of these monuments. But a lot of evidence has surfaced to suggest that it is a mistake to visualize Neolithic people as high-tech scientists. The most convincing aligmnents to the sun and moon are clearly not remnants of a research program, but part of a complex set of religious ideas—many of which we'll never know."

After two centuries of speculative fancy and hard-won fact, what can we finally say about Carnac?

The rich grave goods found in many tombs suggest that in certain centuries megalithic society was highly stratified. The Carnac mounds predicate an immense labor to sanctify the burial grounds of what must have been a small number of people—kings, culture heroes, or priests, perhaps. And the effort of erecting giant menhirs, alignments, and passage graves argues for coordinated workforces of hundreds or even thousands of people. Giot estimates that the industry of megalith building could have occupied as much as 60 percent of the society's "gross national product." Finally, animal bones, hinting at ritual funeral feasts, along with the wealthy objects buried in tombs, suggest a connection with a cult of the dead.

The menhirs and alignments are harder to fathom. Scholars argue that isolated menhirs may have served as topographic markers, or as commemorative stones, or even as icons in a phallic fertility cult. The alignments may have been processional lines, perhaps involving cattle. Menhirs and tombs may pay symbolic homage to a Neolithic awareness of the motions of the sun and moon. As Burl points out, the orientations of the entrances to nearly all the tombs in Brittany lie within a compass range that might be defined by such parameters as the northern and southern extremes of the moon's rising, or the midwinter and midsummer risings of the sun.

Why did these people stop building megaliths? Some scholars believe that the ancient collective values of this stone-working cult gradually faded as a new society took root in the Bronze Age. The long tradition of collective burial places—the passage graves—gave way to more modest mounds, each covering the body of only one wealthy individual.

Whatever its meaning, Carnac is now viewed as one of the great wellsprings of megalithic culture in Europe. But trying to sum up its thousands of years of prehistory, without a single written record to guide us, is a daunting task.

Says Evan Hadingham, "Many mysteries remain. We may never know the exact purpose of the alignments, for instance. But trying to understand megalithic society is easier—the builders left behind many clues, especially in the Carnac mounds. The explosion of wealth represented by these burials tells us of cattle herders who had enormous power—power to build mounds and raise stones, to obtain semiprecious stones traded all the way from the Alps, and to command the sacred images engraved in their ancestors' tombs."

Months after my visit, the sheer strangeness of megalithic Carnac haunts my memory. As my thoughts come apart on the edge of sleep, I see dolmens and menhirs floating by. Runes full of meaning that our minds cannot fathom—such wonders afflict us with a terrible thirst. There is nothing to do but go back, again and again, to touch and stare at those enigmas in granite.

David Roberts is a freelance writer living in Cambridge, Massachusetts. He is the author of eight books, most recently Once They Moved Like the Wind: Cochise, Geronimo, and the Apache Wars. *He writes regularly for* National Geographic, Smithsonian, Men's Journal, Outside, *and other magazines.*

✶

One day we went to Carnac to look at what my friend Pat refers to as the "mogoliths." She was tired out with driving when she coined this term, but I find it excellently descriptive. She was as much impressed by the absence of drifting garbage as she was by the standing stones. If they were ours we'd have written our names and intimations of our libidinous preoccupations on them, and obscured them in empty crisp packets. I got very ratty wondering what they were for. What people would have gone to all the trouble of lining up those colossal boulders for as far as the eye could see, and why would they bother? All those broken fingernails, crushed toes, and pulled muscles. How much of each boulder is buried in the earth and where did they get them from? What's it all about? People keep telling me they're for esoteric astronomical calculations and from them you could figure out when there was going to be an eclipse, but that seems to me a very frivolous explanation. I don't give a monkey's when there's going to be an eclipse. Does anybody? Did they?

Another theory suggests that they have mystical properties, so Pat and I rested our foreheads on one to check this out and see if we got any pre-historic vibes. A passing Frenchman, seeing us thus engaged, observed to his companion, *"Ah, la communication avec les roches,"* as though he'd have expected nothing else from two nutty English dames.

—Alice Thomas Ellis, "French Polish," *The Spectator*

DANIEL ASA ROSE

✦ ✳ ✦

Barging with the Boys

*The buzz of modern life recedes on a float
down the Canal du Midi.*

It's not so much the expense. Nor is it the fact that they
have the metabolism of hummingbirds, requiring food every 75
minutes. No, the supreme challenge for any parent who contem-
plates taking the kids abroad is how to find a place on the
Continent where they can escape the clutch of video arcades.

Which is where a barge trip comes in. Since Double Dragon
took over the world, circa A.D. 1985, it is distinctly more difficult
to expose youngsters to the pleasures once provided by family
travel: a glimpse into other modes of being, a slower pace of living,
the Non-Electronic Path to Enlightenment.

As I discovered taking two sons to Europe for the summer, zip-
pery blue video lights are everywhere, from campsites in the
Ardennes to horse farms on the Costa Brava, beckoning kids to
grow calluses on their thumb pads, just like at home.

Except along the Canal du Midi. Parents may be incredulous,
but here is the unvarnished truth: not once during a week of
lolling and nibbling and basking and sipping, not once did the subject of joysticks come up.

There was, by way of explaining this, the location. Languedoc,
the province traversed by the Canal du Midi, is the deep south of

France, a land of medieval fortresses and misty churches—another century entirely. All 300 miles of leafy canal linking the Atlantic with the Mediterranean feel alive with troubadours, crusaders, the ghosts of things pre-Pacman.

Only occasionally on our leg of canal, a westward stretch from Beziers to Carcassonne, were we reminded with a whoosh of our century: when French Mirage jets would periodically scorch the sky about four feet above our scalps. (Nearby Toulouse is the center of the nation's aerospace industry.)

But time-tripping was only half the pleasure. A barge proved one of the only domesticated spaces my kids didn't seem to mind being confined to: a homey, 100-foot-long pet water monster containing four cabins, a dining area, a galley, and crew quarters. The sun deck was like a floating outdoor café with elbow room, a beamy arena railed like a playpen and dotted with life preservers (a bit overguardedly so, since the canal is only about five feet deep).

With me reading under my umbrella at one wrought-iron table, and the kids sprawled to draw at another, the perfect travel distance from each other was afforded: within earshot but out of each other's hair.

Then there was the question of company. With the clientele getting younger every year, gone are the days when barges catered only to rich widows and sun-happy retirees. Ashore beforehand, the barge company helped me coordinate a week when other young parents with children would be aboard. Afloat, the cheery British skipper, Nick, was more than happy to teach us all to cheat at Dirty Mary, tutor us in history (it's the oldest canal in Gaul, with some humpbacked bridges bearing original dates from the 1600s), or prop up the kids with fishing poles and straw hats so they looked—for hours!—like French Huck Finns.

What evolved were recreations I thought had vanished a generation ago. Conversation: without micro-chip hypno-stimulation, the kids were actually talking to each other. Non-wheelie biking: their greatest treat was pedaling the towpaths under the lush sycamore shade on either side of the canal. Plodding along at less than four mph, the barge maintained the ideal pace at which a child bikes, not to mention the pace at which a recuperating parent takes his Ultimate Jog.

T̸he owners of the Lanikai prefer the French canals to any other because, Alan said, "They're so civilized. Traffic stops at night, and it comes to a complete standstill precisely at noon so the lock keepers can enjoy their lunch; if you're in a lock at the stroke of noon, you're in it for an hour." We noticed, however, that tsk-tsking lock keepers could sometimes be shamelessly bribed to ignore the clock with gifts of cheese or boulangerie leftovers. These hearty, rosy-cheeked individuals, who live beside their lock, are paid approximately a thousand dollars a month for their efforts. Most supplement their income by raising turkeys, geese, a milk cow, and vegetables.

—Rita Ariyoshi, "Canals of France," The Honolulu Advertiser

Alas, swimming was out—microbes and water snakes—but both kids took turns steering the barge from its stern, a sensation, they reported, akin to maneuvering an armored horse with its visor down. Such chivalry! Within 48 hours they had gone back hundreds of years.

What it all added up to was something unprecedented in my travel experience with kids: a languorous time. Away from the zap and sizzle, we had succeeded in fulfilling one of the basic kid requirements of travel—to keep moving—but somehow maintaining a modicum of stillness. Feeling simultaneously nomadic and sedentary, my 1990s kids were becoming calm.

Time slowed.

But it was the unpretentious tiny towns lining the route that, surprisingly, proved the biggest hit of the trip. Except during midday when they took on a guarded mien, presenting nothing but a shuttered exterior onto deserted streets, the labyrinthine byways of these places were far friendlier than in larger French burgs. *"Bonjour, mes petits,"* said the village shopkeeps, tipping their berets to my kids. *Quack,* said the family of mallards screened behind the chicken wire of someone's living room window. A sign announced the next town twelve kilometers away; kids accustomed to jet age speeds realized with a relaxed yawn that it would take all afternoon to get there.

Back on board again, the canal itself took on suspense as each twisted mile brought painterly views my kids had theretofore experienced only in museums: green tufted rolls of hay (not as picturesque as the stacked constructions of the Impressionists, but nice enough); a field of van Gogh sunflowers, all slowly rotating their gaze toward us as we proceeded west with the setting sun. One of the most delightful sensations to work its magic on their skin was also the most ordinary: feeling the different currents of air temperatures, from smoky cool when the water darkened under a passing cloud to brazen hot when sunlight recurred, darned by blue dragonflies.

Snacking on avocado mousse to the hoarse choir of locusts, my kids sat spellbound on deck each evening as the world turned pale sunburn shades, delicate gradations of hue and shadow the likes of which they'd seen on no video screen anywhere.

The last night, a pool hall in a medieval stone-walled village yielded the dastardly sound: blips, jangles, bells. The only game in town, it turned out to emanate from a laughably outdated (read: five years old) MunchMan machine.

Whether it was from their newfound lassitude, a dose of 17th-century languor, or just one of those neat reversals that contented travel seems to bring, I was the only one who wanted to play.

Daniel Asa Rose is a novelist who lives in Rehoboth, Massachusetts with his wife, literary agent Shelly Roth. He is the author of the novels Flipping For It *and* Small Family With Rooster, *the memoir* Hiding Places, *and numerous articles for major U. S. magazines.*

✴

France has 37,300 kilometers (23,300 miles) of navigable rivers and canals, 13,650 put on order by Napoléon I as part of his successful effort to establish a European Common Market by arbitrary rather than elocutional techniques. Since his era, French administrations have successfully improved and deepened her waterways and added frequent *ports de plaisance* (public marinas), which are largely free to the floating population.

—Norris D. Hoyt, "A Concorde of Delights," *Sail Magazine*

Don't Forget Marseille

Saddled with a reputation for vice and violence,
Marseille is, for some, enticing and indefinable.

"*L'AVENIR, L'AVENIR,*" ("THE FUTURE, THE FUTURE") CALLS THE gaudily dressed Gypsy woman opening and closing her deck of tarot cards like a fan on a warmish day. But no one wants the future told in the cafés and restaurants on the Corniche President J. F. Kennedy, which runs along the white limestone cliffs of Marseille's eastern flank. The present is too perfect here—the sea vast, blue, and dazzling, the harbor's tan fortified islands still and serene in the immense light of day—for anyone to be tempted by foreknowledge of that anxiety-producing abstraction, the future. And yet, for few other European cities is the future of such vital concern as it is for Marseille. If the Gypsy were telling the city's future, she might well have laid out cards that signified a fate as grotesque as Beirut's or as vibrant as Miami's.

I had my first inkling of the problem even before departing. "You're going to Marseille?!" exclaimed my accountant, gazing sadly at my returns as if to say, "Why risk your life just as you're entering your peak earning years?" "I've been there," he continued. "I saw the baddest-looking people there I've ever seen in my life."

"I've been held up at gunpoint in New York, attacked by a shark in Belize, and arrested by the KGB in Stalin's hometown." I told him. "I'll get through Marseille. Don't worry, you won't lose a client."

Marseille does indeed have a bad reputation, one that is even worse in Europe, where its name is associated not only with the drug trade but with racism and urban decay. But so is New York's, and it is rare that a city is great in accomplishment without also being great in degradation. I resolved to read nothing about the city, to experience it directly, my senses alert to both beauty and danger, my mind committed to sorting fact from myth.

The city is easily reached by air (a flight of little more than an hour from Paris, with shuttlelike service available), and by France's fine *autoroutes*. But I chose the TGV, Train à Grande Vitesse, which takes four and three-quarters hours from Paris and passes through lovely countryside with glimpses of rivers, nuclear reactors, the Palace of Popes at Avignon. Ever parsimonious, the French pack their own lunches, wisely preferring them to the costly meal available on the train, which could be described as haute Amtrak.

The very first thing that impinged on my senses at the St-Charles railway station in Marseille was that the instruction for the luggage caddies (which the French elegantly call *chariots* and for which they fight or plead most inelegantly) were not

When Roman invaders first pitched their tents on the banks of the Seine at a remote outpost they called Lutetia— now Paris—the magnificent walled city of Marseille, already five centuries old at the time, had long since established itself as the dominant commercial and metropolitan hub of southern Gaul. Two thousand years later, poor, maligned Marseille is a tragic heroine among French cities: still one of Europe's grand old seaports and second only to the French capital in population, she has given her sovereignty to Paris (albeit reluctantly) and her name to the national anthem ("La Marseillaise"), but in her own homeland is more often thought of as a naughty and embarrassing spinster aunt than the wonderfully wicked dowager she really is.

—Morris Dye, "Marseille Revisited," *San Francisco Examiner*

written only in all the usual European languages but in Arabic as
well, with those letters like banners and scimitars, a linguistic jihad.
This first impression is quickly reinforced. The ululations of Arab
speech, the throat-clearing vowels, the prevalence of w's, are heard
on nearly every street. Turbans and other such exotic Islamic head-
gear are commonplace. The older men greet each other in the
time-honored manner, by placing their right hands over their
hearts. Some of the younger men, in transit between two cultures,
first lightly touch their chests then extend their hands for the
equally ritualistic French handshake. Couscous is easier to find
than bouillabaisse.

Facing the sea and Africa, the city could well become a link be-
tween continents, creating new vectors of culture and commerce.
It could just as easily degenerate into a vicious racism fed by the
France-for-the-French nationalism of Jean-Marie Le Pen and his
National Front.

Overt racism is rare. Still, sitting in a small café watching the
waiter feign incomprehension each time an Arab ordered, I knew
that this was in fact how racism had to manifest itself, in hundreds
of petty indignities. The waiter had no trouble understanding me
even though after 30 years of trying I still cannot quite pronounce
"une" or *"vin."* But I was white and foreign, whereas *those* people
had the nerve to be *living* in *his* country. Poverty and humiliation
are always fuel for the resentment that leads to street crime, a law
that holds everywhere. Once, wandering by chance into precisely
that part of the Arab quarter I had been warned against—that
maze of narrow streets covered with chicken wire (to catch the
plaster crumbling off the ancient tenements) that lies directly behind the Vieux Port—I sensed some of the peril of the city, as
some of the "baddest looking" men I had ever seen emerged from
doorways like eels attracted by a fat fish. But that brush with danger never deterred me from wandering alone through the Arab
markets that add such vivid rhythm to the city, nor from sitting in
the Arab cafés, where only once did I ever see a woman seated at
a table. The Arabs I spoke with never scowled on learning I was

an American. Quite the contrary, they seemed to be delighted to actually behold one of those exotic creatures.

But the Algerians and Tunisians, like the city's other minorities—Armenians, Italians, Spaniards, Greeks—are only ethnic spice to a dish that is essentially French, though Mediterranean, Provençal French to be sure. The locals will not correct your faulty pronunciation as Parisians do, and you have all you can do to cut through the patois, which is fond of putting g's in the most unexpected places, "pain" becoming "paing," "vin" becoming "ving." Marseille is entirely un-Parislike, not sharing the capital's ethos of elegance in the least. That is not to say the city lacks elegant quarters, elegant architecture, or elegant restaurants, but rather that it does not constantly regard itself in a gilt-edged mirror, as Paris can seem to.

The mind's first instrument is association, analogy. Miami of the Mediterranean. Or better, a New Orleans, a city rough and sweet, a port of sin and easy laughter. And like New Orleans, Marseille is adorned with innumerable wrought-iron balconies with designs intricate as those on lingerie; it too has above-ground cemeteries, little cities of the dead flashing white in the sun. But analogies are not essence, and the trick, as always, is to catch what makes a thing, a place, itself.

Marseille is both bluntly real and beguilingly elusive. To my knowledge its portrait has never been definitively drawn in literature, along the lines of Joyce's Dublin, Dickens's London, Proust's Paris. Though Pagnol has written a good deal about Marseille, he remains better known both within France and abroad for his portraits of peasant life in the Aubagne area. And, for all its reputation for criminality, it has never even been fixed in the genre of detective fiction as has Maigret's Paris or the London of Sherlock Holmes. The man considered the first French novelist, Honoré Urré, was born in Marseille in 1567 but never so much as mentioned his native city in his works. With the one exception of *The Count of Monte Cristo,* whose famous Château d'If can still be visited by boat from the Vieux Port, the city has not figured greatly in French literature. Flaubert remarked on its "Oriental indo-lence." Lamartine found "more poetry in Marseille than in all the rest of France," and, dying there, Rimbaud cursed the ceaseless brilliance of the sun. Passing through in 1838, Stendhal was aston-ished at the lack of antiquities in a city that had been a going con-cern since 600 B.C.

Unlike nearby Arles and Nîmes, which have entire coliseums and temples, Marseille has only a few marble crumbs from its past. It has been called *"ville antique sans antiquites"* ("a city of antiquity without antiquities"). The little that does remain has been hand-somely arranged and carefully labeled in a small park behind the bourse, a lovely haven for the foot-weary. Yet immediately beside this park is a mall known as the Galleria, which possesses all the bland anywhereness of prefab modernity.

But not quite—this is still Marseille. Acquaintances of mine, noticing an indoor "outdoor" café in the mall, decided to photo-graph it as proof of France's headlong plunge into hi-tech banal-ity, which includes *hypermarchés* with 60 checkout lanes, machines that dispense *frites,* and even computerized tarot machines that, for ten francs, will tell your future—automation threatening even Gypsies. But no sooner had the two Americans documented this instance of France's decline than a young woman and two rough looking men emerged from the café demanding that the camera be opened and the film exposed. The Americans refused and asked the owner to call the police. He agreed but then thought better of it. A man then sidled up to them and whispered— "You're in Marseille. Do as they say if you value your face"—then disappeared himself. Finally, a compromise was reached—the film would be given to a one-hour developer, and any offensive images would be handed over. As usual, life dribbled off into the incon-clusive—whatever they feared was in the photos proved not to be there, and what could have been trouble ended with a handshake. But fiction begins where life leaves off, and this incident could serve as the opening for the suspense novel that puts Marseille on the literary map.

Perhaps there is so little left of ancient Marseille because, as some of the locals insist, the city is so dynamic—always destroying and renewing itself, like Manhattan. Of course not all the destruction was done by the Marseillais themselves. The Nazis found that the twisting streets and tunnels of the Vieux Port made good escape routes for their enemies and posed obstacles to efficient exploitation of the port. They simply leveled the half on the west side of the port—small on their list of crimes, even architectural crimes, but still painful to behold. The buildings that replaced them, ranging from the ugly to the innocuous, are the architectural equivalent of scar tissue. I can't help but suspect that the city fathers of Marseille erected a monument to the Soviet heroes of Stalingrad not only to honor their valor but as a form of vengeance and recompense for what Hilter's armies had done to the heart of their city.

The Vieux Port remains the heart of Marseille; it was there that the Greeks from Asia Minor known as Phoecaeans landed in 600 B.C. to officially found the city. Though Marseille has had a long and tumultuous history—Julius Caesar personally led the conquest of the city as part of the civil war against Pompey in 49 B.C.: it was the launching point for the Seventh Crusade; the venue of a disastrous plague in 1720; a center of the galley slave trade; and the city whose ardor gave its name to the anthem of the French Revolution—some of the most significant changes have happened in the years since World War II. Once the working hub of the city, the Vieux Port is now populated mainly by the sailboats of weekend seafarers and the awe-inspiring yachts of the superrich, while the main working port—where small boats return with their daily catch of eel, bass, scorpion fish, cod, crab, shrimp, and mullet—is now up the coast. The vast building where the vital, vulgar fishwives of Marseille mongered their husbands' catches was known as La Criée, reflecting, no doubt, their voluble cries. The spectral poet of Marseille, the food writer M.F.K. Fisher, pondered the fate of the Criée in her excellent book *A Considerable Town*: "What can be the future of the ugly-beautiful structure, whose tall glassed front looks from the Port somewhat like an early railroad terminal?" Time has answered her question: the Criée is now a theater with only an allegorical mural to commemorate the past. Marseille has been gutted like a fish.

While I neither accepted or deplored what other people report about the French town, and even feel that I understand why they are obliged to use the words they do (Give the public what it wants, etc., etc....), I myself have a different definition of the place, which is as indefinable as Marseille itself: insolite.

There seems to be no proper twin for this word in English; one simply has to sense or feel what is meant. Larousse says that it is somewhat like "contrary to what is usual and normal." Dictionaries such as the Shorter Oxford and Webster's Third International try words like apart, unique, unusual. *This is not enough, though...not quite right. Inwardly I know that it means* mysterious, unknowable, *and in plain fact,* indefinable.

And that is Marseille: indefinable, and therefore insolite. *And the strange word is as good as any to explain why the place haunts me and draws me, with its phoenixlike vitality, its implacably realistic beauty and brutality. The formula is plain: Marseille* = insolite, *therefore* insolite = *Marseille.*

—M. F. K. Fisher,
A Considerable Town

But that's too harsh. The restaurants and cafés of the Vieux Port are thronged until two in the morning most nights of the week. Some bars never quite close, as if it were somehow sinful that someone could be refused food or drink in that city that, for all its shadowy reputation, is a place of light, of the love of life. One sign of that motley vitality is the way the affluent and the indigent brush past each other on the sidewalks, and the way streets suddenly change character. The Canebiére, the city's main street beginning at the Vieux Port, is a mélange of the elegant and seedy by day, to be avoided by night. The rue de La Républicque, which also has its source there, is reminiscent of Paris, with its block-long buildings, bastions of the bourgeoisie, and its colors varying wonderfully from charcoal sketch gray to all the yellows of French *moutarde.*

But a few blocks off to the side in either direction and you're in North Africa; the same sudden changes also occur around the Opera, just behind the Vieux Port. Elegantly dressed couples proceed up the marble stairs and, as soon as they're inside, the square in front becomes a soccer field for street kids, as does every available rectangle in this soccer-mad city. The area around the Opera also offers fine dining, but its real specialty is the *bar américain,* where well-dressed women smile at passersby, and prophylactics are available like Chiclets from wall dispensers.

Still, Marseille remains elusive, as unwilling to have its portrait done as that unsavory trio in the mall were to have their picture taken. If Cézanne had strayed down to Marseille from his beloved Aix-en-Provence, he might have chosen to catch the tone of the place by painting men playing cards, a favorite subject of his. Decks of cards materialize in Marseille as soon as there is a moment's respite from work, and for some of the young men lounging in the cafés of the Vieux Port those respites seem to constitute the greater part of the day. But Cézanne would have preferred the older men with their creased faces, olive-black hair, and gleaming eyes. Unlike the more stolid provincials he usually depicted, these men slap their cards down with a laugh or a curse, then lapse into deep silence that is one of the comforts of the game. They would inevitably be sipping *pastis,* that version of anisette whose first licorice-flavored sip has a medicinal flavor but, as the ice cube melts and water is added from a pitcher, becomes soft as the glow it induces. They would be smoking raffishly and nibbling olives, black or the same green the sea can sometimes turn. Since they would be sitting outside, the city could be seen in the background, a cubist jumble of white houses and red tile roofs. The ancientness of the city, nowhere visible in ruins or monuments, would be there in the very ease of the game, the elbowroom of the centuries.

Richard Lourie is a novelist, literary critic, and translator of Russian and Polish works. Among numerous other books he has translated Andrei Sakharov's Memoirs, *and he is the author of the fictional title* The Autobiography of Joseph Stalin *and* Hunting the Devil, *a true-crime account of a Russian serial killer. He lives in New York.*

✴

La Marseillaise

(National Anthem of France—two verses of seven)

Allons enfants de la Patrie,	Ye sons of France, Awake to glory
Le jour de glorie est arrivé.	Hark! Hark! What myriads bid you rise!
Contre nous, de la tyrannie,	Your children, wives and grandsires hoary,
L'étendard sanglant est levé	Behold their tears and hear their cries,
L'étendard sanglant est levé	Behold their tears and hear their cries!
Entendez vous, dans les campagnes	Shall hateful tyrants, mischief breeding
Mugir ces farouches soldats	With hireling hosts, a ruffian band
Ils viennent jusque dans nos bras	A-fright and desolate the land,
Égorger vos fils, vos compagnes	While peace and liberty lie bleeding?

Aux armes, citoyens! Formez vos	To arms, to arms, ye brave!
bataillons,	Th' avenging sword unsheathe,
Marchons, marchons!	March on! March on!
Qu'un sang impur	All hearts resolved on victory
Abreuve nos sillons!	or death!

Amour sacré de la Patrie,	O sacred love of France, undying,
Conduis, soutiens nos bras vengeurs.	Th' avenging arm uphold and guide.
Liberté, liberté chérie,	Thy defenders, death defying,
Combats avec tes défenseurs; (bis)	Fight with Freedom at their side.
Sous nos drapeaux, que la victoire	Soon thy sons shall be victorious
Accoure à tes mâles accents;	When the banner high is raised;
Que tes ennemis expirants	And thy dying enemies, amazed,
Violent ton trimphe et notre	Shall behold thy triumph, great and
gloire!	glorious!

Aux armes, citoyens! Formez vos	To arms, to arms, ye brave!
bataillons,	Th' avenging sword unsheathe,
Marchons, marchons!	March on! March on!
Qu'un sang impur	All hearts resolved on victory
Abreuve nos sillons!	or death!

—Claude-Joseph Rouget de l'Isle (1760-1836), translated by
Percy Bysshe Shelley and Mary Elizabeth Shaw

INA CARO

* * *

Pilgrim's Path

The author traces the "Age of Faith"
across Southern France.

WE FIRST SAW ROCAMADOUR FROM THE TERRACE OF A LITTLE restaurant on the Hospitalet Road. Our terrace jutted out from a cliff overlooking a deep canyon that separated it from the rugged cliff opposite us, to which Rocamadour was somehow miraculously clinging. Sitting there in the hazy light of a beautiful summer morning, about this deep, wide gorge, I realized I had found an ideal place for a 20th-century skeptic like myself to understand the religious experience of a 12th-century pilgrim. The monks of Rocamadour had taken one of the greatest cliffs of France and built right into its side not only a church but also a bishop's palace, seven chapels, and an entire turreted and fortified medieval town—and had then crowned the cliff with a castle whose battlements are shaped like crosses. From across the gorge, we could see a steady procession of modern-day tourists making their way up the side of the escarpment, up the 216 steps that 12th-century pilgrims once climbed. Because of the distance, the tourists were just a line of dots, and it was easy to imagine them as medieval pilgrims in the Age of Faith. Each year hundreds of thousands of them made their way south across France to three main destinations: Jerusalem, Rome, and Santiago de Compostela in Spain. As they

263

made their way south, the pilgrims would stop for the night at monasteries and abbeys possessing relics—the body or some bones of a saint or martyr—places that had become known for miraculous cures and potential salvation. The pilgrims would make "voluntary" contributions for the relics' upkeep, and monasteries came to realize that such objects constituted a potential source of revenue with which to build greater churches for the glory of God.

First, of course, a monastery had to have a relic—and for monasteries in France, this wasn't always easy. The best relics (the ones believed to have the most power for curing and salvation) were those connected to Christ and his apostles—none of whom, unfortunately, had so much as set foot in France.

So French monasteries attempted to remedy this situation by means both subtle and direct. Foulques Nerra, for example, returned from a pilgrimage to Jerusalem with a large chunk of wood. He said that it was a piece of the True Cross which he had bitten off with his teeth, and he enshrined part of the wood in a church that he renamed the Church of Sainte-Croix—and over the years it became a regular stop for pilgrims heading for Compostela.

The success story of Conques, which we passed as we drove from Albi to Rocamadour, was illustrative of an age in which pilgrimages were big business. Conques was a popular stop on the famous Pilgrim's Path because of its fabulous treasure: a jewel-encrusted reliquary statue of Sainte Foy, which you can still see today. Saint Bernard could have had this statue in mind when, trying to reform the commercial and corrupt practices associated with pilgrimages, he wrote, "Money brings money…[pilgrims'] eyes are feasted and relics cased in gold, and their purse strings are loosed." But Conques had not always been popular. The story of success—how Conques had obtained the statue and the pilgrims who came to see it—was typical of the age.

Sainte Foy was a twelve-year-old girl who was martyred in A.D. 303 at Agen. Her remains had been encased in a gold statue at a monastery there. As early as the 9th century, word spread that the blind were miraculously cured after visiting her remains; so pilgrims came in great numbers with "purse strings loosened." Conques, on the other hand, was attracting few pilgrims. There seemed to be little reason for them to detour through miles of rugged hills and woods, filled with wild animals, robbers, and imagined demons, to this isolated monastery. In fact, the monks who had settled on this rocky site were threatening to leave. To remedy the situation, in 856 Conques's abbot decided to steal Sainte Foy's relics from the Agen monastery. (The solution to his problem was not unique; over a hundred thefts of relics by rival monasteries were recorded during the Age of Faith. Vézelay, for example, stole the relics of Mary Magdalene from another monastery, and in its turn Vézelay was nearly destroyed when monks from yet another monastery, at nearby Autun, tried to steal those remains, which, as it happened, turned out to be fake.) Conques's abbot selected one of his monks, Ariviscus, for the theft from Agen. Arriving at the Agen monastery, Ariviscus discovered that the relics were guarded night and day by trusted monks. Being in no hurry to return to Conques, he joined the monastery and waited. Ten years later the brotherhood at Agen considered Ariviscus trustworthy enough to allow him to guard the treasure. As soon as he was left alone, he grabbed the statue and escaped back to Conques on horseback, with the Agen monks in pursuit.

The treasure in which the relics of Sainte Foy are encased is a nearly three-foot-high statue put together over several centuries. The face is actually a 5th-century gold mask of a Roman emperor, not of the martyred young girl. Monks of the 9th century joined this mask to a wooden core and covered the wood with thin plaques of Merovingian gold. Monks of the 10th century further embellished it with a crown and earrings of precious stones, then placed it on a gold throne. Its reputation for curing the blind followed it from Agen to Conques, so that by 1031 the monks of Conques had accumulated sufficient funds to start construction of a Romanesque cathedral. But any way they looked at it, the monks realized that blind pilgrims constituted a limited source of income, as well as being a group hardly in a position to appreciate fully the beauty of their newly acquired treasure. As the cathedral rose, the

monk in charge of recording miracles noticed that some workmen
who had fallen from steeples during construction were recovering.
That, the monk realized in a moment of inspiration, could be
called a miracle, too. Since at the time cathedrals were being built
all over France, the healing of cathedral construction workers constituted a potential growth industry, and it was announced that visits to Sainte Foy would cure not only blindness but injuries in-
curred by workmen building cathedrals. The resulting
Romanesque church at Conques, with its extraordinary polychrome tympanum of the Last Judgment, is considered a model for
pilgrimage churches of the period.

While 12th-century pilgrims were detouring to nearby Conques in great numbers, they were not stopping at Rocamadour. I
have to admire the inventiveness, if not the piety, displayed by the
monks of Rocamadour to remedy this situation. First, there was
the sword. The miraculous na-
ture of swords was a common
Celtic belief when this area was
still pagan. The evolution of a
legend such as Roland and his
sword Durendal, or King Arthur
and Excalibur, stemmed from the
fact that the Druids, the pagan
priests of Celtic society, were
originally blacksmiths who kept
to themselves the secrets of extracting iron ore from stone and
turning the iron into swords. Pagans saw taking iron from stone
and transforming it into a sword as a magical act, which by the
12th century gave rise to marvelous tales of chivalry in which God
gives the hero a great sword with which to defeat his enemies.
(Joan of Arc, the last hero of the Age of Chivalry, would also
miraculously find a buried sword.) Rocamadour's sword was supposedly Durendal, whose divine properties enabled Roland, personification of the true and faithful Christian knight, to hold off at
Roncesvalles 100,000 Saracens long enough for Charlemagne's
battered army to retreat back to France. In the *Chanson de Roland,*

*The French, though
Catholic in the major-
ity, go to the beach rather more
than they go to church, to wine
bars more than to confession.*

—Richard Bernstein,
*Fragile Glory: A Portrait of France
and the French*

an 11th-century heroic poem—a *chanson de geste,* which is available in paperback and which makes as good reading on a modern pilgrimage as it did in the 12th century when pilgrims recited it as they camped along the road—Roland, wounded and dying, covers Durendal with his body and cries out as he is dying:

> O, Holy Mary, said the Count, help me!
> ...For this sword I grieve and sorrow...
> I should rather die than leave it in pagan hands.
> God, our Father, spare France this disgrace!

The monks of Rocamadour made a slight alteration in the story. In their version Roland did not fall on his sword but, rather, flung it into the air with all his might. And, according to Rocamadour's monks, guess where it landed? The 12th-century pilgrim could see at Rocamadour—as you can see there today—a rusty iron sword embedded in a rock next to the oratory of the Virgin. (Today's tourist office has the good taste to refer to this sword as a replica.)

But the pilgrims still did not come. So in 1166, when a body was discovered near the entrance to the shrine of the Black Virgin, it was announced that it was the body of none other than Zaccheus, a tax collector from Jerusalem who had come to Rocamadour to live as a hermit after his conversion by Christ. According to a contemporary chronicler, the corpse was discovered when an inhabitant of the area, divinely inspired, ordered his family to bury him at the entrance to the Black Virgin's shrine. During the burial Zaccheus's body, miraculously preserved, was uncovered. Zaccheus was renamed Saint Amadour, and the body was placed in the church, close to the altar, for the worship of pilgrims.

Still the pilgrims did not come. In 1188 an ambitious monk produced a list detailing 126 miracles that had occurred at Rocamadour because of the power of its relics. Evidence of the effort to publicize these miracles is found as far north as Mont-Saint-Michel, in Normandy. Still, the pilgrims went to Conques without stopping at Rocamadour.

The monks knew that pilgrims would travel to shrines if they thought important people—medieval celebrities—had also made the trip. So they let it be known that Simon de Montfort had come to Rocamadour to seek forgiveness for his sins. (Actually, Montfort—and his troops—spent the winter of 1212 at Rocamadour not for salvation but for protection: the safety of its fortified location.)

In the 13th century pilgrims finally began to come to Rocamadour. They came not to venerate the Black Virgin or Durendal or Saint Amadour's relics but by choice—their choice being that they could come to Rocamadour or be burned at the stake—for what finally solved Rocamadour's problem was the Inquisition. Rocamadour may not have been the destination for those pilgrims who had taken to the road for adventure, excitement, or salvation, but it was one of the destinations the Albigensian "heretics" were forced to visit by the Inquisitors as penance for their "sins." (Alas, it was not even the Inquisitors' first choice. They had initially sent the Albigensians on a much more oner-ous pilgrimage, to the Holy Land, but found that sending them there was counterproductive, for some of these supposed converts spread their heretical doctrines in Jerusalem.) The penitents were required to return to Albi with signed certificates attesting that they had made the visit. The cult of the Virgin and the worship of saints were particularly reprehensible to Albigensians. Prostrating themselves before this rather barbaric, soot-blackened statue of the Virgin was humiliating to a people who had rebelled, even those

*For anyone trying to un-
derstand the French it
must be remembered that what
came with the French Revolution
was a repudiation of religious values but not of intellectual values.
What this means in practical terms
is that while the French came to
reject religious absolutes, they still
prize the secular opinions of the
rational, well-educated individual.
Hence, the French have retained
the air of the Enlightenment while
around them stumble the descen-
dants of the Celts, Romans,
and Teutons.*

—Sean O'Reilly,
"The Serpent Speaks"

who had considered themselves Catholics, against the more "miraculous" aspects of the Church, which they considered pagan. It was intentional, therefore, that a great number of the heretics who confessed at Albi were sentenced by the Inquisition to prove their conversion by seeking forgiveness from the Black Virgin and Saint Amadour.

The procedure was quite standardized. On the day of his departure from Albi, the pilgrim attended a special Mass at which he received an outfit that had been blessed and sprinkled with holy water. The outfit consisted of a tunic whose back was covered with crosses, a knapsack, a wide-brimmed hat turned up in front, a leather pouch belted around his waist, and a staff. On his arrival at the base of the great cliff of Rocamadour, the pilgrim stripped himself of his clothes, allowed heavy chains to be bound around his arms and neck, and, dragging the chains, climbed on his knees the 216 steps to the shrine of the Black Virgin, stopping on each step to recite the rosary. There was a symbolic reason for the chains, just as for almost everything the pilgrim did during the Age of Faith. They signified the weight of the penitent's sins on his soul. The pouch stood for poverty; the staff, a shepherd's staff, was both protection against the devil and a beam between heaven and earth. The climb up the steps to the shrine was a symbolic climb to God; each step climbed was a symbolic step closer to God. And as he climbed, the pilgrim passed—as the modern tourist does today—scenes representing the fourteen Stations of the Cross. (You now see in the caves of Rocamadour, where 6th-century hermits once lived, scenes depicting each of these stations.)

Once the pilgrim arrived at the shrine and the chapel where Saint Amadour was supposedly buried, he prostrated himself before a statue of the Black Virgin and, with appropriate wailing, begged forgiveness for his sins. The priest who recited prayers of purification then unlocked his chains and presented him with the certificate proving that he had come to Rocamadour. The pilgrim could then buy a *sportelle,* his Badge of Rocamadour. The Rocamadour *sportelle,* an oval medal, showed the Virgin seated on her throne holding a scepter topped by a fleur-de-lis. Little rings on the edge of the medal enabled the pilgrim to attach it to his hat. An average pilgrim's hat would be covered with the medals from the shrines he had already visited—the head of John the Baptist from Amiens; an amulet bearing the words "Thomas makes the best doctor for the worthy sick" from Canterbury; the keys of Saint Peter from Rome; the scallop shell of Saint James (Santiago) from Compostela.

*W*ith the pilgrimage attracting as many as half a million men and women each year, it was about time for an official guidebook. In 1130, Aimeri Picaud, a French monk and himself a pilgrim, answered that need with A Pilgrim's Guide to Saint James of Compostela, written in Latin. It described four well-defined, heavily traveled pilgrimage routes—each tracing ancient Roman roads—that drained France like a vast river system. Picaud's handbook was translated into French earlier in this century and remains a valuable source for modern guidebooks and commentaries.

Each of the routes has a designated starting point that has not changed in a thousand years (except the Via Turonensis, which originally began in Tours, but was soon changed to Paris). Those starting points are important because they became marshaling areas where pilgrims from neighboring countries gathered before beginning the pilgrimage.

—Robert Macdonald, "Pilgrims' Progress," FRANCE Magazine

I looked at my Michelins, Red and Green, open on the table in front of me and thought the more things change, the more they stay the same. These modern French guidebooks list the best places at which to stay and to eat, and advise the traveler which monuments are worth a detour to visit. The medieval pilgrim, I knew, was guided by the *Codex of Callixtus,* a travel guide for pilgrims that listed the best shrines of martyrs and saints to visit for miracles, the best monasteries at which to stay, which inns along the way were bug-infested, which ones had water that was safe to drink, which ones were free from thieves, where and what to eat, which relics were worth a detour to see. Not surprisingly, the pilgrim, like the tourist today, would find that his accommodations improved with the size of the pouch he wore around his waist (although the fresh hay or the addition of fruit and nuts supplied the generous pilgrim might seem an in-adequate improvement to the modern pilgrim). The 12th-century *Codex* was written by a Cluniac monk to divert the pilgrim and his money from Rome to Compostela; the cathedral there was part of Cluny's expanding empire, which would ultimately include over 2,000 Cluniac dependencies, including Conques and Roncevalles. At Roncesvalles, the next stop listed after Conques, for example, the pilgrim was informed by the *Codex* that he would not only see the relics of Roland's famous battle, which took place at that spot, but would be provided with a bed, a bath, and a dinner including almonds and fruit. In order to give the book authority, its author-ship was attributed to Pope Calixtus II—a former Abbot of Cluny who was widely respected in the 12th century for the reforms he had tried to initiate in the Church. This reform Pope would have had difficulty writing the guide, since he had already been dead for twenty years at the time it was written, but the pilgrims were not aware of that—or of how the *Codex* altered the facts of history to enhance the religious experience of some of the pilgrimage sites along the way. In brief, the altered facts relevant to Rocamadour and Conques concerned Charlemagne, who, in 778, had driven the Saracens out of France, crossed the Pyrénées, and gone as far south as Saragossa in Spain, where the Saracens regrouped and drove him back to France. While retreating across the Pyrénées, in August of that year, Charlemagne's rear guard was cut down in the gorge of Roncesvalles by a small group of Basque mountaineers. This historical event was transformed in the *Codex of Callixtus* to authenticate the relics of Santiago de Compostela. Charlemagne's time in Spain was expanded from months to several years, during which he saw a vision of the martyred Saint James arriving at Compostela in a stone boat. Charlemagne's victories in Spain were thus considered the result of the saint's intervention. By taking ad-vantage of the religious fury against the Saracens aroused by the Crusades, the *Codex* created a religious reason for stopping at Roncesvalles. The Christian Basques became pagan Saracens, and Charlemagne's slaughtered rear guard became a company com-manded by Roland.

As I looked across the gorge at the modern pilgrims angling their way up the escarpment, I picked up an American guidebook and read the suggestion that we tourists remain on the Hospitalet side of the gorge and not actually enter Rocamadour, because the town today is overly touristy and commercial. Modern Rocamadour is indeed overly touristy, with booth after booth selling postcards, t-shirts, plastic statues of saints, toy swords, and horns. (The horns on sale at Rocamadour are supposed to represent the Oliphant, the horn Roland blew.) But, of course, Rocamadour was overly touristy in the 12th century, too. Postcards and t-shirts have just replaced *sportelles* and a rusty sword. So, to see Rocamadour is in a way to see the Age of Faith in a very authentic way.

And whatever else it is, Rocamadour is as dramatic a pilgrimage site as any traveler through time could ever hope to visit. I had never seen anything quite like it. To see that great cliff with a church and a town built right into its side must have been an awe-inspiring experience 600 years ago. And it is an awe-inspiring experience today.

Ina Caro also contributed "The Arch of Orange" in Part I. Both stories were excerpted from her book The Road From the Past: Traveling Through History in France.

★

In the Revolution the officials of the Republic seized the treasures of the abbeys and cathedrals and melted them down to coin money for an empty treasury. They had ravished Rodez; and someone warned Conques that they were on their way. So the Mayor of Conques held a village meeting. "We are about to have our Revolution," he said, "and we shall take the abbey treasures and share them among us; every man his piece, and I shall remember which family has which jewel." Then the officials arrived, and called for the Mayor, and told him they were come for the abbey treasure, so that Conques should be privileged to celebrate the Revolution. "But we have had the Revolution!" said the mayor. "Citizen-Comrades, we had it last week. And the citizens, filled with Revolutionary zeal, seized the treasure. And you know that it is not possible to recapture anything that may have been taken by a Rouerguais peasant, particularly from one who is a good revolutionary, as we all are in Conques." With these words, or words to this effect, the Mayor outfaced the officials. And they reflected on the centuries during which the people of this poor country had hidden their small possessions from *routiers,* and taxgatherers, and the abbey bailiffs at the tithing season. So they went away. But when the Terror was over, the people of Conques brought out the abbey treasures from the holes in the walls of their houses, and holes under the trees in their orchards, and gave back every one. So that Conques has one of the very rare medieval treasures of the world.

—Freda White, *Three Rivers of France: Dordogne, Lot, Tarn*

PART THREE

GOING YOUR OWN WAY

RICHARD GOODMAN

Spanish Heart, French Soil

More than just fruit and vegetables thrive
in the countryside.

I THINK EVERY FRENCH VILLAGE SHOULD HAVE AT LEAST ONE
Spanish couple living there. They would bring a certain openness
and heart—a *musicality* to the village that would make it a richer
place in which to live. In St-Sébastien de Caisson, this was provided by a couple from the province of Valencia, a mason and his
wife, Monsieur and Madame Vasquez. They were our first friends
in St-Sébastien.

In Lebanon once, years before the civil wars, I met a young
Jordanian law student. He and I were staying at the same third-class
hotel in Beirut. He befriended
me, acting as my guide and interpreter. "Why?" I asked him
once, since his unending kindness seemed excessive. "We are
all strangers sometime, Richard,"
he said. Those first few weeks
when Iggy and I were isolated and uncertain, when we were
overly polite to people we didn't know and when we were pretending to be capable, Monsieur Vasquez and his wife befriended

*In the interest of privacy,
the author changed the
names of the people and the
village.*

—JO'R, LH, and SO'R

277

us. They took us in. No two people were kinder to us during that year in France. I was very grateful they were there.

Those beginning days, I would take long walks every morning. Each time I walked out of our house, I seemed to see the same short, stocky man seated on the stone bench nearby. He wasn't doing anything, just sitting. Didn't he work? I wondered. I decided to use the excuse of needing to rent a car to begin conversation. Our plan was to drive a rented car to different villages in search of a used one which we would buy.

I walked over to the bench. "Good day," I said.

"Good day," he said and squinted up at me.

"Do you happen to know," I asked him, "where I could rent a car?"

He looked to the side as if he hadn't heard me. I wondered if I'd said the sentence correctly in French. I thought I had, especially since it was one I'd practiced upstairs in our house.

"Oh," he said, "to rent a car you have to go to Alès." His accent was strange. He rolled his rs. I didn't know then he was Spanish.

"Alès? Is that far?"

He looked away again. "Oh, it's not far."

"Uh, how far?" I sat down cautiously next to him.

"Oh, twenty kilometers. Maybe twenty-five."

"Ah," I said. "Is there a bus that can take us there?"

"No." He paused. "There is no bus to Alès." He squinted his eyes as he looked at me.

"We need to rent a car," I said almost to myself. I was thinking aloud now. "I don't know how to get to Alès." I figured I would just hitchhike. Why not? At least I'd get to know the roads.

"Oh," he said, shifting slightly on the bench as if something was disturbing him, "I can take you."

And he did.

He did more than that, too. He took us to his house, and he introduced us to his wife. He asked us in for a drink. He asked us to dinner. And to lunch. We accepted every invitation readily. And when we came, both of them talked and talked and talked. And *we* talked to *them,* ceaselessly it seemed, breathlessly telling them everything we could think of, as if we'd been lost in the mountains in the cold, and they were our rescuers. Which indeed they were. This was only the beginning of their kindness. Now we had friends, thanks to their big Spanish hearts. I never forgot that first kind gesture to us, the strangers.

Going to the Vasquezes' house for a visit—it was a small, cluttered, oddly-built, dark stone house just off the main square— was like going to Spain. It was always a festive occasion and always meant food and *pastis* and talk and laughter. We could drop in unannounced, and often did, spending hours at a time seated in their kitchen gossiping and exchanging information about the village. And learning.

Madame Vasquez was the larger of the couple. She was heavy, with a flat, Valázquez-like forehead, closely cropped black hair, small eyebrows, and a small mouth. She always wore black, in homage to a brother who had died a few years back, but this gesture of respect was often accommodated with just a black sweater, allowing her more latitude with the rest of her wardrobe. When she laughed, she closed her eyes as if she were in pain, and her whole body trembled. She was gossipy and held grudges in a small way and enjoyed complaining. She didn't have a mean bone in her body. It was she, not her husband, who worked and cared for the enormous garden they maintained by the river at the edge of the village. It was unusual for a woman

If there is no preexisting relationship, I am not in a position to ask a favor, unless I thereby wish to establish one. I do not ask "anything of anyone, just like that." And if I am wrong about the nature of our relationship and thus ask for more than it allows, the manner in which the person will perform (or not perform) this "small" favor will make it clear. I will then know if I was "wrong about" him or her.... I do not hesitate to ask for "small favors," such as information. But when it is a matter of a "real" favor, a large favor, asking my friend to do it for me would be the equivalent of imposing it on him or her, since in the name of friendship he or she cannot refuse. In these cases I wait for my friend to offer.

—Raymonde Carroll,
Cultural Misunderstandings:
The French-American Experience

to tend a garden in St-Sébastien de Caisson, especially a garden so immense. But her situation made it necessary. She was a Spanish earth mother.

Monsieur Vasquez was a compact, brown-haired man with a weathered face that had been—to judge from his wedding photograph which hung on the kitchen wall—handsome at one time. He had been a mason, the poverty of his native country urging him to France some twenty years ago. He had built his life in St-Sébastien from virtually nothing. A number of years before we knew him, Monsieur Vasquez had fallen from a scaffolding and broken his leg. Due to improper care, the leg never healed correctly, and so he was in constant pain and limped. He bore this pain bravely, though sometimes, when we were all around his kitchen table drinking, you would see him squeeze his eyes shut and a little cry would escape his lips.

"Your leg?" I would ask.

"Yes. *Merde.* It's worse than usual. *Three* shots I had today already!" His wife administered pain-killing shots supplied by the doctor. His injury prevented him from working—even in the garden. Bending and digging were out of the question.

Monsieur Vasquez smoked heavily, unfiltered Gauloises, and both his teeth and fingers showed the effects, not to mention that he had an ugly, watery cough. The cough became so serious that he gave up smoking while we were in St-Sébastien. And he kept to it. He chewed on a small piece of wood to help him forget the sublime pleasures of tobacco. I admired his discipline, especially since he had nothing to do all day long, and smoking a cigarette to idle the time away must have been so tempting. He was very witty and very quick. Once I found him in the square, his usual haunt, and noticed he didn't have the stick in the side of his mouth.

"Monsieur Vasquez! Where's your stick?" I asked.

"Oh," he said, with only the barest pause, "the tobacconist is closed."

We would speak Spanish together, mostly. At that time, my Spanish was far better than my French. In fact, what French I knew seemed useless to me; people in the village spoke with such a strong accent—for example they said *attand* for "wait," instead of *attend*—and I had great trouble comprehending them. So I was happy to speak Spanish in this French village until I could speak and understand this new language capably.

A visit to the Vasquezes' house meant that we would not return home empty-handed. That was impossible. If it wasn't a jar or two of preserved vegetables from their garden, then it might be a rabbit, even, or some leftover *paella,* or some cake, or perhaps some of their illegal, homemade *pastis,* that licorice-tasting apéritif nearly everyone drinks in the south of France. They *rained* things upon us. We tried refusing at first, but gave up because it took too much energy. Later, when Monsieur Vasquez had an operation on his leg and his wife needed rides to the hospital—she couldn't drive a car—we took her. I was glad to be able to give something in return, at last.

The Vasquezes did not have the best-organized, strictly perfect garden—that honor belonged to Monsieur Noyer—but they had the largest and most chaotic and in many ways the most splendid. It was located, as I mentioned, at the edge of the village, near the little river Darde. I can't begin to tell you everything they grew in it, but it was a catalogue. They also had many fruit trees: apricot, cherry—which we helped them harvest in the spring—fig, apple, more. Oh Lord, I can still taste their cherries now, fat white angels bursting open in my mouth. Madame Vasquez—or Señora Vasquez as I often called her—more than made up for her husband's inability to work. And had no trouble telling me so.

"How's your garden coming along, Señora?" I'd ask.

"Mucho trabajo." Lots of work. She fanned her face with her hand and huffed through her nose.

"Really?"

"Oh, la, la," she said, rolling her eyes, then glancing around to see if anyone else had arrived. She liked to be apprised of every coming and going in the village, a full-time job. She rode to the garden on the *mobilette,* and it was quite a sight to see her huge body perched on the tiny gray machine, bucket hanging from the handlebar, her enormous skirt discreetly tucked away underneath, her face intent. Some days I'd look out of my window and see her there, in front of our house on her *mobilette,* waving up at me.

"Señor Ricardo! Señor Ricardo!"

"Yes, Señora," I'd say, poking my head out of a window.

"From the garden!" She held up some lettuce—or whatever.

"Take! Take!"

"For us?"

"*Sí. Sí.*"

And I would bound down the stairs and receive the just-picked gift.

Going to the Vasquezes' garden was always a treat, and it was even better when both of them came along to give us a detailed tour. Theirs was the first garden we ever saw in St-Sébastien, and what an introduction! Both Monsieur and Madame Vasquez had been eager for Iggy and me to see it. It was in late September, only two weeks after we had arrived in the village. The garden was in its waning stages, but we were still bowled over.

Here was row after row of just about every vegetable you could think of, each one enormous and hardly able to stand up. Madame Vasquez wandered by this and that, plucking, arranging, tearing.

"Here, string beans," she said. "Here, zucchini. *Mucho trabajo.*"

"Those are not zucchini," Monsieur Vasquez said, hobbling along, trying to keep up with us. "Those are eggplant."

Madame Vasquez scowled at him. "Of course they're zucchini!" She clicked her tongue. "Look. Look."

Monsieur Vasquez looked, realized he was wrong, and growled.

"Is this all yours, Señora?" I asked, sweeping my hand to indicate the panorama.

"Yes, all of this. It's too big. Much too big. I must get up every morning at *four o'clock!*" She held up four fingers in front of me.

"Five o'clock," said Monsieur Vasquez.

She frowned. "*Four* o'clock."

He looked away from her, then hobbled over to another plant. She continued walking and surveying.

"Señor Ricardo!" she said. "Look over here. Potatoes! Onions! Beets! Tomatoes!" She reached down, her broad form not seeming to bend, really, but rather to simply lower itself, and ripped a handful of onions from the soft earth. "Take! Take!" She thrust them at me.

I took the onions from her and held them in my fist. Little tough brown whiskers jutted out from the bottom of the bulbs. The skin was sleek and slightly dirty. Their garden seemed to me a paradise, and it seemed to go on forever.

"Eh!" Monsieur Vasquez said. "Over here, Ricardo. Look!" That's when I got the notion, I'm sure. On that warm September day, down by the river, with the village rising up in the distance, the flaming pink schoolhouse atop it all, the sun washing over us. That's when I got the idea, following this generous Spanish woman down the aisle, as it were, my eyes bugged wide open, as she ripped up an old zucchini plant here, a withered artichoke vine there, shaking the dirt off the old roots, then tossing them aside, that maybe somewhere there was a piece of land here in St-Sébastien de Caisson that I might borrow for the spring and summer. To garden.

Richard Goodman also contributed "A Question of Water" in Part I. Both stories were excerpted from French Dirt: The Story of a Garden in the South of France.

✳

French towns are invariably steeped in the character of the particular countryside that surrounds them, supports them, and *to some extent* explains them. In the France of the past in particular, the town was first and foremost, the result of its countryside.

—Fernand Braudel, *The Identity of France,* translated by Siân Reynolds

DAVID ROBERTS

Alone Among the Angels

The author achieves serenity through
hiking in the Alps.

The Alps are among the most vertical of the world's mountains, and even the humblest valley can brag of wild pinnacles and dizzy precipices. In France alone, the lower Alpine massifs include the Jura, the Chablais, the Faucigny, the Aravis, the Bauges, the Beaufortin, the Belledonne, the Dévoluy, the Alpes-Maritimes, the Alpes de Haute Provence, the Chartreuse, and the Vercors.

For climbers, granite is the definitive stone; the clean slabs, plumb cracks, and sharp arêtes of Yosemite, Chamonix, or Patagonia pose challenges so self-evident they set the heart thumping on sight. But for hikers, no rock conjures a more beguiling landscape than limestone. Much of the French Préalpes is made of the stuff, and nowhere does limestone rise to a nobler geologic eloquence than in those twin massifs that bracket Grenoble—Chartreuse on the north, Vercors on the south.

What is it about limestone that so soothes the heart? Its sheer variety, both to the eye and to the tread. Depending on the light and the local whim of Cretaceous deposition, the rock looks graphite-gray, or mottled and creamy, or white so bright you need sunglasses, or even pale orange or streaky rose. It comes in overhanging slabs as smooth as marble, in plates that look grooved by scalpels, or in diced crumbling loaves that seem about to fall apart. Sometimes it spreads as a vast plain scored with gashes and holes, the stone imitation of a badly fractured glacier. To the hand it feels rough like sandpaper or prickly enough to sting. But after a generation of scramblers have grasped its handholds, they grow smooth as mahogany. In its final incarnation, limestone strews grassy slopes as a talus of loose, flat shards, and when you walk across it, it clinks like porcelain.

During the late spring and early fall you can stay in Grenoble, rent a car, and invade both ranges in a series of day hikes. You can also take off from Grenoble and walk for a week or more in either range, choosing each day's itinerary to suit your fancy, just as you would going hut to hut in the higher Alps in August. There will always be a maintained shelter, a country inn, or a small hotel within reach of each day's trek, and you won't have to worry about avalanches. And if you want to rock-climb, there's a lifetime of routes to be done, especially in the Vercors, where some of the world's best alpinists have honed their skills since the 1830s.

Late October, I found the foliage at the peak of its blazing farewell. On the highest slopes, above 6,000 feet, there was a chilly breeze, and a few patches of new snow clung to north-facing ledges. But with a limestone wall on my right, the sun pouring down from the left, I strolled along in a t-shirt. On five successive days of hiking, I ran into only nineteen other people. Four of them were climbers, three were hunters out stalking hare and grouse (and grumbling about the good weather, too dry for game), and four were playing with *parapentes*.

I like the Spartan luxury of hiking alone. With no one else to irk by stopping to admire a flower or retie a shoelace, with no one to query at trail junctions or consult about f-stops, I let myself lapse into ambulatory trance. Silence stifles the fussy nag in my head who is always preaching duty and ambition. Bird-song and leaf-dance become more real than I otherwise allow them to be. And when I leave the trail to pursue some obscure topographic fancy, I like to play with the soloist's habit-forming frisson: *If I slip here and break my ankle, nobody will ever find me.* In the Vercors and the Chartreuse, I made a ritual of shopping for lunch. In a village square at sunrise, I would pick up a baguette at the *boulangerie;* stop next door at the *chacuterie* for a hard, dry sausage; poke into the *fromagerie* for a good local cheese (say a *reblochon* or a *tomme de Savoie*); then walk over to a *primeur* for tomatoes and pears. With a liter of *eau minérale* and a slab of chocolate, I was ready for anything. They do have supermarkets in France— but why, when the point of a good hike is to savor the day, put efficiency before taste?

A peculiarity of limestone is that it dissolves in water. This means that in such ranges as the Vercors and the Chartreuse, the streams carve tortuous valleys, ravines full of secret gloom where the sun never shines and the rivers sometimes disappear underground.

Such valleys, through which it can be hard even to walk, were formidable obstacles to travel and settlement. Today, a network of ingenious roads breaches their defenses. Indeed, the main attraction that draws tourists to the two ranges is their astonishing highways, replete with tunnels, hairpins, and corniced balconies above the void. At ten miles an hour, cars creep "through the verdurous glooms and winding mossy ways" in the Grands Goulets, the Petits Goulets, the Gorges de la Bourne, and the Combe Laval of the Vercors, in the Pas du Frou and the Guiers Vif of the Chartreuse. The names themselves reflect the awe of the pioneers: Pas du Frau, for example, is Dauphinois for Pass of Horror. Following horse-paths, these sinuous highways, built as early as 1895, respect the terrain rather than dynamiting through it like an American interstate.

These ranges also abound in caves. Some are of colossal dimensions, including the Gouffre Berger, whose principal entrance lies atop an innocent-looking plateau not far from the town of Autrans in the Vercors. Pushed over the decades by the best cavers in the world, the Gouffre Berger (Shepherd's Pit) was for a dozen years the deepest known cave. Today, with 4,093 feet of vertical relief, it stands seventh in the world. With its huge galleries and clean shafts, the Berger is, according to one expert source, "still commonly regarded as the finest caving trip in the world."

On a solo hike up the Dent de Crolles in the Chartreuse, I saw on my map that there was a cave called the Grotte Chevalier not far from the trail. No sign pointed me to it, but a faint side-path gave a hint, and I found its 40-foot-wide entrance, a dark, gaping seam where a huge vertical wall met the talus slope at its foot. I am no caver, but I couldn't resist a look inside. A small chamber narrowed to a hole; I dropped through and squatted in the darkness. It was sunny and warm on the surface, but here a breath of winter fanned my face. Wind at a cave mouth, I knew, meant big passages inside. I pulled out a pocket flashlight that needed new batteries and scrambled a little farther. The cold stone slanted down toward another hole: I crawled to the edge and aimed my flashlight inside. Its feeble beam was not much help. Here I knew I had to stop. But before I turned around,

The first time I ever descended into the dark recesses of the prehistoric caves of France, a little girl—the seven-year-old daughter of a friend—led the way. Noticing that I was edging myself extremely slowly down the narrow stairway, whose view of the cavern below was giving me a sudden case of claustrophobia, she blurted out, "If I can do this, so can you!"

I will always be grateful to her for shaming me into entering, flashlight in hand, a pale ivory sanctuary where, in half-trance, I saw white stalactites hanging from the ceilings, golden stalagmites rising from the ground.

I remember holding my breath at the sight of the ancient footprints, heel marks of barefoot children (probably not much older than my friend's daughter) deeply imprinted in the mud and preserved in the hard surfaces of frozen time. Noticing the wrinkled patterns of those small feet, I thought, "This is my childhood." And then: "This is our childhood"—the childhood of the race.

—Jonathan Cott, "Where Art Began," *Travel Holiday*

I shut off the light and sat for a moment in a darkness more profound than we ever know above ground. Silence wrapped me like

cotton, broken every ten seconds by a single drop of water plink-
ing in a shelf somewhere below.

In 1084 a monk named Bruno came to the Chartreuse, hoping
to found a monastic order in the wilderness. Inspired by a vision,
the local bishop guided him and his six followers to "the Desert,"
a secluded region deep in the then-uninhabited range. In a narrow
valley beneath the craggy frown of the Grand Som, Bruno built
the convent of La Grande Chartreuse and began to attract followers. Over the next five centuries, the monastery was destroyed by
avalanche once and by fire nine times. Yet the Carthusian order
flourished; today there are 24 Carthusian monasteries world-wide,
including one in Arlington, Vermont.

Carthusian monks live lives of severe asceticism. Most of their
hours are spent in total silence, alone in their cells; even their meals
are wordlessly delivered, through a hatch in the wall. They devote
themselves to scholarship and the contemplation of God. Bruno
believed in manual labor, and so the monks keep workshops in the
basements of their cells, where they turn out woodcrafts; they also
tend gardens and raise livestock, though they are forbidden to eat
meat; Mondays they go for a hike in the woods.

You cannot visit La Grande Chartreuse today, but you're allowed to hike a mile and a half up the lane that leads to this fortress
of God and admire it from without. It can be an eerie experience.
The lane is lined with stately chestnut trees; the gray precipices of
the Grand Som lean down in claustrophobic threat. The
monastery is vast, austere, magnificent, a 1676 monument in the
style of Versailles. Forty monks today reside in a convent big
enough for hundreds, but you never catch sight of them. A brimming silence reigns over the place, punctured occasionally by the
peal of old, untempered bells. Standing outside the twelve-foot
walls, you find yourself conversing—if you speak at all—in a
furtive whisper.

Since the 18th century, much of the Carthusian revenue has
come from the manufacture of Chartreuse, often called the most
mysterious liqueur in the world. The original recipe, which calls
for 136 different alpine plants to be mixed, macerated, and fer-

mented in a unique process, is said to exist in only one manuscript copy, which is guarded with a vengeance inside the walls of La Grande Chartreuse. To the cellars in Voiron, where the blissful green and yellow liqueurs are distilled, come three Carthusian monks at regular intervals to supervise the production. They are the only three men in the world who know the formula, and no one else is allowed in the blending room where they work their alchemy. For centuries the liqueur has been known as the *élixir de longue vie,* and it is still widely credited with extending the span of human life.

The Vercors has its own sovereign libation, though its fame barely reaches Paris. Clairette de Die, a naturally effervescent white wine, tastes as good as all but the best champagne and can be had for next to nothing. It has been made for centuries in the vineyards around Die, a smiling town set in the valley of the Drôme River, which was a major thoroughfare for the Romans. As Dea Augusta Vocontiorum, Die itself was an important Roman town: though they have been used ten times over, stones from the second century can still be found in the cathedral and the town walls.

One of the most astounding sights in the Vercors is the Roman quarry located on a high *alpage,* a three-hour hike to the southwest of Le Grand Veymont, the Vercors's loftiest peak. A long column of limestone still lies recumbent, squared on three sides, awaiting only a basal incision to free it from the bedrock. A few yards below, as if discarded in haste or perfectionism, are a Corinthian pedestal, part of a cylindrical pillar, and several stone cubes.

From the quarry, the shaped stones were dragged more than ten miles down the contorted Vercors valleys to Die, then 40 miles down the Drôme to the Rhône; then 60 miles up the Rhône to the Roman stronghold of Vienne. What boggles the mind is why, with whole ranges full of limestone, with the banks of the Drôme itself sprouting limestone cliffs, the Romans chose such a high, remote site for their quarry. I asked a Grenoble guide this question. "It is a matter of the particular quality of the stone," he told me with an appreciative smile. "Such was the aesthetic of the times."

The range is also the locus classicus of a more recent heroism.

During the darkest days of World War II, with the Germans in control of France, the high hamlets of the Vercors harbored enclaves of the Resistance. The Germans knew this, but the gorges that separated the interior of the range from the surrounding plains made it hard to attack. On the morning of July 21, 1944, the Nazis made a daring thrust: dozens of troops sailed noiselessly down upon the Vercors in gliders. Storming the nerve centers of Vassieux and La Chapelle, they rounded up the men, shot them on the spot, and burned the villages to the ground. Hundreds lost their lives. The towns, handsomely rebuilt, are now shrines for the French. In La Chapelle, a small courtyard stands as a memorial in the place where sixteen non-combatant villagers, men as young as seventeen, were executed as an example to others. In Vassieux, a pair of German gliders, reduced after 45 years to rusted, skeletal fuselages, stand as grim memento mori, one before the church, one next to the - cemetery. In the graveyard, many of the soldiers' headstones read simply *INCONNU*—"Unknown."

The Resistance took its purest and noblest form in the simple acts of simple people. An extraordinary example, documented in the American film Weapons of the Spirit, *was the small town of Le Chambon-sur-Lignon, 25 miles east of Le Puy. There, the peasants and townspeople of this deeply Huguenot countryside saved the lives of some 5,000 Jewish children and their parents by giving them refuge in their homes. They later said, "It was natural; we did nothing special"—this despite the Wehrmacht's presence and repeated visits by suspicious officials of the Vichy government. When asked about all these visitors to their beautiful hilly area, the villagers stoutly maintained, "No, we know of no Jews!" Until the Liberation, they shared with the refugees the little they had. Years later, when interviewed by the film producer, himself a refugee born in the village, they were embarrassed that risking their lives to save persecuted strangers should be thought remarkable.*

—Henry S. Reuss and Margaret M. Reuss, *The Unknown South of France: A History Buff's Guide*

Driving the crooked roads of the Vercors and the Chartreuse, you can breathe the spirit of the regions. But to plumb the soul of either range, you must walk. In the Chartreuse, the highest mountains stand isolated, gazing upon one another, like a parliament of eminences. Their names are a patois litany: Dent de Crolles, Charmant Som, Grand Som, Chamechaude, Lances de Malissard. Dark forests intervene, through which the trails wind obscurely until you burst into a clearing where one of the saint-named towns appears: St-Pierre-de-Chartreuse, St-Hugues-de-Chartreuse, St-Même, St-Pierre-d'Entremont.

The Vercors is less islanded: the mountains unfold as long escarpments, of which the finest is the succession of linked cirques ranging from the Grande Moucherolle to the Grand Veymont, a bold eastern façade that catches the first light of morning. Behind this escarpment stretches the Vercors's most curious geologic anomaly. For twenty miles from north to south, a plateau stretches high above the valley of the Vernaison, which borders it on the west. (It is on the southern end of this plateau that the Romans had their quarry.) This tableland is lush with fir and pine trees but has never been inhabited, because the porous limestone bedrock allows all the rainfall to soak through it. The rare water-sources, mostly springs and "fountains," are labeled on the map with ancient names such as Trou du Diable (Devil's Hole).

The several hikes I've made on the edges of this great plateau have only whetted my thirst. On my next visit to the Vercors, I'd like to head off for a week, following some spidery path full of impulsive detours and camping by the fountains each night. The Vercors in general, unlike the Chartreuse, abounds in splendid cliff-walks. Some of the best angle east and west from the pass called the Col de Rousset. Here you tread the edge of the range, with a panorama always to the south; on an exceptionally clear day you might see the Mediterranean. Beneath you hang bands of vertical limestone, and on the steep grassy terraces that separate them you are likely to see darting groups of chamois and the alpine deer known as *chevreuil*.

Chamois

The most startling peak in either range is Mont Aiguille, a 6,844-foot plug of vertical limestone that stands alone in the southeastern Vercors. For its relatively small size, it is one of the most remarkable mountains in France. And one of the finest things you can do in the Vercors is to climb it. No route on the peak is less than technical: so sheer are its walls, you would swear at first glance that only experts could get up the thing. But a series of chimneys and ledges on the northwest flank is Mont Aiguille's only weakness; here the route is no harder than 5.2 [a low level technical climb].

An experienced climber, then, feels comfortable scampering up and down Mont Aiguille unroped. I did this in September a few years ago, passing many roped parties who were taking their time. The guides in Grenoble routinely lead clients up the route, for it is a perfect beginner climb.

To ascend Mont Aiguille is to participate in a pilgrimage. Other routes of comparable difficulty in the Alps were not solved until the 1840s, but the first ascent of Mont Aiguille was made in the unthinkably early year of 1492. It was a deed without precedent in Europe, a deed, for that matter, without sequel until well into the 19th century.

On a journey through the Dauphiné in 1489, Charles VIII was stunned by a distant sight of the peak, then called Mont Inaccessible. The locals told him about many strange events in its vicinity: under certain conditions, you could plainly see the tunics of angels floating in the sky near the summit. Charles decided to get to the bottom of this business—or rather, to the top. He appointed his chamberlain, one Antoine de Ville, Dompjulilan de Beaupré, Capitaine de Montélimar, to organize an ascent. De Ville put together a curious team: its members included an almoner, a clerk, a professor of theology, a carpenter, and a lackey. The key figure we may surmise, was Renaud Jubié, ladderman to the king. In June 1492—while Columbus was loading his ships to set out in search of India, while the last Moors were being driven from Spain—this redoubtable gang went to work on Mont Inaccessible. It is a great shame that in the *procès-verbal* he wrote to explain his ascent, de Ville thought it of trifling interest to record his technique. Only two sentences give us clues. The seige of the northwest wall was undertaken "by subtle means and engines." To follow the route "One has to climb for half a league by means of ladders, and for a league by a path which is terrible to look at, and is still more terrible to descend than to ascend." On June 27, de Ville and his cronies topped out.

To their surprise, they found a green meadow on the summit, "a quarter of a league in length, and a crossbow-shot in width...which it would take 40 men or more to mow." Even more surprising, they came upon "a beautiful herd of chamois." God must have put them there, for, as de Ville sadly noted, the animals "will never be able to get away."

Mightily pleased with themselves, de Ville's team hung out on top of Mont Inaccessible for days. Using their route to ferry supplies, they built a little house on the meadow, had the almoner say Mass, baptized the mountain, and renamed it Mont Aiguille. To make sure their bold deed would not later be dismissed as apocryphal, de Ville sent the lackey to Grenoble to come back with witnesses. The parliamentary usher who showed up at the mountain's base did indeed, as de Ville had warned, blanch at the sight of the route; he refused to climb it. But he stayed long enough to take depositions from members of the team, verifying that they "ate, drank, and slept on the said mountain."

The second ascent of Mont Aiguille did not come until 1849. As late as 1899, with iron cables aiding on the tricky spots, the climb was still rated "for experts only." By now, so many pilgrims have climbed de Ville's route that the key holds are polished like glass. As I swung from move to move up the steep wall, I was full of awe for the royal pathfinders of 1492. I kept looking for ledges where Renaud Jubié might have propped his ladders.

Suddenly I emerged from the last chimney. There, just as in the 15th century, the green meadow stretched off towards the summit. I sat down in the grass and broke out my lunch. De Ville had called the top of Mont Aiguille "the most beautiful place that I have ever visited." It is right up there on my own list. No angels' tunics were hovering in the breeze, but the puffy clouds floating by would do just fine.

David Roberts also contributed "Stones of Carnac" in Part II. This story originally appeared in Outside.

★

Of the ancient massifs of France, the largest is the Massif Central (85,000 square kilometres in all), a "fortress almost exactly in the middle of the country" dispatching rivers, roads, and people in every direction. Perhaps it should be accorded more importance than it usually receives from historians for its role in the creation and preservation of France. Its bulk forms a barrier between the different Frances, keeping them apart it is true, yet at the same time linking them together, nourishing them with its waves of emigration, the most abundant in all France.

—Fernand Braudel, *The Identity of France*,
translated by Siân Reynolds

JON CARROLL

Hazy Days in the Dordogne

Sickness has its secret pleasures.

THE ROOM WAS PINK AT NIGHT—PINK WALLS, PINK CURTAINS, PINK bedspread. In the daytime, when the sun streamed through the windows, the color became deeper and more luminescent, and standing in the middle of the room was like being inside a rose. At sunset, it was like being inside a golden rose.

The room was on the third floor of the Esplanade Hotel in Domme, a walled city on a cliff overlooking the Dordogne Valley. On the ground floor of the hotel was a one-star restaurant specializing in the sublime use of fowl fat for human consumption. We ate there the first night; I had to leave before dessert.

I was sick as a dog. No, that's wrong; there were several dogs in the street below my window, and all of them were healthier than I. My head was huge and tight; my throat was small and red.

I took Fuogrip, a charming French antihistamine that made my ears float. I plumped up the pillows in the rose room and gazed mournfully at the far wall. There was a framed tinted photograph of a young girl in Edwardian dress. On the wall to the right, a water-color of a vase of scarlet flowers. In between, a window overlooking the valley.

Much of the Dordogne looks like the cover of a book of fairy tales: castles above precipices, turrets and ramparts, neat squares of farmland yellow and brown in autumn, curling rivers through narrow valleys, picturesque cottages surmounted by wispy pillars of smoke.

That was the view out my window, I had to stand up and go over to the window to see it, however; that struck me as unfair. Having given me a vile continental disease, France could at least provide me with bedside entertainment.

I drifted.

The bell of the church in Domme was rung both sporadically and irregularly. It would suddenly chime at 11:17 or 4:50; one never knew. Just two notes, ding-dong, ding-dong, pause, ding, pause, dong, ding-dong, ding-dong, repeat until weary.

And then ding, ding, ding, ding—I thought that might be the hours, but when it reached 28 I stopped counting. The dings continued long past reason. I pictured an elderly sexton with limited duties and an affection for the great valley-echoing sound of his ancient gong. A church bell in a medieval city on top of a cliff in the waning days of October was almost comically appropriate. Only the dogs disliked it.

I drifted.

Tracy came back from exploring and shopping. She brought quiches, tarts, ham, a baguette. I was sick in the head but not sick in the stomach. I managed to struggle up and eat a tart in three messy mouthfuls. Then I fell back into pink pillows, exhausted from the effort.

Tracy left for more exploring. I drifted.

I read another chapter of *Speak, Memory,* the Nabokov memoir about being young and aristocratic and almost excessively Russian. All the rooms he described seemed much like my rose room, now softer in the afternoon light. The girl in the tinted photograph could have been Tamara, his first great love, with whom he made hopeless damp passionate love at dusk in a shuttered manor in the thick forest near St. Petersburg, an encounter now almost a century old and 600 years younger than Domme, founded in 1283 by

Philip the Bold, as bold as Vlad the Impaler in the smoldering wreck of a huge amber sunset.

I drifted.

I like being sick, always have. I like the excuse for sloth; I like the huge pillows and the solitude and the dreamy way the days pass. Give me a good head cold and a comfortable place to have it in; paradise enough.

I struggled out of bed to see the sunset. I wrapped the pink blanket around me. The sky was gray and liquid, the sun a thin yellow line at the horizon. Tracy came in behind me. "How are you?" she asked.

"About the same," I said, lying.

Jon Carroll is a columnist for the San Francisco Chronicle. *He is also a gardener and a backpacker and a San Francisco Giants fan.*

※

"It was not what France gave you but what it did not take away from you that was important."

—Gertrude Stein, *What Are Masterpieces*

CLAUDIA J. MARTIN

✦ ✦ ✦

Pâtissier's Apprentice

To be Audrey Hepburn or Jerry Lewis,
that is the question.

AS I STOOD ON THE PAVEMENT OUTSIDE 38 RUE CAMBON, I BEGAN
to have misgivings about my reasons for this trip to Paris. On an
impulse I had responded to an advertisement in a magazine, and
now I was looking up at the unassuming sign painted in gold script
over the doorway, "Ecole Ritz-Escoffier." With no professional
training or experience, but a lot of home experimentation, I had
signed up for a week of pastry classes at the Ecole de Gastronomie
Française Ritz-Escoffier.

As I passed through security and down the long corridor that
led to *l'ecole,* two incongruous movie scenarios kept running
through my mind: The first was from the movie *Sabrina,* in which
the awkward chauffeur's daughter, played by Audrey Hepburn,
went off to study cooking in Paris. She returned to New York
miraculously transformed into a sleek marvel of fashion and food
sophistication, thus winning the heart of stolid bachelor
Humphrey Bogart. When I first saw that film at age ten, I longed
to go to Paris, wear slim black outfits and be able to effortlessly
concoct culinary delights. Thirty years later the dream remained.

The other film that came to mind was one of the ubiquitous
Jerry Lewis movies of the same era whose name I could no longer

recall. I remember Jerry standing in a kitchen that was a shambles, covered in batter and wringing his hands. Yellow fingers of yeasty dough were wriggling out of every oven, evidence of Jerry's culinary disaster.

As I seated myself in the small conference room of the school, I wondered if I had made a mistake by using my vacation to try to fulfill a childhood fantasy. I wondered whether 30 years of dreaming and one week of classes could leave me more Audrey than Jerry.

I introduced myself to my four fellow students and Marie-Anne Dufeu, the school's Deputy Director, whose English was flawless. Marie-Anne told us the history of the Ritz Hotel, which opened on the elegant Place Vendôme in 1898, the culmination of a dream for César Ritz. The dream was completed when Ritz enticed the legendary chef, Auguste Escoffier, to leave the Savoy Hotel in London and run the kitchens of his new hotel. The Ritz instantly became the premier hotel of Paris and is still considered by many to be the most luxurious hotel in the world.

The school, located in a portion of the hotel's kitchen area, is a relatively recent innovation. Started in 1985, it is the first private, non-residential school in France offering full diploma programs in cooking, pastry and bread, winemaking and table service. Although French is the school's first language, English is a very close second. In fact, the school's director, Gregory Usher, is an American who formerly was director at two of the other famous French cooking schools, Le Cordon Bleu and La Varenne.

A quick tour of the school followed. First there was the pastry kitchen, with its numerous convection ovens, gleaming stainless steel racks and marble work surfaces. Past the school's small office was the main teaching kitchen, larger than the pastry kitchen and with ornately tiled walls of fruits and vegetables. There was a demonstration island canopied by a mirror which allowed even those in the back of the room to see the instructor's every move.

We were then taken three floors underground to the hotel's laundry to get fitted for our uniforms. The seamstress measured us

quickly, then handed us each a pair of black-checked pants, which
we were warned fit no one properly, a double-breasted white shirt
with the Ritz insignia, a white
neckerchief, apron, towel, and a
small, round hat. Our uniforms
were to make us easily distinguishable from the chefs, who
wear striped-pants and tall,
pleated *toques blanches.*

*There we were, my daugh-
ters and I, in the Haute-
Savoie, watching the French
Mickey Mouse Club on TV. I had
come to loathe the American version, in which everything seems
geared to vapid rock and roll brain-
washing. To my astonishment, the
French host announced a* toast-
buttering *contest. All the children lined up at a table and began
excitedly putting butter to piles of
toast, amid much cheering and ex-
hortation. Well, I said to myself,
that's a nice cultural twist.*

—James O'Reilly,
"Troglodytes in Gaul"

Dufeu brought us back to the
pastry kitchen, gave us each a
glossy blue folder filled with the
week's recipes printed in both
English and French, then introduced Bruno Neveu, the school's
chef pâtissier.

Neveu, a large man in his late
thirties, asked each of us what
our past cooking experience had
been. I was surprised to learn
that except for me, my fellow students, two young women and one
man from Japan, and Gary, the only other American and a former
television news art director, all had prior professional training and
were all staying for the full twelve-week program.

"Oh, well," I thought, "if I come away with a better pie crust
and a bit of French chic, it will be enough."

But there was no time to be reflective. Neveu told us there was
much to learn and hoped that we were all wearing comfortable
shoes because we would be working steadily for five to six hours
each day. We were in for a marathon of mixing, kneading, and
beating butter into submission.

First we would make cream puff pastry. Puff pastry! I had always
bought mine in the frozen food case. We all watched intently as
Neveu whisked together milk, water, butter, and salt in a heating
saucepan. As the milk and butter mix thickened, we sifted the
flour. Sifting adds air and facilitates blending, Neveu told us. We

added the flour to the milk and butter and whisked. We mixed in eggs and whisked some more. The room was a whir of wire beaters whipping the mix into a thick yellow froth.

Then Neveu took out a pastry sleeve, created an opening by holding thumb and forefinger taut under a fold, and using a flat round scoop, gracefully flipped half the mix into the waiting tube. He began squeezing two dozen identical cigar-shapes onto a cookie sheet. "So," he said, "you do this now and make the eclairs."

My fellow students each made a cuff in their pastry sleeves and slid some batter inside the tubes. Twisting the top of the sleeve in imitation of Neveu, they slowly forced thick lines of batter out of the metal tip and onto their trays.

I had never used a pastry sleeve before. The floppy, cone-shaped bag was much more difficult to handle than it had looked. I tried to scoop the mix into the waiting opening, but that graceful gesture, which had seemed so simple in the demonstration, proved elusive to me. Batter dribbled down my arms to the elbow. Batter exploded from the top of the bag as I tried to twist the top closed. Batter squirted into my face.

I looked up to see Neveu smiling. He came over, gave me a new pastry bag, and showed me how to hold the sleeve for filling, the angle to hold the scoop, the upright position of the bag when squeezing the batter out. As if sensing my burgeoning feelings of inadequacy, Neveu told me to relax and not to worry: unlike the others, he said I had no bad habits to unlearn. "You will learn to make friends with the pastry sleeve soon," he assured me.

Under Neveu's tutelage I managed to press wiggling lines of batter onto a tray while laughing. I was looking a bit more like Jerry than Audrey.

Next we grated cheese and added it to the remaining batter. This time, much to my delight, the pastry sleeve and I seemed to be developing a friendship, as I scooped the batter into the opening without too much mess and produced passable flowerettes.

While the eclairs and cheese puffs baked we learned to make sweet short pastry, squeezing chilled butter through our fingers before gradually mixing in icing sugar and flour. "Don't work it too hard or the oil from your hands softens the dough," Neveu warned.

While the pastry dough chilled, we learned to make cookie dough, with less moisture and elasticity. As that chilled, we made the eclair fillings and glaze: coffee cream filling with coffee glaze and chocolate filling with chocolate glaze. Neveu lowered his voice and told us conspiratorially that the secret to the rich chocolate color in the glaze was a few drops of red food coloring. He scoffed at our American eclairs, with their yellow filling and chocolate icing. "These are not true eclairs," he declared.

*I*t is a matter often discussed why bakers are such excellent citizens and good men. For while it is admitted in every country I was ever in that cobblers are argumentative and atheists, while it is public that barbers are garrulous and servile, that millers are cheats, yet—with every trade in the world having some bad quality attached to it—bakers alone are exempt, and every one takes it for granted that they are sterling: indeed, there are some societies in which, no matter how gloomy and churlish the conversation may have become, you have but to mention bakers for voices to brighten suddenly and for good influence to pervade every one. I say this is known for a fact, but not usually explained; the explanation is, that bakers are always up early in the morning and can watch the dawn, and that in this occupation they live in lonely contemplation enjoying the early hours.

—Hilaire Belloc, *The Path to Rome*

I went back to my room that night exhausted. Pastry-making was a very physical activity, at once delicate and vigorous—like dancing.

The next day we beat a half-pound of butter flat with rolling pins and then learned to fold it into our chilled sweet dough, rolling the pastry flat, folding the dough, turning it, chilling it, and then rolling and folding some more. Neveu always had some little tip to give us for each recipe: an extra layer of egg wash for the cookies, or pricking the dough lightly before baking.

Sometimes we would take our doughs into the main kitchens of the Ritz to use a dough press or an oven that made yeast dough rise fast. It was wonderful to see the real chefs at work, skillfully forming breads or carving vegetables to look like flowers or baskets. They glided through the immaculate tiled rooms as if every dish were choreographed and not merely cooked. The chefs all seemed to nod approvingly in our direction as we followed Neveu like chicks with a mother hen.

The pace was relentless. Despite the nonstop work, I found myself taking great pleasure and pride in finishing a cake or bread as Neveu had demonstrated. In just one week I learned to make pear and almond tarts glistening with apricot glaze, light génoise cakes brushed with Cointreau and filled with candied fruit, *beignets*, *sacristains*, snowcakes, *brioches*, croissants thick with butter or rolled with chocolate, and tiny lemon tarts wreathed with delicate meringue leaves and sugared rosebuds. It was especially uplifting to know that these treats looked and tasted as good as anything from a local *boulangerie*.

As we cleaned up on Friday, Neveu asked us to come into the conference room once we had changed back into our street clothes. When we got there, Neveu, Marie-Dufeu, and the other chefs were waiting with several bottles of the Ritz's own Champagne. Champagne flutes were filled, toasts made, and pastries nibbled.

As I raised my glass I thought of how much I had learned in just five days; how much I had enjoyed the learning; how much I wanted to return and continue the course.

When I finally walked back onto rue Cambon, I felt decidedly more Audrey Hepburn than Jerry Lewis, and it wasn't just the Champagne. I knew I would go home and impress everyone with my pastry.

But what seemed more important for me was the satisfaction in knowing that sometimes it's not so foolish to hang on to childhood dreams.

Claudia J. Martin is a travel writer and photographer who lives in the San Francisco Bay Area with her traveling dog, Tralfaz. She had her first gallery showing of photographs in 1994, and although she begrudgingly admits to being a trial lawyer, she spends as much time as she can traveling, writing, taking pictures, and working as an itinerant pastry chef.

★

It is midmorning snack time at rue Fondary Primary School here on the Left Bank, not far from the Eiffel Tower. Estelle Lenotre, the teacher, is passing out tiny pastries shaped like cloverleafs, hearts, and stars.

But this is no ordinary cookie break. Before taking a single bite, the youngsters—nine to eleven years of age—raise each pastry to eye level and examine it. They sniff each one, and run their fingers over it, before biting in. Mme Lenotre asks them to pay particular attention to "the harmony, the subtlety" of flavor in each.

To the three R's, the French public schools these days are adding the letter G—for *goût,* or taste. Concerned about *le fast food*, the French are fighting back. Their recourse: a class to teach youngsters to appreciate quality. Here, that means one thing: French cuisine.

—Judith Valente, "The Land of Cuisine Sees Taste
Besieged By 'Le Big Mac,'" *Wall Street Journal*

JULIA WILKINSON

✱ ✱ ✱

Black Périgord

In a region of truffles and foie gras, *they still talk
about the Hundred Years War.*

IN THE LAND CALLED PÉRIGORD NOIR IN SOUTHWEST FRANCE,
there is a village that I know well. No one can say for sure where
Black Périgord begins and ends, but its pulse beats fastest in the tri-
angle between the great Dordogne river and its tributary to the
north, the Vézère.

My village lies not on the more famous, open-hearted
Dordogne, but on the Vézère, deep and narrow, dark and wooded,
lined with limestone rock shelters. There are more prehistoric sites
here, between Montignac and Les Eyzies, than almost anywhere
else in the world. That knowledge has blurred the people's sense
of time: secrets, myths, and legends from centuries past merge into
strange history in the Vézère Valley, as black a part of Périgord as
you can ever find.

Périgord is an old Celtic name, not as well-known among
tourists as the new term for the region, Dordogne. But no one in
my village would dream of calling themselves "Dordognais." They
are true "Périgourdins" from the nation of Gascons south of the
Pyrénées: a brave, expressive people, warm-hearted and always
hospitable.

"Of course," says Monsieur Estardier, the unofficial *Monseigneur* and wise man of the village, "it is possible we may have some English blood, too. For a while, during the war, the entire Périgord region was in English hands."

"Oh? I didn't realize…"

"Ah, mademoiselle, pardon. It was before your time. I refer to the Hundred Years War. In the 14th century."

Ah, of course, The War.

We always make a point of seeing Monsieur Estardier first when we arrive. In the more than twenty years we have owned a cottage in the hills above the village, we have learnt how delicate is the fabric of relations in a place where nearly everyone is related and where customs are carefully honored. It was many years before we felt we were accepted.

The village itself is small and very old, with narrow, medieval lanes still hugging the wall of a Renaissance château, and creeping out into one main street that for years has hosted nothing more than a post office, grocery store, butcher, baker, and two small *auberges*. The fine Romanesque church lies at the very edge of the Vézère.

It's by the rich meadows along the river, away from the village, that Monsieur Estardier lives. His farmhouse is typical of the area: a huge, old place made from the golden limestone that gives the Dordogne region its special colours. Russet limestone slabs called *lauzes* cover the roof. Each window has berry-red wooden shutters; summers here are fierce, but air-conditioners would be considered an appalling and unnecessary indulgence. More important is the cellar or

> *The Dordogne is not for the trend-setter or the action-seeker. It is a timeless place, charged with history. You can feel the past in the mysterious dark beauty of the landscapes and in the currents of the rivers. Eleanor of Aquitaine married Henry Plantagenet here and set off the chain of intrigues that led to the Hundred Years War. Richard Lion-Heart roamed these hills, and the resistance fighters of the Second World War hid in these forests. I felt graced to live, even for a brief time, in the security of such solid tradition and among so much beauty.*
>
> —Phyllis Raphael, "An American in Périgord," *Vogue*

ground-floor barn, where vegetables, animals, farm tools, preserves, and wine can be kept. And most important is the kitchen, on the first story, accessible by outside stone steps, and the first room you enter. This is the heart of the house, where one of the finest regional cuisines of France is created, and where family and friends gather to talk, eat, and drink.

"*Entrez! Entrez!*"

Madame Estardier bustles us inside, sits us down on the long wooden benches by the long, oak table, and quickly brings out apéritifs. Pernod—or *eau de vie* if they can take it at this hour—for the men. Sweet nut wine for the women. Little biscuits to nibble.

"*Eh bien!*" says Monsieur softly, his round face breaking into a smile that reveals a row of gleaming golden teeth. "So! How are you? How have you been? How is all the family?"

We talk of this and that, of children and grandchildren, births, marriages, and deaths, as people do in the country. We come to the weather. Madame throws up her hands.

"Oh, what a winter that has passed! Snow in April! Such a thing is unheard of. We live like cattle, hardly able to get out at all. *C'était terrible, terrible!*"

In her excitement, Madame begins to slip into the local patois, the ancient *langue d'oc,* halfway between French and Spanish, used in the Middle Ages and by the greatest troubadours in French history. You don't often hear *langue d'oc* these days, but when you do, the rich sound is unmistakable and, to all but the true Périgourdins, totally incomprehensible.

But we understand Monsieur Estardier well enough. He turns the conversation to happier topics. The tobacco crop is doing well; the vines, too. It'll soon be time to kill the geese and look for *cèpe* mushrooms. "Ah, madame," Estardier turns to my mother, "I know you like them. I will bring you a basket. And walnuts, too, of course, when they are ready. Our walnuts should be excellent this year."

A pause. "And in England," Monsieur Estardier asks quizzically, "do you have nuts?"

The Dordogne region produces more walnuts than anywhere else in France. The Périgourdins cook (and dress salads) with walnut oil, make wine from walnut leaves, and use the fresh nuts as one of the most characteristic ingredients of *la nourriture périgour-dine*. Other local culinary treats are *cèpes* (the name comes from the patois for the large berets worn by the men) and *trompette-des-morts* mushrooms. But the most famous ingredient in Périgord cooking must surely be the truffle, the "black diamond of Périgord."

No one knows why this strange subterranean tuber attaches it-self to the roots of only certain oak trees. But everyone in our vil-lage insists that their method of finding truffles is the best: look out for the rust-red midges hovering over the ground, says Estardier. Get a pig to snuffle them out, says Malery. No!—pigs eat the truf-fles! exclaims Manouvrier. Use a dog. Buy them in the Sarlat mar-ket in December, laughs Jardel. Or ask Estardier, whispers Gonzales.

Gonzales lives up the road from Estardier. His Spanish blood has given him an unpredictable, fiery temperament. But his wife—dark, small and round—always wears a smile. "Come in and have an aperitif! Some nut wine perhaps? No? What can I offer you—do you want to buy some pâté, confits, *foie gras?*"

Madame Gonzales makes the best *brou de noix* in the village; and some of the best goose and duck preserves and the richest liver pâtés in Périgord. Her barn below the house contains a secret horde of tinned and fresh *foie gras,* and preserves of goose and duck in the great jars of lard. Sometimes, she will take them to sell in the local markets: Montignac on Wednesdays, Sarlat on Saturdays (and at the *marché aux gras* before Christmas), together with baskets of fresh vegetables grown in her back garden.

It takes only a taste of Madame's *pâté de foie gras* to understand why this rich specialty has made Périgord famous among gourmets throughout the world, and why a certain Reverend Sydney Smith described his idea of heaven as "eating *pâté de foie gras* to the sound of trumpets."

The method of making *foie gras*—force-feeding

Truffles

geese and ducks to fatten their livers—is still done by hand, the old, traditional way, by many women in the village.

"Ah, on est cruel, n'est-ce pas?" laughs Gonzales's neighbour, Madame Malery, as I grimace at her forcing ground maize down a duck's throat. *"Mais!"* she cries, *"le goût est si bien!"* It tastes so good!

The Malerys are our closest, oldest friends in the village. They never seem to change, though Camille has long ago retired from his work as a carpenter. When we first arrived, he made us a solid wooden kitchen table. We woke one morning to find it outside our door; he had brought it from half a mile away, carrying it up the hill on his back. Now Camille stays at home and makes his wine, picking the grapes at the end of September and mixing them with sugar in huge wooden barrels in the cellar. After a week, the smell is so strong you can hardly enter.

France is not one society then but many societies....Of all these societies, the village is the most basic, the smallest in size, and the oldest—predating by far either the church or the feudal system. As a unit, the village had its own territory, its own collective property (the jealously-watched and defended com-munaux). Economically, it was virtually self-sufficient. It had its own customs, festivals, songs, its own way of speech which was not necessarily the same as that of the next village. It had its own assembly, its elected officers with titles that varied (mayors, syndics, consuls), its own legal identity.

—Fernand Braudel, The Identity of France, translated by Siân Reynolds

Her apron splattered with walnut oil or goose fat, her face red and flustered, Marie-Louise Malery is nearly always cooking. But everything stops for guests. Rickety wooden chairs are pulled out and Camille gets the drinks: aperitifs for us, wine for him. An old grandfather clock, made in nearby Montignac, chimes the hour—twice every hour! Périgourdins have a habit of forgetting the time.

Marie-Louise is garrulous; Camille warm-hearted but shy. During the war (the "other" war that is so often mentioned here: the Second World War), Marie-Louise's first husband was killed, and Camille was captured and sent to Germany for four years. The war left many scars in this part of France, where the Resistance was strong. Close to the Malery's house is a memorial plaque—typical of many in the region—to *"Victimes de la Barbarie Nazie 29 June 1944."* Someone still leaves flowers there.

Camille is a die-hard Périgourdin. His beret hardly ever leaves his head, and his patois is so strong that Marie-Louise has to act as interpreter. When we join the Malerys for one of their family banquets, Camille leaves the talking—and the fine wines—to his extrovert son-in-law, Jean-Marc. For himself, he is content with his soup and bread and rough red wine—all of which come together when he stirs a little wine into the last of his soup, picks up his bowl and drinks the dregs. Marie-Louise looks on disapprovingly.

But she is too busy talking to stop him. The village gossip is all about the wedding of the Parisian girl, whose mother owns the old garrison tower next to the chateau.

"Two hundred guests have been invited!" exclaims Marie-Louise, as she serves us *pâté aux truffes.* "And 3,000 white paper flowers have been made to decorate the trees outside the church and in the home. Can you imagine the cost of this? The wedding feast alone…"

The pâté finished, a plate of melon slices appears. Jean-Marc opens another bottle of wine, "A Bergerac," he says loudly, "crisp, dry, white. One of the region's best wines, I think, though the Romans preferred Cahors."

"Of course, there will be musicians outside the church," continues Marie-Louise, "brought all the way from Périgueux. And everyone in the village has been invited to drink champagne with the newlyweds after the service. You must come, too! I invite you! If only to see *les belles robes.…*"

She brings out the next dish—*cou farci,* stuffed goose neck—an old regional specialty rarely served in restaurants. Jean-Marc produces a bottle of Pécharmant, which he labels as "rich, red—you've never heard of it? Quick! Finish the Bergerac. Try it!"

We eat and drink and talk for hours: the next dish is *petits pois,* then guinea-fowl and walnut-oiled salad with another bottle of Pécharmant. The conversation turns to *la chasse,* the hunt, every Périgourdin's passion (though there is little left to shoot), to the forests of Périgord Noir where wild boar once roamed, and to the glory that was once Languedoc and Aquitaine.

Finally, a plate of cheeses signals the start of the end of the meal: a huge apple tart, with Jean-Marc's *pièce de résistance,* a sweet 1959 Monbazillac—"ah, this is truly the finest of wines! The best-kept secret of Périgord!"—coffee, Armagnac, and pink champagne. We stagger up the hill, the sound of crickets and cicadas throbbing in our heads.

Given such hospitality, we find it hard to venture far beyond our village. It has taken us years to see even a little of the treasures that exist, tempted as we were at every stop, from apéritifs at the Malery's or plum wine at Madame Barrière's in the heart of the village, to picnics by the river and simple walks in meadows of willows and wild orchids.

Sometimes we stop to see old Jardel (young Jardel is the village electrician) making baskets in his yard by the chateau. He grumbles jovially about his slow fingers and aching limbs: *"Ah, je suis né trop tôt"*—I was born too soon. It's only later that we ponder the curious poetry of what he has said.

But we always make it to Montignac market on Wednesdays, to wander among stalls of strawberries or *cèpes,* goat's cheese, and Périgord honey, pâté and peaches, meat, fish, and vegetables. On the way back, we visit the trout farm at Plazac. The same old man has served us for years, hobbling out, back bent, apologizing for the smallness of the

> *That evening we sat and rather drowsily talked about the hunt: our natural sorrow and empathy for the stag that all but the most moronic hunter feels for his quarry, but also our sympathy for the hounds, also noble beasts in whose blood runs this ancient urge for the quarry—dogs that had begun anyway as predators and had their instincts refined by man to hunt a particular beast, just as a good bird dog singles out his grouse. The sport is nearly a millennium old in France and in some parts of the world dates back five millennia, as in the stele I had seen in a museum of the great Abyssinian lion dogs upon their own quarry. There is no apologia now for hunting except that the desire is in us.*
>
> —Jim Harrison, *Just Before Dark: Collected Nonfiction*

trout. "I have been ill—my heart, my blood, my lungs—everything!" He potters off to get his net. "Ah yes, I am getting old...I have grown old too quickly."

But he is still agile with the net, tapping the water to drive the trout to one end of the narrow channel, plunging the net in suddenly to catch our four fish, catching one, two and yet another two fish. "Take five," he says, "for the fourth is very small." And he nods his head and hobbles away.

Growing old comes as a sad surprise to the Périgourdin. How can it be otherwise in a land where man has lived so long; where every farmer digs up Stone Age flints in his fields and every child scrambles in the dwellings of cavemen? I have done it myself, as a child, at Castlemerle, an area of dense population in Palaeolithic times, yet better known now among the locals as the site of their favorite restaurant.

But the most famous prehistoric site is Lascaux Cave near Montignac, with its 15,000-year old paintings (though the original cave is closed to the public, there's an excellent facsimile) and the dozens of *grottes* and rock shelters around Les Eyzies. The best of them is Font de Gaume, with its extraordinary polychrome mammoths, bisons, reindeer, and horses.

Atmosphere is all in Périgord Noir. Along the Vézère, passing the fairy-tale chateaux of Losse, Belcayre, and Clérans, it is sparkling and brilliant. The bastions and castles of the Dordogne at Domme, Beynac, Castelnaud, or Montfort are grander by far. But it's Périgord's own dark, deep atmosphere that has always drawn me: the ruins of Château de l'Herm with its murderous history or the awesome remains of Château de Commarque, reaching down through forest-tangled stones, to a troglodyte fort and a cave with Magdalenian engravings.

In the woods around Montignac there is the sombre, decaying bastion of Coulonges which once belonged to the Knights of the Order of St. John, and not far away, tucked in a gentle valley, the astonishing fortified church of St-Amand de Coly, once the home of 200 Augustinian monks.

There are *grandes randonnés*—marked footpaths—everywhere, to lead you to such discoveries; roads with as many curving *cingles* as the river itself or sometimes simply tracks—like the one I took once to the elegant Château de Puymartin—through pine forests carpeted with giant cones, purple heather, and sloe bushes.

The region's most popular atmosphere is in Sarlat, center of Périgord Noir. Its old cobbled streets and golden-stoned Renaissance houses with their sculptured doorways and stairways, mullioned windows, turrets and bell towers are the delight of every visitor. In summer, the place is so full of English tourists that it's almost as if the 1360 Treaty of Brétigny (which gave Périgord to the English crown) had never been superseded. The Saturday market in Goose Square is an event that can't be missed, with its street musicians, jewellery-sellers and profusion of Périgourdin produce.

"Ah, but the December market is better," says Madame Malery. "That's when the best truffles and *foie gras* are sold. Come then, come back for the market!"

When we celebrated twenty years of living above the village in the Valley of the Vézère, we had a dinner under the lime tree and invited all our friends: Estardiers, Malerys, Gonzales, Manouvriers, Barrières, Jardels.

They came dressed in their best, standing nervously at first, refusing drinks. But once we all sat down to eat, the candlelight flickering on the tables, the atmosphere relaxed and the wine began to flow. Someone sang a snippet of an old Périgourdin song. Madame Barrière, bright red spots on her wrinkled cheeks, started to hum.

"Did you ever dance *la bourrée,* madame?" asked a guest from Bordeaux.

"Ah yes, indeed, monsieur!" cried Madame with delight, who tells us of the barrel-organs, the hurdy-gurdies, and *la bourrée,* which she would dance all night.

Monsieur Barrière smiled. In those days, he told me, he was a hairdresser, his father a basket-maker. He has lived all his life in the village. Oh yes, times have changed. There was more comradeship and togetherness then. Even more than now, oh yes!

The evening grew lively, everyone talking at once. For hours we sat under the lime tree until gradually a calm descended. "Listen to

the crickets!" murmured Madame Barrière in a moment of silence.
"We don't have those in the village."

They all left together, at the same time, in a flurry of kissing
cheeks and shaking hands. For a long time afterwards, we could
hear voices in the valley and see lights flickering by the river. And
then the village fell asleep, and even the crickets were quiet.

*Julia Wilkinson is an English freelance travel writer who set off for Australia
sixteen years ago and happily got stuck en route in Hong Kong. She has
traveled extensively throughout Southeast Asia writing for many publications
as well as contributing to several guidebooks. For the last ten years she and
her husband have divided their time between Hong Kong's Cheung Chau
Island and a cottage in the Wiltshire countryside. She visits Périgord every
September and has a passion for flying hot-air balloons, once piloting one
across the English Channel.*

★

There were about 500 geese on this farm, not including the visitors. They
were divided into three groups—the fuzzy little babies, that looked good
enough to eat in one chomp; the breeders, which don't have to do anything but breed, and look rather superior; and the 200 or so producers,
which are kept six to a pen and are fed the hard way three times a day,
little knowing that they are being prepared for a one-way liver transplant.

In the bad old days, geese were force-fed via large funnels, but things
have improved, goosewise. The French fella, whom I shall call Jacques,
rode into the barn on his late-model goose-mobile, a sort of golf cart with
a large container on top for the feed—mainly corn—and a long hose, at
the sight of which the loosey-goosies indeed began begging for it in an
unseemly fashion. Like Pavlov's dogs, I suppose they were salivating. At
any rate, they set up a frightful commotion, extended their necks straight
up and opened wide their beaks. "Come here, *cherie*," said Jacques. He
shoved the nozzle down Cherie's gullet and stepped on the foot pedal that
releases the food. Then he helped things along by massaging the lumpy
grain down Cherie's swanlike neck. "You see?" said Jacques as the other
geese began clamoring for their shots. It really wasn't too awful, and I suppose that giving their swollen livers for the greater glory of France is the
highest honor to which a goose may aspire, but nevertheless I swore off
foie gras on the spot.

—Herb Caen, "Loose as a Goose," *San Francisco Chronicle*

SEÁN DUNNE

✦ ✦ ✦

Finding My Religion

Romantic Paris gives way
to a spiritual Paris.

WHEN NOT AT MY DESK, I WALKED THROUGH THE STREETS OR idled in cafés. I had been to Paris a number of times but something had changed for me. When I went first, as an aspirant writer in my early 20s, I entered a myth. It was the myth of artistic Paris, of bookshops like Shakespeare and Company, and of cafés like Les Deux Magots. Since my late teens and my first reading of Camus, I had been in love with the idea of Paris. Now, in my late 30s, I found that something had changed. Places which once interested me seemed dry and dead. I had no interest in the myths of others. I felt that I would have to create my own Paris and that it was this which would be most truly reflected in my own writing.

On a Saturday morning in June, then, I set out for Saint Gervais with all these things in my mind. I had heard that the church is used by a monastic order known as *Les Fraternités Monastiques de Jérusalem*. I had never heard of this order. I was late for the ceremony, yet from the moment I entered the church, I was drawn by the nature of the way in which Mass was celebrated. The monks and nuns, attired in white, sat or knelt in rows before the altar where a number of icons were set and where candles stood in a menorah. Hundreds of men, women, and children sat on chairs,

315

leaned against wide pillars or simply sat on the floor. The church, one of the oldest in Paris, has a rather tattered air as a result of long closure. This added to the sense of visiting a kind of catacomb.

The Mass was conducted with great care. The ceremony was a mixture of knowledge and love. There were elements which were strange to me: at the Our Father, for example, the monks and nuns raised their arms to Heaven. At the point where people make the sign of peace to each other (a moment that is sometimes met in Irish churches with a wriggling embarrassment), the organ was played with exhilaration and the members of the monastic community moved through the congregation with a true joy. The singing—and the Mass was almost entirely sung—was especially beautiful. The whole affair combined elements of the Roman, Judaic, and Byzantine traditions, but it remained a ceremony where nothing was trendy or shallow.

Without drama, I can say that this hour and 30 minutes in Saint Gervais was among the most moving and joyful experiences that I had ever known. I felt that the experience, at this particular point in my life, was akin to finding a precise word which was waiting to be named. One of the more exciting moments in making a poem occurs when dozens of words are hurled away and the correct one is suddenly found. My experience at Saint Gervais was like that.

Later, I learned a little about the order. It was founded in 1975 by Pierre-Marie Delfieux. A former chaplain at the Sorbonne, Pierre-Marie had spent some years living as a hermit in the Sahara, continuing the tradition started by those hermits known as the Desert Fathers. He became convinced of the need to found a monastic order in the city. The huge cities of today seemed to him to be the equivalent of the desert. The order now includes almost 100 members of many nationalities, with more nuns than monks and with many novices. An explanatory leaflet declares that the church of Saint Gervais "has been entrusted by the Cardinal Archbishop of Paris with the task of growing into a contemplative centre." I met some of the monks and nuns, among them an American, Brother Bradford, and an Irish nun who lives as a hermit.

Monks and nuns live in separate buildings close to the church. The monastery is based in the lower two floors of the large apartment block close to the Monument to the Unknown Jew. I had lunch there with Bradford, as everyone called him. We sat in a crowded refectory where monks and guests ate in silence. A monk placed a record of Handel's *Water Music* on a turntable and the flowing melodies accompanied our meal of ratatouille during which not a word was spoken but for Grace at the start and finish.

> *"French Catholics are like no other Catholics,"* said the famous critic Sainte-Beuve. *"In France, we remain Catholics long after we have ceased being Christians."*
>
> —Alfred Kazin, "River of Life," *Travel Holiday*

This order is deliberately based in the city, just as much of Christ's life was lived in the city of Jerusalem. I found this enormously relevant and attractive since sometimes monasticism is sentimentally seen as a kind of religious pastoralism that denies the value of urban life. As someone who has always lived happily in cities, I immediately responded to this effort to create a sense of contemplation in an urban world. I discovered that the lives of the order at Saint Gervais are not a simplistic outcry against urban life. Rather, they say that they want to "recognise all that is truly beautiful in the city, its creativity, its yearnings, and its innermost values, singing through these the praise and the glory of God." At the heart of Paris, I felt that this order had touched what Eliot, in the book I was studying, called the still point of the turning world.

On the way back to the Irish College, I felt a terrific excitement. I had found the focus where Paris and my inner self met. I had discovered once again that, despite all my arguments with the Catholic Church, there are signs of tremendous tenderness, excitement, and promise. Some are social; some are liturgical; some are monastic. The best of them begin in an interior space that has been shaped by silence and prayer. On that Sunday morning in

Paris, I came into contact with that space as it manifests itself in an urban form.

I went back to Saint Gervais a number of times. Each day, I sat with others before the icons in an oratory and then joined the monks and nuns for Vespers and Mass. It was an experience that seemed at once marginal and central. In that worn church by the Seine, I learned with Eliot what it was to kneel where prayer had been valid, and again I felt that prayer is not simply a matter of words but is often wordless, gathering an accretion of quiet as it deepens and grows. I learned that I could keep this core of silence in my life just as this order keeps it within the heart of Paris. I realised that I had been making the mistake of seeing contemplation and activity as alternatives and that I was creating an unnecessary schism in my mind. Now, I saw them as united, one within the other and running through it like a seam.

That Sunday evening, when I sat at my writing-table and looked across the damp roofs of the Latin Quarter, I knew that I had experienced something that would remain in my memory with the force of an icon in a quiet room.

Seán Dunne was a poet, author, and literary editor for the Cork Examiner *until his untimely death at the age of 39 in August 1995. His books include* In My Father's House, The Cork Anthology, *and* The Road to Silence: An Irish Spiritual Odyssey *from which this story was excerpted.*

★

I remember one starlit stroll that led me unthinking to the Seine, where I reflected on the reflection of the moon: that it would shimmer there the next night, and the next night, and then one night without me.

I stared as if there were some secret to be discerned beneath that dark, sparkling surface. Then the leaves in the plane trees rustled and something rustled inside me and I thought that was all right: that what Paris ultimately gives you, if you are lucky, has everything and nothing to do with the city itself—that it is the gift of cutting through all the laziness and conformity and loss of heart that life develops, to rediscover the passions and goals that you once held fiercely and that are still the fundamental and true you.

In this sense, I thought, there is no leaving Paris. If you have been touched by this magical, passionate place, it flows through you—a cloud-soaring spire, a rain-bejeweled day, a barge, a bookstall, an echoing flute in an ancient archway—as deep and ceaseless as the Seine.

—Donald W. George, "Notes Toward a Portrait of Paris,"
San Francisco Examiner

JON KRAKAUER

★ ✦ ★

A Taste for the Abyss

Derring-do in the birthplace
of modern mountaineering.

IT'S ONLY SEPTEMBER, BUT THE WIND SMELLS LIKE WINTER AS IT gusts through the narrow streets of Chamonix. Each night the snow line, like the hem of a slip, pushes farther down the ample granite hips of Mont Blanc toward the stubble of slate roofs and church steeples on the valley floor. Three weeks ago the sidewalk cafés along the Avenue Michel Croz were choked with vacationers sipping overpriced *citron* and craning their necks at the famous skyline, two vertical miles above their tables and shimmering like a mirage in the August haze. Now most of those same cafés are empty, the hotels deserted, the recently throbbing bistros quiet as libraries. Wandering Chamonix's streets a few minutes before midnight, I am therefore surprised to see a crowd queued up outside the entrance to a nightclub near the center of town. Curious, I fall in at the end of the line.

Twenty-five minutes later, finally inside, it's standing room only. Music is thundering over the sound system with sufficient wattage to rattle the beer glasses, and it's impossible to see from one end of the bar to the other through the blue fog of smoldering Gitanes. The youthful clientele possesses a cocky, self-absorbed allure that brings to mind Shakespeare's line about "the confident and over-lusty French," but there is no dancing; surprisingly few people appear to be on the prowl, hardly anyone is even engaged in conversation. The patrons, I deduce soon enough, come strictly for the videos: every face in the joint is glued to the club's half-dozen giant television screens, transfixed by the flicker of the cathode rays.

The common thread running through all the videos is mortal risk; the grimmer things get, the more rapt the crowd becomes. Indeed, the most popular tape of all is a 45-minute compilation of fatal Grand Prix automobile crashes, a grisly smorgasbord of drivers and spectators being crushed, dismembered, and burned alive—the lot of it enhanced for our viewing pleasure with full-frame closeups and replays in super slo-mo.

At one point in the evening there is some sort of snafu with the video machine, the screens go blank, and I find myself chatting with a young Frenchman from the nearby city of Annecy. Patrick is attired in calf-length floral-print beach trousers, an oversize Batman sweatshirt, and—never mind that the sun set some six hours ago and we are in a dimly lit bar besides—a pair of pink-framed glacier glasses. He allows with characteristic Gallic modesty that he is both an expert *parapente* pilot and a *"superbe"* rock climber. I respond that I, too, happen to be a climber, and that I've been quite pleased with the quality of the routes I've completed in Chamonix thus far; seizing the opportunity to do some chest-thumping of my own, I go on to tell Patrick that I especially enjoyed the route I'd done just the day before, a classic test piece—rated *extrêmement difficile* in the Vallot guidebook—on a slender, improbably steep spire called the Grand Capucin.

"The Capucin?" replies Patrick, clearly impressed. "That must have been a very difficult summit to launch the *parapente* from yes?" No, no, I quickly interject—I simply climbed the peak; I didn't mean to suggest that I'd also flown off it. *"Non?"* says Patrick, momentarily taken aback. "Well, to solo the Capucin, that is a worthwhile undertaking all the same." Actually, I sheepishly explain, I hadn't soloed the peak, either: I'd done it with a partner and a rope. "You did not solo and you did not fly?" asks the

Frenchman, incredulous. "Did you not find the experience a little—how you say in English—*banal?*"

Chamonix, though populated by fewer than 11,000 year-round
residents, has for two centuries been the hippest mountain community on the Continent, maybe
the entire planet, and not merely
in the minds of those who live
there. Chamonix, understand, is
considerably more than the
Aspen of the Alps; it's the very
birthplace of *haute chic*. It's no
accident that when Yvon
Chouinard wanted to establish a
maximally visible retail beach-
head on the far side of the
Atlantic, the first Patagonia store
he opened in Europe was in
downtown Chamonix.

> *he storming of the Bastille
> is called the spark of the
> French Revolution. How many
> know that when the mob actually
> broke down the doors of the most
> dreaded prison in France, the liber-
> ators could find only four lunatics,
> two forgers, and an intimate friend
> of the Marquis de Sade? The real
> event is usually less heroic than the
> official portraits or Major Motion
> Pictures that follow. Also more
> human and more interesting.*
>
> —Martin Cruz Smith, "Martin
> Cruz Smith Flirts with Danger,"
> *Travel & Leisure*

Chamonix proper is overbuilt
and not particularly handsome by
European architectural standards.
There are too many tourist traps, too many megalithic concrete
eyesores, far too many cars and nowhere at all to put them. All the
same, enough Old World remains in the town's twisting cobbled
streets and ancient, thick-walled chalets to make even the most appealing American ski towns seem pseudo-Bavarian theme parks by
comparison. Jammed into the cramped, claustrophobically narrow
valley of the River Arve, just eight miles from the point where Italy,
Switzerland, and France share a common frontier, the community
is hemmed in hard to the north by the 9,000-foot peaks of the
Aiguilles Rouges and even harder to the south by the 15,771-foot
mass of Mont Blanc. The highest point in Western Europe, it towers so near at hand that paragliders routinely touch down in the village center after taking off from the mountain's summit.

The popularity of the nightclub's eclectic video fare isn't surprising: the lifeblood of the entire town, after all, is high-risk recre-

ation and the marketing thereof. As American alpinist Marc Twight—who has been living here intermittently for the past five years—says with great affection and tongue only partially in cheek, Chamonix is nothing less than the "death sport capital of the world." The huge billboard that greets visitors as they motor into Chamonix on the main highway from Italy claims only that they have arrived in the *"Capitale Mondiale du Ski et de l'Alpinisme"*—the World Capital of Skiing and Climbing. And lo, the sign does not exaggerate, for Chamonix and Chamoniards are at the cutting edge of international climbing, perhaps now more than ever before. But in the frenetic, adrenaline-besotted climate of the past decade, Twight's sobriquet has come to seem the more accurate of the two. The impeccably creased knickers and classic guides' sweaters of old have been supplanted by neon-hued Lycra and Gore-Tex, and traditional mountaineering has mutated here into a host of alpine thrill sports that Dr. Paccard would be hard put to recognize.

Dr. Michel-Gabriel Paccard, you'll recall, invented the sport of mountain climbing on August 8, 1786, by making the first ascent of Mont Blanc, in the company of a local chamois hunter named Jacques Balmat. Following the ordeal, Balmat reported, "my eyes were red, my face black, and my lips blue. Everytime I laughed or yawned the blood spouted from my lips and cheeks, and, in addition, I was half-blind." For their inestimable contribution to the future economic base of the community, the two original alpinists received a cash prize of what amounted to 60 U.S. dollars, the village center was designated Place Balmat, and the town's main drag was christened the Rue du Dr. Paccard—along which, two centuries later, you will find not only nightclubs and the spiffy Patagonia store, but merchants selling everything from paragliders, Parisian lingerie, and postcards of climbing stars Jean-Marc Boivin and Catherine Destivelle, to graphite-shafted ice axes, titanium pitons, and state-of-the-art snowboards embossed with likenesses of the Manhattan skyline.

In the decades following the Paccard-Balmat climb, as accounts of that deed and subsequent ascents circulated across the Continent, Chamonix became an exceedingly fashionable destination for the rich and famous, and rapidly developed into the world's first mountain resort (previously, as *New Yorker* writer Jeremy Bernstein has pointed out, mountains were generally regarded as "terrifying, ugly, and an obstacle to travel and commerce, and anyone living in or near them as subhuman"). Goethe, Byron, Ruskin, Percy Shelley, the Prince of Wales, and ex-Empress Josephine all sojourned there. By 1876, 795 men and women had reached the top of Mont Blanc, among them an Englishman named Albert Smith who passed out drunk on the summit after he and his companions put away 96 bottles of wine, champagne, and cognac in the course of their ascent.

As the heavy traffic on Mont Blanc began to rob the climb of its cachet (by its easiest routes, the 15,771-foot peak is not technically demanding or even very steep), ambitious alpinists turned their attention to the hundreds of sheer-walled satellite peaks—the fabled Chamonix Aiguilles—that stud the ridges of the massif like the spines of a stegosaur. In 1881, when Albert Mummery, Alexander Burgener, and Benedict Venetz bagged the fearsome-looking Aiguille du Grepon, it was lauded as a superhuman feat. Nevertheless, in a prescient moment following the climb, Mummery predicted that it would only be a matter of time before the Grepon lost its reputation as "the most difficult ascent in the Alps" and came to be regarded as "an easy day for a lady."

A hundred years after Mummery's heyday, new techniques, better equipment, and a population explosion on the heights have brought about just the sort of devaluation Mummery feared, not only of the Grepon, but of most of the other "last great problems" that followed: the Walker Spur, the Freney Pillar, the north face of Les Droites, the Dru Couloir, to name but a few.

Although Mont Blanc is a mountain of genuinely Himalayan proportions, boasting an uninterrupted vertical rise of nearly 13,000 feet from base to summit, it also happens to sit squarely in the teeming lap of Western Europe, and therein lies the rub. It's this unlikely juxtaposition of radical topography and rarefied Continental culture that, for better and worse, begat modern Chamonix.

On a nice summer day, the streets will be peopled with a mix you'd expect to find in any French tourist town: mink-wrapped matrons, tourists from Cincinnati and Milan, frail old men in wool berets, leggy shop girls in black hose and miniskirts. What's different about Cham—as the village is termed in the local patois—is that fully half the people walking past will be clomping along in climbing boots and have a coil of 8.8-millimeter Perlon slung over a shoulder.

Mont Blanc is now climbed by nearly 6,000 people every year, and tens of thousands of others swarm over the adjacent Aiguilles. A *million* thrill chasers of one kind or another pass through Chamonix annually. The massif is encircled with hotels, peppered with multistory "huts," crisscrossed by 57 chair lifts and aerial trams, and pierced by a seven-mile tunnel through which runs a major European highway. At the apogee of climbing season the Vallée Blanche—the high glacial plateau that feeds the Mer de Glace—is crowded with so many alpinists that from the air it bears an uncanny resemblance to an ant colony. The number of new climbing routes documented in the record books of the Office de Haute Montagne is mind-addling; there's scarcely a square meter of rock or ice left in the entire range that hasn't been ascended by somebody.

One might conclude that every last ounce of challenge has long since been wrung from the mountains above Chamonix, but one would be wrong. The French, being a proud and creative people with a gift for self-dramatization, have had little trouble finding novel forms of alpine stimulation. In addition to the obvious variations—speed climbing, extreme solo climbing, extreme skiing—they have fervently embraced such activities as bungee jumping, *le surf extréme* (extreme snowboarding), *le ski sur herbe* (using wheeled skis to rocket down grassy summer slopes), *ballule* rolling (careering downhill inside giant inflatable balls), and—the most popular new game of all—flying off mountaintops with paragliders, which the French call *parapentes.*

It's a luminous fall afternoon in downtown Cham, and I'm sitting on the terrace of the Brasserie L'M, loitering over a strawberry crêpe and a café au lait, wondering whether I might, given my limited talents, ever rise above the life of the terminally banal. Overhead, a nonstop parade of paragliders is floating across the sky, en route from one or another of the surrounding Alps to a meadow a few blocks away that serves as the town landing field. When I finally get tired of the waiter inquiring every few minutes if I'll be having anything else ("Or will monsieur be leaving now?"), I get up and walk to the meadow, which lies at the base of the Brevent ski lift, to catch a little flying action at close range.

Neither mortal risk nor fear of litigation has slowed the proliferation of paragliding in the Alps: at last count there were an estimated 12,000 parapilots at large in France. And the zeal with which the French have taken up paragliding has nothing to do with some Gallic knack for avoiding accidents: parapilots in Chamonix are forever crashing onto rooftops and busy highways, being blown into ski lifts, and dropping out of the sky like flies. Indeed, within half an hour of my arrival at the Chamonix landing field, I witness two paragliders overshoot the tiny meadow and plow into the trees, and see a third slam face-first into the second-story wall of an apartment building.

The swelling tally of paragliding mishaps, however, is unlikely to move the French to ban the sport from their ski resorts (as Americans have), nor is the annual carnage from climbing ever likely to lead to the curtailment of that activity. This despite the fact that between 40 and 60 people come to unpleasant ends in the mountains above Chamonix in a typical year, and that the overall body count on Mont Blanc now totals more than 2,000, making it far and away the deadliest mountain on earth.

Interestingly enough, routine, lift-served skiing—an activity that few American practitioners think of as life threatening—contributes approximately half the annual death toll. There are eight ski areas in the Chamonix Valley, and their slopes include many runs that are no more challenging than the tamest trails at Stowe or Park City, but there is also a vast amount of lift-served terrain that blurs the line between ordinary skiing and hard core mountaineering. Take a wrong turn, for instance, when you get off the lift on the Grands Montets or the Aiguille du Midi—two of the most popular places to ski—and you could easily wind up in the bottom of a crevasse, or buried under avalanching seracs, or skidding off a 1,000-foot cliff. In the United States, skiers take it for granted that natural hazards, if they exist at all, will be carefully fenced off, marked with signs, or otherwise rendered idiot-proof. In Chamonix personal safety is rightly seen as the responsibility of the skier, not the ski area, and idiots don't last long.

The French, when it comes right down to it, look at riskysports—and sports in general—in a fundamentally different way than Americans do. We go in for team sports like baseball and football, and the athletic heroes we hold up for our kids to emulate tend to be cast in the squeaky-clean Orel Hershiser mold.

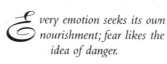

very emotion seeks its own nourishment; fear likes the idea of danger.

—Joubert, *Pensees*

The French, in marked contrast, are notorious individualists with a fondness for the sensational deed, the stylish twist, the dramatic solitary act; their athletic role models tend to chain-smoke Gitanes, drive irresponsibly fast, and excel at activities like long-distance windsurfing or soloing 5.12 rock climbs.

And so, Chamoniards may not be happy about all the bloodshed that occurs in their backyard, but they are adept at shrugging it off. "In Chamonix," a wiry 30-year-old *gendarme* named Luc Bellon explained to me, "there is a special mind. Maybe you are not a guide or a climber—maybe you are a butcher or own a souvenir shop—it makes no difference, the mountains still put food on your table. Like fishermen with the sea, we have learned to accept the danger and the tragedies as a fact of life here."

Although Luc Bellon works as a *gendarme*—a French cop—it should not be inferred that he spends his days arresting pickpockets or directing traffic in a silly pillbox cap. Bellon, rather, belongs to an elite arm of the state police called the Peloton de Gendarmerie de Haute Montagne, PGHM for short, whose job it is to bail out those hapless adventurers who find more excitement then they reckoned on. The *Thwock! Thwock! Thwock!* of a squat

blue PGHM helicopter, speeding off toward the Aiguilles to
retrieve another broken body from the heights, is as common over
Chamonix as is the sound of
police sirens in the Bronx: in July
and August, when the glaciers
and Aiguilles are mobbed with
incautious alpinists from around
the world, Bellon and his cohorts
are frequently called on to perform ten or fifteen rescues or
body recoveries a day.

*It's funny the effect little
things have. We stayed
on in the Chamonix valley in part
because a friendly ski shop owner
volunteered to store our snow tires
for us. Then the local school principal helped us find a house to rent.
And then the butcher, the deli
owner, and the proprietors of our
favorite salon de thé became fonts
of information, gossip, and tips on
how to get along in this corner of
the Alps.*

*—James O'Reilly,
"On and Off the Autoroute"*

Ironically, the skill and vigilance of the PGHM may actually
add to the astounding number of
accidents in Chamonix, for
many would-be Boivins take
even greater chances than they
normally would, knowing that
Bellon and company are standing by round the clock to save their
bacon. According to John Bouchard, an accomplished American
alpinist who has been coming to Chamonix since 1973, "These
days, instead of taking emergency bivouac gear, guys go out on
hard climbs and take nothing but a radio. If things get sketchy they
assume they can just get on the horn and call for a rescue."

I confess to contemplating a similar gambit myself during my
visit last fall. On my second day in Cham, I set out alone up a steep
but oft-ascended groove of ice on a 13,937-foot peak called Mont
Blanc du Tacul. Low on the climb, I repeatedly struck rock as I
slammed my ice axes through the couloir's thin glazing, carelessly
dulling the picks; by the time I was midway up the route, being
both unacclimated and badly out of shape, I began to have difficulty swinging the blunt tools hard enough to make them stick.
Since I hadn't brought along a rope for rappeling down, however,
my only option appeared to be to continue front-pointing the rest
of the way to the top and walk down the easy backside. Just then
a PGHM helicopter buzzed past on a routine flight, and, spying me,

hovered to determine whether or not they'd come across another bonehead in trouble. Immediately, I decided to wave for help. Only the day before, after all, I'd plunked down $70 for rescue insurance, so the impromptu extrication wouldn't cost me a dime.

Problem was, I couldn't figure what sort of story I was going to give to the PGHM to justify the rescue when the guy in the natty blue sweater came down on the winch cable to pluck me from the ice. I hesitated for a moment, then, overcome with guilt, raised one arm—the signal that all was well—and the chopper darted off toward the valley like an overgrown dragonfly, leaving me to my own sorry devices.

It takes about half an hour for the two-stage *téléphérique* to travel the 9,000 vertical feet between Chamonix and the summit of the Aiguille du Midi. Sixty of us have been shoehorned into the rusty box of the cable car for the ride up: Frenchmen in fluorescent orange-and-green outfits with matching backpacks; several teams from an Italian climbing club, singing and farting and laughing enthusiastically; a few silent Japanese tourists incongruously attired in business suits and dresses.

At the summit—a dizzying spike of brown granite, honeycombed with tunnels and barnacled with bizarre steel structures—I find my way to the restaurant for a quick *croque-monsieur,* then board another lift for a ride across the heavily crevassed plain of the Vallée Blanche to the Italian frontier. From there, a short downhill walk takes me to my objective for the day, the north face of a peak called the Tour Ronde. Were this mountain in

It can be argued that the Aiguille du Midi tram defined Chamonix. Prior to the construction of the tram, Chamonix was a small village frequented primarily by climbers, skiers, and a few summer tourists who made a wrong turn in Geneva. Once the tram appeared on the scene, the resulting increase in tourism created a demand for new hotels, shops, and ski lifts, and, in the following decade, Chamonix grew rapidly from a village to an international resort.

—Andrew Slough, "The Greatest Lift on Earth," *SKI*

Alaska, where I have done much of my climbing, I might have spent three or four days laboring beneath an eighty-pound pack to arrive at this point from the Chamonix Valley. Because the peak is in France, the approach has taken me less than two hours (breakfast stop included), my rucksack holds little more than lunch and an extra sweater, and I haven't yet broken a sweat.

Were this peak in Alaska, however, I would probably have had it to myself; as I strap on my crampons at the foot of the Tour Ronde, I count seven climbers on the route above.

The climb follows an hourglass-shaped slab of glassy grey ice straight up for 1,200 feet. By Chamonix standards the route is easy, but I'm concerned, nonetheless, about all the folks above me: in 1983, a pair of climbers fell near the top of the face, and as they plummeted to the glacier, still roped together, they flossed off eighteen people who had been climbing below, killing six and themselves.

The climbers overhead don't pose a problem until I reach the midway point on the wall, the waist of the hourglass, where rock buttresses on either side funnel all the ice kicked loose by those above down through a narrow slot, up which I must climb for 200 feet. Fortunately, most of the ice chips whistling down are small and glance harmlessly off my helmet. Falling ice is to be expected on a climb like this—climbers can't help knocking off small divots when they drive in their axes—but for some incomprehensible reason one of the teams above begins sending down Frisbees of granite, too, some of them weighing eight or ten pounds. "Hey!" I scream up in their direction. "Can't you see there's someone below you?" This, however, only seems to encourage them: when I turn my face upward to yell again, I catch a pebble in the chin. I quickly tuck my head back down and begin front-pointing even faster.

In ten minutes I'm out of the slot and onto the upper face, where it's possible to dodge the fusillade. Forty-five minutes after that I'm on top, where I find the two Frenchmen who rolled the rocks my way lounging beside the bronze statue of the Virgin Mary that marks the summit. Approaching them, I inquire politely,

"What gives, assholes? On the descent maybe I should kick a few boulders down so you can see what it feels like."

The two climbers, who are in their early twenties, act supremely unconcerned. One of them shrugs and tells me, "The falling rocks, they are one of the many natural hazards climbers must face in the Alps. If you do not like the climbing here, perhaps you should return to America, where the mountains are not so big."

By and by, the Frenchmen depart, leaving me alone on the summit, and I begin to settle down. The rock is warm, the September sky crystalline and absolutely still. Around me, so close I can almost reach out and touch them, the Aiguilles rise in wave after endless wave. Here are the crest of Mont Blanc and the thin fingers of the Peuterey Ridge; over there, the Grepon and Charmoz, the immense tusk of the Dent du Géant, the twin summits of the Drus, the formidable profile of the Grandes Jorasses. For most of my life I've read about these peaks, stared at fuzzy photos of them clipped from magazines and scotch-taped to my walls, tried to imagine the texture of their storied granite.

It's getting late. I need to start climbing down, pronto, or I'll miss the last *téléphérique* to the valley. But there's a pleasant, peculiar sort of warmth inching up my spine, and I'm reluctant to cut it short before it has a chance to get wherever it may be going. "Five more minutes," I bargain with myself out loud. A quarter-mile beneath my feet, the shadow of the Tour Ronde stretches across the glacier like a cat.

When I glance at my watch, an hour has passed. Down in Chamonix, the streets are already deep in shade, and the bars are starting to fill with climbers and parapilots back from the heights. If I were down there now, sharing a table with some wild-eyed heir to Messner or Bonatti or Terray, my trip up the Tour Ronde would probably be too banal to mention. Up here on top of the mountain, my ledge affords a different perspective. The summits are still gleaming in the autumn sun. The walls are humming with history, the empty glacier is alive with light. "Five more minutes," I tell myself again. "Just five more minutes, and then I really will start down."

Jon Krakauer has written about a wide variety of subjects for major American magazines including Smithsonian, Rolling Stone, *and* Outside. *Mountaineering is his first love and he is recognized as one of the country's top writers on the subject. He is the author of* Into Thin Air, Into the Wild, *and* Eiger Dreams: Ventures Among Men and Mountains *from which this story was excerpted. He lives in Seattle.*

✦

I'm in a world of white, inching along a knife-edge ridge that sheers 1,000 feet in one direction, 9,000 feet in the other. Does it matter which way I fall? I feel like an ant negotiating the tractionless rim of a bathtub. My head is a bit dizzy, but I'm okay. At least that's what I tell myself. Then, as I take a step, my right crampon snags my baggy left trouser leg and rips the inseam. For a second I lose balance and blood rushes to my head. Then, I continue to climb, too frightened to take my eyes off my feet, but when we stop for a rest, I allow a glance upwards. Just three miles ahead looms the 15,771-foot high peak of Mont Blanc; the mountain that has claimed the lives of 2,000 climbers, more than any other peak in the world. Behind me is a view of the Matterhorn, but I don't dare look. A few steps later the crampon again bites into my pants, and catches, and I start to drop into space. The rope goes taut; I collapse onto my knees and instinctively bury the wrong end of the ice ax into the snow. I'm sprawled, spread-eagle, over this arête, panting, terrified. But Serge turns to me and says, "Don't worry. Take your time. Everything is fine. You're really doing great!" "He's a guide," I say to myself, "I know those words. They're part of the shtick." Nonetheless, I feel better as he repeats them, and I find myself standing up, mustering new confidence, and giving him the "thumbs ups" sign.

—Richard Bangs, "The Guides Must be Crazy," *Just GO!*

Jo's Dog Has His Day

Paris is a dog's best friend.

EVERYONE IN FRANCE HAS ONE, OR SO IT SEEMS. RESTAURANT owners have big ones, taxi drivers have small ones, even prostitutes bring little ones to work.

The French have such a thing for dogs—there are twice as many of them as children in France—that I thought my dog's well-being would be enhanced if he joined Douglas, the man in my life, and me on our annual trip to Paris. In contrast to the way Americans restrict dogs to second-class status, French welcome canines almost everywhere, except maybe Monoprix and the Louvre. If, as Gandhi said, the greatness of a nation can be judged by the way its animals are treated, then the French are way up there—unless you think dog-sitters earning twice as much as baby-sitters is a bit extreme.

My only concern about taking Fromer, my Yorkshire terrier, to France is his feisty behavior. A sculptor who teaches in Paris had reminded me that French dogs are exceptionally well mannered: Fromer should never bark, growl, or snap; he should stay quietly by my side. I worry that my 6-year-old dog, who sometimes still nips at the shoelaces of the UPS man, won't catch on to proper French dog étiquette in the ten quick days of our trip. Just after takeoff from Los Angeles, I lift Fromer out of his carrying case, which is stowed (legally—I'd bought him an excess baggage ticket) under my seat. I camouflage him in my lap in the folds of an airline blanket. Not once am I ordered to "Put that dog back under the seat!" as usually happens when flying in the U.S. Is it because the head flight attendant has two cocker spaniels and a collie shepherd back in San Francisco, or because Fromer never once even barks? Or is it—and I suspect it is this—that we're on our way to Paris and many of the attendants are French?

On disembarking at Charles de Gaulle, Fromer squirms out of my arms and takes his first steps in France on the white airport tile. I look around to see if anyone cares. As if we're still in the U.S., I expect someone will demand that the dog be put back in his kennel. Instead, as we wait in line at immigration, an airport security person walks by and, though he looks at Fromer on his Day-Glo yellow leash, says nothing. At the immigration booth, an official glances at Douglas's and my passports and waves us and the dog by. (The only requirements for bringing a dog into France are certificates of health and origin, which I had but which I didn't have to produce.)

On rue St-Louis-en-l'Ile, the narrow street outside our hotel on the Ile Saint-Louis, Fromer sniffs the surface of every cornerstone, his entire body quivering with the richness of centuries of dogs that have gone before him. (It is *very slow* going.) Although the French feel that with their high taxes they'll be damned if they'll pick up their dog's business, I follow him, California-style, with a handful of tissues.

Because of a sudden downpour, we decide not to go to the other side of town for lunch, but instead dash across the street to L'Ilot Vache. I step over the threshold with a damp Fromer in my arms and feel a familiar dread, as if the proprietor is going to reprimand me for daring to bring a dog into his pretty restaurant—pink tablecloths, fresh peonies, white lace curtains. Yet this is exactly what I've watched the French do for years. We're shown to a lovely table and handed menus, and the waiter lights the candles in our silver candelabra. I breathe easier.

To still his fright from the thunder cracking outside, I hold Fromer tight against my chest. He is there in my lap when the *côte de veau à la Normande* is served. Douglas, a dog person who has two cocker spaniels of his own back in Malibu, nervously looks around the restaurant as I feed Fromer small servings from my plate. There are only two other tables of customers, none of whom is paying any attention to us. Yet I suspect Douglas would be happier if Fromer were having a comfortable snooze under the table or back at the hotel.

But Fromer isn't trained to sleep when succulent platters of veal are being served inches away. Aside from a burger at a Dairy Queen drive-in, this is his first meal out in a restaurant. I give in and let him lick the juices on the plate. Have I gone too far? Am I out-Frenching the French?

The first time I saw a dog eating at the table was at an elegant, dark-paneled restaurant in the old Les Halles district. A large table was bursting with the conviviality of a happy family. I seem to remember they had several dogs—someone had tucked white dinner napkins under the dogs' collars—and they fed them on their laps with forks of food from the plates on the table. Back then I didn't have a dog, and I'd thought, as many Americans still do, Yuck! Nearly twenty years later, here I am copying the very scene that had once turned me off.

We encounter our first NO DOGS ALLOWED—NOT EVEN ON A LEASH sign on the park gate at Notre-Dame. We turn away but later learn that if one of us just carried Fromer we could have entered the park (but probably not the cathedral). It turns out that a dog in one's arms is no longer considered a dog.

We also learn that if it seems there are a lot of dogs in Paris, that's because there are: 55 percent of France's households have one. However, that evening at La Méditerranée, a seafood restaurant on Place de l'Odéon, Fromer is the only dog in the place. I take an immediate dislike to our waiter, who seems not to understand Douglas's excellent French and departs in a huff to wait on another American couple near us but leaves without taking their order either. When he does return, he asks if Fromer—who is now casually resting his chin on the table, his button nose twitching and his big brown eyes growing even larger with expectation—would like some water. The waiter places a red plastic water dish on the table, and then gives Fromer a meringue. He explains that he has a dog (it sounds like a sheepdog), and once he had a Yorkie. My opinion of him softens considerably.

I think we've been managing well enough with our American dog in Paris, but to reduce the tension between Douglas and me— "Darling, notice how the other dogs don't have their feet on the table"—I ask a Parisian friend how a dog owner is supposed to know what to do.

"There's the law," my friend explains, "and then there's what one does. The two are completely different things!"

Because I'd read in *L'Express* that dogs deposit twenty tons of excrement daily in Paris, I also ask what one is supposed to do about this dog business.

She laughs as she describes the fleet of green and white motor-cycles that buzz around the city, vacuuming it up. "It's perverse," she says. "The city is running out of money to pick it up!"

One morning at Le Flore en l'Ile, a café at the corner of our street, a couple is sitting next to us with a long-haired dachshund, and Fromer starts barking. I'd worried about just this sort of thing: a crowded restaurant, tables shoved tight next to one another, and a dog Fromer's decided to hate at the next table.

"He don't like French dogs?" asks the man.

Douglas explains that this is Fromer's first trip to Paris and, be-cause one cannot take dogs to restaurants in America, he's not used to all this commotion.

"You can't take a dog to a restaurant in America!" the man re-peats, surprised, to his wife.

I mumble something about the health department. "Oh, mi-crobes," he says. "Microbes don't bother you if you have a dog."

The waiter serves their *petit déjeuner,* and their dog jumps be-tween our tables, grabbing a slice of toast in his teeth.

"Sorry," says the man, "around food he's like a shark."

One late afternoon, as I'm walking and Fromer is trotting

alongside on rue Royale, we come out at Place de la Concorde, where hundreds of screeching autos are converging like so many bumper cars. He's terrified, shaking so violently that I search for a refuge. The first doorway is the posh Automobile Club of France. The second is the ultra-private Hôtel de Crillon. I wonder if this is one of those rare French hotels that does not allow dogs. The liveried doorman, dressed in black gabardine trimmed in gold, spins the revolving door for us, and instantly we are enveloped in a luxury of quiet. In the gilded chandeliered *salon de thé,* where thick royal blue drapes hang from two stories high, a woman is softly playing Bach on the piano. I sink into a blue velvet couch, while Fromer, whose shaking is subsiding into intermittent spasms, flops onto the cold marble floor.

What was I thinking in bringing this dog to Paris? I'd been so caught up in the fun of his being able to accompany us everywhere, I hadn't thought that he might not want to.

Usually he lives quietly at the beach in Malibu, and although

On sidewalks the dog rules supreme, so it behooves walkers to be constantly alert lest they stand in the dog's merde.

Simply learning the mechanics of walking is not enough. One must also learn a code of behavior. An important courtesy is always to allow a dog to pass. It is even more polite if, when passing, you can make a sidetrack into the gutter yourself. This shows that you understand the nature of the hierarchical order.

It took me some time to discover this particular rule, because on the sidewalks in Paris one often finds a white drawing of a dog and an arrow under this pointing to the gutter. I naïvely believed this meant that dogs should make way for pedestrians until a French friend kindly pointed out (after I had nearly been eaten alive by a passing canine) that this sign meant the outer half of the sidewalk was for the dog and the inner half for the dog owner.

—Mary Hoban, "Paris's Privileged Dogs," *The National Times*

he does go with me to my office, he's not used to cities—Paris or otherwise. Here in Paris, with business people rushing by swinging briefcases and shoppers with bags hanging dangerously near his head, he has started to behave skittishly. Last night at Julien's he was so spooked by all the sounds in that enormous Art Deco room that he didn't eat.

His Paris is so different from mine: not a city of restaurants and bistros, museums and shops, but a city of strange tree trunks and bushes, unfamiliar cornerstones and gutters.

But the French would be the first to understand my impulse to bring him, or so I think as we end our trip with a visit to Provence, and happen upon a country wedding. In a village near Avignon, car horns sound, church bells ring, and a blond Great Pyrénées is decorated with a floppy white bow. This turns out to be Alice, the groom's dog. After the marriage ceremony, the first family photo is taken: it consists of the bride, the groom, and Alice.

Jo Giese is an essayist, author, and TV producer who lives in Malibu, California. She is the author of The Food Almanac, A Woman's Path, *and* The Good Food Compendium, *and her work is included in* Dogs and Their Women.

✻

Dogs are the bane of walkers in France. Every farm has quantities of them and most of the village houses have a couple. None of these dogs is a pet; our meeting with the woman and her spaniel was one of the few times we met someone taking a dog for a walk. They are deterrents. German shepherds are the most popular breed, followed by Dobermans and large terriers. Rottweilers don't seem to have taken hold.

Dogs are the biggest difference between walking in France and in England. We can spend an afternoon ambling around Norfolk byways with hardly a woof; in the Languedoc the house where you don't get barked at is the exception. The ones on the outskirts of towns and villages are the worst; their dogs are kept behind wire fences and skip up and down barking and growling, teeth bared, only a couple of feet away as you walk past. Their confinement turns rage into hysteria. At least the farm dogs have room to roam about and work off their frustration.

—Miles Morland, *Miles Away: A Walk Across France*

NICHOLAS WOODSWORTH

Dining with the Corsican

Jeannot's cousin Pierre has a surprise
in the Corsican interior.

I FIRST HEARD OF PIERRE MILANINI THROUGH HIS COUSIN, Jeannot, as we sat in an elegant little seaside restaurant in the Corsican resort of Porto Vecchio. We were not discussing food, but the insular Corsican mentality.

For an island people, Jeannot was telling me, Corsicans were surprisingly out of their element along their rich coasts. Over the millennia the island has suffered repeated attack and invasion by sea, and Corsicans have survived by seeking the security and peace of the rugged interior— with time, the inhospitable mountains have become their preferred home.

I looked around the restaurant as he talked. The place was full, not of Corsicans but of end-of-summer visitors who came from

France still retains territory not contiguous with the European continent. The Overseas Departments of France are French soil and not merely territories. The departments of Corsica, Guadalupe, (which includes Saint Barts and half of Saint Martin), Martinique, Reunion in the Indian Ocean and French Guiana are part of France. There are also five Oversees Territories: St. Pierre, Miquelon, New Caledonia, French Polynesia (which includes Tahiti), French Southern and Antarctic Territories, and Wallis and Futuna.

—JO'R, LH, and SO'R

everywhere. The food was good, but it might have come from anywhere.

"If you want another Corsica," Jeannot suggested, "why don't you go inland to Quenza? I have a cousin who runs a stable and *gîte d'étape* on the mountain behind the village. He's a bit of a hermit, slightly eccentric, and a real Corsican. And he knows how to cook—every last thing he serves he grows, raises, and prepares himself."

Who could resist a suggestion like that? I left for the hills early the next morning.

Guests would have to know about Pierre Milanini's place to find it. *Gîte d'étapes* exist only in the wilder areas of France and usually serve a specialist clientele of cold and hungry ramblers, mountain climbers, and campers. Their isolation, though, does not affect their quality; they are often the last strongholds of authentic regional cuisine.

The medieval village of Quenza sits lost in a ring of high peaks and hills. I found the *gîte* hidden on a tiny, winding road that disappeared into the chestnut forests above the village. The place was marked only by the well-groomed horses that milled around a paddock beside a ramshackle stone house.

At first, Pierre did not want to know about one more diner. He had closed his *gîte* for the season, he said, shaking his long locks and thick grey beard back and forth. And he was busy preparing his annual trip to Ajaccio—five days through the mountains on horseback. Food, he told me, should be no more hurried an affair than travel.

But when he saw me admiring the ripe, red tomatoes growing in the large garden behind the paddock, his pride got the better of him.

"They are the finest tomatoes around," he beamed. "Same as the rest of my garden, same as my fruit orchard: no pesticides, no herbicides, no chemical fertilisers—just plenty of good, aged horse manure." I was welcome to his tomatoes, he said, if I did not mind sitting down to whatever else he could put together at short notice.

Pierre's house was rustically chaotic. Muddy riding boots stood drying in one corner of a huge, unswept fireplace, mountain walking boots in the other. There was a shotgun leaning against the wall and an ammunition bandolier slung over the back of a threadbare armchair. In the chair itself, a hunting dog lay snoozing with its paws in the air. Three more lay prone on the floor. Half a dozen cats were lounging on the long, scarred farm table that took up most of the room.

He roared, and the animals disappeared in a flurry of hair and dust. "I love animals," he said, slinging one last kitten out the door. "I have 30 horses, 60 pigs, 30 cows, 8 dogs and 11 cats. I'd have more horses if I could afford them, but the damned things don't pay for themselves."

Corsica is different. It's not France and it's not Italy, but a subtle blend, lying 100 miles south of the French Riviera, 50 miles from Italy, and eight miles from Sardinia. The ancient Greeks, one of many groups to inhabit this mountain surrounded by sea, dubbed it "The Most Beautiful."

To Napoleon, born there in 1769, it was "The Perfumed Isle." While exiled on St. Helena, he remarked, "I would recognize Corsica with my eyes closed, just from the fragrance."

—Margaret W. Ketteringham, "A Mediterranean Quartet," *Newsday*

Pierre talked as he put an iron pot of soup on the stove and began slicing tomatoes. An exemplar of Corsican insularity, he is a purist, a die-hard traditionalist, a hold-out against modern civilization. As a cook, he mistrusts all food additives, any kind of pre-mixed concoction or preparation, all time-saving devices, any corner-cutting cooking method.

He has lived all his 60 years in Quenza. When he grew up, producing food was a question of survival. He spent drought-ridden summers watering chestnut trees—without chestnut flour, there was no bread to see the family through the winter. Wheat flour was an unaffordable luxury. "Life was difficult then," Pierre laughed. "We just didn't know it."

We sat down to plates of sliced tomatoes. Mine were accompanied by mild onion rings, parsley, and olive oil, all home-produced, all delicious. Pierre's were accompanied by nothing but a shake of salt.

"We use too many ingredients in our meals," he growled. "Add enough and you kill the taste of what you are trying to eat. People like garnishes and dressings, but do they know what tomatoes are really like?"

Perhaps he had a point, I thought, as I sliced through a tomato with my fork.

"And for God's sake, man, don't massacre," Pierre added. "Tomatoes are delicate things. Here, use this."

He passes over a clasp knife with a long, mean-looking, blade, the kind you imagine gangsters stick into each other. I sighed. No one had instructed me on the use of dining implements since nursery.

Prevention of the violence which could so easily break out at table is, as we have seen, one of the principal aims of table manners. In the West, where knives have not been banished, we are especially sensitive and vigilant about the use of these potential weapons. "When in doubt, do not use your knife" is a good all-purpose rule.

—Margaret Visser,
The Rituals of Dinner: The Origins, Evolution, Eccentricities, and Meaning of Table Manners

A minute later, though, I was learning yet another lesson—to cut bread in the peasant fashion. Copying Pierre, I held his fresh-baked bread—a round loaf the size of a small bicycle tyre—against my chest and drew my knife gingerly through the crust towards me. One slip, I thought, and I shall stab myself fatally.

I was gaining confidence, however, by the time the soup bowls arrived. In them was a thick, fragrant vegetable *minestra,* simmered for hours with herbs and chunks of smoked, salted pork, and wonderful to eat with large slices of crusty bread and red wine.

Again, though, Pierre brought me back to essentials. "All these seasonings and extras are fine—I like thyme, bay, and garlic as much as anyone. But there is just one great secret. It is the onion.

Without the onion, you can do nothing; with it, you can do anything. It is the point of departure." Pierre was emphatic. I was not going to argue. It seemed as good a world view as any.

Silently, we drank in praise of the onion. But I did not remain silent a few moments later when I cut off a thick slice from the leg of cured ham Pierre had set on the table. The flavour was superb.

"Nothing but salt and pepper in that. I slaughtered, cured, and hung that pig five months ago. No flavouring, no herbs, no spices. The taste is in the flesh itself. Elsewhere, pigs are penned up. On this island, pigs wander round all day eating chestnuts and acorns. Come and look at what we make best in Corsica."

In a cool, dark, dry room off the main house, Pierre showed me the produce to which he gives his greatest attention. Hanging from hooks on the ceiling were hams; *coppe* sausages made from pig's necks; *lonze* from their filets; and *figatelli*—smoked sausage from their liver, heart, and kidneys.

And so to cheese. Mysteriously, Pierre kept his soft ewe's cheese in a covered pot and, even more mysteriously, insisted on spreading it on a slice of bread for me. It had a sharp, biting taste which I enjoyed—until I noticed my cheese refused to stay still. Not only were small yellow maggots wriggling to the surface but, once fallen to the table, they began springing about. I think I blanched.

Pierre let go a great haw-haw of laughter. *"Fromage vivant,"* he said. "We call it living cheese. You can't make it, it just makes itself during humid, heavy weather. But when I've got some, people come for miles to eat it. And if we've had a little wine, we like to bet on whose maggots can jump the highest. It's a good time."

I had had a little wine, but I needed a little more before I began to have a good time again. There was coffee; home-made *eau-de-vie;* more talk about the manners and kitchen customs of Corsica; more *eau-de-vie.* By the time I left that rough and ramshackle little *gîte* and was heading back down the mountainside to Porto Vecchio, I was in a quandary. I was wondering how I was ever going to have a good time in elegant little seaside restaurants again.

Nicholas Woodsworth, who lived in Vietnam as a small child, now lives in London and is travel correspondent for the Financial Times.

★

Corsicans are the most clannish, most resolutely parochial of islanders. They build enormous mausoleums for the deceased members of their families even as they let the purported birthplace of Christopher Columbus lapse into a pile of glorified rubble. I mentioned the sorry state of Columbus's house to a resident of Calvi, where the house itself is located. Your people should be proud of it, I told him, or at least keep it in better condition. The man replied, "Ah, that's the problem. Just the problem, monsieur. We are still trying to decide among ourselves whether the discovery of America is something we should be proud of..."

    —Lawrence Millman, "Of Bandits and Bonaparte," *The Sunday Times*

ALICE KAPLAN

Encounters with André

French lessons got under her skin.

I MET ANDRÉ AT THE FIRST PARTY OF THE YEAR IN PARIS, WHERE our junior-year-abroad group had a six-week orientation before settling down in Bordeaux. He came bounding into the room at me. He was long and wiry with shiny black hair and a devil smile on his face. He sat me down on the couch, put one hand on each of my shoulders: *"Alors, ma petite américaine, tu t'appelles comment?"* The room was packed with noisy foreign students. André's voice drowned them out completely. *"Serre-moi,"* he said, taking his arms off my shoulders and holding them out toward me. I didn't know those words in French but I figured out exactly what they meant from André's body: *"Serre-moi"* meant "hold me." Ten minutes later I went with him into the nearest bedroom—I was in love with my own recklessness—and he put his shirt on a lamp for just the right amount of light. We got into bed and his shirt caught on fire. It was like that with him, sudden blazes; he was always jumping up to put out some fire or other, leaping and howling at his own antics. His main activities were mountain climbing (the Pyrénées), painting, and chasing women. He was 27 and he worked for a graphic arts firm, but it was impossible to think of him as an office worker.

I used to wait for him to come into the café around seven. He entered the room like a mannequin, one shoulder slightly behind the other and his legs in front of him. His smile was subtle and controlled; no teeth showed. He had a way of stopping to survey the room before coming over to my table that made me hold my breath for fear he wouldn't come. He looked down his greyhound nose at each of my girlfriends, bent his long frame forward to give the ceremonial kiss on each cheek, all around the table. I was last. I got four kisses, two on each cheek, with the same geometric precision.

I liked to watch André sitting across from me at the café, smoking his cigarette with his head tilted to one side to show off his cheek bones. He exuded an Egyptian beauty, his jet black hair bouncing off his shoulders, his long muscles showing through his skin. There was so much energy in that body, it seemed to be in motion even when he was sitting.

He was a moralist and he had theories. He talked about his "aesthetic folly"—his drunken outings—and about "the bourgeois complacency" of most women (their desire for commitment and stability; his love of freedom). He thought American women talked too much, but he liked me because I was natural. Although I shouldn't wear so much black.

I kept a diary and I started taking notes on André: "André ate a dead bee he found on the steps of the church."

I liked to watch him. I studied André showering. He scrubbed every inch of himself with a soapy washcloth that he wrapped around his hand like an envelope. I watched him washing, I watched all his muscles under the soap, especially the ones around his chest he'd got from climbing mountains. I thought to myself, this is the way a man showers when he only gets a shower once a week. I thought of all the men I knew who showered every day, sloppily, and who had nothing to wash off.

I went to classes, part of our six-week orientation to French culture. In class I spent a lot of time with my head on the desk, nothing but André in it. I went to the language lab for phonetic testing and they said I was starting to get the regional Gascon accent in my "r"s, I should watch out. I had been studying André too hard.

We read André Bazin and learned the difference between Hollywood film and the French *cinéma d'auteur,* film so marked by the style of its director you can say it has an author, like a book. One day we were all bused to the Casino in Pau, to watch Alan Resnais and Marguerite Duras's *Hiroshima mon amour* on a big screen. The movie begins with lovers, a French actress and a Japanese architect. In the first frames, you see their bodies close up, their sweat mixed with shiny sprinkles that look like ash—the ash of the atomic bomb in Hiroshima. I watched their bodies and I heard their voices. The dialogue is sparse in this movie, the sentences are as simple as sentences in a first-year language text, except that they are erotic. One staccato statement after another, the pronoun *"tu"*—the familiar "you"—in every sentence. The movie taught me what *"tu"* means, how intimate, how precious—"You are like a thousand women together," he says, and she: "That is because you don't know me." The sentences are so bare that they seem to mean everything—a thousand sentences packed together in a few words, every sentence an unexploded bomb. She: "You speak French well." He: "Don't I. I'm happy you've finally noticed" (laughter). After it was over, I still felt inside the bare secret world of the movie and went to sit in a park, where I wrote to André in an erotic trance. "When I lose my words in French," I wrote, "a radical transformation occurs. My thoughts are no longer thoughts, they are images, visions. More important—the feeling of power in not being able to communicate, the feeling of being stripped down to the most fundamental communication. I am with you, I see black and then flashes: a leg, a sex, a nose. Seen, felt, tasted. The taste of your body pursues me," I wrote. "Like an essence."

But André wasn't buying it. I still have the letter, stuck between the pages of my diary from that year; it has his corrections all over it. Where I wrote *"la joie de la reverse,"* which is made-up French for "the joy of reversal," he crossed it out and wrote "the joy of anti-conformism." (One of his slogans about himself was that he was an anti-conformist.)

This should have been my first clue that what I really wanted from André was language, but in the short run all it did was make me feel more attached to him, without knowing why I was attached. I can still hear the sound he made when he read my love letter: "t,t,t," with that little ticking sound French people make by putting the tips of their tongues on the roof of their mouths—a fussy, condescending sound, by way of saying, "that's not how one says it." What I wanted more than anything, more than André even, was to make those sounds, which were the true sounds of being French, and so even as he was insulting me and discounting my passion with a vocabulary lesson, I was listening and studying and recording his response.

He decided to take me out for a 96-franc meal, for my education. *Tripes à la mode de Caen*—the stomach of some animal, and the *spécialité de la maison*. I ate it in huge bites, to show him I wasn't squeamish. Before he had too much to drink he made a speech at me, in his high moral style: "You represent the woman I would like to love if I were older and if I dominated myself. I am very happy to have known

*T*utoyer *or not* tutoyer, *that is the question. French teachers make it sound so simple, so indisputable, so transparent: "Use* tu *with intimates and children, and* vous *with everyone else."*

But when have the French ever been simple or transparent? On an airliner bound for France, I want to collar one of those smug pro-fesseurs and subject them to real-life questioning. At what age does a young person cease to be a child? What if I consider someone an intimate but they don't regard me in the same way? Or vice versa? "When in doubt, follow the lead of your conversational partner." That's just fine in one-to-one con-versation, but what of a group dis-cussion? At a large party—say, a wedding reception—I have enough trouble trying to remember names and relationships without having to sort out who might have previously addressed me in the familiar form.

Compounding the dilemma, of course, is my own lack of verbal agility. Unaccustomed as I am to skipping nimbly between alternate sets of pronouns, adjectives and verb endings, I risk committing the faux pas *of responding in too familiar a vein, or, perhaps worse, rejecting a friendly overture by using* vous.

—Joyce Gregory,
"Replaceable You"

you. But I want a woman I can express myself with. You understand my words but not my language—you don't even realize how great a problem it is between us."

(I wrote the whole speech down in my diary afterwards, word for word.) He tried to pronounce the difference between "word" and "world" in English—he thought it was funny they were so alike, and that their similarity had to do with us, with our problem. He couldn't make the "l" sound in "world." He ordered schnapps for two plus a cognac, then another. He drank them all. We raced off to a disco in his Deux Chevaux. He leaped out under the strobe lights, out of my sight. I stood outside the dancing *piste* and watched him sidle up to four different women, one after another, twirling each of them around him in his own athletic interpretation of "le rock." His sister was

Maybe it is fun to sit outside in Paris and drink little cups of coffee. You can watch the French grimace and posture. And then you can guess what they're saying to each other.

"I think, Antoinette, for me the croissant has the aspect existential. It is bread, the staff of life, but no? And yet, there is the paradox marvelous. Because the bread itself, it is a lifeless thing. Is it not true? We must order croissants."

"No, no, no, no, Jacques. To think as this is is to make the miscomprehension of the universe, its nature. To order the croissants would be an act inconceivable. An action of the most bourgeois type..."

Who gives a shit what the French think.

—P. J. O'Rourke, *Holidays in Hell*

at the discothèque. She advised me to grab him and start making out with him if I wanted to get home. Twice on the way home he stopped the car to weep in my lap, sobbing giant tears.

The next day I got a note that said: "I'm sorry Alice. *Hier soir j'avais trop bu. J'espère que tu ne m'en tiendras pas rigueur. Tendresse. André.*" Which means: "I drank too much last night. Don't be too hard on me." I received this note like a haiku and pasted it in my diary.

That week I kept running over his speech in my mind. What was the difference between his words and my words, his world and my world? When I said a French word, why wasn't it the same as when he said one? What could I do to make it be the same? I had to stick it out with him, he was transmitting new words to me every day and I needed more. In fact, while Barbara and Buffy and Kacy (André dubbed us *"l'équipe"*—the team) rolled their eyes about what a raw deal I was getting from this creep, I was all the more determined to be with him. He was in all my daydreams now. I wanted to crawl into his skin, live in his body, be him. The words he used to talk to me, I wanted to use back. I wanted them to be my words.

The last weekend I spent with André, we went to a sleazy hotel in Toulouse. He was on another drinking binge and we both got bitten up by bedbugs—or so I thought at the time. When I got back to the dorm my neck was swollen and my ear was all red. I was hot, and I went into a long sleep that I thought was due to ex-haustion from being with André. Within 48 hours the swelling on my neck felt like a tumor and the whole side of my face was swollen. My right eye was shut. I hid in my dorm room. When I had to go for a meal I wrapped my neck in a scarf and put a hat down over my right eye. I was almost too sick to care that André was spending the night down the hall from me with Maïté, a French woman who was one of the assistants in charge of orient-ing us. She was part Basque, like him, and lanky like him, only softer; she dressed in Indian prints and sheepskin vests.

The doctors didn't really know what was wrong with me, so they did tests. They tried one medicine, then another. Finally they sent me to a convent, where I got free antibiotic shots in my be-hind daily. I went there every day for seven days to get rid of the infection. The stark white cot where I submitted to the treatment, the nuns' quiet efficiency, had a soothing effect on me. I was cleansed by charity.

When I came out of the worst of my sickness I thought about it like this: it was the two of them against me. Two people who had the words and shared the world and were busy communicating in their authentic language, and me, all alone in my room. Maïté had something I couldn't have, her blood and her tongue and a name with accents in it. I was burning with race envy.

I spent a lot of time reading, and sitting in cafés with *"l'équipe,"* my team of girlfriends, and writing in my diary about André and what he meant. He wanted me to be natural, and I wanted him to make me French. When I thought back on the way the right side of me had swelled up, my neck and my ear and my eye, it was as if half of my face had been at war with that project. Half of me, at least, was allergic to André.

The day our group left for Bordeaux, André and Maïté were standing together at the bus stop and André gave me the ceremonial cheek kiss right in front of her, and whispered the possibility of a visit in my tender but healed ear. I could count on his infidelity working both ways.

In Bordeaux we signed up for housing with Monsieur Garcia, the administrative assistant of the University of California program. "You can live with a family or you can have liberty," Garcia said. A family meant nice quarters and no visitors; liberty meant scruffier quarters. Everyone knew that liberty really meant liberty to have sex, and life in France without sex was inconceivable to me.

André showed up in Bordeaux two or three times that year, strictly on the run. Once he claimed he was in town doing a two-week *stage* (the French term for a mini-apprenticeship) on bug extermination with his friend Serge. He rang my doorbell in the middle of the night and leapt into my bed. His breath smelled like rotten fruit and he had one of those stubborn erections that doesn't even respond to sex. Finally he rolled away from me, muttering what I thought was *"Je suis costaud"* (I'm strong), falling into a dead sleep. After a few days of thinking about the phonetic possibilities ("choo-ee-co-stow" or "choo-ee-co-stew"?), and looking through dictionaries, I decided he had actually been saying. "je suis encore saoul" (I'm still drunk), only drunkenly: "J'suis 'co soo," as a way of explaining why he hadn't been able to come. I was still putting up with André, for his beauty and for his words.

Each room of my boardinghouse had a sink and bidet. Outside was the outhouse, with maggots. The other boarders were immigrant workers. Across the hall was Caméra, from the République of Guinée, who had a job in construction and was trying to study math on the side with do-it-yourself tapes. He helped me set up a *camping gaz* so I could make omelets. He took me to the African Student Association dance where I started dancing with the biggest creep there. *"Il ne vaut rien,"* Caméra warned me, "he's worth nothing; a first-rate hustler." The hustler danced like a wild marionette and told me what he liked: "fun, acid, women, music." I made a rendezvous with him, which I didn't keep. Caméra was angry with me, and we stopped speaking.

For weeks I didn't want to open the door of my room, for fear of seeing Caméra, his disapproving glance. I kept the door to my room closed, as though some father had grounded me. When I was out I had the energy of an escaped convict; when I was home the righteousness of a cloistered nun. It felt familiar.

I had to go to the bathroom all the time. The more I dreaded the outhouse, the more I had to go. I planned outings to cafés, to use the bathrooms there. I knew which cafés in my part of town had clean bathrooms, with seats, and which ones had stand-up Turkish toilets. If I timed it right I could go to the best café in town, the Régent, anesthetize myself with steamed milk, go to the bathroom, and make it home for a night of dreams. When I walked home from the café it was pitch black and sometimes a *clochard,* a bum, yelled obscenities at me. I was too lost in my thoughts to be scared.

The room became my world. Clean sheets once a week. I began to recognize the people on my street: the man with no arms, the *tabac* lady with the patchwork shawl, the old concierge and his creaking keys, and Papillon, the pharmacist around the corner. My room and I were together now; night and morning rituals established themselves with pleasantly passing weeks. The bidet was no longer exotic; I soaked my tired feet in it. I had a wool shawl that I wrapped around my nightgowned shoulders and that transported me into timelessness. I put the shawl on to read: *Le Père Goriot,* about a 19th-century boarding house, and *Les Liaisons Dangereuses,* about a woman who controls her world through letters but is destroyed in the end. My room could exist in any century, in any French city.

The administration of the California program arranged all kinds of outings and connections for us students. I babysat for a rich family who lived in a modern house. Their floor was made of polished stones. I was invited to a chateau and I wore my best dress, ready to discuss literature. I got there and my French hosts greeted me in sneakers. They were growing Silver Queen corn in their backyard, and they wanted a fourth for tennis. Of all the Americans in my group the one they liked best was the freckled jock who could hardly speak French and went everywhere on his ten-speed bike. I was waiting to be rewarded for my good French, but he got all the attention. He was having fun playing the American mascot, while I was doing all the hard work of learning their language and what I thought were their social customs. I would have been ready to pose as the Marlboro Man to get the kind of attention he got from the French. But I had veered off in the other direction; I was trying to be French. Besides, I knew his ploy wouldn't work for me: a girl can't be a Marlboro Man.

I was watching and pretending, pretending and watching. I met a guy from Colorado. We were sitting at the French student restaurant together and I was peeling my pear so carefully, he said, he didn't know I was American. We went to the French student restaurant to meet people but no one spoke at the table, just peeled their fruit and left. This guy (his name is gone) and I

> "*When I was a child,*" said Cocteau, "*I believed that foreigners spoke no language, and only pretended among themselves to speak one.*"
>
> —Theodore Zeldin, *The French*

made up stories instead of going to bed together (we weren't supposed to go to bed with each other: we were on our junior year abroad). In one, I would be a prostitute who specialized in American men wanting to meet French girls. The joke would be that I wouldn't be French at all. We figured out where I would have to go and what I would wear and say, and what they would say. He would be my *proxénète,* the entrepreneur, and we would make tons of money and live well.

He went off and found a French girlfriend, a real one, and the next time I saw him they were on his moped, her arms around his waist, her hair in one of those high French pony tails waving in the breeze. When he saw me he waved proudly, a little sheepish to have me see him like that in the middle of his fantasy. I waved back and laughed.

I wanted to travel on my own, be brave, but I wasn't. I was always afraid of making a *faux pas.* I took a taxi to the train station to catch a train and I opened the taxi door just as a car was racing down the street. The car smashed into the taxi door, crumpling it. It was a fancy taxi, a top-of-the-line Renault, and the driver was screaming at me about his insurance and how much my foreigner stupidity was going to cost him. He was so disgusted he wouldn't let me pay the fare. I skulked into the station, my head hung low: this was my great adventure.

In the seventeen years since I met André, my ear has swelled up on me from time to time, although never as dramatically as that September in Pau. When I was writing this book, it happened again. The swelling came on so quickly that I went right to the doctor, who took one look at me and said, "You have herpes simplex on your ear." He'd only seen one case of herpes on the ear in all his years of medical practice: a man who had the cold sore on his mouth kissed his wife on the ear, and she got the virus.

As I searched back in my mind, I could see the tiny little blister on André's upper lip, a neat imperfection I was determined to ignore but that turned into his legacy. My precious ear, my radar, my antenna: the locus of my whole attraction to French, and André went right for it! Maybe he bit me there, maybe he kissed me, or maybe he just whispered some of his words with his lip up against my earlobe, and the virus took.

At the time, when I thought about him and Maïte, I thought, "It's because my French isn't good enough" and "It's because she's French." When he told me I couldn't understand his language,

André had picked the accusation I was most vulnerable to. Afterwards I thought, "I'll show him. I'll know all there is to know about his language, I'll know his language better than he does, someday."

After I had become a French professor, I wrote André, and he wrote back. The nonconformist was still living at the same address and I had moved ten times. I felt glad about that. There were a few spelling mistakes in his letter to me, the kind I'm hired to correct. But I didn't feel gleeful about his spelling because it hadn't been spelling that I wanted from him. I wanted to breathe in French with André, I wanted to sweat French sweat. It was the rhythm and pulse of his French I wanted, the body of it, and he refused me, he told me I could never get that. I had to get it another way.

Alice Kaplan teaches French literature at Duke University. She is the author of Reproductions of Banality: Fascism, Literature, and French Intellectual Life, *and* French Lessons: A Memoir, *from which this story was excerpted.*

✦

The French are far more concerned about words, their usage and meaning, than are the English or Americans. So they have fewer of them.

The total number of English words lies somewhere between 400,000, the number of current entries in the largest English dictionary, and 600,000, the largest figure a library expert is willing to be quoted on.

By comparison, the biggest French dictionaries have only about 150,000 entries. The English language's capacity for adaptation and assimilation, far from limiting, has made English the most widely used and useful language.

—Warren Trabant, "In France, Franglais is Unlawful," *Providence Journal*

PETER MAYLE

⋆

No Spitting in
Châteauneuf-du-Pape

In which the author gets drunk and stuffs himself silly.

AUGUST IN PROVENCE IS A TIME TO LIE LOW, TO SEEK SHADE, TO move slowly, and to limit your excursions to very short distances. Lizards know best, and I should have known better.

It was in the high 80s by nine thirty, and when I got into the car I immediately felt like a piece of chicken about to be sautéed. I looked at the map to find roads that would keep me away from the tourist traffic and heat-maddened truck drivers, and a bead of sweat dropped from my nose to score a direct hit on my destination—Châteauneuf-du-Pape, the small town with the big wine.

Months before, in the winter, I had met a man called Michel at a dinner to celebrate the engagement of two friends of ours. The first bottles of wine came. Toasts were proposed. But I noticed that while the rest of us were merely drinking, Michel was conducting a personal, very intense ritual.

He stared into his glass before picking it up, then cupped it in the palm of his hand and swirled it gently three or four times. Raising the glass to eye level, he peered at the traces of wine that his swirling had caused to trickle down the inner sides. His nose, with nostrils alert and flared, was presented to the wine and made a thorough investigation. Deep sniffing. One final swirl, and he took the first mouthful, but only on trial.

It obviously had to pass several tests before being allowed down the throat. Michel chewed it for a few reflective seconds. He pursed his lips and took a little air into his mouth and made discreet rinsing noises. Lifting his eyes to heaven, he flexed his cheeks in and out to encourage a free flow around tongue and molars and then, apparently satisfied with the wine's ability to withstand an oral assault, he swallowed.

He noticed that I had been watching the performance, and grinned. *"Pas mal, pas mal."* He took another, less elaborate swallow, and saluted the glass with raised eyebrows. "It was a good year, '85."

As I found out during dinner, Michel was a *négociant,* a professional wine drinker, a buyer of grapes and a seller of nectar. He specialized in the wines of the south, from Tavel *rosé* (the favorite wine, so he said, of Louis XIV) through the gold-tinged whites to the heavy, heady reds of Gigondas. But of all the wines in his extensive collection, his *merveille,* the one he would like to die drinking, was the Châteauneuf-du-Pape.

He described it as though he were talking about a woman. His hands caressed the air. Delicate kisses dusted his fingertips, and there was much talk of body and bouquet and *puissance.* It was not unknown, he said, for a Châteauneuf to reach fifteen percent of alcoholic content. And these days, when Bordeaux seems to get thinner every year and the price of Burgundy is only possible for the Japanese, the wines of Châteauneuf are nothing less than bargains. I must come up to his caves and see for myself. He would arrange a *dégustation.*

The time that elapses in Provence between planning a rendezvous and keeping it can often stretch into months, and sometimes years, and so I wasn't expecting an immediate invitation. Winter turned to spring, spring turned to summer, and summer melted into August, the most lethal month of the year to be toying with a 15-degree wine, and then Michel called.

"Tomorrow morning at eleven," he said. "In the *caves* at Châteauneuf. Eat plenty of bread at breakfast."

I had done what he suggested and, as an extra precaution, taken a soupspoonful of neat olive oil, which one of the local gourmets had told me was an excellent way to coat the stomach and cushion the system against repeated assaults by younger powerful wines. In any case, I thought as I drove down the twisting, baked country roads, I wouldn't be swallowing much. I would do as the experts do, rinse and spit.

Châteauneuf came into view, trembling in the heat haze, just before eleven o'clock. It is a place entirely dedicated to wine. Seductive invitations are everywhere, on sun-bleached, peeling boards, on freshly painted posters, hand-lettered on monster bottles, fixed to the wall, propped at the side of vineyards, stuck on pillars at the end of driveways. *Dégustez! Dégustez!*

I drove through the gateway in the high stone wall that protects the *Caves Bessac* from the outside world, parked in the shade, and unstuck myself from the car. I felt the sun come down on the top of my head like a close-fitting hat of hot air. In front of me was a long building, crenellated along the top, its façade blind except for huge double doors. A group of people, outlined against the black interior, were standing in the doorway, holding large bowls that glinted in the sun.

The *cave* felt almost cold, and the glass that Michel gave me was pleasantly cool in my hand. It was one of the biggest glasses I had ever seen, a crystal bucket on a stem, with a bulbous belly narrowing at the top to the circumference of a goldfish bowl. Michel said it could hold three-quarters of a bottle of wine.

My eyes adjusted to the gloom after the glare outside, and I began to realize that this was not a modest *cave*. Twenty-five thousand bottles would have been lost in the murk of one of the distant corners. In fact, there were no bottles to be seen, just boulevards of barrels—enormous barrels lying on their sides supported by waist-high platforms, their upper curves twelve or fifteen feet above the ground. Scrawled in chalk on the flat face of each barrel were descriptions of the contents, and for the first time in my life I was able to walk through a wine list: Côtes-du-Rhône-Villages, Lirac, Vacqueyras, Saint-Joseph, Crozes-Hermitage, Tavel, Gigondas—thousands of liters of each, arranged in vintages and dozing silently toward maturity.

"*Alors,*" said Michel, "you can't walk around with an empty glass. What are you going to have?"

There was too much choice. I didn't know where to start. Would Michel guide me through the barrels? I could see that the others had something in their goldfish bowls; I'd have the same.

Michel nodded. That would be best, he said, because we only had two hours, and he didn't want to waste our time on the very young wines when there were so many treasures that were ready to drink. I was glad I'd had the olive oil. Anything that qualified as a treasure was hardly spitting material. But two hours of swallowing would have me as supine as one of the barrels, and I asked if one was permitted to spit.

Michel waved his glass at a small drain that marked the entrance of the Boulevard Côtes-du-Rhône. "*Crachez si vous voulez, mais...*" It was clear that he thought it would be tragic to deny oneself the pleasure of the swallow, the bursting forth of flavors, the well-rounded finish, and the profound satisfaction that comes from drinking a work of art.

*S*oup should be served at a formal meal, and must at least be tasted: it is rude to leave it untouched. By this means we delicately ensure that everyone present is fortified before wine is served; we also enforce the highly civilized impression that nobody present is anxious to get started on the wine.

—Margaret Visser,
The Rituals of Dinner: The Origins, Evolution, Eccentricities, and Meaning of Table Manners.

The *maître de chai,* a wiry old man in a cotton jacket the color of faded blue sky, appeared with a device that reminded me of a giant eye-dropper—three feet of glass tubing with a fist-sized rubber globe at one end. He aimed the nozzle and squeezed a generous measure of white wine into my glass, muttering a prayer as he squeezed: "*Hermitage '86, bouquet aux arômes de fleurs d'accacia. Sec, mais sans trop d'acidité.*"

I swirled and sniffed and rinsed and swallowed. Delicious. Michel was quite right. It would be a sin to consign this to the drain. With some relief, I saw that the others were tipping what they didn't drink into a large jug that stood on a nearby trestle table. Later, this would be transferred into a jar containing a *mère vinaigre,* and the result would be four-star vinegar.

Slowly, we worked our way down the boulevards. At each stop, the *maître de chai* climbed up his portable ladder to the top of the barrel, knocked out the bung, and inserted his thirsty nozzle, returning down the ladder as carefully as if he were carrying a loaded weapon—which, as the tasting progressed, it began to resemble.

The first few shots had been confined to the whites, the *rosés,* and the lighter reds. But as we moved into the deeper gloom at the back of the *cave,* the wines too became darker. And heavier. And noticeably stronger. Each of them was served to the accompaniment of its own short but reverent litany. The red Hermitage, with its nose of violets, raspberries, and mulberries, was a *vin viril.* The Côtes-du-Rhône *"Grande Cuvée"* was an elegant thoroughbred, *fine* and *étoffé.* I was impressed almost as much by the inventive vocabulary as by the wines themselves—fleshy, animal, muscular, well-built, voluptuous, sinewy— and the *maître* never repeated himself. I wondered whether he had been born with lyrical descriptive powers or whether he took a thesaurus to bed with him every night.

Upon the first goblet he read this inscription, monkey wine; upon the second, lion wine; upon the third, sheep wine; upon the fourth, swine wine. These four inscriptions expressed the four descending degrees of drunkenness: the first, that which enlivens; the second, that which irritates; the third, that which stupefies; finally the last, that which brutalizes.

—Victor Hugo

We finally arrived at Michel's *merveille,* the 1981 Châteauneuf-du-Pape. Although it would keep for several years to come, it was already a masterpiece, with its *robe profonde,* its hints of spice and truffle, its warmth, its balance—not to mention its alcoholic content, which was nudging fifteen percent. I thought Michel was going to take a header into his glass.

It's nice to see a man who loves his work.

With some reluctance, he put down his glass and looked at his watch. "We must go," he said. "I'll get something to drink with lunch." He went to an office at the front of the cave, and came out carrying a crate of a dozen bottles. He was followed by a colleague, carrying another dozen. Eight of us were going to lunch. How many would survive?

We left the *cave* and winced under the force of the sun. I had restrained myself to sips rather than mouthfuls; nevertheless, my head gave one sharp throb in warning as I walked to the car. Water. I must have water before even sniffing any more wine.

Michel thumped me on the back. "There's nothing like a *dégustation* to give you a thirst," he said. "Don't worry. We have a sufficiency." Good grief.

The restaurant Michel had chosen was half an hour away, in the country outside Cavaillon. It was a *ferme auberge*, serving what he described as correct Provençal food in rustic surroundings. It was tucked away and hard to find, so I should stick closely to his car.

Easier said than done. So far as I know, there are no statistics to support my theory, but observa-

There is a certain expression that comes on a middle-to-upper income bracket Frenchman's face when he is about to déguster something really good, cheese, wine, any sort of culinary specialty, that starts out as a sudden interior break in the train of conversation. Silence; he is about to have a gastronomic experience. Then as the fork or glass nears his mouth, his eyes and ears seem to have blanked out; all is concentrated in the power of taste. There follows a stage when the critical faculties are gathering, the head is bent, eyes wander, lips and tongue are working over the evidence. At last comes the climactic moment of judgment, upon which may hang the mood of the meal and with it who knows what devious changes in the course of love, commerce or the body politic. The thing was poor or indifferent; the man shrugs, applies his napkin as though wiping out the whole experience, and goes on with what was interrupted, not quite relaxed; some sense of letdown, a slight disgruntlement lurks in the conversation. It was good, excellent, perfect, and oh what an expansion of frame and spirit; the chair will hardly hold him....

—Eleanor Clark,
The Oysters of Locmariaquer

tion and heart-stopping personal experience have convinced me that a Frenchman with an empty stomach drives twice as fast as a Frenchman with a full stomach (which is already too fast for sanity and speed limits). And so it was with Michel. One minute he was there; the next he was a dust-smudged blur on the shimmering horizon, clipping the dry grass verges on the bends, booming through the narrow streets of villages in their midday coma, his gastronomic juices in overdrive. By the time we reached the restaurant, all pious thoughts of water were gone. I needed a drink.

The dining room of the farm was cool and noisy. A large television set in the corner, ignored by the clientele, jabbered to itself. The other customers, mostly men, were darkened by the sun and dressed for outdoor work in old shirts and sleeveless vests, with the flattened hair and white foreheads that come from wearing a cap. A nondescript dog whiffled in the corner, nose twitching sleepily at the spicy smell of cooking meat coming from the kitchen. I realized that I was ravenous.

We were introduced to André, the *patron,* whose appearance, dark and full-bodied, fitted the description of some of the wines we'd been tasting. There were undertones of garlic, Gauloises, and pastis present in his bouquet. He wore a loose shirt, short shorts, rubber sandals, and an emphatic black moustache. He had a voice that transcended the hubbub of the room.

"*Eh, Michel! Qu'est-ce-que c'est? Orangina? Coca-Cola?*" He started to unpack the crates of wine and reached in the back pocket of his shorts for a corkscrew. "*M'amour! Un seau, des glaçons, s'il te plaît.*"

His wife, sturdy and smiling, came out of the kitchen carrying a tray and unloaded it on the table: two ice buckets, plates of pink *saucisson* dotted with tiny peppercorns, a dish of vivid radishes, and a deep bowl of thick *tapenade,* the olive and anchovy paste that is sometimes called the black butter of Provence. André was uncorking bottles like a machine, sniffing each cork as he drew it and arranging the bottles in a double line down the center of the table. Michel explained that these were some of the wines we hadn't had time to try in the *cave,* young Côtes-du-Rhône for the most part, with half a dozen older and more serious reinforcements from Gigondas to help when the cheese arrived.

There is something about lunch in France that never fails to overcome any small reserves of willpower that I possess. I can sit down, resolved to be moderate, determined to eat and drink lightly, and be there three hours later, nursing my wine and still open to temptation. I don't think it's greed. I think it's the atmosphere generated by a roomful of people who are totally intent on eating and drinking. And while they do it, they talk about it; not about politics or sport or business, but about what is on the plate and in the glass. Sauces are compared, recipes argued over, past meals remembered, and future meals planned. The world and its problems can be dealt with later on, but for the moment, *la bouffe* takes priority and contentment hangs in the air. I find it irresistible.

We eased into lunch like athletes limbering up. A radish, its top split open to hold a sliver of almost white butter and flecked with a pinch of coarse salt; a slice of *saucisson,* prickly with pepper on the tongue; rounds of toast made from yesterday's bread, shining with *tapenade.* Cool pink and white wines. Michel leaned across the table. "No spitting."

The *patron,* who was nipping away at a glass of red in between his duties, presented the first course with as much ceremony as a man in shorts and rubber sandals can muster, placing a deep *terrine,* its sides burnt almost black, on the table. He stuck an old kitchen knife into the pâté, then came back with a tall glass pot of *cornichons* and a dish of onion jam. *"Voilà, mes enfants. Bon appétit."*

The wine changed color as Michel dealt out his young reds, and the terrine was passed around the table for second slices. André came over from his card game to refill his glass. *"Ça va? Ca vous plaît?"* I told him how much I liked his onion jam. He told me to save some room for the next course, which was—he kissed his fingertips loudly—a triumph, *alouettes sans tête,* prepared specially for us by the hands of his adorable Monique.

Despite the rather grisly name (literally, larks without heads), it is a dish made from thin slices of beef rolled around slivers of salt pork, seasoned with chopped garlic and parsley, bathed in olive oil, dry white wine, stock, and tomato *coulis* and served neatly trussed with kitchen twine. It looks nothing like a lark—more like an opulent sausage—but some creative Provençal cook must have thought that larks sounded more appetizing than rolled beef, and the name has survived.

Monique brought in the *alouettes,* which André said he had shot that morning. He was a man who found it difficult to make a joke without delivering the punch line physically, and the nudge he delivered with his forearm almost knocked me into a vast tub of *ratatouille.*

The headless larks were hot and humming with garlic, and Michel decided that they deserved a more solid wine. The Gigondas was promoted from the cheese course, and the collection of dead bottles at the end of the table was by now well into double figures. I asked Michel if he had any plans to work in the afternoon. He looked surprised. "I am working," he said. "This is how I like to sell wine. Have another glass."

Salad came, and then a basketwork tray of cheeses—fat white discs of fresh goat cheese, some mild Cantal, and a wheel of creamy St. Nectaire from the Auvergne. This inspired André, now installed at the head of the table, to produce another joke. There was this little boy in the Auvergne who was asked which he liked best, his mother or his father. The little boy thought for a moment. "I like bacon best," he said. André heaved with laughter. I was relieved to be out of nudging distance.

> *Most of you probably don't know the location or function of your liver, but the French are ever aware of its presence and concerned for its wellbeing. It is an essential part of their obsession with the digestive process—after all, if you have stuffed yourself with food, you have to be sure that it all goes down well. Have you ever suffered from a liver attack? The French do all the time:* "avoir une crise de foie" *is pure indigestion to you and me but, to the French, is more localized. To avoid the dreaded* "crise de foie," *much care is taken to aid and abet the digestive process.*
>
> —Geneviève Edis, *Merde Encore!*

Scoops of sorbet were offered, and an apple tart, sleek with glaze, but I was defeated. When André saw me shake my head, he bellowed down the table. "You must eat. You need your strength. We're going to have a game of *boules.*"

After coffee, he led us outside to show us the goats that he kept in a pen at the side of the restaurant. They were huddled in the shade of an outbuilding, and I envied them; they weren't being asked to play *boules* under a sun that was drilling lasers into the top of my head. It was no good. My eyes were aching from the glare and my stomach wanted desperately to lie down and digest in peace. I made my excuses, found a patch of grass under a plane tree, and lowered my lunch to the ground.

André woke me some time after six and asked if I was staying for dinner. There were *pieds et paquets,* he said, and by some happy chance two or three bottles of the Gigondas had survived. With some difficulty, I escaped and drove home.

My wife had spent a sensible day in the shade and by the pool. She looked at me, a rumpled apparition, and asked if I had enjoyed myself.

"I hope they gave you something to eat," she said.

Peter Mayle also contributed "Les Invalides" *in Part I. Both stories were excerpted from his book,* Toujours Provence.

✳

France as a whole drinks more alcohol per head than any other country in the world, and about five million of the population, almost ten percent, drink far too much, and more than two million are already alcoholics. After heart disease and cancer, cirrhosis of the liver is the third commonest cause of death. The highest proportion of alcoholics is in a band stretching across northern France from Brittany to Belgium, and in the central eastern departments around Strasbourg and Colmar; but this does not mean that there are no heavy drinkers in the South.

—Rex Grizell, *A White House in Gascony: Escape to the Old French South*

JAN MORRIS

✦ ✹ ✦

The Edible City

Wondering if France really exists or is a figment
of her imagination, the author goes
to Dijon to find out.

I SAT AT A TABLE OUTSIDE THE MOULIN À VENT, IN THE PLACE
François Rude, in Dijon, in Burgundy, in France.

The children's carousel in the corner of the square had not
yet opened for business, and its prancing horses were veiled in tar-
paulins, but everything else was wide awake. From the café behind
me issued a murmur of men's voices and a powerful emanation of
coffee. Two or three students sat on the rim of the fountain eating
well-filled baguettes. Crisscrossing here and there, from one baker
of preference to another, housewives marched by with clusters of
long loaves under their arms. Two marvelously powdered and
dewlapped old dames, faces sharpened by lifetimes of probably
fairly malicious gossip, sibilantly continued their conversation as
they heaved themselves, corsets creaking, into the back of a taxi.
The square looked rather like an opera set with backdrops displaying Burgundian architecture of many periods; and the longer I
sat there, the more coffee I drank, the more I wondered if it were
not all indeed some kind of illusion. "Does France exist?" I scribbled rhetorically in my notebook.

I'll tell you why I was there. I had recently read a book by that
mistress of modern American prose, M.F.K. Fisher, about her life

in this very city more than sixty years ago. She had been a young student then, France had yet to undergo the traumas of the Second World War, and even kir, Dijon's supreme contribution to the delight of the nations, had not yet been formally invented. Yet nothing about that book had seemed unfamiliar to me. The France of the 1920s was precisely the France that I cherished in my own fancy in the 1990s. Its mingled images of age, beauty, good living, parochial quirk, and civilized style were just the images that habitually came to my own imagination still, when far away from France I thought of things French. Mrs. Fisher's Dijon truly was a place of the exact and particular memory, but it had long been transmuted, too, I gradually realized, into a place of the mind.

Could it be, I wondered, that this city—the city that is France itself—really no longer existed, but lingered on only in literature, metaphor, or symbolism? I jumped into my car, took a ferry across the English Channel, and drove through France to find out; and there I was in the Place François Rude, on the first morning of my inquiry, considering where to begin. The *mise-en-scène* before me certainly seemed almost too French to be true, embodying as it did so many

When greeting someone you know, the French shake hands and/or give a quick succession of impersonal kisses on alternating cheeks called les bises. *There are lots of nuances here that only experience can sort out, but here a few. Some people give two kisses, some three, and others four. If there are six people in the room and you give four* bises *each, that calls for a lot of kissing. Remember this is just a form of saying* bonjour. *What's interesting to note here is that the French are used to and comfortable with close personal contact. They are not bothered by human proximity or touching. They don't require the same distance Anglo-Saxons insist upon when talking. So get used to* les bises. *Even French people have cute little moments when two people are unsure if it'll be two, three, or four* bises. *Two is the most common, four is more classical; three is for those who want to be a bit different without abandoning tradition. Start on the left cheek and don't really kiss, just touch cheeks and steer your lips inward.*

—David Applefield,
Paris Inside Out: The Insider's Guide for Visitors, Residents, Professionals and Students on Living in Paris

age-old Francophile clichés; but perhaps, I thought, ordering a last coffee, it was only a façade or a happy breakfast camouflage (for whether in fact or in fantasy, almost nothing in life is more pleasurable, in my view, than to wake up one morning and find oneself eating croissants in France).

The gossips had asked to be taken to the railway station, so for a speculative start I followed them there. When I first visited the United States, I was astonished by the spectacle of frail elderly women, hardly to be seen above their steering wheels, driving with every sign of aplomb the vastly finned American automobiles of the time. For a moment I had rather the same sensation as I watched those figures of immemorial France step into a coach of a TGV train, whose bulbous, space-age ambience they took not the slightest notice of as they found themselves seats well placed, I suspected, not for observing the landscape, certainly not for inspecting the equipment, but for eyeing the other passengers.

I stood at the end of the platform to watch the train leave. It was two trains, really, each of ten coaches, with locomotives at the middle and at each end, and it left Dijon with a jerkless and inexorable rumble. As this great thing accelerated swiftly past me, its snout speed-worn like a 747's, its wheels gently hissing, I caught sight of the two old ladies at their window, talking still. Now they did not look in the least anomalous. They seemed to have become organically part of the mechanism; and when the last of the twenty coaches had left the station and was disappearing around the bend beneath a web of electric cables, I found that the tracks left vacant behind were dominated by the medieval towered hulk of Dijon Cathedral protruding above the station buildings. It did not look in the least out of place, either. One might almost have thought it an enormous postmodern signal tower or some kind of transmitter.

So it was not a matter of old ladies versus TGV, or cathedral versus railway station. It was a truce between them, or an understanding. As I walked back toward the city center, past the triumphal arch beneath which they were excavating a car park, past the posh Hotel de la Cloche where the Stars and Stripes billowed beside assorted tricolors, I thought that perhaps the key to my investigation was the French ability to blur things. We think of France as essentially a precise and rational country, but perhaps its genius is really more of a slithery or mollifying kind—generation blended into generation, Gothic into high tech.

There is a splendid covered market in the center of Dijon that is like an exhibition of earthy, rural Frenchness. Such luscious vegetable matter! Such meticulously dissected hunks of meat! Such glorious golden apples, creams, and fat sausages! The stalls spill out of the market hall into the streets outside, elaborating themselves into clothes stalls, too, and stands of toys or candies or kitchen gadgetry; and as they do so, something curious happens. They unite themselves, osmotically, with the fashionable shops of the downtown city, so that mirrored in the plate glass of an aristocratic delicatessen, all exquisitely potted pâtés or chic mustards, you may see the hearty clothes seller in his woolen cap jollying along a couple of housewives, while the violent yellow of the cheap bonbons on one side of life merges with the gentle pinks of bathroom sachets on the other.

In the same way, Dijon's sleek modern buses, linked to their trailers by concertina corridors, ease their way among the venerable offices of Burgundian glory as though they have been doing it since the days of Philip the Bold—whose magnificently colored and angel-guarded fifteenth-century tomb, now in the Musée des Beaux-Arts, conversely looks as though it might have been made yesterday. The computer is part of the furniture here: I once saw a chef call up a recipe for his *spécialité du jour* on his French Minitel. Canned music has been so insidiously admitted that one not only gets drifting slush in some of the best restaurants but majestically recorded organ music in the cathedral. One afternoon there was a parade through Dijon of heavy trucks on their way to a behemoth race. I went into the street to watch them pass, expecting some neo-American display of machismo: but no, the mighty vehicles that came lumbering by, hooting their Klaxons joyously, were decorated with pretty gypsylike paintings of lakes and damsels, flowers and hills, making the event feel remarkably like the latest manifestation of some hoary bucolic festival.

It used to be a temptation to patronize the provincial French—
certainly a distinct element of condescension, I fear, runs through
those standard images of mine. No longer. Nowadays if you dispute
the value of radishes with some quaint peasant at a market stall, he
may very well summon up the market price in Paris, or more
probably Brussels, on his portable computer link.

Yes, more probably Brussels, I came to think as I wandered the
town, because since Mrs. Fisher's day the whole meaning of
Europe has changed. Her Dijon looked back to an eternity of
European squabbling, back through the miseries of the trenches to
the humiliation of the Franco-Prussian War, the triumphs and disasters of Napoleon's adventurings, the Hundred Years War, the
endless pettifogging disputes and rivalries that have punctuated the
history of Europe ever since the end of the Roman Empire. Now
even the capital of Burgundy looks forward, rather than back, as
the continent tentatively shuffles toward some kind of unity.

You might not think it, to look at the place. For several hundred
years Dijon was the seat of a dukedom whose dominion extended,
at the peak of power, as far north as the Netherlands, rivaling the
kingdom of France itself in wealth and pretension. This old consequence gives the place the style of a city-state still. Grand
steepled churches speckle the city center, ancient towers look
down. The dukely palace is now the stateliest of town halls, and
opens still into a formal arcaded square just made for state occasions. Dijon retains the bearing of a capital and is perpetually gaudy
with the flags of ancient heraldry, for all the world as though some
panoplied visiting king or cardinal is expected at any moment.

No doubt all of this made for parochialism, in the days when
only ghastly rutted coach roads linked Dijon with the rest of
France and Europe. I imagine that nowhere could be much more
introspective than a superannuated dukedom in early 19th-century
France, and certainly when the railway came to Dijon in 1851 the
more progressive citizens hailed it as an allegorical liberation of the
civic energies. Now one of Dijon's boasts is its position on the map
of the new Europe. It is true, alas, that the most important of all
the French trains miss Dijon on their hurtling passage from Paris

to Lyon and the south, but almost mystical geographic conjunctions are quoted to demonstrate how absolutely crucial a crossroads Dijon occupies. It stands on the route from the Atlantic to the Alps, from the Mediterranean to the North Sea, from Paris to Geneva, from the Channel Tunnel to Milan, from Spain to Germany, from Dublin, I dare say, to Belgrade. Certainly it is anything but isolated. Paris is only 200 miles to the northwest, Geneva only 130 to the southeast, and at the railway station they schedule trains to Strasbourg, Rome, and Naples too.

If you can't join them...I get the feeling in Dijon that the French, having failed to defy history by sheer force of *la gloire,* have consciously decided to make the most of it instead. If such a French city was still narrow and inward-looking 60 years ago and remains somewhat chauvinistic in most of our stereotypical images, in the 90s it is almost cosmopolitan. Foreigners are everywhere in Dijon now. A regular at the bar of the Moulin à Vent, I soon discovered, was a distinguished but melancholy-looking black man in a long overcoat, sometimes to be seen elegantly drinking at the bar, sometimes selling leather belts in the square outside. Algerians sit in almost every café, huddled threadbare and wistful over their cups. Students talk in many tongues. Busloads of German, Belgian, Dutch tourists spill constantly into the Place de la Libération, and there are always English voices to be heard in the Restaurant Le Prés aux Clercs et Trois Faisans. If you stay at La Cloche you will be able to watch seven television channels in French, three in German, two in Italian, one in English, and two—Euro-Sport and TV 5 Europe—that I assume to be in sort of Eurospeak.

N o foreigner should ever mock the French language, first because he does not understand it properly, and second because it has divine status in France. Every foreigner, however, needs to watch the French mocking each other on how they use their language themselves.

—Theodore Zeldin, *The French*

Plump and definitely replete, those voices at Le Prés Aux Clercs, for of course the Burgundian cuisine remains inviolate, having ridden out the debilitating storms of nouvelle cuisine. The *coq au vin* is still as rich. The pastries are still as crisp. The fish still lie in their sumptuous sauces, or are just as pungently marinaded. The guinea fowl, which look so thin and mingy in the farmyard, are still magically transformed into succulent morsels when they lie amid their duck livers on the plate. Just down the road are the greatest vineyards on earth, and like tokens of tribute there come to Dijon, to be reverently uncorked and sensuously sampled, the precious bottles of the Côte d'Or, bottles with names to send a prickle up a gourmet's spine—like Chevalier Montrachet and Grands Echézeaux, Romanée-Conti and Gevrey-Chambertin—and to leave behind them, when the last glass is poured, the last setting is cleared, and the shutters are down, an aroma spilling out of the restaurant doors like a midnight benediction.

Good living in Dijon demands a bit of purple prose, because it is more than just hedonism. It is faith, or principle, or tradition—tradition especially, for I have the impression that despite their compatibility with the present, Dijoniers are still unusually fond of the past. If change is evidently easily absorbed here, habit is just as delicately sustained. I lunched one day at a Japanese restaurant in town, washing down a plate of sushi with a Kirin beer; but though the place was thoroughly Japanese in appearance and cuisine, somehow in manner it felt to me as fundamentally French as any of those bourgeois corner restaurants, presided over by ladies in black bombazine, that figure so largely in my French imaginings. Probably the best-loved, and certainly the best-known, mechanism in this city is not at all like the TGV but works in a very antique and familial way on the roof of the Church of Notre-Dame. In the 14th century they put up there a figure of a man, a *jaquemart,* to strike the hours of a clock; they called him Jacques, of course, and he banged the bell each hour. In the seventeenth century they added Jacqueline, and the clock sounded the half hours too. A century later little Jacquelinet and Jacquelinette appeared. Now every quarter of an hour this complex, ungainly crew hammers away at the bell with arms, feet, or legs—I can never make out which—still watched, I noticed, after all this time with apparent fond affection by many a citizen below.

Around the corner, on the north wall of the church, there is a very small and almost unrecognizable figure of an owl—*une chouette*. It is just within arm's reach of passersby, and every guidebook says that the people of Dijon habitually stroke it as they walk by, just for luck. I took this bit of folklore with a pinch of salt—it was true that the unfortunate bird had been all but smoothed out of limb and feather by the passage of many hands, but I assumed that to be, like most such European phenomena, merely the patina of ancient superstition. However, when I spent ten minutes in the rue de la Chouette keeping my eye on the owl, I found that many sons and daughters of Dijon really did touch it as they went by— sometimes reaching up casually en passant, sometimes stopping almost reverently, as before an icon, and sometimes lifting a child from a buggy to experience the sensation for itself.

They were young, too; that's the point. It is a happy peculiarity of France that the young seem to be as French as the old—well, not quite so *bottomlessly* French, perhaps, but still far more French than Germans are German or English, English. Dijon is a young city full of students from the University of Burgundy, but its youth does not make it feel any the less rooted in its ways. Young Dijoniers certainly eat hamburgers rather more often than *paillasson de langoustines,* but they do it at what is surely the most discreet Big Mac in the world, urbanely inserted behind a palatial 18th-century façade. I bumped into a parade of agricultural students one afternoon, collecting money for some educational cause. I was slightly disappointed at first to find them dressed up as carrots and potatoes—rather as at a county fair in Iowa, perhaps—and marching, as it happened, to the beat of Sousa. But when I came across them later, at the conclusion of their parade, they were singing a lugubrious Burgundian traditional song around the Place Francois Rude fountain—and how happily I contributed to their collection!

After dinner one night I came across a group of young bloods wildly roller-skating in and out of a pedestrian arcade—out of the arcade, over the sidewalk, into the street, and away in one breakneck motion. Just as I passed one of them came shooting like a bullet out of the arcade and immediately across my tracks. He looked like any other European street kid—jeaned, t-shirted, ear-ringed, ponytailed—but finding me there in his way he swerved abruptly on his skates, circled in front of me, and gave me a bow as courtly as any Burgundy duke's, with a smile as sweet as sorbet.

That's civilization for you, when the rough, tough young can behave with such humorous grace. I am sure there are louts in Dijon not so given to charm, but still the general temper of this city, at all social levels, seems to me polished and considerate. It is one of the last strongholds of the pipe smoker—even Jacques the clock striker smokes a pipe—and this is perhaps a sign of its bal-anced and contemplative temperament.

The longer I looked at Dijon, the more I found myself seduced by its Proustian detail. It is less of a monolithic whole than are comparable cities elsewhere in Western Europe; it is more of a pointillist construction. Like Paris before they let Baron Haussmann loose upon it, even in its center it is a place of wrin-kled back streets and sudden small squares, and the population moves through it not just as an amorphous mass, poll fodder or marketing statistics, but as an ag-gregation of so many individuals. Dijon is anything but homoge-nized, just as most of the cheeses in its markets, thank God, remain resolutely unpasteurized.

> *E*ating out is [vigneron Pierre Ramonet's] only extravagance. Every Sunday the old man changes from his weekday shabbiness into a well-cut suit and takes his family to lunch at Bocuse or Alain Chapelle or another of the famous three-star restaurants of Burgundy. But Ramonet sticks resolutely to the wines of his own corner of the world. There is a story that he once went to Maxim's in Paris, and they gave him a bottle of the fabled '29 Château Latour, intending to honour him. "It is good," said Ramonet, "but it is not wine."
>
> —Simon Loftus, "A Tale of Two Villages," *Discovery*

Here is a man like an Inca striding by, wearing a hat with earflaps and what look like ox-skin boots. Here, five middle-aged women carefully kiss each other, cheek to cheek, pearl to pearl, as they emerge from lunch at Jean-Pierre Billoux's celebrated and extremely, expensive restaurant. A scholarly-looking gent in the Grand Café—philosophy professor?

editor of the local paper?—has his eyes so firmly glued to his book that he must eat his soup tactilely, his spoon feeling its way past his nose, over his mustache, to his listlessly waiting mouth. Outside the cathedral a solitary beggar stands with gaunt dignity, less like a pan-handler than a sculpted figure of a martyr. When it rains in Dijon a wonderful variety of colored umbrellas is sprung into action, and under one of them a student, all alone in a park, is sure to be still working away at this textbook in the spattering shower. Even the sounds of Dijon are curiously compelling—the flowery whistle of a workman somewhere, the clang of a venerable bell, a ducklike quack whenever a car goes over a grate in the Place Darcy.

Dear God, what am I saying? Where do these sentimental and nostalgic meanderings come from—out of my head or out of my observations? Am I back where I started, with the same old im-ages—the age, the beauty, the good living, the parochial quirk, and the civilized style? Could it possibly be that Mrs. Fisher's long-ago France, the France of all my clichés, has been reality all the time?

Search me—I give up; and writing as I am now, under the beneficent influence of a couple of genuine Dijon kirs, I find I don't much care anyway. Ask Jack-o-the-clock, or touch the owl for enlightenment.

Jan Morris has been wandering the world and writing about her experiences for more than 40 years. She is the author of numerous books and her essays on travel are among the classics of the genre. She lives in Wales.

*

We went through a large simple bedroom hung with soft green, past two beds which were low and "modern" and the two shuttered windows which looked out into trees along the rue de la Liberté, and into the bath-room. I felt a kind of quiet nervousness in both myself and my compan-ion: was I going to be annoyed, scoffing, repelled, shocked, by this really ridiculous idea of piping good wine through the walls like water?

"And there it is," Georges said without expression. "You will notice that Monsieur Maillard has very prudently placed it near the washbasin, in case some tipsy guest forgets to turn it off properly, and it dribbles."

"More teasing," Maillard said mildly. "Go right ahead, old fellow. You know such a thing has never occurred."

On the wall to the side of the basin, and about breast-high, was what looked like the front half of a fat little wooden wine cask, with two toy spigots sticking out and two pretty little silver *tastevins,* typically Burgundian, hanging beside them. It was the sort of fakey amusing toy an assistant director in Hollywood might order built into his bar, filled with scotch for his housewarming party and then a dust catcher until he became a producer and ordered a bigger and better one....

Monsieur Maillard rather solemnly took down one of the *tastevins* and half filled it with a couple of tablespoons of red wine. "The reservoir is almost empty," he said as he handed it to me. "It is filled every morning, on the top floor, and of course checked at night. In the summer we keep the white wine chilled, but we leave the red alone."

The wine was a good firm *grand ordinaire,* the same Georges and I had drunk downstairs for lunch. It was, the proprietor's son told us, one of the *passe-tous-grains,* a yield from the noble Pinot Noir grape, stretched with Gamay, which some vintners lied about but he felt proud to serve as what it was. Certainly it was pleasant to drink, and he said smilingly that he had never had any complaints about it, either in his restaurant or up in the bedrooms....

"It never occurred to me to raise the price of the rooms," he went on. "With me it was simply a sort of advertising for Dijon, and not for our hotel."

—M. F. K. Fisher, *As They Were*

NIK COHN

* * *

Riviera Gumshoe

A sometime bass player, sometime private eye,
provides entrée to the world of old Nice.

MIDWAY THROUGH MY FIRST AFTERNOON IN NICE, TOWARD THE
end of March, a sudden storm blows up. The sky turns purplish
black, the color of a bone-deep bruise; a blinding rain sweeps in
off the Baie des Anges. Within minutes, the narrow back streets of
the Old Town, where I have been peacefully loafing, are transformed into swirling rivers, and I take refuge in a bar with no
name. It is a true hole-in-the-wall—a long, narrow cave with a
zinc counter, a few tatterdemalion bullfighting posters, and a terminal case of drains—and it is packed to the bursting point. France
is playing England at rugby football on TV. It is the climax of the
season, Europe's closest approach to a Super Bowl, and massed
drinkers crowd anxiously about the ancient black-and-white
screen, roaring or groaning at every turn of play.

Only one man sits apart, staring glumly into a glass of something pink and sticky. Slouched and rumpled, spilling out of a
baggy white suit, he looks like Walter Matthau's lost brother.

A white panama rests beside him on the bar; his crepe-soled
shoes were once white, too. When I perch on the stool beside him,
he takes a quick sideways peek, just long enough to see that I'm a
stranger. *"Ros bif?* You are English?" he asks.

"Irish."

"A savage potato? A trotter of bogs?" His large yellowed face, the color of nicotine stains, scrunches tight in disgust or acid indigestion. "Godelpus," he says, and drinks deep.

The game approaches its crisis. Flickering like ghost shadows, the French are beautiful to watch, all dazzle and invention, while the English merely plod, and win. "Always the story the same," the man in white complains. "Nothing for virtue. Not a bone."

His English comes out of the side of his mouth, in quasi-American gutturals, a bit like Humphrey Bogart strained through bouillabaisse. On the TV, the French launch one last desperation assault, as gallant and doomed as the rest. Then the final whistle blows, and the English throw up their arms in triumph. All along the bar, strong men groan and blaspheme, curse the fates. But the man in white only sighs. Peeling five 100-franc notes from a billfold of six, he drops them on the zinc bar, turns his face to the wall. "Not a bone. Not a kiss," he says. "For me, the fat lady sings No Cigar."

His name is Jean-Christophe Beziers. What he needs, he says, is a change of air and two, maybe three little glasses. So we venture back into the city. The downpour has slackened to a soft spring rain, sweet to the war-torn spirit, and we paddle serenely downstream till we reach the Cours Saleya.

The Cours is the heart of Vieux Nice. Overlooked by the great rock of the citadel, it is an open-air market and strolling place dazzling to every sense. Eighteenth-century palaces and Baroque churches, pink and gold in sunlight, earth-toned in rain, sit haunch by paunch with tenements; restaurants and cafés—Niçois, Genovese, Tunisian—line both flanks. Even in March, beneath their blue-striped awnings, the stalls are mountainous with aubergines and peaches, *haricots verts* as thin as matchsticks, goat cheeses from the Alpes-Maritimes, strawberries from Spain and scented soaps from Grasse, a dozen species of crystallized fruits and a dozen more of olives; while at the western end, in the shadow of the opera house, there is a flowering jungle riotous with jasmine and tea roses, spiraea, hanging fuchsia, birds of paradise.

Outdoors at the Café les Ponchettes, the Cours's social center, Jean-Christophe plops himself on a sodden wicker chair and calls for ardent spirits. Two cognacs go down seamlessly, without a word or the least flicker of response; but when the third arrives, he raises his glass and half grimaces, half smiles. "To the savage potato," he says.

At our backs, the Old Town is its own tight world, a labyrinth of lanes and back alleys: "A woman's soft stomach. A womb," Jean-Christophe calls it. "Consoling, like some carpet slippers."

He himself took refuge in this fastness more than twenty years ago. On a blistering hot and thunderous day, with a mistral threatening, he was crossing the Cours Saleya in pursuit of the young woman who had his money. His heart was bleeding, his feet were on fire; the young woman, a witch, disappeared like some smoke. Abandoning the chase, Jean-Christophe slumped into the Restaurant Safari, took one small pastis. "And the remains are his tory," he says.

In repose, he looks like a basset hound on downers. Everything about him—shoulders, jowls, soiled white suit—sags at droop, as if pulled down by unseen wires. The overall impression is of a man who was once a few sizes larger but somehow shrank, leaving the bags and folds where solid flesh used to be. Both of his feet are quite flat.

On his ring finger he sports a tarnished gilt heart: "The story of my life," he says.

Now in his 50s, he has lived in Nice all his days. His father, a schoolmaster of geometry, took it for granted that his son would follow the same path. And so, in the beginning, did Jean-Christophe. Until he turned seventeen, he was a shy youth,

I first saw Paris soon after its liberation in 1944.... American literature was suddenly hot, and to my everlasting delight I heard the handsome young Albert Camus say to a G.I. friend of mine, "I love Faulkner because I too am a Southerner. I love the dust and the heat."

—Alfred Kazin, "River of Life," *Travel Holiday*

clumsy, bad at sports, and allergic to all excitements. Then he met Marie-Catherine, who called herself Kitty. She was two years his elder, a bottled redhead with scarlet lips to match, and she lived for Hollywood thrillers, for gangsters, and celluloid gumshoes.

At first she picked him up as a joke; then she made him into a project. She dressed him in double-breasted suits and slouch-brim Borsalinos, drilled him in B-feature Americanese, taught him the use of a pistol. She renamed him Hank Marlow. Finally, she seduced him into giving up geometry and turning private eye.

On the rue Rossini there used to be a famous man called Xavier P. Notari, confidential investigator. To celebrate his eighteenth birthday, Hank Marlow went to work for him as an errand boy. He expected this to lead swiftly to great adventures, to stakeouts and gunplay, showdowns at dawn. But somehow it all went wrong. Love-blinded, he stole a gold heart from a local jeweler's and asked Kitty to be his wife. Before she could answer, he was arrested. And by the time he returned to circulation, it was too late: she had married the jeweler.

"Always the story the same," Jean-Christophe says now. When he takes off his panama to wipe away the sweat, he is revealed as virtually bald, just a few lank strands plastered flat across his scalp. "Not even a wave and the word good-bye," he mourns. "How could such a perfidy be?"

All she'd left him was the gold heart. And even that proved fake. Still, she had changed his life beyond recall. A man who had been Hank Marlow, however fleetingly, can hardly go back to the squares of the hypotenuse. So he has learned to live by sections. Part of him drives limousines for visiting Japanese businessmen; another hires out for surveillance and divorce investigations; yet another plays bass in a trio called Les 3 Diables, available for weddings and bar mitzvahs. The largest portion, however, simply sits around in Old Town bars and waits for savage potatoes.

Now, sipping on a fourth cognac, he gazes across the darkening Cours Saleya, and something strange occurs. It is as if, in contemplating his history, he begins to shift personae. Minute by minute, the crabbed outlines of Jean-Christophe Beziers seem to peel away, fall off him like dead skin, to reveal the Hank Marlow still lurking beneath, a man of vision and derring-do, with all his lost stuffing restored.

Inside the café, a jukebox plays "Here Comes the Night." The market stalls are shutting down, and the Cours is full of home-going housewives, their straw baskets laden with treats. "Oh, how I am famished," says Jean-Christophe, watching these feasts drift past. "We must eat, we must be fat. Such is the duty of all sad men."

Just before dusk, the sun comes out. The citadel rock catches flame, and the whole of the Old Town seems to glow in the re-fraction. Tugging at my arm, Jean-Christophe leads me back into the labyrinth. Cobblers and coffee blenders work sitting in their windows; miniskirted girls in white boots haunt the narrow door-ways. "So why have you come here?" Jean-Christophe asks, steer-ing me down the tight funnel of the rue de Moulin and inside a little restaurant called Le Chapon Fin. "What's your game?"

"My mother sent me."

"Impossible!" He orders *soupe de poisson, salade de poulpes,* and *daurade grillée aux fines herbes,* with one platter of *raviolis à la Niçoise* on the side and another of *aubergines à l'ail et aux anchois.* "Any mother with some white hairs would never so abandon you. She would know, a town like Nice, a country like the Côte d'Azur, they cannot be seen by one man. Alone, he will catch the tourist disease and only lose his time." He refills his wine glass, holds it up against the light. "What he needs," he says, "is a wise man, *une tête forte;* a guide."

"A Virgil in crepe-soled shoes?"

"You may," says Jean-Christophe, "call me Hank."

The line about my Mother is not untrue. In 1926, the Côte d'Azur was her neighborhood. She was then nineteen, a Russian émigrée who had emerged from the Revolution with a broken body and a spot on her lung. In hopes of staving off tuberculosis, she was sent south to Juan-les-Pins, to a sanitarium filled with other malfunctioning Russians, and that was where she first learned to dance the Charleston.

The whole Riviera then, in her memory, had been a land bewitched. Invalids were transported from all over Europe and miraculously made whole. By day, they lounged on deserted beaches or were wheeled through the unspoiled villages of Antibes and Cap Ferrat; at night, they sat out on their balconies by starlight and listened to the nightingales. Hispano Suizas and De Dion-Boutons cruised the Corniche. The casinos were full of exiled royalty. Even the dying wore their flannels well.

"Paradise," my mother said. And the vision passed down to me. As a small child, my bath nights were solemn rituals of remembrance. Although my mother scrubbed my back with coal tar soap, she told me it was juniper, cedar, lavender, all the perfumes of Provence swirled together. "Imagine," she commanded. Then she'd relive the night when she smuggled the consumptive son of Stanislavsky from his hospital bed and they danced the Black Bottom till dawn. Or the time that her friend Kiki, the Parisian flapper, eloped by rowboat with the one-eyed Baron X. Or the solar eclipse through which she had once glimpsed Rudolph Valentino, pursued by shrieking harpies, sweep out of the Hotel Negresco and escape in a chauffeured hearse.

Such images do not fade. By the time I learned to bathe myself, the Côte d'Azur was enshrined forever as my notion of Shangri-la. Now, 40 years on, I have come to see what survives.

I've traveled in March by design. On sundry previous occasions, I have glimpsed the Riviera in high summer, and the place has always seemed like Fort Lauderdale, only not so chic—beaches jammed sardine-tight with broiling flesh; the air choked with the mingled stench of suntan oils, frying fats, and motor exhausts; and blaring over everything, in a ceaseless dissonant fanfare, the furious honking of car horns.

But out of season, in the Mediterranean spring, surely all will be healed. According to the guidebooks, March is the time of blossom, of the cherry trees and the almonds, when the hillsides seem to float on clouds of pink and white and every breeze is heady with scent. The weather, it's true, might prove fickle—"Best to pack a change of heart," the travel agent has advised—but what are a few soakings? "Only foolings. Little pleasantries," says my new guide, "to keep sharp the appetite."

Hank Marlow, as I now think of him, rises to his new duties with a zest. Promptly at eight on the following morning, he waits for me in my hotel lobby, resplendent in a midnight blue zoot suit—"Fresh from the shop of hock"—and a bloodred Hawaiian silk tie with parrots and grass-skirted dancing girls. Through the picture window, I can glimpse the great sweep of the Baie des Anges, bathed in dazzling sunlight. "All is in order. I have arranged every trick," Marlow announces, as if he has just got off the hot line to God. "The *toute* Côte d'Azur salutes you."

For our maiden voyage, I have planned a day's pilgrimage to the stamping grounds of my mother's youth, west from Nice along the coast, through Antibes and Juan-les-Pins to Cannes.

Straightaway, we enter a world deep in love with construction. The coast road is lined with dumpsters and earthmovers, deafened by power drills. Beyond them lie tier upon tier of jerry-built apartment blocks, daubed cream and yellow and bubble gum pink, their postage stamp balconies shaded by plastic awnings, and spray-painted graffiti—A BAS LES JUIFS; RUDE BOYS MARCHENT SUR L'EAU; ELVIS LIVES—besmirching their lower walls. Traffic crawls by inches, gridlocked behind a solid phalanx of steamrollers; beside me, Marlow beams with pride. "Everything bang-bang modern, *le dernier cri,* is not?" he demands. He pats his stomach, then his heart. "Always the progress, progress, more fierce like some gangbusters."

The broken reed of yesterday is now a positive strutter. With each passing hour he seems physically to swell. The empty spaces between his flesh and his clothes are filled again, pumped up to bursting. With his yellow palm pressed down hard on the horn, he honks his way triumphantly through one suburban sprawl after another—St-Augustin, Cagnes-sur-Mer, Villeneuve-Loubet—pointing out a convention hall or municipal swimming pool to our left, the discos and hamburger joints to our right.

And then it starts to rain.

It comes down hard, comes down long. From Antibes on, we

see only a blur of red and yellow lights, a swishing of windshield wipers. "Better turn back," I suggest.

"Not while I breathe." Dripping scorn, Marlow takes a swig from a small hip flask, hammers yet harder at the horn. "The true Niçois, he does not retreat, never of his life," he explains. "He always onward marches, *sauve qui peut,* till death makes him dead."

Inching into Cannes, we seek shelter in a brasserie on the Croisette, the main thoroughfare that overlooks the port. Madonna shrieks at eardrum-damage volume from a half-dozen speakers. Across the street, anchored yachts toss glumly in the storm. *"Du vin rouge,"* I venture.

"Talk English, asshole," our waiter replies.

So it marches. Cannes, a dull commercial town consecrated to media trade fairs, is enlivened only by the Carlton hotel, a new-Baroque wedding cake whose twin domes are said to have been modeled after the breasts of La Belle Otero, the legendary courtesan of the 1890s. La Belle later gambled away her fortune in the Riviera casinos and died a pauper in Nice. In her pomp, however, she was the very grandest of *grandes horizontales,* and the Carlton, a heroic folly, pays her proper tribute: "All is lacking is some peacocks," Marlow says.

"Peacocks?"

"In the lobby, no?" With open hands, he sketches fantails, arched necks, a stiff-legged strut. "More better than dancing bears," he says, nodding briskly. "More class by far."

I ask to visit Le Suquet, the old quarter above the port, where there is said to be a medieval citadel with a 17th-century Gothic church attached. But Marlow will not hear of it. "Just some bunches of old stuff. We have finer, much, in Nice," he

> *To me indelicacy is an abomination. Much worse than debauchery. My ethical beliefs allow me to regard the pleasure of the senses as a splendid thing. They also tell me to respect certain feelings, a certain refinement in friendship, and especially the French language, an amiable and infinitely gracious lady, whose sadness and delight are equally exquisite but upon whom one must never impose obscene poses. That would be to dishonour her beauty.*
>
> —Marcel Proust,
> *Selected Letters 1880-1903*

pronounces. And turning the car toward the east, with a final de-
fiant honk, he sets course for home, the Cours Saleya, and two,
maybe three little glasses.

A daily ritual takes shape. Every morning at eight, Hank
Marlow and I meet in the Cours Saleya and watch the market set
up. I make plans to go visit a museum, a Roman ruin, a mountain
village. Then Marlow drives me to a casino, a power plant, a brand-
new McDonald's.

"The past he is for dead men," he says.

By our third day together, a compromise has been struck. If I
suffer Marlow to show me his Côte d'Azur in the morning, I am
permitted to select my own routes afterward. So we journey to science parks and futuristic soccer stadiums, eat fast food at drive-ins,
then head for the hills. A few miles behind the coastal strip, the
urban sprawl begins to thin, the roads to climb. The hillsides are
still dotted with gimcrack villas, but between them there are indeed cherry orchards and almonds, exactly as the guidebooks
promise. And certain villages, if you grit your teeth through the
outskirts and penetrate their core, have blessedly survived, more or
less intact.

First among these is Vence, walled and mazelike.

Behind its central church square, filled with light and with
brawling children, lies a network of tiny alleys; a souk spilling
over with produce stalls and butchers' slabs, deep caves full of
wine. In summer, a shopkeeper says, the town is abandoned to
strangers. But for now it belongs to a tribe of ancient women. In
their long black skirts and black head scarves, they look little different from their forebears in the sepia postcards sold at the village *brocante*.

At the end of one alley, no wider than an air shaft, sits the Place
Godeau, an almost deserted backwater with a stone fountain, a few
budding plane trees, assorted dogs. The surrounding houses—tall
tenements washed apricot or faded yellow or the palest blush
pink—look down upon a small chapel and an open-air restaurant
serving homemade pizzas of goat cheese and wild mushrooms,
smoked ham and artichoke, red peppers, black olives, and a mite of

fresh grilled sardine. The hill air tastes like springwater; Lili, the house mutt, lies tangled in our feet. "Satisfied?" I ask.

"I endure," Marlow replies.

On a suburban hillside overlooking the town is the Chapel of the Rosary, designed and decorated by Matisse. The nuns of the adjoining Dominican convent nursed him through a wartime sickness, and this chapel was his gift in return. Utterly simple and unpretending—plain benches, a stone altar, some yellow and blue stained-glass windows, a crucifixion drawn in a few black strokes on white—it is a place of such serenity, so perfect in proportion, that even Marlow keeps hush.

Other villages are less impressive. St-Paul, once the town of Picasso, Braque, and Chagall, wallows wall-to-wall in boutiques; Mougins, in the hills behind Cannes, which swarms over with expense account gastronomes; while Haut de Cagnes, Eze, and Tourette-sur-Loup, medieval citadels all, have long since been denatured by sheer gross tonnage of souvenir and crafts shops. Even out of season, the tour buses come and leave in convoys.

From time to time on the twisting mountain backroads, we turn a blind corner and catch a glimpse of how the land looked once—a monumental terrain, harsh but thrilling, where strips of burnt umber rock are interspersed with blocks of dense, dark forest and stark cliffs plunge dizzily into meadows bright with poppies, then we hit another corner and the vision is wiped clean, to be replaced by gas stations and hotel billboards, a hundred more Lego-brick villas.

For respite, we turn to casino towns—Monte Carlo, Beaulieu, Menton. The first, though ringed by skyscrapers so crass as to make downtown Cleveland seem blessed, does at least boast a fine ornamental garden complete with tactfully secluded bowers, so that terminal losers may blow their brains out undisturbed. As for Charles Garnier's Casino, all crystal chandeliers, marbled hallways, and gilt, it is a new-Baroque extravaganza so gloriously overblown that any critique seems prissy. Slot machines now compete with the roulette tables, and piped easy listening fouls the air. Still, the great hall echoes like a cathedral at confession hour, and the croupiers rake in our lost chips with the same sad, priestly eyes that bankrupted La Belle Otero back in the 1920s. "It is a privilege," Marlow says, limping out on his martyred feet, "to be rendered destitute in a style so refined."

When at night, cleaned out and spent, we creep back to Nice and the shelter of the Cours Saleya, it feels like a homecoming from the wars.

Over drinks, I tot up one afternoon's spoils: Menton, the favorite resort of the 19th-century English, had a marvelous foreign cemetery. High above the port and the fine Church of St-Michel, a white marble angel mourned her dead, and the gaunt cypresses, soughing, bent, and twisted in the fierce March winds. At Villefranche, beloved of Jean Cocteau, a 1920s Rolls Royce cruised slowly beside the harbor, driven by a black-mustached chauffeur in a long white duster and matching cap, while from the backseat a lady of a certain age inspected the sidewalk restaurants through a gold-rimmed lorgnette. And outside La Turbie, where the emperor Augustus crushed the rebellious tribes of lower Gaul in 6 B.C., a score of topless Amazons ran shrieking from a pack of pelt-cloaked and woad-painted cavemen while a film director bawled orders.

But all of these, in the end, are merely sights, pictures from a slide show. It is Vieux Nice that tugs the heart. *A woman's soft stomach, a womb, as comforting as some carpet slippers*—Marlow spoke a mouthful.

Everything revolves around the Cours. Behind a high stone wall, which keeps it safe from passing traffic and all loud display, its pace is calm, unchanging, a ritual progression of hours into days. An hour after dawn, the first sunlight touches the upstairs windows of the Opéra, and the cafés open their doors. Beginning in the west, the market loafers work their way serenely from the flower market through the fruit and vegetables to the junk stores in the east, from croissants and coffee for breakfast to pastis before lunch to cold beers in the slumberous afternoon, and on to cognac at dusk, when the last sun dies on the citadel rock and the fake gas lamps flicker on, one by one, all along the deserted parade.

"Never one needs to leave such a place. Never in the life," Marlow says. And increasingly, we do not. With every day, our excursions grow shorter, more cursory. By the end of a week, it takes us all our energies to venture across the Place Masséna into the other neighborhoods of Nice itself.

One doesn't travel to France to be temperate when one can be temperate in Michigan without even trying.

—Jim Harrison, *Just Before Dark: Collected Nonfiction*

There is no great temptation to be sure. Modern Nice is largely 19th century, wrought in a style reminiscent of the Grands Boulevards in Paris. On block after block of unyielding stone, we trudge in search of the Belle Epoque. But most of the great *fin de siècle* palaces have been turned into museums; the Russian Orthodox cathedral, crowned by five onion domes in mosaic tiles, is surrounded by faceless new apartment blocks; in Cimiez, the Matisse Museum is closed for renovation, and the monumental Hôtel Regina, where Queen Victoria stayed, is now offices and condos. Even the Hôtel Negresco, though its exterior is an architectural fireworks display that outblazes the Carlton in Cannes, proves as impersonal as an airport inside, with rows of cheesy gift shops and a toupeed lounge pianist in a shiny red jacket, whose favorite song is "Feelings."

Along the Promenade des Anglais, there is no sign of Russian aristocracy, or even of Anglo-Saxon military. According to a youth at the Church of the Holy Trinity on the rue de la Buffa, where the British Association meets, the last retired colonels vanished some years since. "They are missed," he says, "but not badly missed."

Our only recourse is to turn our backs, stare fixedly out to sea. The pounding of traffic along the front never slackens, but there is a barrier of mighty palm trees that blot out the worst of the ugliness; and the sweep of the Baie des Anges itself, a curve as deep as a crescent moon, is indestructible.

In March the only swimmers are members of the local Polar Bear Club, septuagenarians all, who splash and squeal in the chill waters like so many tots of five. And these waters, in sunlight, dazzle the eye. Their blue is purer, more translucent than seems elementally possible; their calm depths reach out, a lure. "Like the waters of Avalon," Marlow muses, unwontedly poetic, "most beautiful to drown in."

Refreshed, we slide back into the bowels of Vieux Nice and go traveling no more. The whole neighborhood, a triangular wedge, extends for less than a mile. Yet it seems a self-contained universe. At every turn there is some new splendor: a magnificent Baroque doorway squeezed between a hand laundry and a fresh-pasta store; a bell tower, a flight of weathered stone steps; some fountained corner set ablaze by crimson shrubs; or the 17th-century Palais Lascaris, its interior grandiose with stucco and mythological ceiling frescoes; or the fish market on the Place St-François, iridescent with red mullet and bream, forkbeard, conger eel, and the hideous *rascasse:* and everywhere, snaking through the quarter like a blood pulse, the scent of a thousand foods.

Why ever shift? From time to time, perhaps, to keep our appetites sharp, we might take a stroll along the Baie des Anges to the port, or ride the elevator to the ornamental gardens and the old cemetery atop the citadel rock. For the rest, we are content just to sit and fatten.

At last, on the night before I must leave, we return to Le Chapon Fin, where our partnership began. Marlow gorges himself with customary relish. But as the evening progresses and glass succeeds glass, he begins to grow a touch lachrymose. For this, after all, is Hank's last stand. On the morrow, he must revert to Jean-Christophe Beziers. The zoot suit and the tie with the grass-skirted wahines will go back into mothballs. Out will come the baggy white suit, the scuffed crepe-soled shoes. "And what then?" he demands. "What must I become?" He looks as though he might spit, or burst into tears, or both. "A washup," he answers himself.

In vain I try to console him. There is his music to think of, and his surveillance work, and his limousine full of Japanese.

"You have much to live for," I gush.

From across the table, Hank Marlow casts me a look half-angry, half-pitying, and drains his glass as if it were a poisoned chalice.

"With my feet?" he says. His suit looks loose on him, a trifle baggy; patches of sweat begin to splotch his shirt. "Without a doubt," says Jean-Christophe, "the savage potato dreams."

Nik Cohn grew up in Derry, Northern Ireland and has lived in the U.S. since 1975. He is the author of eight books, including the novel Need, Rock Dreams—*a collaboration with artist Guy Peellaert—and* The Heart of the World, *which chronicles a two-year walk up Broadway. His passion in life is "journeys of every kind," and he lives with his wife, children's book author Michaela Muntean, on Shelter Island, New York.*

★

The maître d' fixes you with an intense gaze, and with a sweep of his hand grants permission to leave his exquisite, perfect restaurant. He says only *"Bonsoir, monsieur,"* but his words—so deep, rich (yes, mellifluous)—are a gift, a magnanimous act. You strive to reciprocate, but it comes out too high, absurd: *"Bone-swahr,"* a German dog biscuit which goes skittering across the floor to clatter at the feet of frowning diners. Alas, you are a caveman. You may as well go now to the coat check and ask for your skins and your club and shamble into the night.

—James O'Reilly, "Troglodytes in Gaul"

MARGARET BALKA

Two Moments In France

Everything changes, and nothing.

FORTY-SIX YEARS ON FROM MY FIRST SIGHTING IN FRANCE, I WAS once again on my way in the spring of '93. There was an air of familiarity about our haste through London to catch the train for Folkestone (is anyone ever not in a hurry to catch a train?), and the swiftly passing Kentish countryside was all as I remember.

Once installed, however, in that great little invention, the Hovercraft, bound for Boulogne, I could see that this time, crossing the Channel was going to be roses, roses all the way. The old ferry boat rides, not forgetting the well-used Dover-Calais connection, were often turbulent and disagreeable, as travelers would make a sudden dash for the ship's rail with an offering to Poseidon. I was once slightly rained on in this way, being downwind, and my pretty polka-dot blouse, purchased with precious U.K. clothing coupons, acquired a few more dots which never entirely washed out.

What a luxury, then, after those old three and a half hour journeys, was this smooth 35 minute jaunt in the spring of the year, with the smell of the sea, the waves bravely catching the sun, and the atmosphere of cheerful anticipation among the families with their lovely children. My sister, caught up in the enjoyment of the moment, wondered why on earth a Chunnel was necessary at all, with its daunting cost, its claustrophobic terrors, and the venom it has generated in southern England concerning routings through to London.

The German Occupation was just over and very fresh in people's minds in 1947 as I traveled south by train from Paris to the Landes. Like many of his contemporaries, one young man in his early twenties was still seething with France's humiliation and spoke to me of nothing else for a good part of the journey. He talked chiefly about what his countrymen had done to frustrate the aggressors, and the terrible risks they had run. Once he had started he could not seem to stop, finding, I suppose, some relief in the telling.

I remember, also, a year later in Tours, the aging and kindly M. and Mme Duchesne speaking with the same obsessive intensity about France's suffering. Their chief concern had been to find sufficient to eat and generally survive. They were in no mood to hear anything good about their neighbors to the east.

Oddly enough, my hosts of 1947—vineyard owners in the Landes—did not speak at all of the recent occupation. Did they simply prefer to forget it? Living in the country, they kept a good table, and perhaps their encounter with the invader had been minimal. Despite their comparative comforts, they were very pleased that I had brought them coffee beans, which were in short supply in France at that time.

Now, in the year of grace '93, I am again on French soil, and the world is welcome to come and enjoy France's treasures, spending marks, yen, pounds, and dollars as liberally as possible, *s'il vous plaît* Germans, often in sizable groups, are everywhere, as acceptable as all the others, gazing at the exploits of Harold and his nemesis, William the Conqueror, on the Bayeux Tapestry; treading with reverence the corridors of the Louvre and the wondrous Musée d'Orsay, as humble as the rest of us before the great works of creation.

On one occasion when we went to take an evening ferry ride up the Seine, a large group of German visitors had arrived in good time and were settled in choice seats from which to enjoy the view. Just before the boat set off a little rain fell, and to my surprise, most of them got up to take shelter undercover. Of course, my family moved into vacated seats, the rain ceased, and we had a lovely trip. Our German fellow travelers quickly emerged and in good spirits took what seats were available, reveling as did we all in the glory that is Paris.

The phrase: "Is Paris burning?" kept running through my head. I thought of the brave German general who disobeyed Hitler's order to torch Paris, and how his countrymen in their thousands were now coming to see the treasures he had saved at great risk to himself.

> *itler also took Breker aside and began rhapsodizing on what they had seen the previous morning. "I love Paris—it has been a place of artistic importance since the 19th century—just as you do. And like you, I would have studied here if Fate had not pushed me into politics since my ambitions before the World War were in the field of art."*
>
> —John Toland, *Adolf Hitler*

Asians, especially Japanese, were few and far between in France just after World War II. Now, in the spring of '93, Japanese of all ages blossomed like the lilac trees all over the Loire valley. In Fontainebleau, I vainly attempted to help a young Japanese couple find a lost contact lens. O times, O customs!

Bitterness passes in time, but France remembers her sorrows still through the names of her sons inscribed on the cenotaph in every village. How poignant her choice of words for her lost ones: *Nos Enfants*. This loss of "half the seed of Europe" in war must have contributed to the shortage of help for work on the land, even taking into account the natural exodus of youth to the cities. Our hosts in Maizet, Normandy, worked land that had been in the family for several generations. Life is hard for Gérard, the present owner of the property, who intends to leave farming in a year or two and convert his home to a guest house for travelers. At the beautiful Moulin de Vandon, a Maison d'Hôtes in the Touraine, shortage of help was again a matter of much concern to the hard-pressed owners.

On visits to churches, cathedrals, and attendance at Mass, how familiar that musty odor of damp stone, like the smell of centuries among the soaring columns. Here, too, the same elderly faithful, sparsely disposed among the ample seating. But Vatican II has intervened: the priest faces the congregation; the liturgy is in French; there is, sensibly, one collection instead of two, and while I, like some Rip Van Winkle, automatically intoned the old *"ainsi soit-il"* at the end of the Our Father, everyone else said a pragmatic "Amen."

For getting around the country, the bicycle is still in use, but in my youth it was almost the only inexpensive way, apart from walking. Now, cars are everywhere. I hardly recognized Tours with its bewildering streams of traffic pouring over the bridge. I used to walk over that bridge from St-Symphorien into Tours and do not remember such a frenzy of movement.

Mechanization has of course come a long way, and I suppose the grape pickers at M. de Mauret's estate in the Landes have been mostly supplanted by machines. The vineyard was a great place to flirt: a young man would call attention to himself by throwing grapes at the girl of his choice, and her response would tell him all he needed to know.

Since cars were out of our range in '48, we got around the Loire valley on old, rented bicycles, but were so tired when we arrived anywhere that we would slump behind a glass of *"vin du pays,"* and thereafter dutifully "do" the local château. I remember precious little, being semi-somnolent by that time, though François I's salamander seemed to impinge on my consciousness with much frequency.

Beds do not seem to have changed much. That unique feature of the French bed, the head-wall drapery with a rosette in the middle, gives a sort of silent fanfare to the act of lying down to sleep. In one 17th century farmhouse, my sister and I slept in a large bed with a right royal dust-laden swathe of drapery above our heads. Our laughter put us in high good humor and we slept like babies, with nary a sneeze.

Eating, as distinct from gourmandizing, remains a hedonistic activity. Parisians, especially, dine out with Proustian zeal, as the packed restaurants and frantically busy waiters would attest. Even as France was picking up the pieces in the late 40s, the pleasures of the table did a lot to restore the national spirit. It was in a Paris restaurant that I, a Yorkshire lass, learned of the existence of *Le jambon de Yorkshire*—Yorkshire ham. Until then I had not heard of such a delicacy.

It cannot have been easy for Mme Galimant, my landlady in Tours, to turn out a good dinner every evening for eight students in those austere times, but she managed with a flair. After soup, with lots of bread, there were mushrooms in all sorts of guises, served in scallop shells, and a little cheese to assuage our hunger. Dear Mme Galimant. Such cheerfulness, such a ready smile, such deep shadows under her eyes.

My Tours friend, Mme Duchesne, for all her spleen (for some reason the French love this word) over the Occupation, would turn with pleasure to the subject of good food, traditional recipes, and all the time-honored

ean-Paul said it was too bad everyone didn't work at Nathalie's speed, because then the trailer would still have room. Nathalie made a face and a sharp remark, and he threw a grape at her. She shot one back, and Claude joined the battle.

The older women edged a little into the vines. I sat next to Sebastián, who pitched a few grapes into the melee....

Nathalie's color was high; her mood mingled playfulness and anger. The men kept laughing, but their eyes were heated. They moved to close quarters and began crushing bunches of grapes against her skin and clothes. She wriggled and swore. She clipped Claude on the temple. It looked accidental, but drove him from the field....

Nathalie seemed to lose force, her movements became languid. Jean-Paul gripped her from behind. As he squeezed the grapes into her cotton t-shirt, it clung to her breasts, clearly defined and free, her nipples erect. There were grapes in her hair, stuck to her arms, juice glistened on her neck. Suddenly he let go, and she slipped to the ground, leaned against his legs. She stayed there a moment, then they separated, without a word.

—Thomas Matthews,
A Village in the Vineyards

comforts of the kitchen. I still see her, explaining with precise gestures just how to stir a sauce for some special dish, and in the event,
restoring peace to her soul.

If there is one symbol of continuity that stands proudly among
the icons of France it is the baguette: that slender yet substantial
bâton of bread, warm from the morning oven, its chewy interior
mantled in a delectable crust, begging to be eaten, pulled off com-
pulsively chunk after chunk. Does it, I wonder frivolously, bring
more people back to France than the Mona Lisa?

Though the women these days, like their North American
counterparts, seem to spend less time in the kitchen, a meal *"en
famille,"* as I recently experienced in Normandy, is still an extended, respected activity, with conversation, bonhomie and the
conviviality of wine or home-made cider hospitably pressed upon
the visitor. Nobody had to rush off to be somewhere else.

Talking of taking one's leave: I should have remembered that
unchanged ritual of retiring to bed. One evening, among friends,
I felt very tired and simply announced that I was going to bed.
"Goodnight everyone." The uncomplicated manner of my departure without the customary handshake with the men, and the one,
two, three pecks on the cheek for the women, was a subject for
later comment, though, happily, I hurt no feelings.

Coming from North America with its full-blown vendetta on
smoking, I was somewhat surprised to see so many French, young
and old, still lighting up, as in old Humphrey Bogart movies. The
habit does not seem to bear the same social stigma presently attached to it across the Atlantic. In Amboise, a group of seventeen-
to eighteen-year-old students, having done their educational tour
of Da Vinci's Villa, sat around outside, smoking with a natural ease
containing nothing of guilt or defiance. Our friend, Gérard, cigarette in hand, cheerfully acknowledged that it was not good for the
health. I recalled the old French pre-occupation with the kidneys,
and the often heard phrase: *"Bon/pas bon pour les reins"* (Good/not
good for the kidneys), and wondered bemusedly, if the heart and
lungs were still getting short shrift in vital organ priorities.

It is not always pleasing to note changes wrought by time in a country one loves, but I must say, on the subject of that humble place, the toilet, change has been markedly for the better. Time was, I would summon the resolve to "pay a visit" and come back telling myself stoically: "It's not too bad" or "I'll get used to it." Once, in my hour of need, I was directed to a gloomy corner in which there was set a large flagstone with a hole in the middle. I still think of it in my darker moments. Was that flagstone safe? Could anything pop up as well as down that horrid hole? In Paris, the unsightly *vespasiennes*—rank, corrugated-metal conveniences for male relief, concealing only the midportion of the user—seem, finally, to be gone from the streets. Wherever we went on this recent visit, the toilets were clean and reasonably agreeable places to use: a big plus, I should say, for North Americans.

The French love children and have always looked indulgently on happy displays of spontaneity. As we were crossing the Pont d'Iéna little Mary said: "Let's sing Oats and Beans and Barley O." So grandmother (my sister) and I, with Anna, Noelle and Mary, went happily over the bridge, holding hands and singing our song, while various pedestrians and a couple of roller skaters looked on with a smile. It seemed the most natural thing in the world, that evening in Paris, to go singing across the bridge.

Resourcefulness is also an enduring part of their character. When I first saw the French in their own country they had come through a harrowing time, often surviving by their wits. Nowadays, for many young people, economic survival calls for similar inventiveness. One sunny afternoon on the Place de la Concorde just outside the Tuileries, a young man appeared, dressed in full 17th century court costume. With a harpsichord playing baroque on his cassette, he stood on a low wall, and with considerable miming skill made obeisances and courtly gestures à la Louis XIV. Of course, a little receptacle discreetly placed invited the public's generosity.

It is almost a measure of my own moment in time to have known France in two different phases of her history; just recovering from war, and now coping with the demands of the rapidly dwindling century. Whatever it is that endures to make a country instantly recognizable, like a loved old friend, there, blessedly, it was again, in France, in the spring of '93.

Margaret Balka grew up across from the mill in Bradford, England, went to Oxford (where she got a masters in Medieval French), emigrated to Canada with her Polish husband, where they raised eight children. She lives in Thunder Bay, Ontario.

★

An image from Paris burned into my retinas: one of my daughters wanted to give her monthly allowance (100 francs) to a palsied old man who was begging. I didn't have the right bill, but said ok, I had a fifty franc bill. Noelle went back and gave him the bill and his startled happiness lit up the entire block. As he took the bill, he held her hand and kissed it as though she were a princess. Did the same to her sister Anna who was right behind with more money. Passersby looking on, smiling, smiling.

—James O'Reilly, "On and Off the *Autoroute*"

PART FOUR

IN THE SHADOWS

RONALD KOVEN

The Duty to Remember, the Need to Forget

French history has always been a battle of memories,
and the struggle continues today.

THE FRENCH ARE VERY QUICK TO ACCUSE ONE ANOTHER OF HAV-
ing a special aptitude for forgetting embarrassing episodes in their
history, of having short memories. The real problem, however, is
not forgetfulness. It is that different elements of the French nation
simply can't agree on which parts of French history should be
stressed. Yet these adversaries all seem to agree that there should be
only a single, certified National Memory—their own, of course.
This struggle over which memories should make up the French
psyche reflects a hard-to-accept historical reality: throughout
much of its past, France, more than most other countries, has been
engaged in actual or cold civil wars punctuated by more or less
long periods of national reconciliation that have required a need
to forget.

At least that is what a succession of recent French leaders, including four very different presidents of the Fifth Republic
(Charles de Gaulle, Georges Pompidou, Valéry Giscard d'Estaing
and François Mitterrand), have maintained, explicitly or implicitly.
Their appeals to national unity, implying the sacrifice of certain
grievances, have inevitably met with protests from groups who
have felt that they were being asked to give up pieces of their col-

lective memory. Hence a host of "Lest we forget"-style appeals to remembrance from Royalists, Gaullists, Communists, Catholics, Protestants, Jews, Algerians, and so on.

Yet to observe these calls to remembrance essentially involves dwelling on painful recollections, not pleasant nostalgia. Even exercises in nostalgia seem to turn rapidly into references to collective trauma. A month-long series of daily radio programs broadcast in Paris the summer of 1994, "Songs of the Liberation," featured a detailed commentary on how all the expressions of joy or evocations of faraway places were nothing more than attempts to forget the horrors of the German occupation. The title of the memoirs of the late Simone Signoret, movie star and godmother of a generation of human-rights activists, sums it up nicely: *Nostalgia Is Not What It Used to Be.*

> *It seems a strange idea, though perhaps an appropriate one, to have a rooster—that vain, strutting, loudmouthed, ridiculous creature—as a national symbol. Napoléon's eagle was certainly a more dignified idea, though he got his feathers plucked just as surely as the neighborhood barnyard rooster. The Latin word* gallus *provides the symbol, "gallus" being at the same time "the Gaul" and "the rooster." No fools those Romans, they had already remarked upon the Gauls' loquacity as well as their querulous, aggressive nature. Tacitus reckoned that if the Gauls had stopped quarreling among themselves they would have been nearly invincible.*
>
> —Geneviève Edis, *Merde Encore!*

When memory is that painful, it is hardly surprising that people would sometimes simply prefer to forget. Another title, *Forgetting Our Crimes: National Amnesia, a French Specialty?,* expresses the widespread perception that the French have not yet come to grips with certain aspects of their history. The book may be new, but the theme certainly isn't. For years, many foreigners, including a number of Americans, have gleefully joined French commentators in accusing the French of being unable to accept their past. The most recent debates concern the Vichy government's collaboration with Nazi Germany and the French Army's commission of atrocities during the Algerian war.

Paradoxically, these debates come amid a series of high-profile commemorations ostensibly designed to celebrate national unity: the Bicentennial of the French Revolution, the Millennium of the French monarchy, the Centennial of the birth of Charles de Gaulle and the 50th anniversaries of D-Day and the Liberation of Paris. This recent spate of commemorations has been accompanied by a cult of national heritage, known as *le Patrimoine,* in which even the Nazi bunkers of the Atlantic Wall have been classified as historic monuments. France now has some 40,000 officially listed historic monuments, with some 900 new sites added each year.

This new sensitivity has produced a new concept—"places of memory"—which has been embodied in a seven-volume historical work of the same name. Conceived by historiographer Pierre Nora, this collection of essays is a solemn monument in its own right. For Nora, places of memory are not only the obvious sites and monuments—village war memorials, the prehistoric cave paintings of Lascaux, the Eiffel Tower, or the Panthéon, the republican mausoleum serving as a pendant of Saint Denis Cathedral, the resting place of French kings. Places of memory are also defined as the famous moments in French history expressed in textbooks, proverbs, folktales, and songs—including the national anthem, "La Marseillaise." Nora's definition even embraces the classic Tour de France bicycle race, the French language itself, and culture-defining literature—above all, Marcel Proust's exploration of memory, *The Remembrance of Things Past.*

Nora notes that every French person is aware of the evocative powers that Proust attributes to the madeleine, regardless of whether or not they have personally tasted the cake or, for that matter, read the book. "It's like the metric standard—it is enough to know that it exists; people don't need to actually go see it." As a symbol of memory, Proust's novel has achieved totemic as well as literary value.

Nora concludes that memory is a synonym for national identity. He is concerned not with the spontaneous, natural memory of the individual, but with the memory inculcated in each generation and cultivated for later generations through an institutionalized approach to folk memory.

*A*ristocrats and bourgeois women, royalists and republicans, even the few peasant and working-class women who dictated accounts of their experiences, all were bound together by a common nightmare. Whatever their political loyalties—and indeed there were a few unrepentant republicans like Charlotte Robespierre, Élisabeth Le Bas, and Mme Cavaignac in addition to the more numerous antirevolutionaries—a tragic note prevails. The experience of having survived when so many others had to perish often produced what we in the 20th century, in the aftermath of the Holocaust and Vietnam, have labeled "survivor guilt." Their testimonials spring from an inner urgency to bear witness for those who had been silenced, and they derive their haunting grandeur from the pervasive mark of death.

—Marilyn Yalom, *Blood Sisters: The French Revolution in Women's Memory*

French self-flagellation over its modern history concerns episodes that proceed in a straight line from the beheading of King Louis XVI during the French Revolution to the present. Not that there aren't plenty of pre-revolutionary events that remain unresolved in the French psyche, for example, medieval carnages such as the destruction of Provençal culture by the northern powers during the 13th century Crusades against the Albigensian and Cathar heretics or the Saint Bartholomew's Day Massacre of Protestants, in 1572. In the 1930s, French political scientist André Siegfried demonstrated that the southern tradition of voting for the far left was traceable to the perhaps subconscious desire of Provençal people to defy a northern authority that had never made amends for the horrors perpetrated against their real or imagined ancestors.

Henry Rousso, author of the *Vichy Syndrome,* notes that the study of "the history of memory" in France stresses "profound crises of French unity and identity...those crises feed upon one another, with the memory of each preceding crisis playing a role in the next: the French Revolution in the Dreyfus Affair, Dreyfus in Vichy, Vichy in the Algerian war, and so on."

Indeed, it may be argued, French memories are not too short but too long. I recall meeting a descendant of Georges Clemenceau, the leading World War I ally of England, France's former hereditary enemy, against Germany, its more recent hereditary enemy. Speaking in the 1960s, he said he could forgive the English for a list of relatively recent affronts, including Mers el Kebir (where the British Royal Navy destroyed a French fleet in 1940 lest it fall into German hands). "But for what they did to Joan of Arc—never!" In response to my laughter, the younger Clemenceau replied, "What's so funny? I'm very serious."

However old the historical grudges the French bear against one another or others, crimes committed with the tacit or overt blessings of the French state since the Revolution of 1789 have a special meaning. Since that date, France has considered itself a country with a universal message, contained in the Declaration of the Rights of Man and of the Citizen and summed up by the French republican slogan *Liberté, Égalité, Fraternité.* The Declaration proclaimed the State of Law, equal for all, and abolished the legitimate exercise of arbitrary power. It notably inspired the European constitutional movement and Latin American independence struggles. Since then, any actions by France that have contradicted that message—massacres, deportations, summary justice, invocations of "reasons of state" to justify illegal actions—have appeared as so many denials of that universality.

From the start, of course, many French rejected the message as a transgression of the eternal verities taught by the Church and the Monarchy. For

> *France is gifted not so much for battle as for civil war. Apart from 1914, she has had no experience of a long and truly patriotic war. Every one of the conflicts waged by the nation that takes greatest pride in its military renown, have contained elements of civil war. This is obvious of 1939-45, but is no less true of the Revolutionary and Napoleonic wars, of the age of Joan of Arc and the Burgundians, of Henri IV, the Ligue or Richelieu. Even in 1870, there was a party which secretly or openly desired the defeat of the country's leaders.*
>
> —Mark Ferro, historian, quoted by Fernand Braudel, *The Identity of France,* translated by Siân Reynolds

them, the French Republic was born in the original sin of the execution of Louis XVI. The guillotining of the deposed royal couple was a national trauma that still has not fully healed. Contemporary republicans discuss it defensively, and historical debate continues to rage over whether Louis and Marie Antoinette deserved to die. The debate has even been turned into a large-scale parlor game by actor-director Robert Hossein, who stages reenactments of Marie Antoinette's trial. The audience votes electronically from their seats; invariably, the verdict is overwhelmingly against putting the queen to death.

Ever since the decapitation of Louis and his consort, France has appeared to be a country living largely on the brink of civil war. Yet it was almost always recognized that beyond the internal passions of the moment, beyond the consecrated monarchy and the secular republic, the French nation was an underlying entity worthy of general defense against aggression.

So France reinvented the Athenian republican notion of amnesty—the effacement of political crimes. For the sake of national consensus, the crimes and their punishments were deemed no longer to exist. The word amnesty is rooted in the Greek word amnesia—loss of memory.

As Stéphane Gacon, a young historian of amnesty, notes, "All the Franco-French wars have had their amnesties: the Commune's in 1879-80, Boulangisme's in 1895, the Dreyfus Affair's in 1900, the collaboration's [partially] in 1951-53, the Algerian war's from 1962-68." It is a system for recreating national unity.

The French press law of 1881, still in force, makes it illegal to publish, or discuss in public, any punishments, including those that have been amnestied. That the published facts are true is no defense in cases involving amnestied crimes, or for that matter, any legal punishments that are more than ten years old.

Each successive amnesty has different rules and case law to interpret it. But precedent is much weaker in the French legal system than in Anglo-American practice, and the general framework is still the 1881 law banning public discussion of amnestied crimes. That law has a chilling effect on editors, making them very cautious about printing historic facts that could involve them in costly, prolonged lawsuits, even if they are likely to win.

Although amnesty may have obvious advantages for society as a whole, it complicates dealing with national memory. At the very least, it makes it difficult to discuss recent history whose actors are still alive. There are prominent Frenchmen active today who are generally known to have been torturers in Algeria, but it is at least technically illegal to recall publicly that they have been accused of atrocities. And transgressors have regularly lost defamation suits in the courts.

Moreover, the ban does not end with the death of the amnestied person; the family may sue for harm to "the honor or the reputation of the living heirs or spouses." In practice, nobody gets sued for discussing major historical figures such as Pétain, Pierre Laval, or Joseph Darnand, the chief of Vichy's anti-Resistance force, the paramilitary Militia. But recalling the past or the postwar punishment of a simple Militiaman could lead to a lawsuit.

The loss is not merely to history. A sociology professor recounts how one of her graduate students was emotionally traumatized upon learning that his family had moved from one village to another to hide his grandfather's service in the Vichy Militia. "The family was living a lie," she said, "and my student was completely overwhelmed when he finally realized it."

French colonial rule in Algeria lasted 132 years, ending in 1961. But the French-Algerian connection is anything but over, and it remains a troubled one for both sides. The French struggle with immigration and terrorism issues, the Algerians with bitter independence war memories and civil unrest aimed at a ruling elite which has remained Francophile over the years.

—JO'R, LH, and SO'R

This makes it all too easy to perpetuate the myth that the French can't and don't deal with crimes committed in the name of France. There are countless articles that say, for example, that the French have never faced up to the reality that wartime collaboration was widespread. But thousands of suspected collaborators were publicly disgraced or executed by the Resistance at the Liberation, often without even the benefit of a kangaroo court. Such justice was often summary enough to be suspect. De Gaulle appealed to his compatriots: "Frenchmen, don't take it upon yourselves to administer justice."

Vichy Premier Pierre Laval was tried, sentenced, and executed by a firing squad, as was the writer/propagandist Robert Brasillach. The talented but openly anti-Semitic writer Céline escaped to permanent exile in Denmark. Pétain was condemned to death and the sentence commuted to internment on a small island off the Atlantic coast. Many collaborators were sentenced to periods of "national indignity" during which they were denied the right to vote or other civic rights.

Yet somehow the myth still persists that France did not deal with its collaborators. This is partly the work of De Gaulle himself. He had to erase the humiliation of France's defeat in 1940 and lead a vanquished but liberated nation to its seat among the victors. And he had to administer a country in need of reconstruction. Merely having worked under Vichy as a civil servant, plant manager, policeman, or judge was not reason enough to be purged. Some administrators with dirty hands inevitably slipped through the nets.

During the Cold War, there was a conscious effort to rally all non-Communists in France and elsewhere in the West against the Soviet threat. The political will to prosecute wartime collaborators dwindled. This fit in with De Gaulle's conscious attempt to wipe out the shame of the French defeat in 1940. De Gaulle's hostility toward U.S. President Franklin D. Roosevelt was in large part based on Roosevelt's refusal to accept Gaullist mythmaking.

In competition with the Gaullists, the French Communists pressed their own version of the Resistance, calling theirs "the party of the 75,000 firing squad victims," when, in fact, "only" 35,000 Resistance members were executed, a large proportion of whom were not Communists.

No one can really say how many French citizens were collaborators and how many were in the Resistance. It is partly a problem of definition, degree, and timing. Many early collaborators later joined the Resistance. Motives were mixed. Clearly, throughout much of the Occupation, it was Vichy—and not De Gaulle and the Resistance—that was considered the true representative of France. Many of the world's major powers, including the United States, maintained diplomatic relations with Vichy for as long as they could.

Far more numerous even than the *collabos* or the *résistants* were the fence-sitters, those whose main objective was survival or, perhaps, not to compromise the safe return to France of relatives held in German prisoner-of-war camps (two million of them), or of the young men drafted into forced labor in Germany (600,000). Given this record, it is not really surprising that so many people went along with De Gaulle's implied urging to forget an inglorious era.

That said, it would be wrong to dismiss the Resistance as having made no meaningful contribution. Allied Supreme Commander Dwight D. Eisenhower, who commanded 85 Allied divisions in the Battle of Normandy, said that the Resistance was worth another fifteen divisions to him.

It also, of course, had the value that De Gaulle was so adept at exploiting—the creation of a record, of a socially and politically useful memory. It was just this kind of thing that General Henning Von Tresckow, one of the participants in the almost successful July 20, 1944, assassination plot against Hitler, had in mind when he said before the attempt: "It is no longer a matter of its practicality but a matter of demonstrating to the world and before history that the Resistance movement dared the decisive gamble. Beside that, everything else is a matter of indifference."

French documentary-filmmaker Marcel Ophuls, whose 1971 movie *The Sorrow and the Pity* set off the French public's reassessment of the French wartime record, says, "It is the same problem in France as in Germany, in different proportions to be sure. The French had to invent a victorious history. It was nonsense, but it was understandable. History was easier to deal with in Germany because they were the vanquished. They did rewrite their history books to acknowledge their guilt and so forth. But this problem remains at the center of French preoccupations, whether they admit it or not."

Ophuls, the French son of a prominent German Jewish moviemaker who took refuge in France, has devoted much of his career to the problem of memory. His latest film, *The Troubles We've Seen,* is about the role of memory in Sarajevo. And in 1976, he made *The Memory of Justice,* which opens with the Nuremburg trial of Nazi war criminals and wraps in such Allied crimes as the devastating firebombing of the German city of Dresden, an act that had no military justification and continues through France's war in Algeria and the U.S. war in Vietnam.

Ophuls interviewed, among others, Albert Speer, Hitler's chief architect and a Nuremburg defendant released after a prison term, and former French Premier Edgar Faure, an Allied prosecutor at Nuremburg. Speer dealt with questions about atrocities by escaping into disembodied abstract verbiage. Faure, however, spoke of the Nazi crimes in clear, direct, down-to-earth terms. Then Ophuls asked Faure about French actions in Algeria (admittedly a very different kind of war). The Frenchman's flight into abstrac-

> *In all he reigned his second time for eleven years, not very long compared to the Sun King, Louis XIV, who sat on the throne for 67 years, or to his dissolute great-grandson, Louis XV, 59 years. Even Napoleon in one guise or another lasted longer, about fifteen years. But none of these men could have seemed more regal than Charles de Gaulle, even though they wore crowns and ermine and he did not. Command was in his bearing, in his eyes. He was, or at least became, a more austere, more unapproachable figure than any king. Note his press conferences, for instance. They represented at once an approach to the people and a godlike performance from on high....*
> *When he took his seat at the table in front of the television lights he sometimes wore his brigadier general's uniform; at other times he wore a business suit. He would recognize each questioner in turn, listen attentively to questions that were sometimes long and intricate but never frivolous. At the end of each question he would nod and say: "Bon."...*
>
> *Finally he would begin a speech that answered them all one by one, and if an impromptu question had somehow got included he would answer that too.*
>
> —Robert Daley, *Portraits of France*

tion was suddenly and hauntingly similar to the German's.

In France, a country with a major film industry, cinema is a key vector of national memory. Most French film producers, however, are loath to deal with historical controversy, an attitude that contrasts with Hollywood's willingness to tackle such subjects as the Vietnam War without waiting for the wounds to heal. Ophuls attributes this reluctance to commercial-minded "cowardice" and dependency on co-financing by TV decision-makers who are even more prone to prudence. "It's self-censorship," he says. "Collectively speaking, French producers have been that way since the silent pictures. Look at the Germans; they've made lots of movies about the Nazi era. But what kind of country is this that hasn't made a real movie about the Dreyfus Affair, the most fantastic courtroom drama that you could imagine? My father tried to do things like that. But there was never any question of anyone allowing it, and there's still no question of it."

Despite their apparent reluctance to be entertained by their own defeats, the French do, paradoxically, like to think of themselves as victims or martyrs. Most of the great legendary heroes of French history have died tragically: Vercingétorix defeated by Caesar; Roland betrayed by his companion-in-arms while commanding Charlemagne's rear guard; Joan of Arc burned at the stake after being abandoned by the weak king she had enthroned; Napoleon exiled as a prisoner of the English enemy. This is psychological preparation not for self-examination but for *La Revanche* (as in Gambetta's dictum after Bismarck seized Alsace-

> *The Dreyfus Affair was a flashpoint in the struggle between the right and left, the military and intellectuals. Captain Alfred Dreyfus was falsely accused and convicted of passing secrets to the German military attaché in Paris in 1894. The case became a* cause célèbre *in 1898 with the publication of novelist Emile Zola's letter "J'Accuse!" and exposed deep veins of anti-Semitism and paranoia. Dreyfus was ultimately exonerated, but the case created a profound political crisis which discredited the army and helped the French develop a secular state.*
>
> —JO'R, LH, and SO'R

412 *Travelers' Tales ⋆ France*

Lorraine from France during the Franco-Prussian war: "Think of it always, speak of it never."). It is also preparation for the deep-rooted sense that the essence of history is tragedy. Pétain's sense that the defeat of 1940 was a useful lesson in combating moral rot and encouraging national regeneration placed him firmly in the French tradition of heroic victims. Even his role as the victor of Verdun in World War I seems tragic because of the million men who died in history's bloodiest battle. De Gaulle's insistence that the French were victorious heroes thus appears to break with the image of the French as virtuous losers.

Perhaps it is because the French see themselves as victims in World War II that it is so difficult for them to admit that it was the French police, not the Germans, who rounded up 76,000 Jews in France for deportation; that Pierre Laval went beyond Nazi demands by insisting that these Jews should be deported eastward, "without forgetting the children," and that it was not even Vichy but the democratic French Third Republic that created the first French internment camps for Spanish Republican refugees and later for German, Austrian, and Italian antifascist refugees (including Jews) viewed as potential Fifth Columnists. Vichy only "inherited" such camps, noted a collaborationist trial defendant.

Yet those who try to paint the French as somehow sharing in Nazi guilt are obviously wide of the mark. There were 300,000 Jews in France before the war, and the 225,000 who survived did not do so by accident. Many non-Jews, including some of the police involved in the roundups, took risks to help them. The Jews in Germany and Nazi-occupied Eastern Europe were virtually wiped out, and they still don't find those countries congenial places to live. Today's French Jewish community is more than twice as large as it was before the war.

France's colonial past is another chapter of French history that is still being digested. Endless ridicule has been heaped upon the classic French history manual used to teach black Africans about "our ancestors, the Gauls." There was nothing ridiculous about the intent: to assimilate the colonized elites as Frenchmen. France claimed to be bringing them culture and civilization. The colonized people's previous history could not be destroyed, but their memories could be erased and replaced with French history. It was an attempt to rewrite not History but Memory, a real-life example of George Orwell's fictional description of how communist regimes shoved inconvenient history "down the memory hole."

Talking of wartime France, there is an interesting explanation of why Jean-Paul Sartre became famous. His masterwork L'Etre et le Néant [Being and Nothingness] was published during the German Occupation. At this time the Germans had seized all the brass weights for melting down to make munitions. The book in question weighed exactly a kilo, and quickly became a bestseller. He never looked back.

—Bill and Laurel Cooper, A Spell in Wild France

In mainland France, this same policy of assimilation created a tense ambivalence between the centralizing French culture and the cultural identities of the Alsatians, Algerians, Armenians, Basques, Bretons, Catalans, Corsicans, Flemish, Jews, Poles, Protestants, Provençals, and others who make up the French people. Assimilation meant a community had to give up its collective memory. Discrimination meant that the message of the Rights of Man was flawed.

France's attempt to turn immigrants and colonized peoples into Frenchmen made credible its insistence that the French were not racists—a policy that French spokesmen contrasted with that of Britain, which never tried to turn Indians into Englishmen. Now, of course, Britain returns the compliment by saying that it was more respectful of cultural identity.

Both approaches, however, beg the question of dealing with memories of colonial atrocities. The French public was far too focused on celebrating the German surrender on May 8, 1945, to notice that the French Army was that same day massacring 30,000 Algerian nationalists in Sétif to reassert French authority. Stirrings of conscience over similar massacres in Madagascar in 1947, over the thousands who died in forced labor building the Congo railway, and so on have still not been fully assimilated by official French memory.

The same fundamental debate about how much memory is good for a society is only just beginning in Eastern Europe (not to mention Argentina or Chile), with all the same competing principles—purge vs. pardon, social catharsis vs. consensus, justice vs. amnesty—in sum, remembering vs. forgetting. If the French experience is any indication, those questions will take a long time to sort out, and only much more history will settle them.

Perhaps the easing of the pains of memory really started in France back in 1959 with the birth of *Astérix,* the comic-book series that has sold hundreds of thousands of copies by mocking such official historical myths as "our ancestors, the Gauls." The French could finally make fun of themselves; laughter proved to be at least one useful complement to the "Duty to Remember."

Ronald Koven was born in Paris of a French father and American mother and educated in the United States. In the 1960s he was the "De Gaulle-watcher" of the International Herald Tribune *in Paris. He became the foreign editor of* The Washington Post, *and in 1977 returned to Paris as the* Post's *correspondent for Latin Europe and the Maghreb. He was the Paris correspondent of* The Boston Globe *from 1981-1994 and has been the European representative of the World Press Freedom Committee since 1981.*

★

In the final analysis, France, more perhaps even than my own country, is an idea toward which a great collective effort has tried to shape reality. The ineluctable element of size and the force of global homogenization are against it. So, too, are the forces of history. And yet both the French and the rest of the world believe now and will continue to believe in a certain imaginary country, a France of the mind, an ideal both to remember and to strive for.

"Our country," Michel Charzat, a Socialist parliamentarian, has written, "has been, all during its past, a history of illusion. Each generation has forged a certain image of France.... Few nations owe as much as ours does to the imagination and to the violence of its people." There are discrepancies between what is imagined about France and what actually exists, between the country's goals and reality, between esteem and unblinkered judgment. There is something at times pathetic and laughable, or perhaps it is only sorrowful, in seeing a country that no longer enjoys great power attempt to portray itself as a colossus. There is a sense in which the French live on a kind of past capital, nibbling unconsciously away at the foundations of their very imaginings.

—Richard Bernstein, *Fragile Glory: A Portrait of France and the French*

MOSHE SAPERSTEIN

⋆ * ⋆

Service Non Compris

Sometimes Parisian waiters live down
to the stereotype.

A DOCUMENTARY FILM, "CITY OF DOGS," CLAIMED THERE ARE NINE
million dogs in France, more dogs than there are children between
the ages of one and ten. Under normal circumstances this would
be of no interest to me whatever. On a scale of things that please
me least, the French rank just above spiders, and any phenomenon
that indicates the number of Frenchmen in the world is declining
is a cause for cheers.

As to the problem of how to deal with puppy proliferation, a
people that consider snails a delicacy will doubtless learn to love
nouvelle cuisine pooch-oir if given the opportunity. And I suspect
that after the long history of French control of Indo-China, where
Lassie would be the main course at a family banquet rather than
the guest of honor, there are many Frenchmen who would not be
averse to nibbling on dog biscuits.

No, what fascinated me was the French capacity to combine in-
cisive analysis with hypocritical self-deception. Thus many of
those interviewed stated that la belle France was being buried in a
tidal wave of doggy-doo, while others related with a straight face
that though their pets had mauled them, often savagely and repeatedly, they loved the beasts anyway.

416

While taking a walk on our first evening in Paris, and finding ourselves before a tobacconist, my wife suggested I try a local brand. We entered the shop, I held my pipe aloft and asked for tobacco. The rotund soul behind the counter stared at me with what I can only describe as stupid malevolence. Holding up my pipe, I repeated "Tobacco please, for my pipe." He replied in French, I repeated myself in English, my wife laughed in Esperanto.

He then handed me a small packet, unlike any tobacco pouch I had ever seen. "Is this tobacco?" I asked. *"Oui, monsieur,"* he answered. Out on the street, my wife urged me to try it. "French tobacco," she said hopefully, "might not stink as bad as what you usually smoke."

With some misgivings I opened the packet, filled my pipe with what did look like tobacco, and applied a match.... A spike of flame shot out of the pipe's bole, singeing my eyelids, and startling my wife. And pungent fumes seared my throat. My lips were numbed, my teeth rattled, I gasped for breath. The pipe dropped to the sidewalk and shattered.

It took a few moments to regain my composure, and I still shook. But now I shook with anger instead of fear. We returned to the shop. The proprietor was collapsed against the counter, convulsed with laughter.

"Poor monsieur did not know that snuff is to be pinched in the nose, like so?" He demonstrated.

"Snuff? SNUFF? I held up my pipe. I asked for pipe tobacco."

"Ah, monsieur wanted tobacco *aromatique*.... Why did monsieur not say so? How am I to understand the strange requests of *les Américains?*" Staggering down the street, my throat feeling like the Roto-Rooter man had been at it, I let my wife lead me to a café. A picturesque, sidewalk café. The café was deserted but for a waiter. We sat at a table. The waiter glanced at us, then walked inside to chat with the barman. Five minutes passed. We would have drawn more attention had we been specks of dust.

"You sit here and relax," my wife said. "I'll go inside and get us some Cokes."

"No you won't," I gasped, still unable to speak normally. "You're too pretty. I don't want you alone with those two." And so saying, I entered the café. The waiter and the barman continued their discussion as if I weren't there. I tried to dramatically clear my throat. Nothing came out but a squeak.

"Could we have some Coca-Cola please?" I finally managed.

Without even looking at me, the waiter said, "If the gentleman will return to his table, he will be served in due course."

Waiters generally intimidate me. This French waiter terrified me. So I returned to my sidewalk seat. Another ten minutes went by and, indignation overpowering good sense, I again entered the bar. The waiter was not in sight. The barman was reading a newspaper as I approached. Before I could say a word, he started to grow shorter. Shorter? No doubt about it. Or I was growing taller.

"Jump!" my wife shouted. Accustomed as I am to incomprehensible orders from my spouse, I did as commanded. And probably saved myself from serious injury. The reason I had seemed to be growing taller was that I had been standing on an elevator rising from the bowels of the café. Now sprawled on the floor, I watched the elevator continue to rise until the waiter stepped out. "If monsieur will return to his seat, I shall serve him presently."

Showing his disdain for us by waiting another ten minutes, the waiter finally made an appearance at our table. My wife asked for the Coca-Colas, the waiter sneered, then returned with our drinks. They were warm, and fizzless. He then presented us with a bill, verbalizing the letters in heavy black type, *"Service non compris."*

"Good," said my wife, "because we have received no service." I then placed the exact amount atop the bill, and we rose to depart.

"Service non compris," he shouted. "You must leave something for the waiter."

At which my wife took a tissue from her handbag, daintily blew her nose in it, and left the sodden mess on the table. *"Pour vous, mon-sewer,"* I said, and we walked away as quickly as dignity would allow, to the sound of juicily expressive French curses rendered in very bad English.

Life is made up of large defeats and small victories. It is these victories that make the defeats bearable. Especially if they are won at the expense of the French.

Moshe Saperstein wrote this story for The Jerusalem Post.

✳

First of all, let's dispense with this absurd stereotypical notion that the French are rude. The French are *not* rude. They just happen to hate *you*. But that is no reason to bypass this beautiful country, whose master chefs have a well-deserved worldwide reputation for trying to trick people into eating snails. Nobody is sure how this got started. Probably a couple of French master chefs were standing around one day, and they found a snail, and one of them said: "I bet that if we called this something like *'escargot,'* tourists would eat it." They had a hearty laugh, because *"escargot"* is the French word for "fat crawling bag of phlegm."

This spirit of daring culinary innovation persists in France, which has also pioneered such advances as:

– The entrée that costs as much as a set of radial tires and consists of a very large plate that appears at first to be totally empty except for a tiny speck of dirt that turns out, upon closer inspection, to be the entree. (A top French chef can carry an entire year's supply of entrees in his wallet.)

– The waiter who makes it extremely clear that he did not get into the waiter business to waste his valuable time actually *waiting on* people, especially not lowlife scum such as yourself who clearly would not know the difference between fine French cuisine and Cheez Whiz.

– The tip that is automatically included For Your Convenience even if your food arrives festooned with armpit hairs (*les haires du pitte*).

—Dave Barry, *Dave Barry's Only Travel Guide You'll Ever Need*

LAWRENCE OSBORNE

White Night by St–Denis

Civilization and history are peeled like an onion
in a stroll down one Parisian street.

GUIDES TO THE CITY ARE ALWAYS OBLIGED TO MAKE SOME MENtion of the rue St-Denis. The conscientious tourist is advised to steer well clear of the City's most humid red-light district, or if he must pass through there, to wear an appropriate expression of disgust, embarrassment, or sneering superiority riveted dutifully to his face. In this way he will be equipped with the right mask behind which to hide. But on no account must he express curiosity, a quickening of the cardiac tempo, naked fear, or blind lust. On no account must he feel that he is in the City's heart, an organ which is complex, palpitating with incessant activity and filled with assorted ventricles, tubes, valves, and chambers. Behind those leprous medieval façades and bulging timber frames rotting slowly through the centuries he must imagine masochistic circuses and sad little dramas of incontinence and relief such as are appropriate to the subdued and fraudulent sexualities of bald septuagenarians in crinkled raincoats and hordes of industrial managers from the Ruhr in white shoes and rhinoceros-skin belts.

Oh, how superior you feel here, how permeated with luminous and omniscient perceptions, how above it all you are, how astrally inclined, how desexualized, how contemptuous, and politically subversive! What a little Engels you suddenly become, confronted with all this social and sexual misery! Not for you these pathetic displays of prostitution; not for you all this crass genital tourism. After all, in the City of Light, you have better things to do and more enlightened ways to spend your evenings than patrolling up and down a half-lit street half a kilometre long in the company of such hideous types, leering lechers, bunny-rabbit women swathed in cuddly fur, bored cops, and the endless stream of white-clad Nordic visitors. What could be more sad, dismal, or dangerous?

Our peasant, however, is not of the same opinion. He spends a truly inordinate amount of his free time patrolling the rue St-Denis in just this way and not for a minute is he dissuaded from doing so by the thought that one of his cultured and disapproving friends, passing through perhaps safely ensconced in a car (those cars that crawl at the slowest possible speed down the street manned by drivers who can hardly keep their eyes on the road), might accidentally catch sight of him chatting to one of the hookers...perhaps—what could be more excruciatingly embarrassing!—the twenty-stone mama from Zaire at the corner of rue d'Aboukir or the giant blonde sabre-toothed tiger loitering around the end of the rue Blondel baring her teeth at the terrified and puny male specimens edging their way nervously around her. What shame and consternation! What universal condemnation! The rows of beady eyes...the accusing looks...the knowing winks. But we might as well come clean: our hero is an addict and that's that. Neither chains nor fire could keep him away. He has to have his fix, even if it is only in the form of an evening's voyeurism. And, in addition, it should not be forgotten that this fertile thoroughfare is not just a sexual bazaar: sweat-shops, secret and graceful covered arcades, the passages that remind us of the subvitreous shopping malls which once ran from one end of Paris to the other in the 19th century, swarming boutiques and its proximity to the *pêle-mêle* of the garment district make the zone an ant-hill of relentless activity, a restless nest of termites where the human density is suffocating and intense.

Although at certain times of the week the street can suddenly empty itself and revert to its rustic quiet, there are times, in the heat of summer, when the ancient world comes alive again between the triumphal arch of St-Denis and the rue de Turbigo. Chains, chinchilla, brocatelle and stockings, leather straps and studs, nightshade lipsticks, SS boots, body-nets, gladiator belts, stillettos, leopard skins, matador hats, beryl earrings, watered silk elbow gloves, French Resistance outfits, the Girl Next Door outfits, Your Worst Nightmare-Fantasy outfits, Bat from Hell outfits, I'm Waiting for My Favourite Bullfighter outfits, Wouldn't You Like to Squash Me outfits, Snow Queen outfits, Wicked Fairy outfits, Naked Savage outfits, You Tarzan outfits, Be Sweet, Gentle but Naughty outfits, Eat Raspberries off My Tongue outfits, Inca Princess outfits, Blue Angel outfits, Let Me Suck Your Neck outfits...how can you remain so cold and aloof? Do you mean to say that none of this interests you in the slightest? All the races of mankind are present here, from Eskimos to Melanesians and every fantasy is ticking over somewhere in the dark, and you stand by with your hands in your pockets wondering why it is allowed? The spangles and G-strings drift in front of you...you are in a sea of opium, the pungent opium of paid sex. Why not recline like the pasha you have suddenly become and float in the current of sexism? Mashers of the world unite! You have nothing to lose, after all, but your erections.

A few years ago, during a turbulent summer, the peasant rented a flat on the top floor of no. 265 at the Strasbourg-St-Denis end of the street. The large building has a courtyard lined on one side with tall mirrors belonging to the Ateliers Sandra clothes shop on the ground floor. Over the impressive doorway a stone ogre gapes flanked by sculpted pine-cones and the usual twisted laurel leaves. The apartment is surrounded on all sides by rooms rented to prostitutes and gives on to another court on the inner side, at the bottom of which is the glass roof of a textile factory. Through the missing panes of glass in this roof can be seen rows of Pakistani faces sweating over sewing machines and racks of multi-coloured coats. Opposite, dozens of windows arrayed below the skyline, a forest of aerials and, far away, the dome of the Opéra. In these end-less lines of windows can be seen the pullulating dramas which are played out under the aegis of St-Denis. At every landing window, a pimp idling away empty hours, and in the adjacent windows, al-ways empty in the stagnant heat of summer, the peeling walls of the love-nests. Projected against them, flashes of naked bodies, the flicker of money and the odd bra tossed in the air.

While brushing his teeth by his bathroom window, for exam-ple, our impressionable hero was confronted, in the flat just oppo-site, with the daily sight of a small shabby bed next to which, carefully plugged in at the wall, reposed two giant electric dildos in a metal box. Below this room nothing could be seen except the continuous exercising of a pair of brown thighs clasped frantically around pairs of white bouncing buttocks. But usually only the feet were visible and so the casual spectator-voyeur was treated to a tango of red high heels and white brogues danced according to rigid rules of engagement, never missing a step or skipping a heart-beat. The dizzying speed of these multiple consummations, all taking place simultaneously as on a hundred different television screens, called for a certain agility of the eye and brain. A hundred copulations a minute! Multiplied by a hundred down the length of the street…a staggering calculation! Nor did the dances stop for a minute, from eight in the morning to eight. Millions, no, tens of millions of feet dancing the tango of sex, millions of times a year. What an industry worthy of the Age of Efficiency, more impressive even than the building of the Great Wall of China. He could not stop himself trying to imagine, in the most vulgar and horrific way, the sheer quantity of semen being

My most memorable encounter in Paris was running into a lady of the night, or early morning in this case since I was out for a walk. She asked in bad but adequate English if I wanted to, and here she made lewd movements that no Proustian Parisian lady would ever make. I said "No, mademoiselle," and she demanded, "Why not?" I was too surprised by this response to con-tinue further conversation, so I quickly walked away.

—Rajendra S. Khadka, "Lost Days in Paris"

expended every week. Enough to multiply the population of the globe by ten. And enough money to buy Paraguay.

The various comings and goings of the three or four blocks assembled around this large interior space were governed, however, by secret forces that only occasionally showed their faces to reveal where all this money was destined. One night a pimp was murdered at the bottom of the stairs opposite, knifed by the Tong, pandemonium exploded on the staircases and a flock of Arab girls came crashing down them screaming *"Les jaunes! Les jaunes!"* Was it the Tong who were rumoured to control the building, the prostitutes and the drugs they used, or does the fantasizing intelligence of the dumb witness like to jump to such conclusions? There is no reason it should not have been a hired Tong killer, for shortly afterwards our peasant certainly heard an intruder beating up a street girl in the flat next to his...slaps, shouting, incrimination, and then the sound of a television set hurled from the window crashing into the glass roof five storeys below followed by its owner, who was found in several pieces among the spangled coats, apparently with fingerprints all over her. They say that a Tong man will kill any casual or accidental witness and so it was not prudent to lean out of the window too far and observe what was going on. But the thought of Chinese hit-men armed with machetes and .38s fitted with silencers creeping through the warren of rooms regulating everything from behind the scenes is too irresistible for our peasant, weaned as he has been on *films noirs* and the adventures of Fantômas so closely fitted into the Parisian landscape. In any case, the duels that are fought behind the façades of the rue St-Denis are in no way inferior in violence and exoticism to the marginal brutalities of mythic cities of 20th-century crime elsewhere, only it is a violence that is discreet, unnoticed, and hallucinatory. The day after the body and the television set hit the roof, the glass had been swept away, the sweat-shop was back to normal, and nothing was mentioned in any newspaper if not the usual single sentence under a cryptic small headline on page eighteen. No other city sweeps its crumbs so swiftly under the carefully brushed carpet.

During his months here, however, the peasant gradually acclimatized himself until even the feminine Gestapo thugs hanging about in his doorway called him by his first name and it was then that he became a self-taught expert in the system of prostitution, the rules, regulations, and nuances of which must be carefully observed if transactions with the denizens of St-Denis are to pass off smoothly and normally.

The rue St-Denis extends from the Porte St-Denis by the Strasbourg-St-Denis Métro station as far as the rue de Rivoli near the Place du Châtelet, but it is only the stretch from the Porte to the junction of the rue de Turbigo and the rue Etienne Marcel that is given over to prostitution proper. This red-light zone also includes the several side streets, passageways and alleys that subtend to the rue St-Denis itself.

On certain nights, a vast congestion of heaving heads, torsos, thighs, and mouths blocks the main street and the alleys, the rue Blondel, the Passage Basfour and the junction of rue Réaumur, where the run of sex shops begins. In the Passage Basfour, in the southern half, shattered old tarts pose in the half-darkness on the saddles of motorbikes and in the rue Blondel, in the northern half, half-naked atrapas in beaver coats stand against the walls of the tiny street all night, as white or Asiatically light-tinted as the Ghanaians of the parallel rue Ste-Apolline are blue.

In the city of the future, the spatial organization of pleasure will

> *The era of the maisons closes ended in 1946, following a crusade by a no-nonsense woman named Marthe Richard. For a long time, I had heard of a mythic directory of these places called the* Guide Rose— *the color was probably chosen to set it apart from the more conventional* Guide Bleu, *which is a standard and lists, in sometimes tedious detail, all there is to see throughout France. The* Guide Rose, *more modest in scope, listed only the brothels, by town, street number, and sometimes name of the madame. After 1946 it was of no practical value, but I searched for a copy anyway as an evocation of a France I had always heard of, the France of between the wars.*
>
> —James Salter,
> "When Evening Falls," GQ

be far more convenient than today's random and chancy gambles. Instead of playing with the possibility that in descending Blondel at two in the morning the imperious male perambulist, feeling dangerous swellings in his *corpus spongiosum,* might just find the cute Eurasian in leather jodhpurs who hangs around the Escale bar, but then again might not, the masher of the future will have at his disposal a system derived from the highly moral English example of grovellingly euphemistic newsagent ads. Of course, those oblique notices pasted in the windows by desperate night nurses and unemployed "school mistresses" desperate to exert a bit of gratifying discipline will have to be replaced with something a little more appetizing. After all, the English tone in these matters is anything but appealing. No, the Paris masher of Futuropolis will want it full in the face, no punches withheld. Obeying future laws that will nevertheless govern the propriety of the streets (yet again following the noble British example of urban antisepsis), the customer will find along the walls of the rue Blondel or the rue du Ponceau not the hordes of beautiful and exotic sex slaves he sees there today but rows of video installations, which—rather like the information screens in the Les Halles underground complex—will provide reams of searing information at the mere touch of a finger. Vital statistics, date of birth, racial composition, blood group, medical history and certificates, relevant vaccination record, full colour photographs of all bodily parts, and even clips of explicit films which will show the wonder-struck john just what his prize-to-be looks like on the job—all will flash before his eyes on the screen as he selects each section with his index finger. Not only that, but the sound of the woman's voice, listing her prices in a happy and convivial tone, will be activated by the simple push of a button. In short, it will have been understood once and for all that the object of what is now called prostitution (but which in the future will go by more pleasant names—"empathetic release procedures" "physical reciprocity procurement" "love-finance systems" is to remove, without fear of retaliation of sudden moral exposure, the mystical element of chance that governs the obtaining of sexual gratifications. Even the faintest possibility of female refusal or frigidity is categorically removed. Possession is instanta-neous. It is a commercial idea of genius, attributable, so they say, to the cynical but alluring priestesses of Ur who…but the priestesses of Ur will be nonexistent to the masher of the future who, strolling lecherously down the babbling rue Blondel, will have only the fu-ture on his mind and who, in addition, will have instantaneous possession in its most perfected form. Push a button and there she is, with a pink computer-coded receipt between her teeth and a magnetic tape stuck to her buttocks. You will be able to choose her clothes, her make up, her smell, her underwear; you will stick your bank card into her socket and watch your time expire on a digital clock carved into her neck.

How, then, will it be possible to imagine the open-air barless cages of today when they have disappeared? They will be as re-mote as the 100,000 girls of the *fin de siècle* participating in the golden age of whoredom. And how is it possible to imagine the age, the age of Cora Pearl and Mademoiselle Maximum, the glo-rious epoch of the courtesan chronicled in the fantastical pages of Arsène Houssaye and that strange and obscure historian, "Zed?" The vampire-whore of the Second Empire, with her block shares in Royal Dutch and Transoccidental Spices and her spectacular *im-broglios* hatched in the infamous Room 16 of the Café Anglais, her wad of calling cards from the collective membership of the Jockey Club and the footloose aristocrats of the Age of Pleasure, the Grammont-Caderousses and Ducs de Morny…she is as unimag-inable today as the hysterical black heroines of Shakespeare or the Didos of rococo ceilings. There is no means of associating the sex-ual remnants of the tradition of the *"grandes horizontales"* who loi-ter in the network of St-Denis alleys, the purple Pigalle bars with open windows and the indexes of contemporary dating agencies with the *filles de joie* of that lost century. The open air gardens of the Bal Mabille with their hanging lamps and promiscuous shaded *promenoirs* are as unimaginable as the "revues" of the Marquis de Massa. The political and financial power of the prostitute has evap-orated along with her cultural prestige, sealed by the opulent por-traits and group pieces of Meissonier and Alfred Stevens.

Regardless of factual knowledge of the empire of syphilis and the secret history of spirogyra that underlies it, the age of the courtesan succeeds in imposing its atmosphere of nostalgia and romance, the meteoric lives of the cocottes—Otéro winning thousands at the Monte Carlo casino at the age of thirteen, Léonide Leblanc burning thaler notes as Maryland cigarettes at the galas of Baden-Baden, Paiva demanding that Adolphe Gaiffe burn 1,000-franc notes for the duration of his passage through her *lit d'apparat*—will never be repeated, just as their props, the *bouchon de carafe* diamonds, the Duleep Singhs and upholstered broughams, have become as unthinkable as the possibility of thoughtful life on Uranus. From the social apogee of Chrystianne de Chatou's Inca Ball held at the courtesan's house on the rue Fortuny in the year 1900, for which Massenet composed what is now the national anthem of El Salvador, the prostitute has subsided to the figures of the rue Blondel, pastiches of air stewardesses, lion tamers, schoolgirls, and the mythic courtesans themselves. The prostitute for the first time is in danger of becoming a pastiche of herself. She no longer belongs: she is doomed to ever-accelerating convenience. She is on her way to the video screens of the ideal future.

In the glare of day the rue St-Denis is crossed and recrossed millions of times an hour by the hordes of ephemeral Pakistani and Indian porters hired by the garment district, who whiz and weave their way through the maze of parked cars, matted pedestrians and tarts, with their small steel trolleys and tow-wheel lifters piled high with enormous packages or whole clothes racks on castors laden with astrakhan coats or embroidered pyjamas. The covered arcades come alive and the whores take a back seat. In the doorways of the boutiques immaculately turned-out managers and salesgirls stand surveying the influx of their wealth, a small-scale flow of cash, perhaps, but intense and pregnant with kitsch nevertheless. In the innumerable courtyards and functional passageways that open up on either side of the street sewing machines hum, needles click and tiny warehouses clatter with frenetic deliveries. The richest and most important thoroughfare of medieval Paris relives in echoes the forgotten glories of its silk merchants, milliners, goldsmiths, bankers, and tailors, those proud and prosperous merchants capable of covering the street with a "sky" of silk sheets during the progress of the monarch on his way to Notre-Dame and who, during the said procession of Louis XI following his coronation in 1461, were able to fill the street's four public fountains with milk, wine, and hippocras. The rue St-Denis remained a district of luxury boutiques, despite the departure of many firms during the Fronde for the rue St-Honoré, until well into the 19th century. Perceiving the efficacy of the St-Denis barricades during the revolution of 1830 Napoleon III decided to pierce the *quartier* with the large Boulevard de Sébastopol, opened in 1858, so initiating the rapid decline of the rue St-Denis....

The rue St-Denis once flowed with lace and handkerchieves. Madeleine Clergease, the handkerchief-maker, was its patron saint. It flowed with gold and copper, and Guillaume Desaufiers was its guardian angel. Today there are the Pakistanis and their obsolete Singer machines, pantyhose production lines, seas of panties and nylon bras, thermal underwear and string vests, tweed trilbies and polyester ties, sweat-absorbent soles and plastic shoes to go with them. In the process of becoming a cloaca, the royal thoroughfare has made the vertiginous descent from gowns of silk to disposable raincoats with synthetic linings. The "skies" of satin have turned into a forest of vertical plastic signs and the lines of spacious, accommodating shops transformed into the crannies of

> *The sweetest taste of Paris is always outdoors, preferably at lunch outside a café. In a happy mix, with equally satisfied people at the next table, wine, food, sunshine, and every scent in the air combine to make you feel that height of enjoyment that Germans fondly described as feeling* wie Gott in Frankreich, *"like God in France." Sitting there, you think of Henry James's* The Ambassadors, *in which a repressed New England widower, bewitched by a garden party somewhere on the Right Bank, realizes that before coming to Paris he had never really lived. "Live all you can!" he suddenly cries out to a young American at the party. "It's a mistake not to.... This place and these impressions…wind a man up so."*
>
> —Alfred Kazin, "River of Life," *Travel Holiday*

the honeycomb, the pickets of space where there is a frenzied, maddening crepitation of insects...the buzzing of anthropomorphic bees. And like bees they are busy copulating, hoarding, running, dancing, carrying, flying, working, and copulating again. The cloaca of Paris are filled with the miraculous industry of bees...and in the Passage du Prado, as in all the "underground" arcades which are the best mementoes of a violated past, the spirit of the hive is alive, the world of the insect is alert.

A peasant's head is always full of memories...the highway of whores fills him with involuntary reminiscence.

putas
pilares de la noche vana

The Mexican poet is not describing Paris, nor even Mexico City, he is observing the eternal return at the crux of the flesh trade. It is a hot summer evening and the peasant approaches an Arab girl by the grocery store of the rue Greneta. There is nothing attractive about her, nothing extraordinary. She is dressed in a fluffy white woolly cardigan and black dress. The light fails and turns green as they cross the street and mount the stairs. There is an excruciating queue outside the rented room, muffled sounds, sly grins all round, the Algerian pimp shaking everyone's hand. Almost like a family picnic, sympathetic and informal. It seems that the girl is Berber, not Arab. She hardly speaks a word of French. Their discussion slides into absurdity. She tries to name figures, throws up fingers. Her face is shaped like a strange crystal, bulging at the sides, and in the middle of her forehead (it is this which no doubt attracted him to her) is a paling blue tattoo. She is naïve and nervous. Her teeth are black at the edges, he remembers those teeth from the Sahara. Finally the door opens and out steps a lithe and charming tart with a radiant smile. Behind her, clumsy, awkwardly self-conscious, a fat fellow with straggling hair slipping across his face, stuck down with sweat. It's been a heavy session. He looks devastated. Her purse is bulging with notes. So he went the whole way, 500 francs! Through some desire to please, the Algerian ushers in the Berber girl and the peasant and they find themselves alone. An awkward moment.

He opens up conversation and she throws up the same fingers. But at the same time they smile at each other. There is resignation in the air. She undresses slowly, takes off her tights, looks over at his body with curiosity, her own is coffee-brown, fragile and thin except around the hips, the slender beauty of the desert. He touches her arms. They are breakable. She doesn't know what to say, although it is clear she wants to say something. They sit side by side on the bed—a ridiculous gesture. They can't stop smiling. For once, there is nothing uneasy in the movements, the room is warm and well decorated, a far cry from the cubicles on the rue de Budapest equipped only with a candle and box of tissues. What is happening? The blue tattoo…it seems to smudge under the trickles of sweat appearing on her forehead. And suddenly he sees what it is about the tattoo. It's in the shape of the Cross of Lorraine, the symbol of the old Action Française or the Free French, he can't remember, in any case a potent symbol of national purity. The Cross of Holy France is emblazoned in her forehead and trembling under its pool of sweat. She turns her face sideways. She says something in her Berber dialect. Perhaps she would like him for a husband. Her working papers are stuffed carelessly into her wallet, along with his money. Is she smiling about that? Her lips are covered with faded rose lipstick clumsily applied and her teeth peep out when she smiles, hideous and irregular, black at the crown, brownish at the root. And yet he likes her teeth as much as her Cross of Lorraine tattoo, they are suffused with the same gentleness and absence of calculation. The almost-black aureoles of her breasts are the same colour as the rotted crowns of her teeth. It is perfect, everything tied up into a quiet whole. She could be dreaming about the oases of the Draa. She could be dreaming about castration. She could be dreaming about retirement.

They take a long time and there is a tap on the little door. They help each other dress. Small intimacies, like a married couple! At last the door is opened. She hangs back, waiting for him to go out first. No, he wants her to go out first. She doesn't understand. It's politeness, he insinuates. You're the man, she insinuates back. A small fiasco ensues. Neither of them moves. It is imperative, after their wholly unexpected interlude of tenderness, that a wholesome etiquette be observed. In the end, seeing her absolute refusal to be impolite or to fail to do what a woman is expected to do, he grabs her by the shoulders and propels her through the door. But after that there is another door to get out into the hallway and the same thing repeats itself. He pushes her firmly out in front of him. What slaves of form they both are! But at least she is enjoying herself. Yes, she's really quite pleased to be propelled through doorways by her client! She is confused at the same time. And at the final door giving on to the street she resists, through the power of instinct and education, a third time, then, apologizing for no reason, steps through the door of her own accord. It is night, as always. They say goodbye. She invites him to look her up for a drink one of these nights, and she does this miraculously, using just her fingers. It is extraordinary, the power of fingers. She walks off and the moon rises over the rue de Turbigo, inflamed, melon-orange, glacial. Despite all climatical, astrological and meteorological declarations to the contrary, it is another white night by St-Denis.

Lawrence Osborne also contributed "Métro Metaphysics" in Part I. Both stories were excerpted from his book Paris Dreambook: An Unconventional Guide to the Splendor and Squalor of the City.

★

Decadent scenes of the rue Saint Denis are represented in masterful paintings and novels by Charles Dickens, Victor Hugo, Emile Zola, and Toulouse-Lautrec. The street was the home of Irma La Douce and serves as the setting for numerous plays and films depicting "the fallen angel."

Walk the route with resolution—don't loiter, and button down your wallets. Working girls in the shadowy doorways don't appreciate mere curiosity seekers. You'll be able to observe enough, without staring, to satisfy your imaginations for a long time. Check out the shop windows displaying surprising merchandise, which serves the local clientele. Avoid a detour down the side streets, don't sample the goods, and resist stopping in the neighborhood dives. At the end of the experience, you'll rejoice in the good fortune of going home with someone you know and adore.

—Edith Kunz, *Paris Passion Places: A Guide to Romantic Paris*

DONOVAN WEBSTER

Remnants of Hell

*Millions of acres in France remain littered with explosives
from the two world wars. A special corp of experts
is doing its best to remove the deadly debris.*

ACROSS THE CENTURIES, FRANCE HAS OFTEN BEEN A BATTLE-
ground. On this particular morning, a Tuesday in late September,
we're cleaning up after World War I. Six of us are walking through
a dense forest just outside the town of Verdun, 160 miles east of
Paris. Scattered across the uneven ground, in and among the still-
extant bomb craters and trench lines, unexploded artillery shells
are everywhere. A 170-millimeter shell (long as a man's leg; bigger
around than his thigh) rests like a leaf-swaddled child at the edge
of a crater. It is picked up and carried back to the truck by one of
the *démineurs*.

A few steps away, at the edge of a trench, sits a stockpile of 75-
millimeter shells, the most widely used artillery pieces of the war.
From today's perspective, they resemble nothing so much as a stack
of corroded hairspray cans. One by one, the rusted, moss-blanketed
shells are lifted from their 75-year rest and transferred to the truck
by the *démineurs*.

In a nearby foxhole are a dozen German grenades: they're the
"racquet type," which means their baseball-size explosive charges
are lashed to foot-long (and now rotted) throwing sticks of wood.
They look like potato mashers. And that, in fact, is what the

American soldiers nicknamed them. One by one, they are scooped up and carried to the truck.

All around me the *démineurs* ("de-miners"), as France's bomb-disposal experts are called, are clearing the forest of explosives, carrying them to the beds of the four-wheel-drive Land Rovers we've driven into this forest. The men work quickly and confidently. Each wears the uniform of France's Department du Déminage: blue coveralls, made from special antistatic material, with their pant legs tucked into the tops of high rubber boots. Each *démineur*'s hands are gloved, too, as protection against any mustard gas or phosgene or chlorine that might seep through the rusted shells to blister or even kill the men instantly.

Twenty more minutes of explosives-collecting passes. Then another hour. The *démineurs* work steadily. They lift the projectiles from their long sleep on the forest floor, and, being careful not to trip over the tree roots or rusty trench wire as they cross the forest, they gently lower each shell into the wooden transport racks in the Land Rovers. The dark, pitted skins of the shells are corroded and flaking; the shells themselves smell damp and old—like the darkest corner of an unused basement.

After three hours, I survey the forest we're clearing. There are still shells everywhere. It seems we haven't even started working. My interest shifts, and I walk away, deeper into the trees. These forests were home to some of World War I's worst fighting. And back in mid-November 1918, just after the Armistice, the hills above Verdun were so thick with unexploded weapons and grenades (plus the still-uncollected dead) that the French Government simply cordoned them off. In fact, they closed nearly sixteen million acres above Verdun, placing them inside the Cordon Rouge, the "red line." Much of the area has been closed to visitors ever since by fences with big, red-lettered signs that read TERRAIN INTERDIT ("forbidden ground").

A breeze has autumn's final leaves fluttering in the canopy. At my feet, a trench winds across the ground; it's deeper than a man is tall. I follow it. Its wooden supports (which once kept it from collapsing under the shelling as they now keep it from crumbling) remain in place—though the wood has rotted and become painted with dark moss. Where two trenches intersect, there is a 1918 vintage of liquor bottles among the mushrooms and downed leaves. Farther along, in the trench's bottom, I find the sole of a man's boot and a rusted canteen. A few steps beyond that, the ball-like end of a human thigh bone protrudes; it has shattered along its length and looks like a dagger. I lift the bone, then toss it up and down in my hand. It's pale, clean, and white. It feels light but solid, like a hunk of cork. I let it fall back to the leafy trench.

The *démineurs* estimate that today, more than 75 years after the end of World War I, twelve million unexploded shells from that conflict still lie in the soil near Verdun. Millions more await discovery in the battle zones along the Marne and Somme rivers, southwest and northwest, respectively, of where we now stand. And, of course, millions of still-undiscovered artillery shells and aerial bombs from World War II remain embedded in the beaches of Normandy and Brittany. Everywhere in France—in potato fields and orchards, under town squares and back porches—the fallout from two world wars has turned the national soil into an enormous booby trap. Since 1946, the year the Déminage department was officially established, 630 *démineurs* have died in the line of duty. In that time, the department has collected and destroyed more than 18 million artillery shells, ten million grenades, 600,000 aerial bombs and 600,000 underwater mines. Those in a position to estimate the *démineurs'* progress admit they're not sure how far along the de-mining of France is. They'll freely admit that, through the efforts of the *démineurs*, more than two million acres have been reclaimed from the explosive and toxic tools of war. Still, when pressed, they'll allow that at least that many acres, littered with unexploded bombs, are still cordoned off. They'll also say that, because not all ordnance are found in the ground-clearing process, even places considered safe continue to spit up unexploded ordnance. In 1991, for instance, 36 farmers died when their machinery hit unexploded shells. Another 51 citizens were injured

when they happened on a bomb unexpectedly. It is the job of the
démineurs—123 men in eighteen districts stretching the length and
width of France—to clean the
place up.

*ort Douaumont [near
Verdun, a fortress that
would eventually inspire the disastrous Maginot Line] is possibly the
most enormous single chunk of
concrete in the world. It is half a
mile long, a quarter of a mile wide,
a concrete carapace whose walls and
roof are said to be more than eight
feet thick. It was the strongest fort
in existence at the time.*

*It was so vast that, standing in the
snow on its roof, I can't even see
all of it.... The view to all sides is
stupendous, which of course was
why the fort was built there in the
first place. Although clearly im-
pregnable, Fort Douaumont fell to
the Germans without a shot being
fired. It was retaken eight months
later almost to the day, also virtually without a shot being fired. In
between it cost the French
100,000 lives. All it ever was, was
a symbol. How they did believe in
symbols in those days. In that war
men died for symbols by the millions. Verdun itself was a symbol—
the German generals had mounted
their offensive against the one spot
in the 300-mile-long front that
French honor would feel obligated
to defend to the last man.*

—Robert Daley, *Portraits of France*

We are now at lunch, six
démineurs and myself, in a fine little Alsatian restaurant in the village of Eix-Abaucourt, a wide
spot in the road between Verdun
and Metz. As we eat herring in
white wine, then sautéed chicken
breasts in cream sauce, I'm listening to the chief of the *démineurs*,
a sturdy, crew-cut man named
Henry Belot; he's giving me a
taste for how many ordnance
pieces are still around. In 1991
and 1992, he says, as the French
national railway dug a new bed
for its TGV bullet train—for a
line connecting Paris and London through the new Channel
tunnel—the *démineurs* in that region, home to the battlefields of
the Somme, were on constant
duty, with daily collections of five
tons of shells and bombs being
the norm. Miraculously, in the
two years of digging the railbed,
no one has been injured. The
same record can't be claimed by
the project's excavation machinery. So far, Belot says, four front-
end loaders have been exploded,

as have a number of earthmovers. "They still keep digging," he says.
"The railroad is a point of French pride."

"Here's another story," says a stout, blond *démineur* named Christian Cleret. "Just recently, a farmer near Soissons was tilling his beet field along the Aisne River. There was a large German offensive there in 1918, and apparently not all of the bombs have been cleaned up. The farmer's implement hit a buried shell. He gave his life among the furrows."

Henry Belot tells of an explosion the previous winter. A group of five lumberjacks was working in the steep hills of the Argonne Forest. It began to snow, so the men built a fire to warm up. Unknowingly, they had set their fire over an artillery shell just beneath the dirt's surface. Boom! All were killed.

What's the *démineurs'* least-favorite type of shell? I ask. "The toxic ones," they all reply. I ask why.

"Two reasons," Belot says. He lifts his right hand into the air, holding it as if he's gripping something loosely. "First, you never know how solid their skins are. They are often very rusty, so they may leak gas and kill you as you lift them. Also, they are harder to destroy."

To destroy the usual explosive shells, I am told, deep pits are dug, which the *démineurs* then fill partway with the ordnance they've collected. Then they attach plastic explosives to the top of the pile and blow the whole thing up. "The blast is directed straight into the air," another of the *démineurs* says. "No one gets hurt."

Until recently, toxic shells had been detonated in the English Channel. On a beach with a 50-foot tide range, *démineurs* would drive out on the flats at low tide, dig pits and carefully stack toxic shells in them, attach explosives and unreel wire back to the high-tide mark. At high tide, when the pits were underwater, the charges would be set off, exploding the shells, burning off the gas and sending plumes of the water a half-mile into the air. Protests from environmentalists stopped the practice, however; now the Deminage is looking for alternative methods.

I ask how many *démineurs* were killed or injured in the past year, and Belot tells me that five were killed, eleven hurt. "It was a good year," he says. "We didn't lose too many."

Then Belot takes a final bite of his chicken and, after swallowing it, says, "Every day, you can die. It's something you remember each morning. You never know when. You can't anticipate it.

elot was gravely injured by a poison gas shell after this story was written. We were unable to get an update on his condition because the Department du Déminage does not release this kind of information, preferring to keep its activities out of the public eye.

—JO'R, LH, and SO'R

These bombs look old on the outside, but inside"—he points to his wristwatch— "they are as clean as a new clock. Out there is a bomb with your name. Today, if you lift that bomb, you are in the past."

Christian Cleret puts down his silverware and lifts a piece of bread. The *démineur* takes a bite, then points the rest of the bread at me. "It is very sad when one of us dies," he says, "since all the other *démineurs* know him. There are so few of us, we are all friends, we know each other's families. When one of us dies, it is very sad."

Then, for a long minute, no one says anything more. I look around the table; everyone has finished eating. All of the men are staring down at their plates.

The next day, a misty Wednesday, the final day of September, I'm in another Déminage Land Rover, rolling through the flat farmland just north of the Marne River, 90 miles northeast of Paris. The brown and furrowed earth in this part of France is nearly shaved of trees, and in every direction I can see the horizon as it bends against the dark, stormy-looking sky. It's harvest time, and the fields are full of farm machinery. The farmers of this region serve up much of France's food; its potatoes and sugar beets and wheat come from here. In this century, six different battlefronts have moved through the area. The remnants are everywhere.

We're rolling down an empty two-lane road, looking for a tiny village, but it's taking us longer to get there than we'd figured because we have to keep making stops. Every mile or so, a shell stands along the road's shoulder like a miniature, dirt-encrusted obelisk. Each one has been uncovered by a farmer who has climbed down from his harvester, lifted the shell from the furrow lines and lugged it to the roadside. These are known as "incidentals."

A *démineur* named Remy Deleuze is telling me the history of this road between the fields. It is called the Chemin des Dames— the "Path of the Women"—and got its name when King Louis XV's daughters used it for carriage rides through the countryside. It was also the site of two major battles in World War I. The first was a failed French counterattack in April 1917, when more than eleven million artillery shells were dumped on the well-fortified Germans. The second was on May 27, 1918, when in four hours of furious shelling more than 700,000 German bombs fell, allowing the Kaiser's army to blow through the dead and dazed French Sixth Army like floodwaters through a picket fence. On that day, in one bound, the Germans leapt thirteen miles closer to Paris, the largest single-day movement of the war till then. "That was a bad day," Deleuze says, "a terrible day for France."

Deleuze, second in command of his squadron, is just 27 years old. As we roll down the Chemin des Dames, he sits on the passenger side. Driving is another *démineur,* a man named Patrice Delannoy. Delannoy is short and solid, with intense gray eyes. His hair is cropped and dark, and he has a thick, graying mustache. For the past half-hour, Deleuze has done all the talking while Delannoy—who is hard at work, scanning the road for explosives—has yet to say a word. Up ahead, Delannoy spots another bomb in the roadside grass. After he brakes the truck to a stop, we walk closer. When Deleuze sees what kind of bomb it is, he claps his hands. "Ah!" he says. "A *crapouillot.*" It does not resemble the aerodynamic artillery shells we've been lifting for days; four pinwheel fins extend from its sides, and a shaft from its base. It looks like a large spear. Deleuze bends to lift the shell, his gloved hands grasping the bomb's nose and tailward shaft. He tells me that *crapouillot*s are French-made cousins to the modern mortar shell. Their shafts fit into smooth-bore cannon barrels; when the cannons were fired, the *crapouillots* were spit out to fly short distances. The fins, he says, helped the bomb to spin, gyroscopically stabilizing it to enhance its accuracy.

Deleuze says that, though the fields around the Chemin des Dames have long ago been "officially cleared" by the *démineurs*, each year the earth continues to give off bits of deeper-buried ordnance, just as stones continually work their way to the surface of a New England farm field.

We return to the truck and start off again. Deleuze says that it will take centuries for some shells to work their way to the sunshine. He waves a hand, then shrugs. "Any dreams France has of feeling completely safe from the First War," he says, "they are exactly that: dreams."

Delannoy brings the Land Rover to a stop once again, and Deleuze and I step out. This time we find a World War I British 155-millimeter shell sitting next to a house-size pile of sugar beets. The beets await a collection truck that will take them to a sugar refinery; the bomb awaits us. As Deleuze lifts the shell from the ground, he flits it back and forth. From inside the corrosion-pitted shell comes a sloshy swish, swish.

"Hear that?" Deleuze asks. "That's the mustard gas." As he walks the shell to the rear of the truck, Deleuze tells me that while the poison in each toxic shell is called "gas," it is generally fired as a liquid, which is vaporized at the moment of explosion. He places the shell into the truck's rack, then slips a wooden shim beneath it to secure it solidly. "We find 900 tons of bombs a year," he says. "At least 30 tons of those are toxic." With his gloved hand, he scrubs at the shell's dirty, rusty skin. The gritty patina falls away, and stripes of white paint become faintly visible on the shell's body. He points at the rings: "These mean toxic."

We get back into the truck and keep rolling. Delannoy turns off the Chemin des Dames and follows the side road toward a clump of dark, prim, stone houses. Each house appears to have two rooms downstairs and two up; most still have their windows shuttered against the mist and rain. We pass a grove of trees, and beyond that a graveyard of French crosses from World War I. Then we follow the pavement through an opening between two buildings, and we're inside the village walls. We find the place we're looking for: No. 1 Place St-Georges. Inside a gravel courtyard, Delannoy stops the truck. "This is the home of Madame Painvin," Deleuze says. "She has a bomb in her garden."

Deleuze gets out and climbs a set of steps to the front door. He knocks, and Madame Painvin opens it. She appears to be about 30 years old.

"I'm from the Department du Déminage," Deleuze announces himself.

"Ah," says Madame Painvin, "the bomb is across the road. I'll show you. Let me get my shoes."

A minute later, she is leading us out of the courtyard and across the narrow street to her walled garden. The contents of the garden have pretty much been picked through. In the far corner, a thick shrub is growing against the garden wall, and Madame Painvin stops walking and points at the bush.

"There," she says. "Get it out of here."

Remy Deleuze slips on his gloves, drops to one knee and, reaching between the base of the shrub and the wall, finds an un-fired artillery shell with its propellant cartridge still attached. He lifts the shell from behind the bush and sets it gently on the ground at our feet. It looks like a two-foot-long bullet. "Well, what's this?" he says. "An unfired 75-millimeter shell. American. From the Second World War."

"Get it away!" Madame Painvin says, almost shouting. "Get it out of my garden. My children found it yesterday. I looked out the window, and they were playing in the garden with it."

"Certainly, certainly," Deleuze responds, "but I think there are more surprises here." He reaches through the shrub's branches into a deep cavity in the wall and extracts another American 75. He lays the shell gently on the dirt and carefully examines it for danger signs. Then, still kneeling, he hands both shells to his partner. As Deleuze stands, slapping the grit from the knees of his coveralls, he says, "Voilà! No more bombs in the garden today."

As we start walking toward the truck, Deleuze tells Madame Painvin the probable scenario: back in World War II—most likely during the Allied push from the Normandy beaches toward Germany in late 1944—an American soldier set these bombs into the wall's crevice during a skirmish, then forgot to retrieve them. It is, he continues, the kind of thing he sees all the time. "The *démineurs*," he says, "we make 11,000 stops at citizens' houses each year. To collect shells and grenades."

As we leave, Deleuze smiles and shrugs. "It's nothing strange," he says. "Only the usual story. The soldiers moved on. The war moved on. The bombs stayed."

Late on a Friday night I drive back to Verdun, passing the 13th-century cathedral in Reims, its squared-off twin towers silhouetted against a dark, misty sky. Like the towers, my plans are symbolic yet vague. I figure I'll spend Saturday and Sunday in Verdun, coming to know why men bomb and shoot one another. I'll picnic in the hills and walk among the half-timber buildings of the historic towns.

Despite the homey hotel and the fine poached pike I have for dinner (with plenty of wine), I don't sleep very well. By 6:45 the next morning I've left the hotel to drive into the World War I battlefields in the hills above town. The road I'm following runs north along the banks of the Meuse; the river's smooth water slides past in the growing daylight. Poplars line both sides of the road at intervals: it's something out of a French travel poster. In the village of Bras the road turns away from the river, and I see a large white arrow that points up a side road. The words on it read: *"Louvemont, village détruit."*

Louvemont is one of the area's nine obliterated villages, one of the places scraped from the earth by a single day of war. At 7:15 on the snow-bright morning of February 21, 1916, after an eight-month buildup, German shells began to fall in the hills around Verdun, and Louvemont was in the way. By noon of that day, no habitable structure was left in the village, and the heat from exploding bombs melted the snow that only hours earlier had coated the fields and rooftops.

The shelling went on all day. It was the most fearful offensive of World War I. Trees were shattered. Explosives cratered the landscape, then cratered the craters. The barrage continued through the afternoon, and, in the long string of trenches above Verdun, the

French forces—hunched over and praying—waited for the shelling to end. Thousands of Frenchmen were already dead from shell fragmentation or direct hits. The rest were merely deafened and dazed. In the bottom of the trenches, snowmelt began to refreeze.

As the sun began to set, the first wave of German infantry advanced, employing their newest weapon: the flamethrower. Downed trees and brush exploded into fire. Smoke fouled the air. The Frenchmen who could still move crawled to the tops of their trenches. They steadied their rifles on the mud and began firing. Many Germans fell. Others kept coming. Mortar shells flew. Soldiers were exploded. Still they kept coming and soon reached the trenches. Skulls were pulped with rifle butts. Men were pinned to the cold mud with bayonets. Soldiers from both sides were shot at close range. Others were blown apart by grenades.

The Germans had made a tactical mistake, however. They had bombed too long and had not allowed time for the infantry to clear the battlefield. They had also miscalculated the French

When you subject men to the conditions of the Bois des Caures, the conditions that generally obtained throughout that war, when you leave them eating, sleeping, shitting, freezing, day after day in the same two feet of muddy trench and then subject them to a ten-hour bombardment—when you do this you remove from them all dignity. You reduce them to the level of slavering animals. They exist on the level of animals. Their psyches are overpowered by the most basic and also the basest (we have mostly been taught to think) of emotions, namely fear and rage. They become crazed. Are crazed men responsible for their actions? Some become catatonic and are killed where they cower, sometimes by their own men. Others in their hysteria fight like demons, a more accurate word than most people commonly realize. They literally no longer know what they are doing. The difference between coward and hero may even be chemical, the presence or absence of a single hormone, perhaps, something that could be added or subtracted from their soup. The hero may have no more control of himself than the coward. To me, especially in that snowy woods this morning, it seems as unreal to call one man coward as to call another hero.

—Robert Daley, *Portraits of France*

Army's ability to defend itself. At about six o'clock, as the mid-winter night began to settle on these fields, the offensive stalled. The German infantrymen could do nothing but bed down in the open fields. In the dark, the French opened a counteroffensive. They moved silently along their trenches to get close to the Germans, then crawled up and over and slithered closer. More soldiers were blown up. By ten, the battlefield was quiet again.

In the hills above Verdun, that kind of fighting went on for months. Before the siege was over, nearly a million souls had been chewed up in the maw of war. In what may be the most grisly statistic ever, fewer than 160,000 identifiable bodies were recovered. The rest were impossible to recognize or had simply been swallowed up by the explosions and mud.

The sun is just coming up now, rising over the forests and long, rounded ridgelines above Verdun. The road climbs a hillside, then flattens. And then I am in Louvemont.

There's not much. A marble monument. A chapel. A few beech trees. To this day, after all these years, the ground beyond the beeches is broken and uneven. The shells did more than tear up the soil. They destroyed the village, too. There is nothing left of Louvemont. No little stone houses. No barns. No town square with a fountain. Nothing.

I hurry back to the car and drive from Louvemont. The road continues to twist and turn uphill. Above the treetops to the right—sticking up like a fifteen-story concrete missile—is the tower of the Ossuary of Douaumont, strikingly white in the morning sun. The tower dips behind the treetops as I crest the hill, and now ahead of the car is the National Cemetery, where 15,000 crosses of white marble jut from the perfectly tended grass. The crosses spread across the hillside—each of them was once a life. A rosebush is planted at the base of each cross, and the roses are just beginning to open for the day, tens of thousands of crimson buds in the morning light. Yet they number nothing compared with what is inside the ossuary, the quarter-mile-long blockhouse and spire that waits at the upper end of the huge cemetery. Inside that building, the remains of 130,000 human beings are entombed.

The ossuary is made of white stone. Its shape is long, rounded and low, like a loaf of French bread. From its center rises the fifteen-story spire, which has been fashioned to look like an artillery shell. The interior is a narrow hallway with a rounded ceiling that runs the building's length; it feels like the inside of a gun barrel. The floor is perfectly laid marble. The only light inside comes from sun shining through stained-glass windows. Dozens of granite tombs are arranged in alcoves that have been built into the ossuary walls. There are no names on the tombs; lettering denotes the sector of the Verdun battlefield from which the remains were taken. Beneath the marble floor are the remains. The floor plan has been divided into sectors that correspond with those on the tombs; the bodies—or parts of bodies—that came from those zones and could not be identified are buried here.

I walk outside to take a deep breath of the cool, sunny, autumn morning. I start across the gravel toward my car, then see a row of windows in the white stone along the building's base. I kneel and peer inside. There are bones everywhere, as far as the daylight can penetrate. Vertebrae. Skulls. Tiny little bones that seem fragile and white, like lumps of talcum powder. There are ribs and ribs and ribs; the bony remains of thousands of torsos are piled so deep that the jumble of rib ends looks like a fish's scales. In the window's center sits a jawless skull. It's been pierced behind the left ear and in the forehead. The holes are asymmetrical, no doubt the

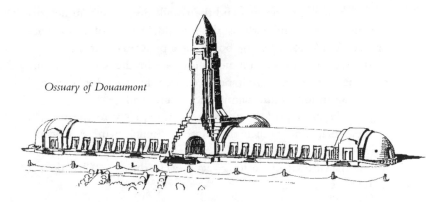

Ossuary of Douaumont

legacy of the British officer Henry Shrapnel, who was the first to put bullets into an exploding projectile.

In back of the ossuary there is a small shop with books and slides for sale. There is a multimedia show devoted to the siege of Verdun, too. When I enter the shop, I find that the show does not begin until ten o'clock. I ask the shopkeeper about it, and he says that no one ever visits the ossuary before ten. "Why would you want to spoil a new day with a place like this?" he replies. I'm drawn to the rows of stereoscopic viewers lining one of the walls. In three-dimensional, black-and-white images, the Battle of Verdun comes to life. The French soldiers in the pictures are slightly built and pale. They seem poised on the edge of moving, of gesticulating, of shouting to me. Most are smiling, most have thick mustaches and bright, dark eyes. In some of the photographs, the men are bivouacking in the remains of obliterated villages. In others, they are digging new trenches or buttressing with wooden supports the trenches they've already dug. Their uniforms are muddy, but they look happy and cocky—even a little hopeful.

Finally, there's one picture that makes me pull my head from the viewer with a snap. A severed forearm lies on the mud. Ahead of it, there's only the bald, hilly horizon. The arm is beautifully pre-served. It's just lying there, clean from the rain, the fingers of the hand slightly opened, palm to the sky.

The shopkeeper, who's seated near the cash register, asks, "What did you see?"

I tell him about the arm and then walk over to where he's sit-ting. He is skinny and perhaps 35 years old. In front of him are na-ture handbooks for sale. The books have pictures of birds and trees on their covers; they're intended for use in the sectors of sur-rounding forests that have been cleared by the *démineurs* and opened again for picture-taking and nature walks.

To make conversation and pass the time, I say to the man, "I wonder what kind of arm that was? A French arm? A German arm?"

The man frowns for a long second. He shrugs. "What does it matter?" he says.

Donovan Webster's work has appeared in major American magazines including The New Yorker, The New York Times, *and* National Geographic. *This story, which originally appeared in* Smithsonian, *became part of his book* Aftermath: Cleaning Up a Century of World War. *He lives with his wife and family outside Charlottesville, Virginia.*

*

There is no place on earth where death cannot find us—even if we constantly twist our heads about in all directions as in a dubious and suspect land.... If there were any way of sheltering from death's blows—I am not the man to recoil from it.... But it is madness to think that you can succeed....

Men come and they go and they trot and they dance, and never a word about death. All well and good. Yet when death does come—to them, their wives, their children, their friends—catching them unawares and unprepared, then what storms of passion overwhelm them, what cries, what fury, what despair!...

To begin depriving death of its greatest advantage over us, let us adopt a way clean contrary to that common one; let us deprive death of its strangeness, let us frequent it, let us get used to it; let us have nothing more often in mind than death.... We do not know where death awaits us: so let us wait for it everywhere. To practice death is to practice freedom. A man who has learned how to die has unlearned how to be a slave.

—Michel de Montaigne, *Essays*

PART FIVE

The Last Word

SIMON LOFTUS

Windows on a Village

Bread, wine, and friendship remain staples
of life in Burgundy.

THERE IS ONE SPOT IN THE SQUARE [IN PULIGNY-MONTRACHET],
a simple bench beneath the trees, which is to its habitués the centre of village society, a place to meet, chat and watch the world go
by. From this quiet corner you can observe Michel Mourlin re-
pairing a window of his house or Madame Robaire going home
after a long day's work at the hotel or an English wine merchant
crossing the square on his way to see Olivier Leflaive. A cluster of
cronies congregates on the bench in the afternoon, but it's a good
vantage point at any time from which to enjoy the restful patterns
and small surprises of the passing day.

One morning in early spring my daydreaming was disturbed by
the clatter of a cement-mixer—the men were mending the roof
of the house behind me. Then it stopped and in the sudden stillness I heard one of the workmen calling down to his mate on the
pavement, a dog barking, and an unexpected cuckoo, the first of
the year, repeating itself among the trees in the park of the
Château de Puligny. A fat woman emerged from the house next
door, purse in hand and dog at heel, still barking. I had a bet with
myself that she was heading for the bakery. A few minutes later she
returned, smiling, with three baguettes. Then out popped the

451

baker, leaving his wife to mind the shop while he went to have a word with the butcher, whose van was parked at the entrance to the rue de la Mairie.

Two old fellows stopped for a chat in the middle of the road, one leaning on a bicycle, the other on a stick. Ten minutes later the stick waved goodbye, just as a younger man and his child came walking down from the post office and paused to greet the cyclist. With foot to pedal the old boy remained gossiping in the road for a while longer before heaving himself on to the saddle and wobbling off towards the Mairie. At which moment an elderly woman who was trotting up the pavement with her bag of groceries stopped for a word with the father and his son. And so it continued, like a slow dance choreographed with perfect timing to weave together the erratic pathways of disparate lives.

The intersection of these meanderings shifts during the course of the day. In the mornings you could pinpoint a spot in the middle of the road, just outside the bakery, but in the afternoon all the paths lead to the bench under the trees, which catches the warmth of the westerly sun.

At three o'clock, if the day is fine, the first of the regulars arrive. André Goudrand and his wife Marguerite have returned to Puligny from Chalon, where he kept a pharmacy and she worked as chambermaid at the hotel. He walks with some difficulty, leaning on a crutch, and she is beginning to show signs of arthritis in the wrists, but they take cheerful pleasure in each other's company and are amiable gossips. "Of course it's expensive living here, everything in the shops costs so much and with his leg he can't drive so we don't go out to the supermarkets in the big towns like everyone else does. We're dependent on the *épicerie* here, and the baker, and the butcher who comes here on Tuesdays and Fridays. But we have friends." There's a contented sigh from both of them. André slaps his hands on his knees and leans forward as he gazes across the square. "Ah yes," he says, eventually, and leans back again on the bench.

Although they are both in their sixties they don't go much to weekly meetings of the Club du Troisième Age, when the old people get together to play cards or plan a coach trip abroad or, this year, to make flowers for the decorations which will cover the village at the Fête St-Vincent. "No, I prefer to make my flowers at home...and we meet our friends here."

Next to arrive is Michel Boissard, a *vigneron* who worked for Domaine Chartron before his retirement and who now, in his seventies, seems as fit as a fiddle; a walking advertisement for wine. Finally, at four o'clock precisely, along comes the doyen of the group, Pierrot Lombard. His is an unmistakably French figure: large beret, prominent nose and walrus moustache, blue workman's trousers which flap around the ankles of his sturdy boots. Pierrot walks slightly stooped, slowly and with the aid of a stick, but his voice is firm and he chews his words with pleasure, looking back on a long and dignified life.

"I'm 92, the oldest vigneron in the village. I've lived here always, except for the war. But I'm not the oldest inhabitant. No, that's Monsieur Beck, who used to be a railwayman at Paris. He's 94. But he doesn't get about much now." This is said with a degree of satisfaction at his own vigorous longevity as he plumps himself down on the bench beside the others and rests his hands on his stick, enjoying the autumn sunshine while the first yellowing leaves fall gently, almost silently, to the ground.

An hour later they are still there, chatting peaceably together between interludes of companionable silence, as they do every day while the fine weather lasts....

There used to be two butchers in Puligny but the last one closed in the mid-seventies. Since then the villagers have had to rely on the travelling butcher, Monsieur Bruchard. He takes his van to Volnay on Wednesday and Saturday mornings, St-Romain on Saturday afternoons and Puligny on Tuesday and Friday mornings. The rest of the week he spends behind the counter of his shop at Meursault.

Parked in a side street just off the Place du Monument, Monsieur Bruchard serves customers from a neatly organized cold shelf which is revealed when he swings up the side of the van.

"Our little shops are all disappearing, it's happening all over the world. There used to be half a dozen butchers on the square in Meursault, now there are three. With us it's a family clientele—you have to wait your turn, they talk, you know them. The old people and the middle-aged are still faithful, but the young couldn't care less about you. They buy their beefsteak at the supermarkets. The mentality has changed. It's quality that keeps me going. I can't compete with the big shops on price but I can on quality."

I watch in queasy fascination as he slices some ham, noticing that three fingers of his left hand have been chopped off at the first joint. "I make all my own pâtés, my *saucisson sec,* my *jambon cru.* My speciality is *jambon persillé.*"

A middle-aged lady comes up to buy a kilo of beef. The purchase is wrapped and paid for. As the woman turns to go she asks Monsieur Bruchard, "For Boeuf Bourguignon, you use water?" It seems astounding that she doesn't know. "Wine," says the butcher firmly, then seeing her glance of dismay he adds, "And water. Wine and water...."

Marital relations are a mystery to outsiders—who knows the hidden strengths or stresses of any partnership? But the business of being a baker's wife seems a dull *métier,* especially during the vintage. For most of the year Madame Fontaine works alongside her husband throughout the day (Patrick bakes, Sandrine sells the results of his labour). In the afternoon, while the shop is quiet and he is preparing the elaborate range of *pâtisserie* in which they both take considerable pride, there is the chance of a few minutes' gossip. But in the evening he goes to bed early, soon after supper, because he has to get up at three a.m. in order to fire the stove and knead the first batch of dough for the breakfast baguettes. And for two or three weeks during the harvest they hardly see one another at all. Hundreds of pickers need feeding, dozens more loaves need baking. Monsieur Fontaine abandons the *pâtisserie* for the duration, starts work at ten in the evening, bakes all night and sleeps as best he can through the clear autumn days. His wife continues to serve in the shop and comforts herself by counting the takings. They have

a monopoly in the village and they are appreciated by their neighbours. *"Ça marche bien ici"* (i.e. they are doing well financially).
In other ways they are less content. The Fontaines came to
Puligny from the Morvan in 1986. They had been used to living
in a small friendly village near Saulieu where everyone talked to
each other and all the children played together in the street, running in and out of each other's houses. "Here it's different, our boy
has no companions when he plays. It's not as if there aren't any
other children—it's just that everyone stays shut up, separate. The
thing that disturbs me most about Puligny is that when you cross
paths with someone in the street you never know whether they're
going to say hello or not." Challenged as to whether she says hello
in such circumstances, Madame has to admit that she's often too
shy to do so. This business of greeting one another has enormous
implications at every level of society in France: *"Elle me dit bonjour"* is resonant with meaning, far beyond the basic recognition
of neighbours.

But the business is good and the Fontaines take considerable
pride in what they bake. "We make up to ten different types of
bread, from simple baguettes to *pain à l'oignon*. All the bread is
made *sans fèves*, without any bean flour [unlike much commercial
bread in France]. It's yellower in colour, like old-time bread, and
it's entitled to the appellation Banette, which means that it's made
from pure cereal flour, without any additives. We buy the flour
from a mill at Chagny. It goes well here. We also make croûtons
and *gougères*. And *pâtisserie*—every day we make something different. *Boules de neige* [snowballs] are my husband's speciality. They're
made with strawberries, cream, mousseline mixed with chantilly
and they're covered in white chocolate. It's our own recipe and we
only make it at weekends or on special occasions but the people
here like it very much."

All of which is produced in a startlingly small kitchen at the side
of the shop and baked in a gas oven from Germany of which the
Fontaines are exceedingly proud. It's a compact family operation.

I was standing in front of the counter one morning in mid-
October, chatting to Madame about local education (her son is at

the Puligny infants' school), when the door opened suddenly and in came a woman in a hurry. "Only 25 today," she said breathlessly and began loading a couple of dozen baguettes into the two large bags she carried with her. I recognized Madame Boudot, from Domaine Sauzet, who explained that the vintage was nearly over, some of the pickers had already gone and the rest would be leaving tomorrow. She was looking forward to the end of it, and not having to cook for the masses. But today they were still picking, it was close to noon and she must rush back with the bread for the midday meal.

I realized then that only two commodities continue to be made and sold in Puligny, the biblical staples of bread and wine. The more the business of wine becomes all-pervasive, to the point of obsession, the more the village needs that small bakery on the Place du Monument to leaven the loaf of daily life. The bakery has always been there (the street is marked "rue du Four" on the 18th-century map of Puligny), and I hope it always will be. As long as the warm smell of the morning's bread continues to waft down the street and mingle with the scent of fermenting wine, so long is it possible to have faith in the promise of Ecclesiastes: "Go thy way, eat thy bread with joy and drink thy wine with a merry heart; for God now accepteth thy works."

Simon Loftus is a British wine merchant, hotelier, restaurateur, and writer. He writes often about wine and travel for numerous publications and is the author of Anatomy of the Wine Trade, A Pike in the Basement, *and* Puligny-Montrachet: Journal of a Village in Burgundy, *from which this story was excerpted.*

WHAT YOU NEED TO KNOW

$\mathcal{W}$HEN TO GO/WEATHER

The right time to visit France is any time, 365 days a year. It all depends on your personality, interests, and of course, your budget. However, if you want to avoid crowds, don't even consider Paris or the Riviera in July or August, and be aware that late spring and early fall are also very popular times for visitors; the main tourism regions and sites will be thronged and in many cases choked by buses, cars, and people. Would you prefer to visit Versailles in a driving rain and negligible ticket lines, or in lovely weather with teeming crowds?

Weather can vary widely from region to region and season to season (Provence's climate may remind you of California, just as Brittany's may remind you of Ireland), but is in general reasonably temperate. Springtime in Paris is legendary, but if you enjoy winter activities, consider a trip to the Alps followed by a January or February visit to Paris, which even if bitterly cold has a romance all its own—and far fewer visitors. The summers can be particulaly hot in Ardèche and the Drôme Provençale, with autumn fantastically colorful and mild.

Provence is known for the Mistral, winds blowing up from North Africa. This phenomenon mostly occurs during the winter and can last anywhere from a few days to a few weeks. The Mistral is not something to be avoided if you enjoy experiencing forces of nature, but if it goes on for too long, like anything else, it can drive you a bit batty.

$\mathcal{V}$ISAS AND TOURIST CARDS

Visas are not required for Americans, European Union (EU) nationals, or visitors from Canada or New Zealand staying less than 90 days in France. However you will need a valid passport and one form of identification on you at all times.

THE NEXT STEP

If you lose your passport, you can obtain a temporary three-month passport from the U.S. consulate in Paris at 2, rue St-Florentin (1st), Tel: 01-42-96-12-02. There are also U.S. consulates in Bordeaux, Lyon, Marseille, and Strasbourg.

If you plan to stay in France more than three months, you must get a residence permit from the Prefecture de Police, Service des Estrangers, 1, rue de Lutèce, 75195 Paris, Tel: 01-53-71-53-71, Information 01-53-71-51-68.

CUSTOMS AND ARRIVAL

Citizens of non-European Union countries are allowed to bring in duty-free: 200 cigarettes or 100 cigarillos or 50 cigars or 250 grams of smoking tobacco; 1 liter of hard alcohol, 2 liters of wine, 2 liters of sparkling wine; 50 grams of perfume, a quarter liter of toilet water; 500 grams of coffee, and 100 grams of tea. Visitors from EU countries are allowed slightly more of each category.

Be aware that in France and other EU countries prices will include a 5%–25% sales tax (Value Added Tax). In France it is called TVA. If non-EU residents spend at least F1,200 in one shop, then they are entitled to a refund. Just fill out a *détaxe* form and turn it in to customs when you leave. Exceptions to the rebate are food and alcohol, medicines, tobacco, cars, and motorcycles.

Getting into Paris

Getting into Paris from Roissy-Charles de Gaulle Airport, or from Orly Airport is straightforward, with quite a few options. Roissy-Charles de Gaulle Airport is nineteen miles north of Paris. You have the choice of R.E.R. express trains, Air France buses, Roissybus, and taxis. Taxis are by far the most expensive mode, sometimes costing four times as much as trains and buses, and they won't save that much time, especially if you get caught in traffic. The R.E.R. trains depart regularly from the Aérogare 2 and SNCF train station at the airport. Line B will stop at the Gare du Nord, Châtelet, St-Michel, and Denfert-Rochereau Métro stations. Air

France buses run regularly from Port Maillot and the Arc de Triomphe, and to and from the Gare de Lyon and Gare Montparnasse. You can also get to Lille, Lyon, and the French Riviera from Roissy-de Gaulle by taking the TGV high-speed trains at the SNCF station.

Orly Airport is only nine miles south of Paris. You can take the Orlyval automatic train, the Orlyrail shuttle bus, Air France buses, Orly Bus, or taxis. The Orlyval departs every ten minutes and connects with the R.E.R. line B. The shuttle bus that conncects to R.E.R. C, Orlyrail, stops at the Gare d'Austerlitz, St-Michel, Musée d'Orsay, Invalides, Champs de Mars-Tour Eiffel, and Javel stations. The Air France buses run regularly to and from the Gare Montparnasse and Les Invalides. The Orly Bus also departs frequently and runs to and from Denfert-Rochereau Métro station.

If you are going to use taxis in Paris, get familiar with the extra charges posted in the vehicles, and take your time paying the driver. It is all too easy to be overcharged by a Parisian driver, and it is a rare one who shows any of the grace of a London cab driver.

France has an excellent rail system (and of course you can now arrive in Paris from London via the Chunnel), and a very good highway (*autoroute*) system. Driving in France is a bit more civilized (Paris excepted) than driving in Italy, Spain, Greece, and Germany, but still takes some getting used to if you are new to driving overseas.

H EALTH

There are no vaccines required to enter France from the U.S. and most countries. If you have health questions while in France, ask the clerk at a local pharmacy for help. Pharmacies throughout France are well-marked with green neon crosses. If your condition is more serious, consult one of the medical services listed below.

Some Helpful Tips:

- See a doctor and a dentist for general checkups before you leave home.

$\mathcal{T}$HE NEXT STEP

- ◆ If you wear prescription glasses or contact lenses, bring an extra pair along with your prescription.
- ◆ Stay hydrated.

Pack a medical kit which includes: aspirin or acetaminophen, antihistamine, antibiotics, Lomotil or Imodium for diarrhea, rehydration mixture, antiseptic such as iodine or Betadine, Calamine lotion, bandages, bandaids, tweezers, scissors, thermometer, cold and flu tablets, insect repellent, sunscreen, and chapstick.

Also consider taking a travel kit of basic homeopathic remedies and a homeopathic first aid book. Such remedies are available all over France and can provide rapid relief from common travel ailments including gastrointestinal problems and fevers. Of course if relief doesn't come, get yourself to a doctor!

Emergency Assistance

Emergency phone numbers throughout France:
Medical emergencies and SAMU (24-hour ambulance) 15
Police 17
Fire & other 18

Several companies in the U.S. and Europe provide emergency medical assistance for travelers worldwide, including 24-hour help lines, English-speaking doctors, and air evacuation in extreme cases. Consult your travel agent or try:

Global Care
2001 Westside Drive #120, Alpharetta, GA 30004
tel. (800) 249-2533; fax (770) 475-0058
www.globalems.com

International Association for Medical Assistance to Travelers (IAMAT)
In the U.S.:
417 Center Street, Lewiston, NY 14092
tel. (716) 754-4883; fax (519) 836-3412
email: iamat@sentex.net; http://www.sentex.net/~iamat

SOS Help (English language crisis line)
01-47-23-80-80

American Hospital in Paris
63 blvd. Victor-Hugo, 92202 Neuilly
01-46-41-25-25

American Citizen Services
2, rue Saint-Florentín
75001 Paris
www.amb-usa.fr/consul/oas_home.htm

The Hertford British Hospital
3 rue Barbès, 92300 Levallois-Perret
01-46-39-22-22

Dhéry Pharmacy (open 24 hrs)
84 av des Champs-Elysées, 8e.
75008 Paris
01-42-25-49-95

IME

France is one hour ahead of Greenwich Mean Time. Thus, when it's noon in Paris, it's:

3 a.m. in San Francisco
6 a.m. in New York
11 a.m. in London
6 p.m. in Hong Kong
7 p.m. in Tokyo
8 p.m. in Sydney

*B*USINESS HOURS

Most banks in northern France are open Monday through Friday from 9:00 a.m. to 4:30 p.m. In Southern France banks tend to be open Tuesday

through Saturday from 8 a.m. to 4:30 p.m. Stores are generally open between 10 a.m. and 7 p.m., with some stores staying open until 10 p.m. in
the larger cities. In the provinces and the outskirts of Paris, businesses are
often closed for lunch between 1 p.m. and 3 p.m. and all day on Mondays.
National museums are usually closed on Tuesdays and sometimes on
Mondays. Expect everything to be closed on public holidays and often the
afternoon of the day before.

ℳONEY

In France, the unit of currency is the franc (F). One franc equals 100 cen-
times. All French coins are either copper, silver, or a mixture of both. 5,
10 and 20 centime coins are copper. 1, 2 and 5 franc coins are silver. 10
and 20 franc coins have silver centers with copper on the outside. Paper
money comes in denominations of 20, 50, 100, 200, and 500 francs. Avoid
getting 500 franc bills as they can be difficult to break.

ATM machines are the easiest and most affordable way of exchanging
money these days. They take Visa and MasterCard, and most are linked to
the Cirrus and Plus systems so you can use your bank cards too. Money
can also be exchanged at banks or a *bureau de change*.

If your credit card is lost or stolen, report it to the police and the appropriate office:

American Express: 01-47-77-72-00
American Express Travelers' Checks: 08-00-90-86-00
Diner's Club: 01-47-62-75-50
Eurocard-Mastercard: 01-45-67-84-84
Visa: 01-42-77-11-90

ℰLECTRICITY

Electric current is 220 volts, 50 cycles. If you are used to traveling with a
notebook computer or other electrical appliances, take a voltage trans-
former and a plug adapter.

*M*EDIA: NEWSPAPERS, RADIO, TELEVISION ——————

International publications are widely available in France. Newspapers and magazines such as the *Wall Street Journal-Europe, USA Today,* the *Economist,* and *Newsweek* can be bought at many newstands and shops in major urban areas. There are two English-language newspapers published in France, the *International Herald Tribune,* a daily, and the *European,* a weekly. The *Boulevard,* a monthly, and *France-US Contacts,* a bi-weekly, are also published in English. France's top newspapers are: *Le Monde, Le Figaro, France Soir, Libération,* and *L'Humanité.* To find out what's going on and get listings for local events, pick up *Pariscope* and *L'Official des Spectacles.*

News is broadcast in English between 4–5 p.m. daily on Radio France Internationale. English language news can also be heard on the BBC World Service on 648 khz. The Voice of America transmits on 90.5, 98.8, and 102.4 Mhz. For French news around-the-clock try Infos on 105.5 Mhz, or the state-run France Inter on 87.8 FM.

French TV is broadcast on six channels: F2, Arte, and F3, which are public; Canal Plus, the main movie channel, is subscription; and TF1 and M6, are commercially open broadcasts. French news comes on at 8:30 p.m. on Arte and 1:00 and 8:00 p.m. on F2, or you can watch the American CBS evening news at 7 a.m. on Canal Plus.

Check the France Online section below for France media websites.

*T*OUCHING BASE: PHONE, FAX, POSTAGE, EMAIL ——————

France converted to a ten-digit direct-dial phone system in 1996. This means that there are no area codes and you dial ten numbers direct instead of the old eight-digit system. However, if by chance you encounter an eight-digit number, just add the following regional numbers to the front: Paris-01; Loire, Normandy, and Brittany in the northwest-02; Burgundy and Alsace in the northeast-03; Provence, Riviera, and the Alps in the southeast-04; and Dordogne in the southwest-05.

It is very easy to make phone calls from public phones using "Télécarte" cards. Télécartes are similar to American calling cards in that they are bought in different monetary amounts, but they are "smart"; one doesn't call an 800 number and punch in a code; instead, the amount of the call is electronically deducted when you make the call. Télécartes can be bought at post offices, airports, large stores, train stations, and most tobacco shops (*tabac*) and newstands.

To dial out of France, prefix your call with its international code, 00, then the country's code, and then your number. To call into France from another country, begin your call with the international access code of the country you're calling from (011 from the US, and 00 from most European countries), then dial France's country code (33), omit the first 0 of the ten-digit local number, and finish with the remaining digits.

It is also easy to call back to the United States if you have an AT&T, Sprint, or MCI calling card. Each of these companies have toll-free numbers in each European country that put you in touch with English-speaking operators.

Post offices (*La Poste*) are usually open Monday to Friday from 9 a.m. to 6 p.m., and from 8 a.m. to 12 noon on Saturdays, with smaller towns having shorter hours. In addition to regular mail services, main post offices have fax, telex, telephone services, and can cash or send international postal checks and money orders.

The main post office in Paris is open 24 hours: 52 rue du Louvre, 75001. Stamps can also be bought at *tabacs*, hotels and some newstands.

Travelers with American Express cards or AmEx traveler's checks can receive mail at American Express, 11, rue Scribe 9ème (tel: 01-47-77-77-07). They are open Monday through Friday 9:30 a.m. to 6:00 p.m., Saturday 10 a.m. to 5:00 p.m.

Internet access is available at various cybercafés and in some larger hotels. Check with your email or Internet Service Provider for access from France.

CULTURAL CONSIDERATIONS

*L*OCAL CUSTOMS: A FEW SIMPLE DO'S AND DON'TS

- The French are in general a well-mannered people. Always say *bonjour* before asking what you want in a shop, and be sure to follow it with a *merci*, after you receive your purchase and change. As you leave the shop, add *merci, au revoir*.

- Shake hands when being introduced to someone. Firmer is not necessarily better, as in America, but rather a brief handhold to acknowledge that the greeting is important. At the beginning and end of the day, the French tend to shake everyone's hand. When you are included in this, be sure not to leave anyone out. If you are in a restaurant, shake hands with everyone at the table.

- Try to speak French, no matter how poor your accent or limited your vocabulary. A valiant effort will get you more respect than if you insist on speaking English.

- The French greet or part with close acquaintances with a double kiss. (Usually one on each cheek starting with the right cheek.) The double kiss is sometimes reduced to kissing the air, instead of actually making lip to cheek contact. This version is acceptable, as is a third kiss back on the starting cheek as a symbol of further intimacy.

- When counting in France, start with your thumb. Starting with your index finger might confuse someone since your thumb and index fingers equals the number two.

- The French use a lot of body language and often speak with their hands. Avoid putting your hands in your pockets—some might consider it impolite.

- Don't be surprised if you run across rude waiters in Paris or at tourist sites such as Mt. St. Michel. Consider it a game, and a challenge. If you remain polite, you just might find the rudeness fading to something resembling acceptance. At the same time, do not be a doormat. If rudeness persists, or is extreme, make your displeasure known—or leave.

- The French—if you can make generalizations about such a diverse group of people— have a wonderful sense of elegance and style, both in dress and personal poise. If you are a slob by nature or habit, consider dressing up just a bit.

◆ Don't be surprised if you find yourself seated next to other foreigners in restaurants. The French find it offensive when Americans or other foreigners talk loudly at the table. In crowded spaces, lower your voice out of courtesy to others.

◆ Be on time if you have been invited as a guest to a French home. And don't come empty handed. Bring a plant, chocolates, or a bottle of wine for the host.

◆ Cocktails or *apéritifs* will be served before the meal. Don't ask for wine—it will come with the meal.

◆ As you're introduced to other dinner guests, don't ask them what they do for a living as a means for conversation. To the French, that's as private as asking an American for his or her bank account balance.

◆ France remains a very Catholic country, despite the oft-proclaimed agnosticism or indifference of many urbanites. Be respectful and quiet in cathedrals and churches.

ℰVENTS & HOLIDAYS

There are thousands of festivals and events that occur throughout France. Celebrations of all kinds, whether they are being held on a national or spontaneous local level, are an integral part of French culture and not to be missed. Here is a general guide to national holidays, but check with your travel agent and regional tourist office about local events that will be taking place in the towns you're visiting.

Public Holidays

January 1	New Year's Day
April 12 & 13	Easter Sunday and Monday
May 1	Labor Day
May 8	V.E. Day (Victory in Europe—End of World War II)
May 21	Ascension Thursday (40 days after Easter)
June 1	Whit Monday

July 14	Bastille Day
August 15	Feast of the Assumption
November 1	All Saint's Day
November 11	Armistice Day (End of World War I)
December 25	Christmas

January

Monte Carlo Motor Rally—mid-January, is the world's most famous car race.

International Ready-to-Wear Fashion Shows—mid-January to mid-February, get a glimpse of what the public will be wearing in six months as various couture houses present their shows.

February

Carnival of Nice—mid-February to early March, an ancient celebration with parades, boat processions and races, masked balls, fireworks, and battles with flowers.

March

Foire du Trône—March to late June, an enormous amusement park in Paris on the Neuilly Lawn in the Bois de Vincennes.

April

Paris International Marathon—weekend of April 2, runners from around the world come to compete. The participants run from place du Concorde to Château de Vincennes.

May

Cannes International Film Festival—second and third week of May, over fifty years of cinematic tradition, the highly celebrated film festival takes place in the Palais des Festivals. Don't be surprised to see melodramas acted out in hotel lobbies, on sidewalks, and in local cafes.

THE NEXT STEP

End of World War II—May 5–8, big celebrations in Paris and Reims.

Gypsy Pilgramage—May 24–26, is a gypsy pilgrimage to the Les Stes-Maries-de-la-Mer church in the Camargue marks the arrival by boat of Mary Magdalene, St. Martha, and the sister of the Virgin Mary.

Monaco Grand Prix—Ascension weekend, visitors come from all over the world to see the infamous car race through the narrow streets of Monaco.

June

French Tennis Open—last week in May-first week in June, at the Stade Roland-Garros, Paris.

Festival de Musique de St-Denis—throughout June in Paris, music is played in the burial place of the French Kings.

Cinéscénie de Puy du Fou—early June to September, *son et lumière* at the Château du Puy du Fou, Les Epesses, Vendée in celebration of the achievements of the Middle Ages.

July

Le Tour de France—July 1 to 23, the world's most famous bicycle race. The grand final leg of the race takes place on the Champs-Elysées, Paris.

Festival d'Avignon—mid-July to mid-August, France's largest festival. Featuring avant-garde theatre, dance, and music from around the world.

Bastille Day—July 14, festivities all over in celebration of the birth of modern-day France.

Grand Parade du Jazz—mid-July, the largest most prestigious jazz festival in Europe. Concerts are on the Arènes de Cimiez, a hill above Nice.

August

Festival International de Folklore et Fête de la Vigne—first two weeks in

August, in Dijon, Beaune, and near 20 villages in the Côte d'Or. An international festival celebrating the famous wines of Burgundy.

Lourdes Pilgrimage— Palm Sunday to August 25. Pilgrims come from all over to one of Catholicism's most beloved shrines where a young peasant girl saw 18 visions of the Virgin Mary in 1858.

September

Festival d'Automne— mid-September until just before Christmas in Paris, one of the most famous and eclectic festivals in France. The focus is on modern music, theater, ballet, and art.

Le Puy "Roi de l'Oiseau"— third week of September, a costumed Renaissance carnival celebrating the city's best archers.

Grape Harvest Festival—the whole month in Cognac.

October

Paris Auto Show —ten days in early October at the Parc des Expositions in Paris.

Prix del'Arc de Triomphe—early October in Longchamp, France's most important horse race.

Espelette Red Pepper Festival—last weekend in October, a festival in this small Pyrenees village honoring the red pimento pepper.

November

Armistice Day—November 11, a military parade in Paris from the Arc de Triomphe to the Hôtel des Invalides celebrating the signing of the codument that ended World War I.

Dijon International Food and Wine Festival—first two weeks of November.

Les Trois Glorieuses—ate November to early December, France's most important wine festival celebrated in Clos-de-Vougeot, Beaune, and Meursault.

December

Christmas Fairs—around Christmas, Strasbourg continues to celebrate a traditional Christmas that has lasted over 430 years. Over 35 Alsatian villages do the same.

Fête de St-Sylvestre—December 31, New Year's Eve. This national celebration gets the most rowdy in the Quartier Latin around the Sorbonne.

IMPORTANT CONTACTS

FOREIGN EMBASSIES IN PARIS AND THEIR PHONE NUMBERS

* Australia: 1/40-59-33-00
* Canada: 1/44-43-29-00
* Ireland: 01/44-17-67-00
* New Zealand: 1/45-00-24-11
* United Kingdom: 1/44-51-31-00
* United States: 1/43-12-22-22

TOURIST OFFICES AND THEIR PHONE NUMBERS

Every town in France has a tourist office, Office de Tourisme or Syndicat d'Initiative. They are marked with a blue "I" sign and are usually located in the city center. For advance information, the National Federation of Tourist Offices has a website with links to thousands of local tourist offices: http://www.tourisme.fr

Paris
127, avenue des Champs-Elysées
01-49-52-53-54

Ile-de-France
Versailles
2, bis Avenue de Paris
01-39-24-88-88

Southwest France
La Rochelle
place de la Petite Sirène
05-46-41-14-68

Bordeaux
12 cours du 30 Juillet
05-56-00-66-00

Toulouse
Donjon du Capitole, rue Lafayette
05-61-11-02-22

Languedoc-Roussillon
Comite Regional du Tourisme Languedoc-Roussillon
20, rue de la Republique
34000 Montpellier
04-67-22-81-00

Carcassonne
15 bd. Camille-Pelletan
04-68-10-24-30

Perpignan
Palais des Congrès, place Armand-Lanoux
04-68-66-30-30

Eastern France
Reims
2 rue Guillaume-de-Machault
03-26-77-45-25

Strasbourg
place de la Cathédrale
03-88-52-28-28

Troyes
16 bd. Carnot
03-25-82-62-70

THE NEXT STEP

Provence
Avignon
41 cours Jean-Jaurès
04-32-74-32-74

Marseille
4 La Canebière
04-91-13-89-00

Western France
Pont-Aven
place de l'Hôtel-de-Ville
02-98-06-04-70

Carnac
avenue des Druides
02-97-52-13-52

Tours
78, rue Bernard Palissy
02-47-70-37-37

Orleans
6, rue Albert 1er
02-38-24-05-05

Riviera-Côte d'Azur
Cannes
Palais des Festivals-1, La Croisette
04-93-39-24-53

Monaco
2A bd. des Moulins
04-92-16-61-16

Nice
Thiers at the Station Centrale
04-93-87-07-07

Rhône Alps
Lyon
place Bellecour
04-72-77-69-69

Grenoble
14 rue de la République
04-76-42-41-41

Normandy
Caen
place St-Pierre
02-31-27-14-14

Rouen
25 place de la Cathédrale
02-32-08-32-40

Burgundy
Autun
2, avenue Charles-de-Gaulle
03-85-86-80-38

Beaune
rue de l'Hôtel-Dieu
03-80-26-21-30

Dijon
34, rue des Forges
03-80-44-11-44

Vézelay
rue St-Pierre
03-86-33-23-69

ACTIVITIES

* Stay at a farm bed and breakfast. These *"maison d'hôtes"* are typically a few rooms in a family's home, and will give you a view of country life in France. Watch a baby goat being born, learn how to churn butter, meet ordinary French people.
* If Mt. St. Michel is on your itinerary, spend the night on the island. After all the day tourists leave, it becomes an utterly magical place, especially in the off-season.
* Listen to a concert in the Sainte-Chapelle in Paris. The combination of Gothic architecture and stupendous stained glass makes it seem as if you're enjoying music while sitting in a box of jewels.
* View the passage of migratory birds from the Dune du Pilat in Southwest France. This immense stretch of sand is the largest dune in Europe.
* Take a backstage tour of the Comédie Français in Paris where the classic French theatre is performed.
* Visit the gardens of Giverny in Normandy where the father of French Impressionism, Claude Monet, lived and painted. There are originals of his 19th- and 20th-century artwork in the Musée d'Art Américain Giverny nearby.
* See the Jurquet-Metge family make the famous yellow green-and-ocher Vases d'Anduze as they've been doing since 1610. The famous garden vases are decorated with original 1750s molds and seals. The Terralha ceramics fair is in the medieval village of St-Quentin-la-Poterie mid-July.
* Mountain bike among the ruins of medieval castles in the Parc Naturel Régional des Vosges du Nord in Alsace. There are also castle-to-castle hikes for those who like to stay on their feet.
* Whether you are a skier or not, ride the tram which rises from the Chamonix valley floor at the base of Mont Blanc to an amazing rocky

pinnacle from which you can see the summit of Mont Blanc and the Matterhorn in Switzerland on a clear day.

- Tour the historic eastern Loire region by a drive-it-yourself houseboat, easily rented from moorings in Montargis, Montbouy, Châtillon-sur-Loire, and Briare.
- Sunbathe on the Ile de Ré outside La Rochelle on the Atlantic Coast. It is much less developed and populated than the other beaches, and has 18 miles of sand dotted by white-washed cottages and tiny villages.
- Take La Route des Crêtes, a countryside drive between Alsace and Lorraine. It is one of the oldest mountain ranges in France and is engulfed in rich forests of hardwood trees and firs. There are marked hiking trails on all points of this routes.
- Take a sailing trip off the coasts of Brittany or Corsica.
- Children will love sailing a toy boat in the Luxembourg Gardens in Paris. It is a wonderful spot to watch Parisians of all ages enjoying life.
- Trace the history of ceramics from early Greek to present day porcelain pieces at the Musée National Adrien-Dubouché in Limoges.

ADDITIONAL RESOURCES

RANCE ONLINE

There are a wealth of websites on the Internet focusing on France. The following list is by no means comprehensive but will at least get you started. There are a lot of Francofiles out there on the World Wide Web.

French Government Tourist Office: www.francetourism.com

French Ministry of Culture: www.culture.fr

France Online: www.france.com

Maison de la France: www.franceguide.com

THE NEXT STEP

Paris Tourist Office: www.paris.org

SNCF French National Railroad: www.sncf.fr

Eurostar: www.eurostar.com

Rail Europe:www.raileurope.com

French Embassy in the United States: www.info-France-USA.org

Pariscope: www.pariscope.fr

Eiffel Tower: www.tour-eiffel.fr

Hotels in France: www.hotel-france.com

Camping in France: www.camping-france.com

FRENCH MUSEUMS ONLINE

Centre George Pompidou: www.cnac-gp.fr

City of Sciences La Villette: www.cite-sciences.fr

National Conservancy of Arts: www.cnam.fr

Musée du Louvre: www.louvre.fr

Musée d'Orsay: www.musee-orsay.fr

National Museum of Anthropology: www.mnhn.fr

National Library of France: www.bnf.fr

Museums and Monuments Pass:
www.gotoparis.net/gotoparis/musee.html

FRENCH MEDIA ONLINE

LeMonde (general information): www.lemonde.fr

LeMonde Diplomatique: www.ina.fr/CP/MondeDiplo

France Amérique: www.france-amerique.com

Paris Match: www.Parismatch.com

France 2 (TV Channel number 2): www.france2.fr

Canal Plus (TV Channel number 4): www.cplus.fr

Radio France (national radio station): www.radio-france.fr

RECOMMENDED READING

Applefield, David. *Paris Inside Out: The Insider's Handbook to Life in Paris.* Old Saybrook, Conn.: Globe Pequot, 2000.

Applefield, David. *The Unofficial Guide to Paris.* Hungry Minds, 2000.

Barclay, Steven. *A Place in the World Called Paris.* San Francisco: Chronicle Books, 2002.

Barry, Dave. *Dave Barry's Only Travel Guide You'll Ever Need.* New York: Ballantine Books, 1999.

Bernstein, Richard. *Fragile Glory: A Portrait of France and the French.* New York: Plume, 1991.

Botting, Douglas (ed.). *Wild France.* San Francisco: Sierra Club Books, 1994.

Braudel, Fernand. *The Identity of France.* English translation by Siân Reynolds. New York: HarperCollins Publishers, Inc., 1989.

Bryson, Bill. *Neither Here nor There: Travels in Europe.* New York: Avon Books, 1993.

Caro, Ina. *The Road From the Past: Traveling Through History in France.* New York: Harvest, 1996.

Carroll, Raymonde. *Cultural Misunderstandings: The French-American Experience.* Chicago: The University of Chicago Press, 1990.

Cooper, Bill and Laurel. *A Spell in Wild France.* London: Methuen London, 1992.

Cooper, Bill and Laurel. *Watersteps Through France: To the Camargue by Canal.* Dobbs Ferry, NY: Sheridan House, 1996.

Daley, Robert. *Portraits of France.* New York: Little, Brown & Co., 1995.

Delbanco, Nicholas. *Running in Place: Scenes from the South of France.* New York: Grove Press, 2001.

Dunne, Seán. *The Road to Silence: An Irish Spiritual Odyssey.* Dublin: New Island Books, 1994.

Fisher, M. F. K. *As They Were.* New York: Alfred A. Knopf, Inc., 1982.

Goodman, Richard. *French Dirt: The Story of a Garden in the South of France.* Chapel Hill, North Carolina: Algonquin Books of Chapel Hill, 1991.

Gopnik, Adam. *Paris to the Moon.* New York: Random House, 2001.

Grizell, Rex. *A White House in Gascony: Escape to the Old French South.* London: Victor Gollancz Ltd., 1992.

Hanbury-Tenison, Robin. *White Horses Over France: From the Camargue to Cornwall.* London: Granada Publishing Limited, 1985.

Harrison, Jim. *Just Before Dark: Collected Nonfiction.* New York: Houghton Mifflin, 1992.

Kaplan, Alice. *French Lessons: A Memoir.* Chicago: The University of Chicago Press, 1994.

Krakauer, Jon. *Eiger Dreams: Ventures Among Men and Mountains.* New York: Anchor, 1997.

Loftus, Simon. *Puligny-Montrachet: Journal of a Village in Burgundy.* London: Ebury Press, New York: Alfred A. Knopf, Inc., 1993.

Loomis, Susan Herrmann. *On Rue Tatin: Living and Cooking in a French Town.* New York: Broadway Books, 2001.

Mayle, Peter. *A Year in Provence.* London: Hamish Hamilton, Ltd., New York: Alfred A. Knopf, Inc., 1990.

Mayle, Peter. *Toujours Provence.* London: Hamish Hamilton, Ltd., New York: Alfred A. Knopf, Inc., 1991.

Mayle, Peter. *French Lessons: Adventures with Knife, Fork, and Corkscrew.* New York: Alfred A. Knopf, 2001.

Matthews, Thomas. *A Village in the Vineyards.* Toronto, Ontario: HarperCollins Canada Ltd., 1993.

More, Julian. *Views From a French Farmhouse.* London: Pavilion Books Limited, 1985.

Morland, Miles. *Miles Away: A Walk Across France.* London: Bloomsbury Publishing Ltd., 1992.

O'Rourke, P. J. *Holidays in Hell.* New York: Grove Press, 2000.

Osborne, Lawrence. *Paris Dreambook: An Unconventional Guide to the Splendor and Squalor of the City.* London: Bloomsbury Publishing Ltd., 1990.

Reuss, Henry S. and Margaret M. *The Unknown South of France: A History Buff's Guide.* Boston: The Harvard Common Press, 1991.

Rosenblum, Mort. *A Goose in Toulouse and Other Culinary Adventures in France.* New York: Hyperion, 2000.

Rosenblum, Mort. *The Secret Life of the Seine.* Reading, Massachusetts: Addison-Wesley, 1994.

Sedaris, David. *Me Talk Pretty One Day.* New York: Little, Brown & Co., 2001.

Visser, Margaret. *The Rituals of Dinner: The Origins, Evolution, Eccentricities, and Meaning of Table Manners.* New York: Penguin, 1992.

White, Edmund. *The Flaneur: A Stroll Through the Paradoxes of Paris.* London: Bloomsbury, 2001.

Wilcock, John and Elizabeth Pepper DaCosta. *Magical and Mystical Sites: Europe and the British Isles.* New York: HarperCollins, 2000.

Glossary

allons-y	go ahead	*gîte*	home
alpage	high mountain pasture	*haricots verts*	green beans
		ici	here
amie	friend	*mais non*	of course not
arrondissement	district	*méchoui*	whole sheep barbecue
ausfahrts	exit road		
bateaux-bains	floating baths	*métropole*	metropolis
bateaux-mouche	tour boats	*n'oubliez pas*	do not forget
billet-doux	love letter	*naturellement*	naturally, of course
boule	bowling green		
		parapentes	sport parachute
boulangerie	bakery		
bouquinistes	booksellers	*pâtisserie*	pastry
cave	cellar; wine cellar	*pétanque*	bowl game
		poubelle	garbage can
chanson	song	*rayonnement*	radiance
cordonnier	cobbler	*robinet*	faucet
cornichons	gherkin	*rouge*	red
croque-monsieur	toasted ham and cheese sandwich	*routier*	mercenary soldier
		salon de thé	tearoom
etape	stopping place	*sorties*	exits
feu	light	*tableaux*	pictures, paintings
filets	nets		
froid	cold	*wagon-lit*	Pullman, sleeper

Index

Index of Contributors

Acknowledgments

Heartfelt thanks to Wenda Brewster O'Reilly, Andrea, Noelle, and Mariele O'Reilly, Paula Mc Cabe, Brenda O'Reilly, Timothy O'Reilly, Anne O'Reilly, Cindy Collins, Trisha Schwartz, Raj Khadka, Susan Brady, Nancy Priest, Edie Freedman, Jennifer Niederst, and Linda Sirola. Thanks also to Gary Kray, Paul O'Leary, Anne Sengès, Kim Guptill, Madame Anne Richard of the Confédération Générale de Roquefort, the staff of the periodical department at the Phoenix Central Library, and the staff of the Luke Air Base library in Glendale, Arizona [for the use of their facilities].

In Normandy, special thanks for extraordinary hospitality to Jacques Pochon and Chantal Pochon-Lesage, Lucy and Nicolas Robin, Anne, Gerard, and Mathilde LeCorsu, and in the Haute-Savoie, to Jacques and Jeannette Tomei, Veronique Boud, Anne Baniel, Agnes Tandy and Jean-Pierre Berthoud, Catherine Vu, Madame Armand Charlet, Jean-Claude and Clo Charlet, Pierre and Charlotte Ténot, Philippe Dilloard, Bruno Mea and Elisabeth Lenoir, Paul, Mireille, and Jean-François Coquoz, Claude Benvenuto, Claude Prosper, Jacky and Chantal Chaudun, Pierre Cupelin, Jean-Jacques Bonenfant, Sylvie Mannoni, Hanne and Peter Borggaard and the staff of their hotel, Les Becs Rouges. In big and small ways these folks effortlessly embody what is most wonderful about France.

486

1991 by Richard Goodman. Reprinted by permission of Algonquin Books of Chapel Hill, a division of Workman Publishing Company, Inc.

"River of Light" by Mort Rosenblum excerpted from *The Secret Life of the Seine* (pp. 3-7, 9-15, 17-23), © 1994 by Mort Rosenblum. Reprinted by permission of Addison-Wesley Publishing Company, Inc.

"April Fool" by Nicholas Delbanco excerpted from *Running in Place: Scenes from the South of France* by Nicholas Delbanco. Copyright © 1989 by Nicholas Delbanco. Used by permission of Grove/ Atlantic Inc.

"Covert Operations" by Debbie Seaman reprinted by permission of the author. Copyright © 1991 by Debbie Seaman.

"War and Remembrance" by Clive Irving reprinted from the February 1994 issue of *Condé Nast Traveler.* Courtesy *Condé Naste Traveler.* Copyright © 1994 by The Condé Nast Publications Inc.

"Love among the Apples" by Judy Wade reprinted by permission of the author. Copyright © 1995 by Judy Wade.

"In the Land of the Musketeers" by Rex Grizell excerpted from *A White House in Gascony: Escape to the Old French South.* Reprinted by permission of Victor Gollancz Ltd. Copyright © 1992 by Rex Grizell.

"*Cinema en Plein Air*" by Jenny Woolf reprinted by permission of the author. Copyright © 1995 by Jenny Woolf.

"Métro Metaphysics" by Lawrence Osborne excerpted from *Paris Dreambook: An Unconventional Guide to the Splendor and Squalor of the City* by Lawrence Osborne. Copyright © 1990 by Lawrence Osborne. Reprinted by permission of Pantheon Books, a division of Random House, Inc. and A.M. Heath & Co. Ltd.

"Three Women of Nice" by Donald W. George reprinted from the August 15, 1993 issue of the *San Francisco Examiner.* Reprinted with permission from the *San Francisco Examiner.* Copyright © 1993 by the *San Francisco Examiner.*

"The Arch of Orange" by Ina Caro excerpted from *The Road from the Past: Traveling Through History in France* by Ina Caro. Copyright © 1994 by Ina Caro. A Nan A. Talese Book. Used by permission of Doubleday, a division of Bantam Doubleday Dell Publishing Group, Inc.

"I Was Really Very Hungry" by M. F. K. Fisher excerpted from *As They Were* by M. F. K. Fisher. Reprinted by permission of Alfred A. Knopf, Inc. Copyright © 1982 by M. F. K. Fisher.

"*Les Invalides*" by Peter Mayle excerpted from *Toujours Provence* by Peter Mayle. Reprinted by permssion of Alfred A. Knopf. Inc. and Hamish Hamilton, Ltd. Copyright © 1991 by Peter Mayle.

"The Cave Where It Lives" by Roy Andries de Groot reprinted from the November 1980 issue of *Cuisine.* Copyright © 1980 by Roy Andries de Groot.

"Road Scholars" by James O'Reilly reprinted by permission of the author. Copyright © 1993 by James O'Reilly.

"Loving the Middle Ages" by Jo Broyles Yohay reprinted with permission from *Travel & Leisure,* December 1991. Copyright © 1991 by American Express Publishing Corporation. All rights reserved.

"Bovary Country" by Mort Rosenblum excerpted from *The Secret Life of the Seine*

"Black Périgord" by Julia Wilkinson reprinted from the October 1988 issue of *Discovery Magazine*, the in-flight magazine of Cathay Pacific Airways. Reprinted by permission of the author. Copyright © 1988 by Julia Wilkinson.

"Finding My Religion" by Seán Dunne excerpted from *The Road to Silence: An Irish Spiritual Odyssey* by Seán Dunne. Reprinted by permission of New Island Books. Copyright © 1994 by Seán Dunne.

"A Taste for the Abyss" by Jon Krakauer reprinted with permission from *Eiger Dreams: Ventures Among Men and Mountains* by Jon Krakauer. Copyright © 1990, Lyons & Burford, Publishers.

"Jo's Dog Has His Day" by Jo Giese reprinted by permission of the author. Copyright © 1991 by Jo Giese.

"Dining with the Corsican" by Nicholas Woodsworth reprinted from the January 1, 1994 issue of *The Financial Times*. Reprinted by permission of The Financial Times Syndication. Copyright © 1994 by The Financial Times Syndication.

"Encounters with André" by Alice Kaplan excerpted from *French Lessons: A Memoir* by Alice Kaplan. Reprinted by permission of The University of Chicago Press and the author. Copyright © 1993 by The University of Chicago Press.

"No Spitting in Chateauneuf-du-Pape" by Peter Mayle excerpted from *Toujours Provence* by Peter Mayle. Copyright © 1991 by Peter Mayle. Reprinted by permission of Alfred A. Knopf. Inc. and Hamish Hamilton Ltd.

"The Edible City" by Jan Morris reprinted from the October 1991 issue of *Condé Nast Traveler*. Reprinted by permission of Julian Bach Literary Agency and the author. Copyright © 1991 by Jan Morris.

"Riviera Gumshoe" by Nik Cohn reprinted from the March 1992 issue of *Condé Nast Traveler*. Reprinted by permission of the author. Copyright © 1992 by Nik Cohn.

"Two Moments in France" by Margaret Balka reprinted by permission of the author. Copyright © 1995 by Margaret Balka.

"The Duty to Remember, the Need to Forget" by Ronald Koven reprinted from the Fall 1994 issue of *FRANCE Magazine*. Reprinted by permission of *FRANCE Magazine* and the author. Copyright © 1994 by Ronald Koven.

"*Service Non Compris*" by Moshe Saperstein reprinted from the January 28, 1991 issue of *The Jerusalem Post*. Reprinted by permission of *The Jerusalem Post*. Copyright © 1991 by *The Jerusalem Post*.

"White Night by St-Denis" by Lawrence Osborne excerpted from *Paris Dreambook: An Unconventional Guide to the Splendor and Squalor of the City* by Lawrence Osborne. Copyright © 1990 by Lawrence Osborne. Reprinted by permission of Pantheon Books, a division of Random House, Inc. and A.M. Heath & Co. Ltd.

"Remnants of Hell" by Donovan Webster reprinted from the February 1994 issue of *Smithsonian* magazine. Reprinted by permission of the author. Copyright © 1994 by Donovan Webster.

"Windows on a Village" by Simon Loftus excerpted from *Puligny-Montrachet: Journal of a Village in Burgundy* by Simon Loftus. Copyright © 1992 by Simon Loftus. Reprinted by permission of Alfred A. Knopf, Inc. and Ebury Press.

Whitehill © 1993. Quoted with permission of the publisher from *France by Bike*, by Karen and Terry Whitehill, The Mountaineers, Seattle.

Selections from *The French* by Theodore Zeldin reprinted by permission of HarperCollins Publishers Limited. Copyright © 1983 by Theodore Zeldin.

Selection from "French Polish" by Alice Thomas Ellis reprinted from the September 3, 1988 issue of *The Spectator*. Reprinted by permission of *The Spectator*. Copyright © 1988 by *The Spectator*.

Selection from "French Town Doesn't Miss Humor, Irony, Tales Galore" by Mike Harden reprinted from the May 24, 1994 issue of *The Columbus* (Ohio) *Dispatch*. Reprinted, with permission, from *The Columbus* (Ohio) *Dispatch*. Copyright © 1994 by *The Columbus Dispatch*.

Selection from "Gallic Gall" by Richard Bernstein reprinted from the August 17, 1986 issue of *The New York Times Magazine*. Copyright © 1986 by The New York Times Company. Reprinted by permission.

Selection from "The Greatest Lift on Earth" by Andrew Slough reprinted from the November 1991 issue of *SKI* magazine. Reprinted by permission of Times Mirror Magazines, Inc. Copyright © 1991 by Times Mirror Magazines, Inc.

Selection from "The Guides Must Be Crazy" by Richard Bangs reprinted from the Summer 1993 issue of *Just GO!* Reprinted by permission of the author. Copyright © 1993 by Richard Bangs.

Selection from *Holidays in Hell* by P. J. O'Rourke. Copyright © 1988 by P. J. O'Rourke. Used by permission of Grove/Atlantic, Inc.

Selection from "How to Make the Most of Your Speaking Engagements" by Kay Eldredge reprinted from the February 1990 issue of *European Travel & Life*. Copyright © 1990 by Kay Eldredge.

Selection from *The Identity of France* by Fernand Braudel and translated by Siân Reynolds. English language translation copyright © 1989 by Siân Reynolds. Reprinted by permission of HarperCollins Publishers, Inc.

Selection from "Imagine Paris" by John Berger reprinted from the January 1987 issue of *Harper's Magazine*. Copyright © 1987 by John Berger, reprinted with the permission of Wylie, Aitken & Stone, Inc.

Selection from "In France, Franglais is Unlawful" by Warren Trabant reprinted from the *Providence* (Rhode Island) *Journal*. Copyright © 1994 by Warren Trabant.

Selections from *Just Before Dark: Collected Nonfiction* by Jim Harrison. Reprinted by permission of Clark City Press. Copyright © 1991 by Jim Harrison.

Selection from "The Land of Cuisine Sees Taste Besieged by 'Le Big Mac'" by Judith Valente reprinted from the May 25, 1994 issue of *The Wall Street Journal*. Reprinted by permission of *The Wall Street Journal*. Copyright © 1994 by *The Wall Street Journal*.

Selection from "Learning the *Langue*" by Richard Reeves reprinted with permission from *Travel & Leisure*, March 1987. Copyright © 1987 American Express Publishing Corporation. All rights reserved.

Selection from *Letters Home: A War Memoir* by John Ausland. Copyright © 1993 by John Ausland.

Selection from "Linger in the Châteaux of the Loire" by Gail Russell Chaddock

Pitman Publishing Corporation. Copyright © 1940, 1970 by Gertude Stein.

Selection from "When Evening Falls" by James Salter reprinted from the February 1992 issue of *GQ*. Reprinted by permission of the author. Copyright © 1992 by James Salter.

Selection from "Where Art Began" by Jonathan Cott reprinted from the May 1991 issue of *Travel Holiday*. Reprinted by permission of the author. Copyright © 1991 by Jonathan Cott.

Selections from *White Horses Over France: From the Camargue to Cornwall* by Robin Hanbury-Tenison reprinted by permission of Arrow Books Limited and the Peters, Fraser & Dunlop Group Ltd. Copyright © 1985 by Robin Hanbury-Tenison.

Selections from *A White House in Gascony: Escape to the Old French South* by Rex Grizell reprinted by permission of Victor Gollancz Ltd. Copyright © 1992 by Rex Grizell.

Selections from *Wild France* edited by Douglas Botting reprinted by permission of Sierra Club Books and courtesy of Sheldrake Press. Copyright © 1992 by Sheldrake Publishing Ltd.

About the Editors

James O'Reilly, president and co-publisher of Travelers' Tales, wrote mystery serials before becoming a travel writer in the early 1980s. He's visited more than forty countries, along the way meditating with monks in Tibet, participating in West African voodoo rituals, and hanging out the laundry with nuns in Florence. He travels extensively with his wife Wenda and their three daughters. They live in Palo Alto, California when they're not in Leavenworth, Washington.

Larry Habegger, executive editor of Travelers' Tales, has been writing about travel since 1980. He has visited almost fifty countries and five of the six continents, traveling from the frozen arctic to equatorial rain forest, the high Himalayas to the Dead Sea. In the early 1980s he co-authored mystery serials for the *San Francisco Examiner* with James O'Reilly, and in 1985 the two of them began a syndicated newspaper column, "World Travel Watch," which still appears in major newspapers throughout the USA. He was born and raised in Minnesota and lives with his family on Telegraph Hill in San Francisco.

Sean O'Reilly is a former seminarian, stockbroker, and prison instructor who lives in Arizona with his wife Brenda and their six children. He's had a life-long interest in philosophy and theology, and has recently published a book called *How to Manage Your DICK: Redirect Sexual Energy and Discover Your More Spiritually Enlightened, Evolved Self.* Widely traveled, Sean most recently completed an 18,000-mile van journey around the United States, sharing the treasures of the open road with his family. He is editor-at-large and director of international sales for Travelers' Tales.

TRAVELERS' TALES

THE SOUL OF TRAVEL

Footsteps Series

THE FIRE NEVER DIES

One Man's Raucous Romp
Down the Road of Food,
Passion, and Adventure
By Richard Sterling
ISBN 1-885-211-70-8
$14.95

"Sterling's writing is like spit-
fire, foursquare and jazzy with crackle...."
—*Kirkus Reviews*

ONE YEAR OFF

Leaving It All Behind for a
Round-the-World Journey
with Our Children
By David Elliot Cohen
ISBN 1-885-211-65-1
$14.95

A once-in-a-lifetime
adventure generously shared.

TAKE ME WITH YOU

A Round-the-World
Journey to Invite a
Stranger Home
By Brad Newsham
ISBN 1-885-211-51-1
$24.00 (cloth)

"Newsham is an ideal guide. His journey, at
heart, is into humanity." —Pico Iyer, author
of *Video Night in Kathmandu*

THE SWORD OF HEAVEN

A Five Continent Odyssey
to Save the World
By Mikkel Aaland
ISBN 1-885-211-44-9
$24.00 (cloth)

"Few books capture the soul
of the road like *The Sword of Heaven*,
a sharp-edged, beautifully rendered memoir
that will inspire anyone." —Phil Cousineau,
author of *The Art of Pilgrimage*

LAST TROUT IN VENICE

The Far-Flung Escapades
of an Accidental
Adventurer
By Doug Lansky
ISBN 1-885-211-63-5
$14.95

"Traveling with Doug Lansky might result in
a considerably shortened life expectancy...but
what a way to go." —Tony Wheeler,
Lonely Planet Publications

THE WAY OF THE WANDERER

Discover Your True Self
Through Travel
By David Yeadon
ISBN 1-885-211-60-0
$14.95

Experience transformation through travel
with this delightful, illustrated collection by
award-winning author David Yeadon.

KITE STRINGS OF THE SOUTHERN CROSS

A Woman's
Travel Odyssey
By Laurie Gough
ISBN 1-885-211-54-6
$14.95

— ✦★✦ —

ForeWord Silver Medal Winner
— *Travel Book of the Year*

STORM

A Motorcycle Journey
of Love, Endurance,
and Transformation
By Allen Noren
ISBN 1-885-211-45-7
$24.00 (cloth)

— ✦★✦ —

ForeWord Gold Medal Winner
— *Travel Book of the Year*

Travelers' Tales Classics

COAST TO COAST
A Journey Across 1950s America
By Jan Morris
ISBN 1-885-211-79-1
$16.95

After reporting on the first Everest ascent in 1953, Morris spent a year journeying by car, train, ship, and aircraft across the United States. In her brilliant prose, Morris records with exuberance and curiosity a time of innocence in the U.S.

THE ROYAL ROAD TO ROMANCE
By Richard Halliburton
ISBN 1-885-211-53-8
$14.95

"Laughing at hardships, dreaming of beauty, ardent for adventure, Halliburton has managed to sing into the pages of this glorious book his own exultant spirit of youth and freedom."
— *Chicago Post*

THE RIVERS RAN EAST
By Leonard Clark
ISBN 1-885-211-66-X
$16.95

Clark is the original Indiana Jones, relaying a breathtaking account of his search for the legendary El Dorado gold in the Amazon.

THERE'S NO TOILET PAPER...ON THE ROAD LESS TRAVELED
The Best of Travel Humor and Misadventure
Edited by Doug Lansky
ISBN 1-885-211-27-9
$12.95

★ ★ ★

Humor Book of the Year
— *Independent Publisher's Book Award*

ForeWord Gold Medal Winner— *Humor Book of the Year*

TRADER HORN
A Young Man's Astounding Adventures in 19th Century Equatorial Africa
By Alfred Aloysius Horn
ISBN 1-885-211-81-3
$16.95

Here is the stuff of legends —tale of thrills and danger, wild beasts, serpents, and savages. An unforgettable and vivid portrait of a vanished late-19th century Africa.

UNBEATEN TRACKS IN JAPAN
By Isabella L. Bird
ISBN 1-885-211-57-0
$14.95

Isabella Bird was one of the most adventurous women travelers of the 19th century with journeys to Tibet, Canada, Korea, Turkey, Hawaii, and Japan. A fascinating read for anyone interested in women's travel, spirituality, and Asian culture.

Travel Humor

NOT SO FUNNY WHEN IT HAPPENED
The Best of Travel Humor and Misadventure
Edited by Tim Cahill
ISBN 1-885-211-55-4
$12.95

Laugh with Bill Bryson, Dave Barry, Anne Lamott, Adair Lara, and many more.

LAST TROUT IN VENICE
The Far-Flung Escapades of an Accidental Adventurer
By Doug Lansky
ISBN 1-885-211-63-5
$14.95

"Traveling with Doug Lansky might result in a considerably shortened life expectancy...but what a way to go."
—Tony Wheeler, Lonely Planet Publications

Women's Travel

A WOMAN'S PASSION FOR TRAVEL
More True Stories from A Woman's World
Edited by Marybeth Bond & Pamela Michael
ISBN 1-885-211-36-8
$17.95

"A diverse and gripping series of stories!" —Arlene Blum, author of *Annapurna: A Woman's Place*

A WOMAN'S WORLD
True Stories of Life on the Road
Edited by Marybeth Bond
Introduction by Dervla Murphy
ISBN 1-885-211-06-6
$17.95

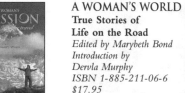

★ ★ ★

Winner of the Lowell Thomas Award for Best Travel Book— Society of American Travel Writers

WOMEN IN THE WILD
True Stories of Adventure and Connection
Edited by Lucy McCauley
ISBN 1-885-211-21-X
$17.95

"A spiritual, moving, and totally female book to take you around the world and back." —*Mademoiselle*

A MOTHER'S WORLD
Journeys of the Heart
Edited by Marybeth Bond & Pamela Michael
ISBN 1-885-211-26-0
$14.95

"These stories remind us that motherhood is one of the great unifying forces in the world" —*San Francisco Examiner*

Food

ADVENTURES IN WINE
True Stories of Vineyards and Vintages around the World
Edited by Thom Elkjer
ISBN 1-885-211-80-5
$17.95

Humanity, community, and brotherhood comprise the marvelous virtues of the wine world. This collection toasts the warmth and wonders of this large, extended family in stories by travelers who are wine novices and experts alike.

FOOD (Updated)
A Taste of the Road
Edited by Richard Sterling
Introduction by Margo True
ISBN 1-885-211-77-5
$18.95

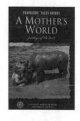

★ ★ ★

Silver Medal Winner of the Lowell Thomas Award for Best Travel Book— Society of American Travel Writers

HER FORK IN THE ROAD
Women Celebrate Food and Travel
Edited by Lisa Bach
ISBN 1-885-211-71-6
$16.95

A savory sampling of stories by some of the best writers in and out of the food and travel fields.

THE ADVENTURE OF FOOD
True Stories of Eating Everything
Edited by Richard Sterling
ISBN 1-885-211-37-6
$17.95

"These stories are bound to whet appetites for more than food."

—*Publishers Weekly*

Spiritual Travel

THE SPIRITUAL GIFTS OF TRAVEL
The Best of Travelers' Tales
Edited by James O'Reilly and Sean O'Reilly
ISBN 1-885-211-69-4
$16.95

A collection of favorite stories of transformation on the road from our award-winning Travelers' Tales series that shows the myriad ways travel indelibly alters our inner landscapes.

THE WAY OF THE WANDERER
Discover Your True Self Through Travel
By David Yeadon
ISBN 1-885-211-60-0
$14.95

Experience transformation through travel with this delightful, illustrated collection by award-winning author David Yeadon.

PILGRIMAGE
Adventures of the Spirit
Edited by Sean O'Reilly & James O'Reilly
Introduction by Phil Cousineau
ISBN 1-885-211-56-2
$16.95

——★*★——

ForeWord Silver Medal Winner
— Travel Book of the Year

A WOMAN'S PATH
Women's Best Spiritual Travel Writing
Edited by Lucy McCauley, Amy G. Carlson & Jennifer Leo
ISBN 1-885-211-48-1
$16.95

"A sensitive exploration of women's lives that have been unexpectedly and spiritually touched by travel experiences.... Highly recommended."
—*Library Journal*

THE ROAD WITHIN
True Stories of Transformation and the Soul
Edited by Sean O'Reilly, James O'Reilly & Tim O'Reilly
ISBN 1-885-211-19-8
$17.95

——★*★——

Best Spiritual Book—Independent Publisher's Book Award

THE ULTIMATE JOURNEY
Inspiring Stories of Living and Dying
James O'Reilly, Sean O'Reilly & Richard Sterling
ISBN 1-885-211-38-4
$17.95

"A glorious collection of writings about the ultimate adventure. A book to keep by one's bedside—and close to one's heart." —Philip Zaleski, editor,
The Best Spiritual Writing series

Adventure

TESTOSTERONE PLANET
True Stories from a Man's World
Edited by Sean O'Reilly, Larry Habegger & James O'Reilly
ISBN 1-885-211-43-0
$17.95

Thrills and laughter with some of today's best writers: Sebastian Junger, Tim Cahill, Bill Bryson, and Jon Krakauer.

DANGER!
True Stories of Trouble and Survival
Edited by James O'Reilly, Larry Habegger & Sean O'Reilly
ISBN 1-885-211-32-5
$17.95

"Exciting...for those who enjoy living on the edge or prefer to read the survival stories of others, this is a good pick."
—*Library Journal*

Special Interest

365 TRAVEL
A Daily Book of Journeys, Meditations, and Adventures
Edited by Lisa Bach
ISBN 1-885-211-67-8
$14.95
An illuminating collection of travel wisdom and adventures that reminds us all of the lessons we learn while on the road.

THE GIFT OF RIVERS
True Stories of Life on the Water
Edited by Pamela Michael
Introduction by Robert Hass
ISBN 1-885-211-42-2
$14.95
"*The Gift of Rivers* is a soulful compendium of wonderful stories that illuminate, educate, inspire, and delight."
—David Brower, Chairman of Earth Island Institute

FAMILY TRAVEL
The Farther You Go, the Closer You Get
Edited by Laura Manske
ISBN 1-885-211-33-3
$17.95
"This is family travel at its finest." —*Working Mother*

LOVE & ROMANCE
True Stories of Passion on the Road
Edited by Judith Babcock Wylie
ISBN 1-885-211-18-X
$17.95
"A wonderful book to read by a crackling fire."
—*Romantic Traveling*

THE GIFT OF BIRDS
True Encounters with Avian Spirits
Edited by Larry Habegger & Amy G. Carlson
ISBN 1-885-211-41-4
$17.95
"These are all wonderful, entertaining stories offering a *bird's-eye view!* of our avian friends."
—*Booklist*

A DOG'S WORLD
True Stories of Man's Best Friend on the Road
Edited by Christine Hunsicker
ISBN 1-885-211-23-6
$12.95
This extraordinary collection includes stories by John Steinbeck, Helen Thayer, James Herriot, Pico Iyer, and many others.

THE GIFT OF TRAVEL
The Best of Travelers' Tales
Edited by Larry Habegger, James O'Reilly & Sean O'Reilly
ISBN 1-885-211-25-2
$14.95
"Like gourmet chefs in a French market, the editors of Travelers' Tales pick, sift, and prod their way through the weighty shelves of contemporary travel writing, creaming off the very best."
—William Dalrymple, author of *City of Djinns*

Travel Advice

SHITTING PRETTY
How to Stay Clean and Healthy While Traveling
By Dr. Jane Wilson-Howarth
ISBN 1-885-211-47-3
$12.95

A light-hearted book about a serious subject for millions of travelers— staying healthy on the road—written by international health expert, Dr. Jane Wilson-Howarth.

THE FEARLESS SHOPPER
How to Get the Best Deals on the Planet
By Kathy Borrus
ISBN 1-885-211-39-2
$14.95

"Anyone who reads *The Fearless Shopper* will come away a smarter, more responsible shopper and a more curious, culturally attuned traveler."

—Jo Mancuso, *The Shopologist*

GUTSY WOMEN
More Travel Tips and Wisdom for the Road
By Marybeth Bond
ISBN 1-885-211-61-9
$12.95

Second Edition—Packed with funny, instructive, and inspiring advice for women heading out to see the world.

SAFETY AND SECURITY FOR WOMEN WHO TRAVEL
By Sheila Swan & Peter Laufer
ISBN 1-885-211-29-5
$12.95

A must for every woman traveler!

THE FEARLESS DINER
Travel Tips and Wisdom for Eating around the World
By Richard Sterling
ISBN 1-885-211-22-8
$7.95

Combines practical advice on foodstuffs, habits, and etiquette, with hilarious accounts of others' eating adventures.

THE PENNY PINCHER'S PASSPORT TO LUXURY TRAVEL
The Art of Cultivating Preferred Customer Status
By Joel L. Widzer
ISBN 1-885-211-31-7
$12.95

Proven techniques on how to travel first class at discount prices, even if you're not a frequent flyer.

GUTSY MAMAS
Travel Tips and Wisdom for Mothers on the Road
By Marybeth Bond
ISBN 1-885-211-20-1
$7.95

A delightful guide for mothers traveling with their children— or without them!